C000121719

1,000,000 Books

are available to read at

www.ForgottenBooks.com

Read online
Download PDF
Purchase in print

ISBN 978-1-334-66901-9
PIBN 10699616

This book is a reproduction of an important historical work. Forgotten Books uses state-of-the-art technology to digitally reconstruct the work, preserving the original format whilst repairing imperfections present in the aged copy. In rare cases, an imperfection in the original, such as a blemish or missing page, may be replicated in our edition. We do, however, repair the vast majority of imperfections successfully; any imperfections that remain are intentionally left to preserve the state of such historical works.

Forgotten Books is a registered trademark of FB &c Ltd.
Copyright © 2018 FB &c Ltd.
FB &c Ltd, Dalton House, 60 Windsor Avenue, London, SW19 2RR.
Company number 08720141. Registered in England and Wales.

For support please visit www.forgottenbooks.com

1 MONTH OF
FREE
READING

at

www.ForgottenBooks.com

By purchasing this book you are eligible for one month membership to ForgottenBooks.com, giving you unlimited access to our entire collection of over 1,000,000 titles via our web site and mobile apps.

To claim your free month visit:

www.forgottenbooks.com/free699616

* Offer is valid for 45 days from date of purchase. Terms and conditions apply.

English
Français
Deutsche
Italiano
Español
Português

www.forgottenbooks.com

Mythology Photography **Fiction** Fishing Christianity **Art** Cooking Essays Buddhism Freemasonry Medicine **Biology** Music **Ancient Egypt** Evolution Carpentry Physics Dance Geology **Mathematics** Fitness Shakespeare **Folklore** Yoga Marketing **Confidence** Immortality Biographies Poetry **Psychology** Witchcraft Electronics Chemistry History **Law** Accounting **Philosophy** Anthropology Alchemy Drama Quantum Mechanics Atheism Sexual Health **Ancient History** **Entrepreneurship** Languages Sport Paleontology Needlework Islam **Metaphysics** Investment Archaeology Parenting Statistics Criminology **Motivational**

LIFE OF

VISCOUNT PALMERSTON

VOL. II.

LONDON: PRINTED BY
SPOTTISWOODE AND CO., NEW-STREET SQUARE.
AND PARLIAMENT STREET

LIFE OF

VISCOUNT PALMERSTON

VOL. II.

LONDON: PRINTED BY
SPOTTISWOODE AND CO., NEW-STREET SQUARE
AND PARLIAMENT STREET

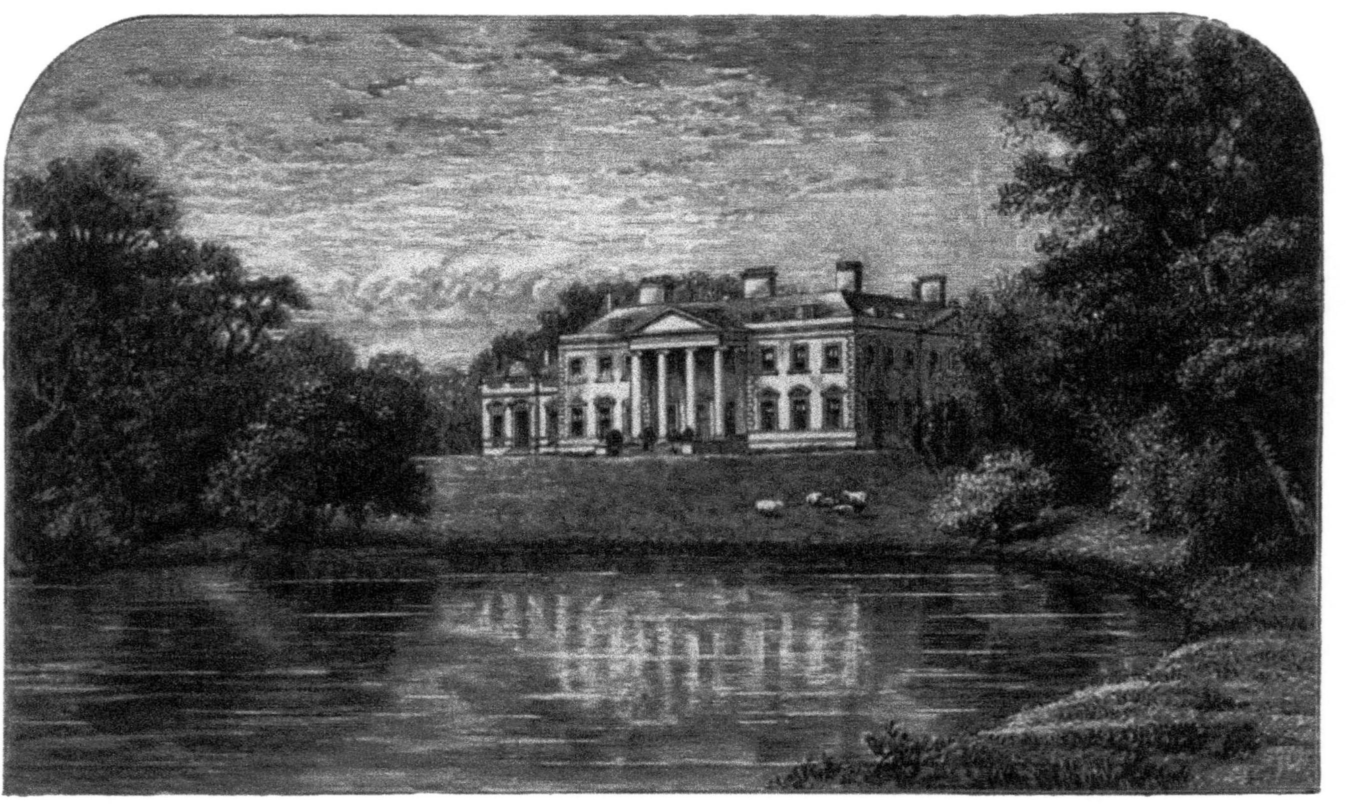

Frontispiece

BROADLANDS

THE LIFE AND CORRESPONDENCE OF HENRY JOHN TEMPLE VISCOUNT PALMERSTON

BY THE

HON. EVELYN ASHLEY, M.P.

IN TWO VOLUMES

VOL. II.

LONDON
RICHARD BENTLEY & SON, NEW BURLINGTON STREET
Publishers in Ordinary to Her Majesty the Queen
1879

All rights reserved

CONTENTS

OF

THE SECOND VOLUME.

Book II.

CHAPTER I.

CHAPTER II.

CHAPTER III.

CHAPTER IV.

CHAPTER V.

CHAPTER VI.

CHAPTER VII.

CHAPTER VIII.

CHAPTER IX.

CHAPTER X.

CHAPTER XI.

CHAPTER XII.

CHAPTER XIII.

CHAPTER XIV.

CHAPTER XV.

CHAPTER XVI.

CHAPTER XVII.

CHAPTER XVIII.

LIFE AND CORRESPONDENCE

OF

HENRY JOHN TEMPLE

THIRD VISCOUNT PALMERSTON, K.G., G.C.B.

BOOK II.

CHAPTER I.

THIRD TENURE OF THE FOREIGN OFFICE—SWITZERLAND—SPANISH MARRIAGES—PORTUGAL—ANNEXATION OF THE PUNJAUB.

LORD PALMERSTON was close upon sixty-two years of age when, in 1846, he went to the Foreign Office for the third and last time. Nearly twenty years elapsed before he died, but death found him still in harness and the working head of a powerful Administration. During this long space, with only two short intervals, he was continuously in office—first as Foreign Secretary, next as Home Secretary, and twice as Prime Minister.

Of these years the five given up to 'Foreign Affairs' were the most unquiet which, with his own country at peace, could fall to any man's lot, and culminated in his abrupt retirement at the close of 1851. The year which immediately succeeded his taking the seals was sufficiently full of anxious events, such as the Spanish marriages, civil wars in Spain and Portugal, and the disturbances in Switzerland, which, at one moment, seriously threatened the independence of that sturdy little republic; but these formed but a fit prelude to the storm which broke over Europe in 1848, and continued to rage throughout the following year.

To aid, by his countenance and counsel, the triumph and maintenance of constitutional freedom, was Lord Palmerston's desire. He foresaw clearly enough the results of despotic repression. The events of the revolutionary year were, in his opinion, but the natural fruits of the growths planted by the hands of absolute sovereigns. To prune betimes was, as he incessantly pointed out, the only check which kings, ministers, and patriots could usefully apply. In fact, during the whole of 1847, he was bent on giving such aid as was in his power to those Governments which were willing and able to 'put their house in order.' While, however, he recognised the necessity, he was little hopeful in the prospect. History admonishes us, he used to say, that rulers seldom have the forecast to substitute, in good time, reform for revolution. They take no note of changes around them, and forget that it is the pre-existing spirit of slavery in the people that has made tyrants in all ages of the world. No tyrant ever made a slave who was not one already—no community, however small, having the spirit of freemen ever had a master for long. When subjects change their spirit, they will also restrain or else change their rulers.

The following extract from a circular despatch sent to the British representatives in Italy, in January, 1848, gives such a clear compendium of his views and of his previous endeavours in other directions that I here insert it:—

The situation of the sovereigns of Italy towards their subjects is one of which advantage may be taken by the enemies of both. It is not difficult to convey to the sovereigns false reports that risings are intended, and to create in their minds

... revolutionary plots are in agitation. ... agency may be employed to repre... their sovereigns are insincere in their ... thus the people, being stimulated to ... of securing political reforms, the very ... have been delusively led on may be con... for depriving them of the objects of their ...

... to counteract, as far as possible, these ... are instructed to say to the Minister that ... of reform and improvement is still ... sovereigns, but that it is now too late for ... distrust reasonable progress; and that re... petitions is sure to lead ere long to the ... to irresistible demands. That it is better ... to frame its measures of improvement with ... and to grant them with the grace of sponta... than to be compelled to adopt, on the sudden, ... insufficiently matured, and which, being wrung ... pressure of imperious circumstances, invert ... of things, and being of the nature of a capi... sovereign to the subject, may not always be a ... for permanent harmony between the Crown and ...

... leaders with whom you may have inter... should use language of the same tendency and argu... from the same considerations. You should tell ... put upon the inclinations of their sovereigns ... ill-will and repugnance, which must lead their ... part, to be constantly looking out for an oppor... off the yoke which they may have been obliged ... mutual distrust will thus be created between the ... the governed. That this distrust will break out ... each side, intended perhaps defensively by those ... but regarded as offensive by the other party. ... will thence ensue, and foreign interference ... result.

... imbued with these sentiments that Lord ... scanned the horizon, and one of the first ... his attention was the state of Swit... naturally viewed with the greatest concern ... of any such interference by the Great ...

Powers with that free confederacy as might compromise her political independence, or endanger the position which she held as the home and refuge of liberty on the Continent. His influence, as will be seen, contributed very materially to avert any such intervention.

To understand the events which were occurring in that country, it is necessary to remember that, up to the commencement of the present century, the condition of a Swiss canton was like that of a feudal lord with an aggregate of seigneurial and subject properties. It had two councils, great and small, but the real powers of government were all exercised by the small or executive council, while the great or legislative council had neither initiative, independence, nor publicity of debate. In 1846, of the 2,400,000 inhabitants of Switzerland, about 900,000 were Roman Catholics, and the remainder Protestants, while each of the twenty-two cantons had an equal voice in the Diet whatever the disparity as to size, wealth, or, we may add, intelligence. In the Catholic cantons the clergy enjoyed great privileges and power, and the people generally were in a state of ignorant submission to their directions.

The French Revolution of 1830 gave an impetus to a movement towards more liberal and popular institutions, and the Radical party booame speedily opposed to the Conservative. The Roman Catholic priests and Jesuits in three of the small cantons took, as might have been expected, an active part on the Conservative side, and were incessant workers in a series of counter-revolutions.

The introduction of the Jesuits into the important canton of Lucerne, which had, up to the year 1844, been free from their noisome presence, put the torch to materials which had thus long been piling up ready for the flame. The seven Roman Catholic cantons found it necessary, if they wished to resist the decrees of the rest of the Federation, to form themselves into a

offensive and defensive. This new name of the 'Sonderbund.'
July, 1846, the Federal Diet voted illegal, and decreed, on the 3rd of Sep- of the Jesuits from the four can- Schwytz, Freyburg, and Valais, in established. A civil war was the in- quence.

however, the French Government had England, France, Austria, Russia, and make a collective declaration recom- arbitration of the Pope in the dispute suits—proposing a conference for modify- al compact, and announcing to the Swiss they refused these propositions and pro- the war, the five Powers would consider ation as no longer existing—in other posal to compel the Swiss by force of t the views of the Great Powers. Lord behalf of the British Government, re- this proposal. He stood at first alone, ights of Prussia over Neufchatel prompted ere, although, as a Protestant Power, she athy for the seceders; and the Austrian, he Russian, was not more with him than n. The view that Prince Metternich took neutrality of Switzerland could only be long as she was one Federal Republic— y being founded on her Federal consti- he view of Lord Palmerston was, that her would be equally necessary and equally r she was federated or not. Metternich ere both jealous of Switzerland becoming therefore, powerful military state. They, secretly aided the seven cantons, and, in Lamartine, almost treated the Diet as a

er was, no doubt, for a time one full of r. Morier had reported from Berne in

October, 1846: 'Altogether it may be safely affirmed, that from this time forth the Federal Bund is virtually dissolved, and Switzerland, as a political body, in a state of decomposition;' and Chevalier Bunsen, Prussian Minister in London, becoming at length alarmed, wrote to Lord Palmerston: 'Don't let the affair slip out of your hands; it is very serious.'

The following letter to Lord Minto, who had gone on a mission to Italy, gives the views of the British Government:—

F. O.: November 11, 1847.

If the Diet get possession of the canton of Freyburg and dispose of the Jesuits there, it will go some way towards settling the pending questions, and if the Diet can also get a friendly Government established at Lucerne, and by that means drive the Jesuits out of that canton, I should think that they need not very much care about their remaining in some of the smaller cantons. But the best would be if the Pope would take some step to induce them to evacuate Switzerland altogether.

Broglie[1] says that there will be no difficulty in getting the Pope to take some steps about the Jesuits, but then he says that they are not the real object, but only a pretence, and that when they are got rid of some other demand will be made which will be found unreasonable. I say, in reply, yield to-day that which is reasonably asked, and resist to-morrow that which you will be borne out in resisting, but do not let us put ourselves in the wrong to-day merely for fear that we may find ourselves in the right to-morrow. I send you copies of the communication which we have received from the French Government on Swiss affairs; I am going immediately to write an answer. It will be in substance that we are willing to join the other Powers in an endeavour to put an end to the civil war by an offer of mediation, but not willing to meddle with the revision of the Federal compact. But that before the five Powers make a joint offer of mediation, it seems desirable that they should be agreed as to the conditions of settlement which they would think fair between the parties. That our notion is this: We think that the Jesuit question is a political as well as, and much more than a religious question, and that it is at the bottom of the whole of the present quarrel. We therefore propose that the Sonderbund cantons

[1] French ambassador in London.

to abide by any decision which question, and that the five Powers the Diet to use all their influence the Pope the recall of the Jesuits from they receiving, of course, compensa- which they might be thus obliged to removed, we should propose that the all hostile intentions against the seven renew their often-made declaration that mean to respect the sovereignty of the which the Confederation is composed. This having no further pretence for their should be dissolved, and then the whole matter would then go to work, in the manner Federal compact, to make any alterations or that compact which they might wish or want. that the five Powers will agree to this scheme; and perhaps Russia take part openly with and Guizot's despatch only repeats the propo- the Sonderbund, and rejected by the Diet, and that effect made by the five Powers would of same fate. Guizot's object, of course, is to try et apparently in the wrong, so as to afford him ome kind of pretext for violent measures after- raft of note is a paraphrase of the manifesto of ers last year about the extinction of Cracow. I bly put my name to such a paper, and I wonder uld defend himself to the deputies for having put

November 17 he writes to the same:—

have to choose between us and the three Powers; that his draft of note was suggested by Austria. low Austria; and the Prussian Government have d his plan. Broglie, however, says his own per- vate opinion is with us; and it seems to me that in France would not go along with Guizot in the proposed to us. We shall lie on our oars till we from Paris to the despatch which went thither the meantime, if the Pope would take any steps uits, he would increase the chances of peace; but e too far in Switzerland to admit of a settlement le of the mere recall of the Jesuits from Lucerne.

France having accepted the modifications proposed by Lord Palmerston in the plan of mediation, he writes to Lord Ponsonby at Vienna on the 20th:—

F. O.: November 20, 1847.

You will see that the French Government are willing to agree to our proposal as to the offer of mediation between the contending parties in Switzerland. The explanations which they wish us to accept, and to which we have no objection, are, that the Jesuits should be withdrawn, by the joint concurrence of the seven cantons and of the Pope. All we require is, that the foundation of the arrangements should be that the Jesuits should be removed from the whole of the territory of the Confederation, because we are now quite convinced that things have now gone so far, and popular feeling has been so strongly roused against them, that unless they leave Switzerland entirely there is no chance of peace in that country. The next explanation of the French is, that they understand the separate sovereignty of the confederated cantons to carry with it the result, that no change can be made in the Federal compact without the consent of all the cantons, and they hold that this principle ought to be admitted by the Diet. We think this reasonable, and are willing to agree to it as the foundation of the settlement which is to be proposed. The French, thirdly, say that, in agreeing to our proposal that the refusal of the joint offer of mediation, if it should be unfortunately refused, is not to be used as a pretext for armed interference, they must make this reserve, that all parties are to remain after such refusal possessed of all the rights in regard to measures with respect to Switzerland which they at present possess. To this we can, of course, make no objection.

The French agree to the conference being in London, and we hope that P. Metternich will not object to this. I do not think that we should willingly consent to join a conference to be held anywhere but here.

Meanwhile, however, the capture of Freyburg by the forces of the Diet under General Dufour brought the war to an abrupt termination, and obviated the necessity of the proposed mediation. Lord Palmerston's object had been gained, and the delay had been of incalculable service to the cause of Swiss independence.

…, who was on his way to his …, had been instructed by Lord … Berne on his way, where his cha… might be of service in enforcing … English Foreign Office. Lord Pal… him :—

F. O.: December 18, 1847.

… be able to persuade the Diet to give up … against their opponents at Freyburg … really would be very disgraceful of them if … use of their victory; and they might re… wheel of fortune has many turns, and that it …, in some future change of things, the measure …w mete out to others might be measured back …selves. At all events, such confiscations and … enduring resentments and perpetuate party … any counterbalancing advantage, except … who thus transfer to themselves the property … belongs to others. Besides, there is not in … of a principle to justify their proscriptions. …, or Polish, or Galician nobles revolt against …, they are clearly on the wrong side of the law; …, they must abide by the consequences. If a …tes the constitution of his country, and fails in … may partly be made to pay in person and in …nalty of his illegal acts. But in the case of Frey…erne there was no violation of the laws of the …e was a decision taken by the sovereign authority …which the Federal Government thought at variance …ral obligations and engagements of those cantons; …ot, by any fair construction of words, be called … Treason means the violation of some duty to… …ereign power of the state of which the accused is …ect; but such a crime cannot be committed by …t of a sovereign state towards the confederates … Freyburg and Lucerne were not subjects of the … and could not be guilty of high treason towards it.

…ing still some danger of an Austrian inter… …d Palmerston sent the following to Lord

F. O.: December 21, 1847.

It seems to me, from Canning's accounts of his conversations with Ochsenbein,[1] that the Swiss will pursue a more moderate line of conduct than at first appeared likely; and it seems quite certain that they will afford the four Powers no valid reason for interference. At the same time, I wish you to lose no opportunity of endeavouring to dissuade Metternich from any attempt of the kind. He could not interfere without France doing so too; and whatever may be the professions or even the sincere intentions of Louis Philippe and Guizot, he may depend upon it, as sure as he is alive, that any interference of France in the internal affairs of Switzerland would turn to the account of France, and would be adverse to the interests of Austria.

In fact, if French troops were to enter Switzerland, they would sympathise with the Liberals, and not with the party which Metternich would wish to favour. If there is one maxim of policy which Metternich ought to hold by more than another, it is to keep the French out of Switzerland and out of Italy; but if Austrian troops enter one or the other, French troops will follow, and Austria will rue the day when she paved the way for such a military movement by France.

Spain was once described by the Duke of Wellington as the only country where two and two did not make four, and the unexpected events of which it has so often been the theatre might appear to justify the assertion. Few of them, however, have been so whimsically sudden, or so uselessly mischievous, as that which towards the end of the year 1846 startled and irritated England under the name of the 'Spanish Marriages.'

Queen Isabella and her sister the Infanta were young and unmarried. To secure the succession it was necessary to find them husbands. The question in debate was, who these were to be.

It had been the settled policy of England—as indeed of the other European Powers—ever since the War of the Spanish Succession, to provide against the contingency of a union of the crowns of France and Spain, in the person of one sovereign or in the same

[1] President of the Diet.

rance occupied 500 miles of the
rica with a large naval station at
ld, therefore, to be a great and
th us, that Spain should be com-
and that her policy should not be
h considerations; so that if ever
at war with France, we should not
unt find ourselves involved in war
rd Palmerston, therefore, when he
erdeen at the Foreign Office, re-
which had been expressed by his
ich had elicited from the French
t pledges that no son of Louis
rry Isabella, or even the Infanta
to the Spanish throne had been se-
becoming a mother. These pledges
n of 1846 broken both in their
was suddenly announced that the
her cousin, Don Francisco, and
on the same day become the wife
tpensier, the youngest son of the
n. Apart from the discreditable
h characterised this intrigue, the
he transaction lay in the fact that
l his Minister had ascertained that
sue of the marriage between the
a, and calculated on securing by a
which they were solemnly bound
ements to prevent. Yet Guizot's
wrong, of honour and dishonour,
ed by his feelings of antagonism to
it, regardless of the universal con-
s conduct and that of his master
gland and throughout Europe, he

actually boasted to the French Chamber, when they met, that the Spanish marriages constituted the first great thing France had accomplished completely single-handed in Europe since 1830. Retribution, however, soon fell on all concerned, and the objects aimed at were not attained. Montpensier's wife never came to the throne, while Louis Philippe had to descend from his own. The fall of his Government and of his dynasty was undoubtedly hastened by the position of isolation, distrust, and contempt in which they were placed by this act and by the feelings which it provoked among the French people themselves as well as abroad. England only suffered in this respect, that from the date of this transaction the close alliance between the two countries was broken—distrust succeeded to confidence, causing, indeed, one of those periodical invasion scares to which the English people are liable—and the absolutist courts of Europe took advantage of this state of things to carry out their high-handed proceedings in Poland and elsewhere.

The following letter is amongst the first private papers of Lord Palmerston after his return to office. It is interesting, because we see in it the germ of his policy as to Italy, which found so many detractors and defenders. He foresaw that if Rome remained as it was, a French army would eventually enter it. He foresaw also, that if Italy remained as it was, a war between France and Austria was inevitable:—

Foreign Office: July 30, 1846.

My dear John Russell,—I send you a copy of the Memorandum which, in 1831, was presented to the Pope on behalf of the five Powers, and which was defeated by adverse influences, although the recommendations which it contains were entirely approved by Cardinal Bernetti and others in authority at Rome.

The matter is really one of great and serious importance, and has bearings much more extensive than at first sight might appear. Italy is the weak part of Europe, and the next war that breaks out in Europe will probably arise out of Italian

[illegible] of the Papal States is intolerably
[illegible] submit to such misrule, but phy-
[illegible] external assistance.
[illegible] formerly municipal institutions of great
[illegible] much civil security. These insti-
[illegible] by the French invasion, and were not
[illegible] peace of 1815. Outbreaks and insurrec-
[illegible] have followed each other in rapid succes-
[illegible] there was, often when there was not, a
[illegible] from without. The French Revolution of
[illegible] explosion in the Roman States, and that
[illegible] the conferences out of which the Mem. arose.
[illegible] and discontent has more than once been since
[illegible] acts. Leave things as they are, and you
[illegible] power of disturbing the peace of Europe when-
[illegible] Two or three millions of francs, properly
[illegible] an insurrection at any time, and the as-
[illegible] Liberal party at Paris, whenever it may happen,
[illegible] of an election or by the death of the king,
[illegible] followed by an outbreak in Italy. That is the
[illegible] the French Liberals look; they know that if
[illegible] back to the Rhine they would have against
[illegible] many united, Russia, and more or less England;
[illegible] an insurrection in Italy against Papal mis-
[illegible] they would stand in a very different position.
[illegible] probably take no part against them; Prussia
[illegible] a foot; Russia would not be very active, and,
[illegible] not displeased at anything that might humble
[illegible] Austria. But Austria *would* interfere, and could
[illegible] doing so, even though not very efficiently backed
[illegible] France and Austria would then fight each other in
[illegible] France would have all the Italians on her side. But
[illegible] in Italy, would probably spread to Germany,
[illegible] events, we can have no wish to see Austria broken
[illegible] France aggrandised, and the military vanity and love
[illegible] the French revived and strengthened by success.
[illegible] should happen, and they may not be so distant
[illegible] suppose, people will naturally ask what the Whig
[illegible] of 1846 was about, and why they did not take
[illegible] the liberal inclinations of the new Pope to en-
[illegible] him to make reforms, which, if then made,
[illegible] prevented such events. I own that I for one should
[illegible] loss for any answer to such an interrogation.

If, on the other hand, we take the step which I propose to take towards the other four Powers, we shall either succeed or fail. If we succeed in getting any one or more to join us, I believe we shall be doing a thing agreeable, as well as useful, to the Pope, and shall strengthen and support him in effecting reforms which every enlightened member of the Roman Government has long seen and acknowledged to be necessary. If, on the contrary, we fail, and if all four should refuse to do anything, we shall at least stand justified, and shall be able to show that we are wholly absolved from the responsibility of any misfortunes which may hereafter arise from that quarter.

Far from being animated by the passions of the revolutionist—as it was the fashion of party then to describe him—Lord Palmerston wished to turn revolution everywhere aside by compromise.

His error, if error it was, consisted in thinking that a government of priests would willingly resign any portion of their power to laics; and that men of the stamp of Mazzini and his disciples would care two straws about moderate constitutional government. The first idea was to open diplomatic relations with Rome, and send a regular ambassador. No regular ambassador or minister, however, was ever named; and thus Lord Minto was ultimately sent on a special mission, which will presently be spoken of. The affairs of Italy were not alone in demanding attention at this time. In Portugal, the intrigues of France and Spain to undermine the traditional influence of England had created a confused variety of factions; whilst the want of tact and judgment on the part of the Court, both as to the measures it adopted and the men it employed, had produced dissatisfaction, terminating in insurrection. The civil war which broke out with the revolutionary supreme Junta was caused by the arbitrary acts of the Royal Government, who hoped for a Spanish intervention in their behalf. As the Crown could neither subdue the rebels, nor the rebels triumph over the Crown, the country was in a state of anarchy, amidst which the Queen was not unlikely to lose her

... its last chance of reviving pros-

... endeavours, from October, 1846, ... were directed to persuade the ... to come to terms with the ... Spain from interfering by force ... of 1847, he found that the ... would not come to terms with ... that the Spanish Government would ... of England, if the throne of Donna ... in imminent danger. None could ... was in such danger, and that the ... going to ruin by reason of the war. ... therefore, at last, determined to ... conjunction with the naval forces of Spain, brought the conflict to an end on ... amnesty and the constitution. By this serving the interests of British commerce, ... ton was enabled to secure to the Portu- those concessions which would not have Spain had interfered singly at the request ... Party, and saved the Portuguese from that political dependence on Spain have been the result of obligations due to

... glaring violation of the Whig principle of ... tion could hardly be cited; but it was a ... nd served to add to the many proofs that ... en of the absurdity of establishing general ... to be practically applicable to every ... se. In the mutable condition of human ... is but one universal doctrine that a states- ... preach to a sensible people—the necessity of ... h a manner as, according to circumstances, ... est for the particular country he governs, ... vantageous to mankind at large.

... wing correspondence gives somewhat more ... onsecutive account of the action taken by ... Government in the matter:—

Foreign Office : Oct. 30, 1846.

My dear Normanby,—I am this afternoon returned from Windsor, where I have been for two days. The Queen and Prince are very anxious and uneasy about the state of Portugal. We send off to-morrow Colonel Wylde, who goes in the *Cyclops*, from Portsmouth to Oporto and Lisbon, to see and report on the state of things, and we shall order a reinforcement of our naval force in the Tagus. But this is all we can at present do, and our interference must be confined to giving advice and taking care of the personal safety of the Queen. It is a most unfortunate state of things; but I trust the danger is somewhat exaggerated; still it is great; and what makes matters worse, it has been brought on by the folly of the Court, instigated I believe by the German tutor, Diez.[1] It was foreseen that, if the elections went on and the new Chambers should meet, one of their first acts would be to address the Queen to remove the intermeddling tutor. Thereupon he set to work to secure himself, little caring for or little foreseeing the danger in which he was involving the King and Queen. The only way, as he thought, to avoid the address was to prevent the meeting of the Cortes, this could only be done by getting rid of the Government which was pledged to call them; the way in which that could be accomplished was by making a *coup d'état*; and so it was made, against the advice of all persons whose judgment was worth having, and without consulting Lord Howard, because they knew he would have been against it; and contrary to the opinion of our Court, though I believe that opinion arrived too late.

Carlton Terrace : Nov. 1, 1846.

My dear Normanby,—We have heard of Parker's arrival at Lisbon, with his whole squadron, so that our naval force in the Tagus will now be respectable. No doubt his presence will produce a useful effect; when people see a strong force, they do not exactly know how far such a force may be authorised to act, and they fear the worst, and guide themselves accordingly. Parker will be instructed to protect the persons of the Royal Family, if they should be obliged to take refuge on board their own line-of-battle ship in the Tagus, or on board one of ours; and in case of need he will be authorised to garrison the fort of Belem with his marines; but you had better say nothing about

[1] This gentleman had been placed by his family about the young King.

French should intrigue to prevent it.
having been done, you will know
sanctioned by the British Government.
tonight that he heard from Paris that
they should not mind our squadron
provided we did not send any land troops.
have said this, because they know well
old and special treaties with Portugal,
casus were to arise we should not inquire
Government minded or not that which we
called upon by our treaty engagements

under the influence and auspices of
who was once termed in a debate in the
as the 'Jonathan Wild' of European
who had started life as a furious
Portuguese Government had entered
of exasperating tyranny. Soon after
compelled to fly, the Marquis de Sal-
the post of President of the Council,
led to the taint of Cabral's policy and
its. The head-quarters of the rebels
lutionary supreme Junta of Government
. Lord Palmerston, on the eve of an
at place by the Royal troops, determined
tiate between the parties, and so avoid
e and property which the capture of
m would necessarily involve. He wrote,
lonel Wylde, under the date of January
acting him to go to Oporto and to enter
g negotiation:—

gotiation must be a declaration and engagement
n, to you, as the representative in this matter
vernment, that immediately on the termination
she will establish constitutional government,
without delay. Unless this assurance is given
d and positive manner, we cannot meddle with
ought, I think, also to assure us that she
present at least, bring into office the Cabrals,
revolt has taken place. Of course she would

not be expected to exclude them for ever from power; their turn may come; but to replace them just now would be to irritate and provoke a large portion of the country. With these assurances in your hand, you may be well entitled to urge the Junta to lay down their arms and submit to the Queen's authority. Of course they would say, the assurances given may be satisfactory as to the nation, but what is to become of us as individuals, and how are we to be secured?

The general basis of the conditions should, I think, be amnesty for the mass of the insurgents; precautions as to some of the chiefs and leaders. That security was wisely and liberally stated in Saldanha's Articles to consist in their temporary retirement from Portugal; the military so retiring to have half-pay for their support. For the civilians no provision was proposed by Saldanha, because, I presume, he concluded that most of them had means of their own; and I infer and take for granted, that no confiscations or sequestrations of property are thought of. The difficulty, and it is one which we in this country have no personal knowledge which would enable us to solve, is, how far these voluntary and temporary banishments are to go. There may be a certain number of men whom it would be better for their own sakes and for the peace of the country for a short time to remove from Portugal. But if the list is made large, and I think Saldanha's Articles make it much too comprehensive, the Queen will lose the services of many men who, though they have been opposed to her Government and Ministers on the present occasion, might, when the contest is over, become very useful servants of the Crown; and it must also be remembered that if all the leading men of the Liberal party are to be compelled to leave the country, though only for a time, the conduct of affairs must necessarily fall into the hands of the opposite set of men, who have been clearly proved to be hateful to a large portion of the nation; and that is not the way to restore contentment in the country.

Sir Hamilton Seymour had now succeeded Lord Howard as English Minister at Lisbon.

Carlton Gardens: Feb. 5, 1847.

My dear Seymour,—The Queen should remember that unless she shows herself to be the sovereign of the whole nation, she cannot expect the whole nation to regard and love her as their sovereign; and that a throne whose stability rests on the point of the bayonet has a very ticklish and uncertain basis.

... and such others as may occur to ... the Court and the Govern- ... understand that they must expect ... help them to continue a system of ... England will take care that no sup- ... them by Spain.

Foreign Office: Feb. 17, 1847.

... for full powers to conclude some fresh ... in the event of Don Miguel's returning ... warn the Court against giving in to the ... will by such means obtain aid against the ... party; we shall take uncommon good ... If the Queen fears Don Miguel, she must ... up matters with the Junta, and to be able ... parties who are for constitutional government ... against the adherents of Don Miguel. If ... governed despotically and by sword and bayonet, ... a woman for such purpose, and it matters ... despot is called by one Christian name or ... make this very civilly to be understood by the ...; and endeavour also to explain to them in ... the sending off the Torres Vedras prisoners ... Africa[1] has done the Queen irreparable injury in ...; and if it turns out that they are sent to a ...n, you may observe how unfortunate it is that ...d have incurred unnecessarily the odium of a ...e did not mean to inflict.

... trust that Diez will be shipped off too; but ... do lives after them,' and the mischief done ... tinue to be felt long after he has re-crossed the ... It will be something gained, however, not to ... evil counsellor always at the Royal ear; and ... will have more chance of swaying decisions upon ... may arise.

... to think that Miguel has no intention at ... to Portugal, and that he will not do so until, ... is a considerable force in the field under his ... came overland from Italy as servant to a Captain ... ived here on the 2nd inst. from Calais.

[1] ...itulated on honourable terms, but were shipped off to

Foreign Office: Feb. 26, 1847.

I wish you to press in the strongest manner upon the Queen and King, and on any of the people about them who may be worth talking to, that it becomes every day more and more absolutely necessary for them to make overtures to the Junta, and to come to some amicable settlement, so as to put an end to the civil war. Tell them plainly that if they speculate upon a Miguelite insurrection, to bring in foreign troops to put down the Junta, they deceive themselves. We shall take good care that any measures to be adopted against Miguel, if he should return to Portugal, which he will probably not do, shall not be perverted into an interference between the Camarilla and Junta, between whom in reality the civil war is waged.

Tell them as to our guaranteeing a loan, they might as well ask us to give them a slice of the moon.

The only way in which the Queen can make herself strong against Miguel is by rallying again round her that portion of her subjects by whose exertions, devotion, and sacrifices she was placed upon the throne; but if the Constitution on which she rode in triumph is to be abrogated, and despotism is to be set up in its stead, such of the Portuguese who are for despotism will naturally say that it is Miguel, and not Maria, who is best entitled to be their despotic sovereign.

In the following Memorandum, Lord Palmerston puts on record the views which were afterwards embodied in the formal Convention of May, made between England, France, Spain and Portugal:—

Carlton Gardens: March 25, 1847.

I entirely concur in the view taken by Lord John Russell, of the nature of the present state of affairs in Portugal, and of the bearing of the letter and spirit of the Quadruple Treaty upon that state of things; and I am decidedly of opinion with him, that 'there is at present no case for interference, either by the letter or the spirit of the Quadruple Treaty.'

But it may be argued, by those who ask for interference, that there may be ground for such interference, independently of that treaty, upon general principles of policy, and not in virtue of any anterior engagements. The Quadruple Treaty itself was, it may be said, the record of a determination taken upon general grounds of policy, and was not the fulfilment of

... the question may be asked, is ... for interfering by force of arms in ... grounds of general policy, and ... engagements?

... writers on the Law of Nations that, ... regularly established in any country, ... has been divided into two contending ... marshalled in two opposing camps, foreign ... conflicting parties in the same manner as if ... nations; and may allowably side with ... in the civil war, as they would with one ... in a war between two independent ... to do so is acknowledged to exist in all ... expediency of doing so must depend on the ... particular case.

... of any third party in such a case must depend ... which it could give to two questions—First, ... party whose side we think of taking, a just ... Is it for our interest to give that just cause ...

... case of a civil war which originates in a dis... both of these questions may generally be ... difficulty, either one way or the other. The ... a foreign State may easily make up its mind as ... is right in regard to a disputed succession, ... upon which the decision is to turn are known ... the country where the dispute exists as in it; and ... which such foreign Government may have in the ... easily appreciated. Such was the case out of ... Quadruple Treaty arose. The civil war arose out of ... succession in Portugal and in Spain; and the inte... England had in the matter was a matter of compara... simple calculation.

... different when a civil war arises out of a contest ... parties in a country, who differ in regard to ... forms of government, and who, without pretend... the reigning dynasty, stand up for different ... organisation.

... difficult, in such a case, for the Government of ... to pronounce with certainty that either party ... is absolutely in the right; and when the ... conflicting systems of government is mixed up with ... of illegal or unconstitutional proceedings, the task of judging between them is rendered still more difficult. In such a case, too, it is far less easy to answer the second of the above-mentioned questions, even after having formed an opinion on the first; for, supposing the right to be pretty clearly on one side or the other, there are a vast number of considerations to be taken into account before a foreign Government could decidedly determine that it was for its well-understood interests to interfere by force of arms. But this is the present case of Portugal; and there would be much difficulty for the English Government to answer the two foregoing questions affirmatively in favour of the Queen of Portugal. At the same time, England has a great interest in the welfare of Portugal as a State; and the present course of events seems likely to ruin Portugal for a long time to come as a European Power.

Is there, then, any way open for England by which, without violating principles on which her foreign policy has always been founded, and without taking steps which would make enemies of the majority of the Portuguese nation, she might speedily put an end to this disastrous war?

England has offered the Queen of Portugal mediation between her Government and the Junta; the offer has been declined, because Marshal Saldanha does not choose the war to end by negotiation and reconcilement, and because he insists upon it that what is plainly the minority of the nation shall, by aid of a Spanish force, be enabled to crush the majority. But such an end would not be lasting; the defeated majority would wait their opportunity, and, whenever a party sympathising with them should rise to power in Spain, they would again try the fate of arms in Portugal. Saldanha's plan is, therefore, objectionable in policy, as well as in principle.

But might not the English Government renew its offer; but giving to its offer the character of arbitration rather than of mediation? Might some such communication as the following be made to the Queen?—The course you are following is fatal, end as it may; for it is evident that it will not end in your Majesty's triumph over the Junta and their adherents, by your own means. England is your ancient ally, and is bound to come to your aid in times of difficulty and danger. She is ready to do so now; but you must allow her to prescribe for Portugal such remedies as her disorders require. We demand, therefore, of you *carte blanche* as to the offers which we require you to authorise us to make in your name to your revolted subjects. These offers, however, we intend to be generally these: General

... tender their submission on or before a ... amnesty, of course, to include retention of ... property; and of military commissions, ... for officers, according to the discretion ... and restoration to the Queen's service for ... officers and privates as choose to be so ... and very few—*probably not above ten—of* ... *of the Junta to retire for two or three* ... A new Ministry to be formed, consisting ... neither to the Junta nor to the Cabral ... by which the Constitution has, in any of ... whole, been suspended, to be immediately ... Constitution, as it stood before the 6th of ... to be immediately restored. The Cortes to be ... on some specified day, not too distant; and ... take place at a proper interval before their ... to leave Portugal by the very next packet; ... of Camarilla Government to be for ever left off. ... should agree to these terms, the civil war would ... the fair and just demands of the Portuguese be satisfied. The Junta, therefore, might be told, ... conditions were proposed to them, that if they should ... the British Government would then be prepared ... active part in favour of the Queen, and would join ... in order to restore peace to Portugal. Of ... case, the British Government must, however ... it might be to do so, guarantee to the Junta the ... of these conditions by the Queen; and ... would, in such a case, be no difficulty in en- ... execution. There can be little doubt that such a ... put an end to the war in a fortnight after it was ...

... Queen should say that she could not adopt such a ... Saldanha would resign, the answer would be: ... would render his resignation a matter of indifference; ... offer you Colonel Wylde to take his place at once, ... Wylde shall be Chef d'Etat-Major, to assist, with his ... judgment, any Portuguese General whom you may ... general command.

... war could be terminated in this manner, by ... without Spanish or French interference, the ... Queen would be saved, the liberties of the Por- ... would be respected, and the tie between England

and Portugal would remain unbroken. The despatches received this afternoon, from Lisbon and Oporto, seem to show the urgency of some energetic measure for putting an end to the calamities with which Portugal is now afflicted.

PALMERSTON.

Foreign Office: April 3, 1847.

My dear Seymour,—I send you instructions which I hope will put an end to the civil war. The only difficulty which I anticipate will be with the Queen, and with the people who govern her without her knowing it. But the recent change of Ministers at Madrid will probably help us,[1] because if the new Ministers have any predilections towards Portugal, I should think it might be rather towards Oporto than towards Lisbon. At all events, we may be pretty sure that they will not let their troops enter Portugal without our consent, and, therefore, the Queen of Portugal must feel that her chances of assistance from Spain are much lessened, if not extinct. I trust she will agree to our terms. If she does not, we must rest upon our oars, and wait till one side or the other is fairly worn out by fatigue and exhaustion.

I say in my despatch that the amnesty ought to be full and general; and you should try all you can to get it made so. The Queen must be made to understand that we are greatly stretching our established principles of foreign policy by engaging to coerce the Junta in any case, and that unless she gives us the broadest possible ground to take our stand upon, we could not justify our course to Parliament and the country; and therefore she ought to make the amnesty without exception.

There certainly was little in the conduct of the British Foreign Office compatible with the principle of non-intervention, and it was only on the ground that we were saving the Sovereign from ruin, and the country from confusion, and establishing something like a system of liberality, moderation, and equity, that we could justify our course; but if we did that, we might fairly contend that we did justify it, considering our peculiar relations with Portugal, and admitting that States, like individuals, have duties which may inspire them with an interest in their neighbours' welfare.

[1] The Pacheco Government.

however, as the next letter which were unworthy of them, character of men who were being themselves.

F. O.: April 30, 1847.

—Our monetary affairs look better; and the funds rising; and the notion, which that the Emperor of Russia is going to sterling of his hoardings in our funds has in the City to-day.

that the Queen of Portugal, or rather her about sending a dozen men to live at the Portuguese Government for six months at Paris. matter were less serious, one should call this infatuation. They seem determined to put the Queen upon the result of a battle. If they have fight, they will not essentially mend their position, e the worst of it, the Queen will be in great peril; ts, if saved by us, will undergo the humiliation after defeat, to terms which, before the battle, worn the appearance of imposing. If we were rers between the Government and the Junta, we y have conveyed the Queen's demand for the ishment of the sixteen or eighteen persons in we had taken the resolution to combine with ain to compel the Junta to submit, on the terms ed to them. It was necessary that we should be e terms were such that a refusal of the Junta to would justify us and our allies in undertaking the rtugal, for such the compelling operation would ent temper of the Portuguese; and whether that t be difficult or easy, whether a short or a long ould be an undertaking to which heavy responsi- ecessarily attach, and which the English Govern- ought to be able to justify to Parliament and to ow we think that, supposing, as is probable, that uld agree to submit on the terms offered them, mnesty were general, but should refuse to consent banishment, the expulsion for six months of a lf of men would not be an object of sufficient im- stify the conquest and subjugation of Portugal in

Firmness, however, carried the day, as it usually does when it has right on its side.

F. O.: May 6, 1847.

My dear Seymour,—We have received your despatch giving us an account of the Queen's acceptance of our terms. I am delighted; it is indeed good news, and I trust we shall soon hear that the Junta have accepted also, and that this calamitous civil war has been brought to a close.

The Cortes ought to meet as soon as the preliminary arrangements can be made for it, and the sooner the Queen can substitute tongues for muskets, as instruments of civil and political strife, the better for her and her kingdom.

Saldanha's army is full of Cabralist officers. It is not very likely that Saldanha and his officers should attempt any prank, and fall back towards Lisbon, to coerce the Queen, and prevent her from acceding to our terms; but if he were to do so, he might be told that we will coerce him just as readily as the Junta, and that he had better take care what he is about.

The British fleet was now directed to protect the Queen of Portugal's Government from an attack by the Viscount Sa da Bandiera, or any other of the leaders of the Revolutionary party. But Lord Palmerston considered the desired work was only half done so long as the constitution was dormant, and Parliamentary government not firmly re-established.

C. G.: May 26, 1847.

My dear Seymour,—I hope you will not have had occasion to employ force to protect Lisbon from attack by Sa da Bandiera: but if it has become necessary, I have no doubt it will have been done with effect, and the means at Sir William Parker's disposal will have proved amply sufficient. As to the demands of the Junta, we must be as firm in resisting any unreasonable pretentions of theirs as we were in refusing to comply with the overstrained expectations of the Court. Napier has been appointed to the *St. Vincent*, that he may go to Lisbon and take the command there when Parker moves on to the Mediterranean. We want to collect a larger force within that sea than we now have there; and with Parker and Napier, both with their flags flying there and thereabouts, we shall probably have Joinville on his good behaviour.

C. G.: June 13, 1847.

...satisfactory than the course of things ... as we have hitherto learned them, and I ... the Junta will have submitted, and ... the people in Algarve and in the other ... followed the example thus set them, the civil ... completely ended, and tranquillity will ... restored. Now then comes the time for ... on the Portuguese Government, as to ... immediate execution of the four conditions, ... not, under any pretence whatever, evade. ... power will try to put off the elections and ... the Cortes, because they will fear that the ... against them, and that the majority in the ... the Liberal party, will turn them out, and put ... in. But to this they must make their minds ... have intended to do, and what the Portuguese ... pledged to us to do, is to transfer from the field ... floor of Parliament the conflict of political ... The people, or at least a large portion of ... had grievances which required redress. The ... told them they should have no Parliament ... and represent those grievances. The reply of ... natural and just: they flew to arms. Driven ... and from Parliament, they sought refuge in ... have said to the Queen's Government that they ...ck a Parliament, and that then the people must ...ir arms. The people have laid down, or are about ... their arms. The Queen must give back the Parlia... this point there must be no mistake.

C. G.: July 6, 1847.

...t come home, at half-past one, from the House of ... my letter will not be long. I am glad to find ...rto Junta have at last given in. This puts an end ...ar for the moment; whether it will be renewed or ...n the Queen. If she fulfils faithfully her engage... ...verns in the true spirit of the Constitution, the ... may be content with wielding power according to ...ng no longer fearful of being stripped of it, may be ...out upsetting or attacking the throne. But if the ...s faith, or allows herself to follow the lead of the ..., she will be, as you said in a former letter, a doomed woman. We must try to save her against her will, [illegible] against her tendencies; you cannot therefore be too fi[illegible] insisting upon the fulfilment both of the letter and spirit [illegible] Four Articles. The Torres Vedras prisoners must be sen[illegible] immediately, and I would rather that an English ship [illegible] were sent to fetch them than that they were left to the [illegible] ness and delays of a Portuguese ship of war, such as it [illegible] would be, with ostensible orders for despatch, and secret [illegible] structions to be slow. I should wish, therefore, that you [illegible] Parker should determine at once to send off the *Sidon*, or [illegible] other vessel of suitable dimensions, which Parker can spare, [illegible] bring these people back, and the ship should be off immedia[illegible] She ought to carry out orders *open* and *unsealed*, and [illegible] others, to the Governors of Angola and Benguela, to collect [illegible] give up all the prisoners at once, in order that they may [illegible] brought back. A list of them should be sent, and the [illegible] should carry medical means for such as may be suffering from wounds or sickness, and bedding and other accommodation for them.

The honour of the British Crown and the good faith of the British Government is pledged to the strict fulfilment of the Four Articles, and there must be no exceptions. You will see that the tone of the debate last night was not a bit more favourable to the Queen, her present Ministers, and the Cabral party than the discussion which took place before. Moncorvo came to me this morning, and was evidently nettled at the things which were said, but I told him that Parliamentary privilege has no limit.

Portugal was not the only case in which—non-intervention being laid down as the Whig rule—intervention was the exception. The war between Monte Video and Buenos Ayres had long been the curse of La Plata, and not only injurious to the belligerents themselves but to the trade of the world. The Speech from the Throne, while Sir Robert Peel was still in office, announced an alliance between the French and English Governments for the purpose of suppressing it. This alliance was maintained by Sir Robert's successor, although Lord Palmerston clearly intimated to the French that the game of Algiers was not to be played over again in the river Plate; and, though the agents of

differed wherever their instruc- to differ—the French showing a for the Monte Videans—the final and peace and commerce once their wings in that quarter of the

Prince Talleyrand had incidentally re- Lord Palmerston that Spain had always in the same relation which Portugal England. Monsieur Guizot is known to the same sentiment in 1847, and, further, that such close dependence was one of French foreign policy. It is not, matter of wonder that the prospect of the of the Infanta with the Duc de Montpensier ne of Spain alarmed English statesmen, the ative being Montemolin, son of Don Carlos, absolute monarchy, and condemned before- the Quadruple Treaty to be expelled the foreign forces. Portugal, meanwhile, torn factions, offered a sorry prospect to those her independent stability. Thus it hap- the idea of a union of Spain and Portugal Portuguese Prince, after the death of the Queen, found some favour. The view taken, great free State extending from the Pyrenees would in all future times be a counterpoise and thus save Belgium and the Rhenish from the invading propensities of the French. It was also asserted that the Progressists were ready to hold up their hands for the Portugal as a successor to Queen Isabella. merston, however, did not at all fall in with as is shown in the following letter:—

Broadlands: August 9, 1847.

John Russell,—With regard to the possible with Portugal, or, rather, the incorporation of with Spain, it may be said that if Spain is not now by itself a great free State forming a counterpoise to France, and securing by that means Belgium and the Rhenish provinces; it is not because Spain is not large enough in territory, population, and natural resources; nor would the acquisition of Portugal give her, in this respect, any means the want of which cripples her at present, neither can it be said that by such incorporation Spain would be freed from controlling dangers in her rear which prevent her from facing France boldly to her front; because as long as Portugal is closely connected with England, Portugal would be a help and not a clog to Spain in the pursuit of such a policy. There seems no reason, therefore, to think that Spain, after having swallowed up Portugal, would be a bit more politically independent of France than she is or will be, without having so absorbed her neighbour, and, consequently, the probable result of such an annexation would be, that some fine day England would not only find Spain become a satellite of France, but would lose all the counterbalancing resources which, in such a case, Portugal, as a separate State, would afford us. Those advantages are many, great, and obvious; commercial, political, military, and naval, and if we were thus to lose them, some of them would not be mere loss, but would become formidable weapons of attack against us in the hands of a hostile Power. For instance, the naval position of the Tagus ought never to be in the hands of any Power, whether French or Spanish, which might become hostile to England, and it is only by maintaining Portugal in its separate existence, and in its intimate and protected state of alliance with England, that we can be sure of having the Tagus as a friendly instead of its being a hostile naval station. Only fancy for a moment Portugal forming part of Spain, and Spain led away by France into war with England, and what would be our naval condition with all the ports from Calais to Marseilles hostile to us, St. Malo, Cherbourg, Brest, Rochefort, Corunna, Vigo, the Tagus, Cadiz, Carthagena, Port Mahon, Toulon, and with nothing between us and Malta but Gibraltar, the capture of which would be the bait which France would hold out to Spain to induce her to go to war with us. If, on the contrary, the Tagus were at our command, we should occupy an intermediate position greatly impeding the naval movements of France and Spain. Perhaps, if the scheme of an Iberian Republic could be realised, such a State might be more likely to remain independent of France than a Spanish Monarchy promises to be; but such a republic would soon fall back to be

… be created without sweeping away … allied to us by treaty engagements, and … certainly take the field.

… matters which engaged the atten… Office at this time was the violence … Alliance' to the Republic of Cracow. … 1845, a conspiracy was discovered in … the independence of Poland. An … in the early part of the following … of Cracow, and the Senate applied to …, and Russia for their intervention. … shortly after occupied the city, but … expelled, and Russian troops, coming to …, recaptured it. Although the inde… the Republic had been guaranteed by the …, the three protecting Powers pro… incorporation to Austria in November 1846, … accomplished the extinction of the last rem… nationality.

…lmerston says to Lord Normanby:—

Nov. 19, 1846.

…pared an answer about Cracow, which I shall …enna without waiting for Guizot. Our answer is, … admit the necessity of doing what the three …ing to do; and that we deny their competency to … against it as a clear violation of the Treaty of … comes very awkwardly at the present moment. … as no doubt long intended it, and thinks the time … England and France have differed, and when … would be willing to gain his support about Spain … with him about Cracow.

…ll make a show of resistance, but the fact is that … and England had been on good terms, they have … action on the spot in question, and could only have … thing by a threat of war, which, however, the … would have known we should never utter for the …ow. The measure is an abominable shame, and … most hollow pretences and the most groundless

… that Prussia consents to it unwillingly; that

Austria is urged on by her own covetousness and hatred of freedom and independence, even in name, and is pushed on by Russia, who wants to have an example set, which may hereafter be quoted by her as an excusing precedent when she swallows and assimilates the kingdom of Poland.

Foreign Office: Jan. 21, 1847.

My dear Ponsonby,—I have seen Hummelauer and have had a preliminary conversation with him and Dietrichstein. He is to send me his papers to read. I have told him that if he is able to show that Cracow was the source of danger to the Austrian dominions, and if I am authorised to publish the proofs, that may go far to mitigate public opinion here; though, of course, the question will still remain why the three Powers did not previously consult England and France, and the other parties to the Treaty of Vienna; and the stronger the case the three Powers can make out for the necessity of some alteration in the political condition of Cracow, the less reason there was for fearing that they should not obtain the consent of those other Powers to some reasonable and fair arrangement.

Dietrichstein, Brunnow, and Bunsen stayed away from the House of Lords when the Queen made her speech, and I think that they were right, as it might have been unpleasant for them to have stood by to hear their Courts taxed with having violated a treaty.[1]

During the first Session of 1847, Mr. Hume moved a resolution condemning the conduct of Russia, Prussia, and Austria in the affair of Cracow, and declaring that the payments to Russia by Great Britain on account of the Russo-Dutch Loan should be discontinued on account of her violation of the Treaty of Vienna without any previous communication with this country. A long discussion followed, one prominent feature of which was an eulogium of the conduct of the three despotic Courts by Lord George Bentinck as the leader of the Tory party. In a letter to Lord Normanby, Lord Palmerston

[1] 'The extinction of the free State of Cracow has appeared to me to be so manifest a violation of the Treaty of Vienna, that I have commanded that a protest against that act should be delivered to the Courts of Vienna, Petersburg, and Berlin, which were parties to it.' (*Extract from Queen's Speech, January* 19, 1847.)

made a very good and very
Bentinck distinguished him-
which he is likely also to extin-
for office.' Lord Palmerston
briefly, merely declaring that the
by Austria was undoubtedly
of Vienna, and had received
but that to meet it by such a
the Russian Government was, in
a legal nor a dignified course of
after this, withdrew his motion.

letter[1] is quoted because the course
with Asiatic countries has sometimes
and the principle maintained that
them exactly as we should European
according to a policy which they can-
and will not appreciate. When their
usages become European, then we should
with them as Europeans; but as long
and usages are Chinese, we must
as Chinese. The moral nature of these
the point to be considered, and that is not
in treatises on international law:—

Broadlands: January 9, 1847.

lose all the vantage ground which we have gained
in China, if we take the low tone which seems
adopted of late by us at Canton. We have given
a most exemplary drubbing, and that brought
their senses, because they never were deceived
we were; but it brought them to leave off the
contempt, under which they had so long
fear. They will not forget that drubbing in a
we set them the example by forgetting it ourselves;
take especial care not to descend from the rela-
which we have acquired. If we maintain that
by the force of our intercourse, we shall not
recover it by forcible acts; but if we permit the
at Canton or elsewhere, to resume, as they will,

[1] To Sir John Davis.

no doubt, be always endeavouring to do, their former tone of affected superiority, we shall very soon be compelled to come to blows with them again.

Of course we ought—and, by we, I mean all the English in China—to abstain from giving the Chinese any ground of complaint, and much more from anything like provocation or affront; but we must stop on the very threshold any attempt on their part to treat us otherwise than as their equals, and we must make them all clearly understand, though in the civillest terms, that our treaty rights must be respected, unless they choose to have their seaports knocked about their ears. The Chinese must learn and be convinced that if they attack our people and our factories they will be shot; and that if they illtreat innocent Englishmen who are quietly exercising their treaty right of walking about the streets of Canton, they will be punished. So far from objecting to the armed association, I think it a wise security against the necessity of using force. Depend upon it, that the best way of keeping any men quiet is to let them see that you are able and determined to repel force by force; and the Chinese are not in the least different in this respect from the rest of mankind.

The Irish famine occupied so entirely the attention of the country and of Parliament that little else was debated in the House of Commons during the session of 1847. The subject of education, however, was taken up by the Government, but they had to encounter the jealousy which various Dissenting bodies felt at any further sum being placed under the control of the Established Church.

When, therefore, Lord John Russell proposed an additional grant of 100,000*l.*, Mr. Duncombe moved an amendment, not, as he stated, from want of confidence in Her Majesty's Government, but from distrust in the Committee of Privy Council, who were to administer the grant. In spite of strong opposition the vote was carried, and Lord Palmerston comments on this result and on the general state of parties as follows:—[1]

You will have been as much surprised and pleased as we have been at the division last night about the Education question.

[1] To Lord Normanby, April 23, 1847.

House that, with a general election combination of Dissenters against our been such an overwhelming majo- creditable to the Government that proposed should have been intrinsi- great body of the House should have of their constituents from approval of suppose that the result of last night will to Louis Philippe and Guizot. It must that, for the present, we are the only can be found to stand; and, unless I am general election will not materially alter

have made up his mind that for a year or hope to form a party, and that he must give time to forget the events of last year;[1] in the evident that he does not wish that any other should be formed out of the people on his side of of that Government he would not be a these reasons, and also because he sincerely that we should, for the present, remain in, he cordial support, as far as he can, without losing his position. Graham[2]—who sits up under his old ever comes down to Peel's bench, even for personal on—seems to keep himself aloof from everybody, himself free to act according to circumstances; but, not considered as the head of any party. George entirely broken down as a candidate for minis- ; and thus we are left masters of the field, not of our own merits, which, though we say it great, but by virtue of the absence of any efficient

ttles of Moodkee, Sobraon, and Goojerat had possession of the Punjaub. The question her we were to annex it. Lord Palmerston's o this, and the opinions of Lord Hardinge uke of Wellington, are still interesting, as the relations of England and Russia in the

[1] the Corn Laws.
[2] Graham had been Home Secretary under Sir Robert Peel.

Carlton Gardens: June 9, 1847.

My dear John Russell,—I return you Hardinge's letter and the Duke of Wellington's. These two generals are great military authorities; but the Duke is a far greater one than Hardinge, of whose judgment I have no opinion, though his bravery in the field is undoubted. Both seem to agree in thinking that the Russians cannot conquer India, and in this opinion they are clearly right. I do not think, however, that Hardinge has demonstrated that the Russians might not give us much trouble and put us to much expense in India.

I would observe that Hardinge seems to think Scinde of no value in a military point of view, whereas the Duke considers the possession of it as a great security; and, as regards the Punjaub, Hardinge is evidently against our possessing it, while, on the other hand, he says that the only gate through which an invader could attack India is through the Khyber Pass, which cannot be occupied and defended by us unless we do possess the Punjaub; and he shows the necessity for this, because he says that it is only to the eastward of the Chenab that a large army could find subsistence. It is only there, consequently, that we could station a large army; and, therefore, as the Khyber Pass, being narrow, could be penetrated by only one column at a time, our best means of stopping an invading enemy would be either to occupy the pass with a small force beforehand, or to station a small force at the outlet of the pass, to attack in succession the heads of the columns of march as they might open out into the plain. But, to do this, we must have the country up to the pass; for we could not in such a case risk a small force three hundred miles from our main body through a country which, not being ours, might at the moment become hostile. If the Khyber Pass is the only gate to India, and if it is there we are to defend India, we ought to have, and must have, military occupation of the country up to that gate; otherwise the pass is of no more defensive value to us than any other defile which the invaders would have to pass between Astrabad and Cabul. The advance of a Russian army is, however, far from being as impossible as Hardinge seems to think it. Persia must, I fear, now be looked upon as an advanced post for Russia, whenever she chooses to make use of it. She will command it either by overpowering force or by bribing the State by prospects of acquisitions in Afghanistan. There would be no insurmountable difficulty to prevent Russia from assembling a considerable force at Astrabad. The roads through

... the Caspian gives additional facilities. ... Afghanistan are very practicable mili... distance from Astrabad to Attock is not ... than eight hundred miles, considerably ... from Attock to Calcutta.

... in occupation of Afghanistan might not ... Calcutta, but it might convert Afghanistan ... of Russia, instead of that advanced post ... and, whatever Hardinge may say of the secu... of our frontier, you would find in such case a ... displayed by the Burmese, by the Nepaulese, ... unincorporated States scattered about the surface ... possessions. These things would lead to great ... require great efforts, and might create consider... The best method of preventing these embarrass... be to take up such a military position on the ... in posse, as Hardinge would do, but in *esse*, as ... plain to everybody that we could not be taken ... that the decisive position could neither be snatched ... rapid movement, nor be wrested from us by a ...

... there are further considerations to which Har... not advert, namely, that while Russia was thus ... India, we should not be idle in Europe; but still ... strong in her European defences, whether in the ... the Black Sea, and it is well that we should be able ... India in Asia, as well as in Europe.

...act from Letter of Lord Hardinge, dated Simla, April 20, 1847.

...gards the intentions of Russia, I am confident no ...empt will be made. They are confined to the exten... trade with China and parts of Central Asia. A ...rce can only enter India through Afghanistan and ...yber Pass.

... and Afghan force intermixed with Russians, on ... principle as in our Indian Army, would be required, ...ern system of war, to be supported by a large and ... field-train of artillery, with all its numerous ... modern necessity entails great difficulty in moving ... through a sterile and mountainous country. The more ... to make your army efficient in artillery in such countries, the greater becomes your difficulty of rapidly moving forward.

If Russia could afford the means of getting through the Khyber Pass with a well-equipped army, it must be an operation of time, and could not be disguised. The concentration of our military means would be comparatively easy. We have now 50,000 men and 100 field pieces, and 100 siege guns, with 500 rounds a gun, on this frontier. We should have the choice of meeting this Russian army where we pleased. Peshawur is a very small and poor district; Attock still more; and the country between the Indus and the Jehun, or Hydaspes, is so poor and barren it could not support an army. Between the Jehun and the Chenab, or Acesines, the case is the same, and it is only on this side, between the Chenab and the Sutlej, that a large army could be subsisted, with rivers intersecting the approach at right angles, of which we have no idea in Europe, one, two, and even six and seven miles broad, from June till October, when the snow melts and the rain falls, running five or six knots an hour.

Look at the map and you will find, from our new frontier on the Byar at Noorpor, passing to the eastward along the mountains which now bring us into contact with Chinese Tartary at Spitti, and the Nepaul hills, and thence by the Tennasserim provinces to the Straits at Singapoor, that there is no enemy which can give this Government any uneasiness by an external attack for a distance of nearly 6,000 miles of land frontier.

Passing from Noorpoor to the westward, down to Kurrachee on the sea, the only entrance into India is by the Khyber Pass. No general in his senses would attack India through the Bolan Pass for the sake of occupying Scinde, having then an impassable desert before him, or a flank movement of 700 miles through Bhawulpoor before he could reach this frontier.

Consequently, any attack on India is limited to a space of about 100 miles on the Sutlej, from Ferozepore to Rampoor. For 100 miles from Ferozepore down to Kurrachee no hostile attack could be made. Our coast, from Kurrachee down to the Straits, is between 5,000 and 6,000 miles. The land frontier from Kurrachee to the Straits, about 7,000 miles. Therefore, out of 13,000 miles of sea and land frontier by which the empire is encircled, the only practicable attack is confined to 100 miles between Ferozepore and the foot of the hills at Rampoor, or, if you please, the Khyber Pass, 300 miles in advance of the Sutlej.

... to be a navigable river, and ... for troops and stores could ... Kurrachee by the Indus, the Punjaub ... military value; but that route has ... real military communication between ... However, I won't enter into the ... of the Punjaub. I have shown you ... of any importance can be made except ... Sutlej; and, lastly, I give you my opinion ... the Khyber Pass for a Russian army with ... and munitions of war is very nearly as im-... other of the entrances into India.

... has solved the problem of the possibility ... Afghanistan has no resources: it is by ... to feed a large invading army; and even if ... reach the Indus, our British means are at ... overwhelm it.

... of Russia are restricted, I should say, to the ... trading speculations. She now supplies Chinese ... Cashmere, and Turkestan with broadcloths, ... hardware, &c., and receives shawls and shawl ... &c., in return. We should, in addition to what ... export opium, sugar, indigo, and English cotton

... have no cause for apprehension. Let us get rid ... annual deficit by a surplus; pay off the five per ... the country—and you may do what you like; ... Russian invasion of India, depend upon it, my dear ... is a political nightmare.

Letter from Duke of Wellington, dated Windsor Castle, June 3, 1847.

... is quite correct in his account and descrip-... frontier. You may rely upon it that you have ... apprehend from Russia in that quarter. The pos-... is a great security.'

... system of government, which was ruin-... monarchy in France, produced a scandal, to ... reference is made in the following letters. ... was a Peer of France, and M. Teste ... of Public Works. In order to obtain a concession of a salt mine for a company in which he was interested, the General had given large bribes to the Minister. In July a State trial took place with reference to these transactions, and the culprits were condemned to fine and imprisonment. Meanwhile, however, M. Teste had attempted suicide by placing a pistol to his mouth, which missed fire. He then discharged a second, so close to his breast that the ball did not penetrate, but fell to the ground, leaving only a bruise. Lord Palmerston seems to have had his doubts about the intensity of M. Teste's desire to die.

F. O.: May 7, 1847.

My dear Normanby,—These revelations about Cubieres and Teste will, no doubt, lead to other disclosures of a similar kind, because such exposures follow each other as murders do in this country; and if the system by which majorities have hitherto been obtained is laid bare, either the Ministry must fall by public disrespect for it, or it will be weakened by the cessation of the abuses upon which it lived. In either way, these things must be a blow to Guizot and the Philippine system.

What dashing fellows our cousins Transatlantic are! Who would have thought of Ulloa[1] surrendering without being attacked? I remember a Greek line which says that "silver spears will conquer all things." No doubt the fort was a little bombarded with dollars while they were shelling the town. The Yankees will end by becoming masters of the greater part of Mexico. We cannot prevent it without going to war with the United States; and to go to war with them for such a set of people as the Mexicans would not go down with the House of Commons in the best of times, and least of all just now. If the Union becomes very large, it will either split, or else the multitude of conflicting interests which will belong to its various component parts will be an obstacle to any unnecessary war with a great maritime Power and wealthy customer like England. Moreover, a great extent of fine land to the south will render the Americans less anxious to strip us of Canada. I hear that they are already become careless about Oregon, satisfied with having the ownership.

[1] The fortress of St. John d'Ulloa, which commanded the town of Vera Cruz.

C. G.: July 16, 1847.

...'s attempted suicide was a reality, or ...? It looks like the latter. In former ... Meadows, in our service, was brought into ... affairs of the same kind which had happened ... discharged a pistol at his own head; the ball ..., and friends who heard the report rushed in ... bathing his forehead in cold water; and he said, ..., that he had had an affair of honour with ... having stood the shot, he had declared himself ... though Teste has escaped the shot, the Ministry ... between wind and water, which, sooner or later, ... even if it tells in no other way than by making ... difficult, because more dangerous, it will in that ... Government which relies so much upon such ... support. I get on very agreeably with Broglie, ... have only talked about Switzerland and Greece, ... both of which we 'agree to differ.' We shall ... up by Thursday or Friday of next week, then ... then comes the tug of war. It is said we are to ... new Parliament an absolute majority of our own of ...ty out of the whole House. Be this as it may, ...ly win many seats.

...nent was dissolved on July 23. There was ...usiasm on either side during the general ...hich followed. The Free Trade question ...settled; and though a more vigorous policy ...pated from a Russell than from a Melbourne ...ation, no great organic changes were expected ...On the other hand, the remnants of the Con... party had nothing to hold out beyond vague ... of attachment to our ancient institutions. ...sence of party feeling the men in possession ...ew votes, although among their nominal sup... ...ere many independent members in no way ... go with the Government if they disapproved

CHAPTER II.

LORD MINTO'S MISSION TO ITALY—IRELAND—SICILY.

LORD MINTO, as has been stated above, went about this time to Italy, on a mission which deserves some notice. The whole land was in a ferment, and was clamouring for liberal institutions. Sardinia led the way, despite the unconcealed disapproval of her Imperial neighbour. Tuscany followed, though with laggard steps, and the Papal Court suffered for its prostration under the general fever by the occupation of Ferrara by Austrian forces. Charles Albert at once notified to the Pope his readiness to assist him with a Piedmontese army if the Imperial troops made any further advance. Meanwhile Pius IX., being engaged in administrative reforms, had expressed to the English Government a wish to have the assistance of some person of rank and experience who might aid him by advice, and at the same time afford him the moral support of England. Lord Minto therefore went off to Rome in November, 1847, with directions to visit Turin and Florence on his way. His aim was so to represent the English Government as to strengthen the authority of the constitutional governments in Italy, but he did not profess to believe that English mediation or interposition in territorial questions was likely to turn to much account. He only thought it probable that, by taking a firm and decided line, England might enable the wise friends of order and freedom to cope in their domestic affairs with the sedition of the young Italy and Mazzini firebrands.

Lord Palmerston's instructions to Lord Minto were, first of all, to convey to the King of Sardinia the

Government, and the ex-
and regret that Austria should
possibility of an entry by her troops
territory, if the King, in the exercise
rights of sovereignty, should make
arrangements within his own dominions
displeasing to the Government of
was to add that Her Majesty's
learnt with much pleasure the assur-
and defensive support which his Sar-
had recently caused to be conveyed to
which did great honour to His Majesty
Prince and as an Italian Sovereign.'

Grand Duke of Tuscany Lord Minto was
address himself in a tone of encourage-
him to persevere in that independent
enlightened progress which he at that moment
to pursue.

at Rome [proceeded Lord Palmerston], not as
credited to the Pope, but as an authentic organ of
Government, enabled to explain its views and to
sentiments upon events which are now passing in
which, both from their local importance and from
on the general interests of Europe, Her Majesty's
are watching with great attention and anxiety.

Majesty's Government are deeply impressed with the
it is wise for sovereigns and their governments
the administration of their affairs, a system of pro-
improvement; to apply remedies to such evils as, upon
they may find to exist, and to remodel, from time
ancient institutions of their country, so as to render
suitable to the gradual growth of intelligence and to
diffusion of political knowledge; and Her Ma-
Government consider it to be an undeniable truth, that
independent sovereign, in the exercise of his deliberate
shall think fit to make within his dominions such
in the laws and institutions of his country as he
conducive to the welfare of his people, no other
can have any right to attempt to restrain or to
such an employment of one of the inherent attri-
independent sovereignty.

Lord Palmerston concluded by authorising L[illegible] Minto to say 'that Her Majesty's Government wo[illegible] not see with indifference any aggression commi[illegible] upon the Roman territories, with a view to preven[illegible] the Papal Government from carrying into effect th[illegible] internal improvements which it might think prope[illegible] adopt.'

Lord Minto was received with great ovations. [illegible] Avezzo, Genoa, and other places, he was called upon [illegible] address the people from the balcony amid flags a[illegible] music. With wise discretion, he usually confined hi[illegible] speech to a cry of 'Viva l' Indipendenza Italiana!' which satisfied the crowds and caused their dispersion, to the sound of 'Viva l' Italia!'

On reaching Rome he placed himself in communication with the Papal Government, so as to carry out his instructions. Pio Nono was at this time apparently about to enter on a career of progressive and successful reform, but Lord Minto was evidently not sanguine as to His Holiness's ability 'to ride the whirlwind and direct the storm.' Writing home during the early troubles of 1848, he says:—

> The Pope is a most amiable, agreeable, and honest man, and sincerely pious to boot, which is much for a Pope; but he is not made to drive the State coach. To-day be is in very good spirits, although he foresees the dangers of the country, because he has recovered a saint's skull which had been sacrilegiously stolen.

The fact is that Pio Nono was at that time, and always remained, far more anxious for his power as Head of the Catholic Church than for his position as a temporal sovereign; but the British Government songht to turn to account whatever anxiety he might feel in his temporal capacity by obtaining, in return for their good offices, the exercise of his influence in Ireland to second their efforts in the cause of national education, and to restrain the lawlessness of the priests.

In the following letters Lord Palmerston refers to

...that the newly-established Queen's ... fact that agrarian outrages were, ... at any rate not condemned by the ... the people. England had commu... as her old ally, her hope that the ... be interrupted by foreign force. She ... the means of opening formal com... Rome, and naturally expected mean... attitude on the part of the Head of ... had many adherents across the Irish

F. O.: October 29, 1847.

...Minto,—Nothing could be better nor, I trust, ... your negotiations at Turin, upon which I ... you official approvals. That Italian Commer... will be an excellent thing if it is placed upon a ... commercial and political.

...Austrians, they have been headed, and will not ...wards Italy. Many things have contributed to ...we had our share in the merit, and were the first ... view hollos which scared them. The Pope ought ...l to us for this, and if he does so, he ought to give ...ns of his thankfulness. I send you a copy of ... sent some little time ago by Clarendon for your ... the main, good. There is a little inconsistency ... in one part he assumes that the priests have no ... Ireland, and in another part he assumes that they ...deal. But the fact is so: they have influence and ...t; they have it in some things and not in others. ... to make to the Pope the plain, and simple, and ...quest that he would exert his authority over the ...od, to induce them to abstain from meddling in ... on the contrary, to confine themselves to their ...es; and in these duties to exhort their flocks to ...d conduct, obedience to the law, and abstinence ... violence and crime, and, moreover, to inculcate on ...the propriety of not only obeying the law them... aiding honestly and fearlessly in the execution of ... in the attainment of the ends of justice by faith... ...ing their functions, as magistrates, jurymen, and ... disagree entirely with Clarendon as to the expe... ...ing or inviting the Pope to send any confidential agent to Ireland. I should fear that such person, unless [illegible] well chosen indeed, would be got hold of by McHale rather [illegible] by Clarendon, and then if his reports were to be unfavour[illegible] to us, we should have increased our difficulties instead of [illegible]nishing them. I shall be able to send you by the next me[illegible] a Memorandum about the letter which has recently been rec[illegible] by McHale from Rome, upon the subject of Irish coll[illegible] This is an unkind and a most mischievous measure, and [illegible] little to be expected at the hands of the Pope at the [illegible] moment that we were stepping out of our way to be of [illegible] him. It is an ungrateful return, and can only be explained [illegible] the supposition that it was extorted by intrigue and false repre-sentations made at Rome by McHale, and that the Pope acted ignorantly and without knowing the mischief he was doing. But you should lose no time in making him aware of his mis-take, and you should say that if he expects the English Go-vernment to be of any use to him, and to take any interest in his affairs, he must not strike blows at our interior. You may also say that an Act of Parliament will be necessary to enable us to establish diplomatic relations with him. Things of this kind may have so bad an effect upon public opinion in England as to make it impossible for us to obtain the consent of Parlia-ment to any such measure.

' 'College of the Sacred Congregation for the Propagation of the Faith, Rome, October 9, 1847. The Sacred Congregation has felt it its duty to caution the archbishops and bishops of Ireland against taking any part in establishing them. But as it would have wished, before some of the prelates had entered into any negotiations with the Government for amending the law regarding the aforesaid colleges and procuring other measures in their favour, that they had taken the opinion of the Holy See, so it doubts not but that, from the profound obedience which the prelates of Ireland have invariably exhibited towards it, they will retract those things which they have done to the contrary.

* * * * * * * *

'Above all things, the Sacred Congregation would deem it advan-tageous that the bishops, uniting their exertions, should procure the erection in Ireland of such a Catholic academy as the prelates of Bel-gium have founded in the city of Louvain.

* * * * * * * *

'With these things you will, we are sure, comply with the greater alacrity since they are in all points in conformity with the judgment of our most Holy Lord Pius IX., who has sanctioned with his appro-bation the decision of the Sacred Congregation, and gave to it the supreme weight of his authority.

'J. PHIL. CARDINAL FRANSONI, P.D.P.F.
'ALEXANDER BARNABO, Pro-Secretary.'

... is lessening, but still severe, and will ... to come. The grain which was ... United Kingdom in the first nine months of ... cost and freight rather more than twenty- ... We had to advance upwards of six ... in Ireland, and the nation has spent ... millions in railways at home, and upwards ... railways abroad. The wonder is not that we ... that we are not all of us bankrupt.

... dum on the 'Irish Colleges' referred ... letter was as follows:—

... nally or ignorantly I know not, but the ... against the Irish colleges, committed a ... and unnecessary act. It was hostile, because ... announced and directed the Roman Catholic ... a measure which had received the sanction ... and Parliament of England. It was ill-judged, ... no regard for the opinion of the Roman ... and a great proportion of the Roman Catholic ..., who consider the colleges an important boon, ... to supply a want that has been long and ... and who are determined not to be deprived of ... from which they expect much good. It has pro- ... of resentment and irritation among the Pro- ... reat Britain, and, I may add, among many of the ... Ireland, that will not easily be allayed, and that are ... by all those who desire to soothe animosity be- ... two creeds, and to promote the establishment of ... tions with Rome.

... Lieutenant was in communication with the ... Crolly, with Archbishops Murray and Nicholson. ... stion of theirs had been scrupulously attended to ... the religious instruction and moral conduct of the ... holic students, and in conformity with their wishes ... were under revision as soon after the long vacation ... idential Board could assemble. When these facts ... to the knowledge of the Pope, it is hoped that His ... ill see that he has been led into error, and that ... suspection will be desirable in listening to malicious ... reports transmitted from Ireland, and which ... hitherto too readily believed at Rome. There are ... Roman Catholic prelates of Ireland men of great intelligence and activity, who lend themselves to politi[illegible] agitation, and who seek to obtain the sanction of the R[illegible] authority towards the maintenance of hostile feelings ag[illegible] the British Government, and between the Protestants [illegible] Catholics of the United Kingdom. These men untruly as[illegible] to speak in the name of the entire hierarchy, and their st[illegible]ments have in consequence had an importance given them [illegible] Rome to which they are not entitled. It is probable that [illegible] this time the Pope has received certain resolutions against [illegible] colleges, and against the national system of education in the name of the archbishop and bishops of Ireland in Syn[illegible] assembled; but these resolutions were not passed in Synod at all. Many of the prelates had left Dublin at the time they were framed, and even Archbishop Murray, who was in Dublin, never heard of or saw them till he read them in the newspapers, when he highly disapproved of them, and felt sure that many of his brethren would do the same. His example, among many that might be quoted, will show the unscrupulous character of certain prelates, and the necessity of receiving with caution any facts or opinions put forward by them. The best course for the Pope now to pursue is to remain entirely passive until he receives further and more correct information. He may rest assured that in the establishment of these colleges the British Government have had no other object than to supply the best possible education to the middle classes in Ireland, and, as a consequence of that object, to promote religion and morality among the students of different denominations alike. The British Government has no ulterior or sinister design, as has been most falsely asserted. It uses no disguise. The Lord Lieutenant has freely communicated with the Primate, and Archbishop Murray has received and acted upon their suggestions, and will communicate to them the statutes as soon as they are revised, and before they are definitively determined upon. It may perhaps be desirable, in whatever form Lord Minto shall think best, to let the Pope understand that the Roman Catholics of Ireland have neither the means nor disposition to establish at their own expense such seminaries as are recommended in the rescript, and that they can only be provided for out of the public funds. That a large proportion of the Roman Catholic laity are so convinced of the desirableness of these colleges, that nothing will prevent them from sending their sons there when once they are satisfied that religious instruction is duly provided for, and that if the opposition of Dr. McHale and

... prove successful under the supposed ... of the Pope's name against the national ... by which four hundred thousand children ... ignorance and its consequences, the large ... to this object by the Legislature will ... the exclusive management of the Pro... large proportion of these children will be ... who are acquainted with Ireland must be ... the influence of the priesthood can check ... desire for education that exists among the ... will greatly prefer to receive it from Catholics, ... forego its benefits, they will gladly accept it ...

CLARENDON.

... 30, 1847.

F. O.: December 3, 1847.

... Minto,—I send you a letter from Clarendon, the ... you may, I think, read to anybody with whom ... communication on the part of the Pope. But you ... further than Clarendon has chosen to do, and ... confidently assure the Papal authorities that at ... Ireland, misconduct is the rule, and good conduct ... in the Catholic priests. That they, in a multi... are the open, and fearless, and shameless in... disorder, to violence, and murder, and that every ... week the better conducted, who are by con... ... nature the most quiet and timid, are being ... fellow-priests, as well as by their flocks, from a ... in any efforts to give good counsel and to restrain ... crime. Major Mahon, who was shot the other ... ounced by his priest at the altar the Sunday before ... ered. He might have been murdered all the same ... had not denounced him, but that denunciation of ... all the people in the neighbourhood think the deed ... stead of a diabolical one. The irritation and ex... ... growing up in the public mind against the ... thood is extreme, and scarcely anybody now talks ... murders without uttering a fervent wish that a ... might be hung forthwith, and the most effectual ... has been suggested, and which seems the most ... hat whenever a man is murdered in Ireland the ... parish should be transported.

... meanwhile I begin to doubt whether it would be

prudent at present to bring in our proposed Bill for Legalising Diplomatic Intercourse with the Court of Rome. The sectarian prejudices which, under any circumstances, would give strong opposition to such a Bill, but which, in a better state of things we should be able to conquer, would find such sympathy in public opinion at present, that our task would be more difficult; however, we do not give up our intention, but must postpone its execution till after the Christmas recess. I really believe there never has been in modern times, in any country professing to be civilised and Christian, nor anywhere out of the central regions of Africa, such a state of crime as now exists in Ireland. There is evidently a deliberate and extensive conspiracy among the priests and the peasantry to kill off or drive away all the proprietors of land, to prevent and deter any of their agents from collecting rent, and thus practically to transfer the land of the country from the landowner to the tenant. I trust, however, that some of these murderers will be taken; some indeed have already been apprehended, and if evidence can be got against them, the hanging of a dozen of these miscreants all in a row may have some effect in deterring others from following their example, and if we could but get a priest in the lot it would be like a ptarmigan in a bag of grouse, or a pied or ring-necked pheasant in a battue.

Extract from Letter of Earl of Clarendon, dated V. R. Lodge, November 26, 1847.

McHale is a dangerous demagogue, whose proceedings as a citizen, and irrespective of their ecclesiastical indecorum, no Government in the world but ours would tolerate. Political agitation, popular elections, and inflammatory publications are his favourite pursuits. His object seems to be to set the people against their rulers; and if he could have his way their ignorance and their turbulence would be perpetual, and throughout his province those priests have the greatest share of his favour who most promote his sinister designs. The majority of the bishops dislike his proceedings and his character, but they succumb because he is audacious and overbearing, and they are afraid of making public the grave dissensions that exist among the Roman Catholic hierarchy. Such a man, however, and such a bitter opponent of the British Government and the true interests of Ireland, is not an adviser upon whom the Pope should rely.

With respect to the priests, I must again repeat that, as a

... world a more zealous, faithful, hard-... of the older priests are friendly to ... to the general improvement of the ... however, some unfortunate exceptions, but ... clergy, the curates and coadjutors, that ... are to be found, and if they could be ... to religion and social order would ... however, cannot much longer go on in ... the duty of a Government towards the ... disposed portions of the community will ... necessary for a state of things which ... if the existing laws should become in-... the timely exercise of spiritual authority be ... held.

... at this moment numerous cases in which, if ... be procured, a prosecution could be sustained ... as accessories to atrocious crimes, by the inciting ... held to people over whose minds they exer-... control.

... endeavoured to procure such evidence, because it is ... Government to punish misconduct that tends to the ... every social tie, and in the administration of the ... tion of persons can be admitted; but such evidence ... form is not to be procured. From different ... country, and from persons upon whose veracity I ... hear either that a landlord has been denounced ... the altar, in a manner which is equivalent to his ... or that persons giving evidence against criminals ... public enemies and traitors, or that people are ... semble in mobs and enforce their demands upon ... It was only yesterday that I heard of a priest (in ... Dr. McHale) addressing a man in the chapel, and ... at he would not curse him, because the last man ... died directly, but that before *the blossom fell from* ... would be a corpse. This man's offence was having ... in a court of justice against a party that had ... his house and robbed him. I have sworn deposi-... on my table in proof of acts of this kind, but ... dare not come forward and openly give their ... they say—and I know it to be true—that their ... is worth four-and-twenty hours' purchase. In-... any misunderstanding upon the subject, the priest usually defies any person to give information of what he has been saying, and warns them of the consequences.

The result of all this is, not only that crime is encouraged, but that the priesthood must fall into contempt, and that the wholesome restraint and humanising influence of religion will decline; that the people will become more barbarous; and that the clergy, to maintain their position, must still pander to the passions of their flocks. In places—and there are many—where a priest friendly to order and anxious for the real welfare of his people has given good advice, and intimated that among those present in the chapel there were some who had been guilty of such and such crimes, the individuals alluded to will come forward and bid him hold his tongue, and threaten him with vengeance if he proceeds. I could multiply facts and details *ad infinitum*, for every day some fresh ones come to my knowledge, but the above are sufficient to exhibit the state of things in certain parts of Ireland, and all its evil tendencies; for wherever the priests so misconduct themselves, there the people are always found to be the most turbulent and wretched. The indignation, and I may add shame, of the respectable Roman Catholic classes are extreme: they consider that the course pursued by these unruly priests is calculated to give a false impression of their (the Roman Catholic) religion and their politics; to exasperate against them the entire Protestant people of England, and to check effectually any intentions on the part of the Government to place the two churches on a footing of equality.

The Pope may well hesitate to believe in things the like of which exist in no other part of the world; but we don't ask him to take our words for them. He has himself proposed to send some person over here to examine and report, and I am sure that will be the best mode of proceeding, if any one sufficiently unprejudiced, and likely to resist the evil influences by which he will be surrounded immediately on his arrival, can be found to undertake the mission. He should not come in any public capacity, or with pomp and circumstance, but privately, and with instructions whom he should consult, and with powers to act, but not to go beyond the sphere of spiritual jurisdiction. The Primate and Archbishop Murray, and some of the metropolitan clergy, who well understand the interests of their Church, and are acquainted with all that is going on in the country, would be safe guides; and I feel sure that a Papal prohibition to take part in political agitations, and to make use of the purpose, would be received as a disposed priests (i.e. the majority of the become agitators, yield to intimidation, against their judgment. If they could of the Pope's authority for confining spiritual duties, they would not fear to have and thus find themselves destitute of the

belief, the bishops are not in the habit of as those I have alluded to. They may neither official nor private knowledge of the their interference is not very successful.

had several interviews with Pius IX., Papal rescript against the Queen's also about the conduct of certain bishops Ireland who took so leading a part in the and terrorism. Neither the Pope Ferretti was versed in public affairs, and evidently much astonished at the state of enquiry revealed to them as existing in Pope expressed his entire disapprobation activity of the Irish clergy, and he Minto not only of his readiness but of to do whatever might be in his power remedy to these clerical disorders. He also regret of the effect which the missive of the against the new Colleges appeared likely saying that he had postponed as long as he his sanction to the report of the Sacred which he had finally done as undertanding represented the deliberate opinion of the great the Irish Bishops.

Diplomatic Relations with Rome Bill,' to Palmerston refers, passed through Parliament Lord Eglinton, in the House of Lords, against the Government by which the an ecclesiastic as Papal Nuncio in London. This condition was regarded at Rome that the Pope refused to send any

Minister, and also declined to receive an envoy from England on a unilateral footing. The truth was that representations made to him from Ireland induced him to imagine that we were in such straits in Irish affairs that we should be compelled to yield. When Lord Minto asked whether he would, on his part, receive as English Minister one of our Archbishops or the Moderator of the Church of Scotland in full canonicals, he frankly owned that he could not; but reciprocity has never been a weakness of the Vatican.

Lord Palmerston was in favour of the Eglinton clause. To Lord Clarendon he writes:—[1]

> I could not have consented to make myself responsible for receiving an ecclesiastic as Roman envoy, and it is much better that our refusal should stand upon a prohibitory law than upon our own voluntary determination. I quite concur in the view taken of that question by Aberdeen and Stanley, and I am convinced, by my diplomatic experience, that there would be no end to the embarrassments and inconveniences which we should suffer from having a Roman priest invested with diplomatic privilege holding his court in London, surrounded by English and Irish Catholics, and wielding a power of immense though secret extent, and capable of becoming an engine of political intrigue to serve all kinds of foreign interests.
>
> As for the idea that we could manage the Irish priests by means of a Roman priest in London, I am convinced that the presence of such a man would only have given the Irish priests an additional means of managing us.
>
> Cappucini, a liberal and enlightened man, was offered to be nuncio at Paris; he declined, and gave to his private friends the reason—that he knew he should have been obliged, by his official position, to side with the most ultra of the Catholic and Jesuit party in France, and as his opinions were against them, he would not place himself in so disagreeable a position.

Very shortly after Lord Minto arrived in Rome—namely, in January, 1848—an insurrection broke out at Palermo, the Sicilians demanding from the King of Naples the Constitution of 1812. Both parties applied to Lord Napier, then our *chargé d'affaires* at Naples, to

[1] F. O., March 9, 1848.

[illegible]. The Sicilians founded their [illegible] the former connection between Eng-[illegible] upon the share which the British [illegible] had in the remodelling of the Sicilian [illegible] in 1812. The Neapolitan Government [illegible] application upon the well-known interest [illegible] been taken by the British Govern-[illegible] of the kingdom of Naples. Lord [illegible] did not undertake the office, because [illegible] Government was not willing at that time [illegible] such proposals as were alone likely to lead [illegible]. Soon, however, the King invited [illegible] to Naples, and requested him to employ [illegible] to effect a reconciliation between the [illegible] the Home Government.

Foreign Office: Feb. 24,[1] 1848.

[illegible] Minto,—I have now but five minutes to write to [illegible] enough to give you all the instructions you [illegible] to act according to your own good judgment as [illegible] each other. I most sincerely hope that you will [illegible]ble to bring the Naples Government round to your [illegible] Sicily. Your scheme of amalgamation is excellent, [illegible] afford the best chance of a permanent connection [illegible] two countries; but one fears the blind obstinacy [illegible]. The Sicilians, moreover, doubt his future good [illegible]ings have gone much too far for it to be possible for [illegible]er to retract; and as to our guarantee, that is out [illegible]ion, and would lead us into future embarrassments [illegible]ibilities of the most difficult and inconvenient kind. [illegible]e position of a foreign Power who should be guaran-[illegible] a sovereign and a portion of his subjects would be [illegible] for such Power, and inconsistent with the inde-[illegible] such sovereign. Probably the King of Naples [illegible]onsent to it.

[illegible] poor Pope, I live in daily dread of hearing of [illegible] having befallen him. Events have gone too [illegible] a slow sailer as he is. I only hope he will not be [illegible] the swell in the wake of those who have outstripped

[1] Two days before the Revolution at Paris.

him, for this would perhaps bring the Austrians into the Roman States; and then we should have a regular European row. One thing, however, might prevent this, and that is, the change of Government which happened yesterday at Paris;[1] for Metternich, if he hears of it in time, will not be disposed to take any step which will irretrievably commit him until he is able to learn the views and intentions and policy of this new Government in France. It will, however, of course, be much more liberal than Guizot's, both at home and abroad, and especially in regard to Italian affairs. What had been happening in Italy ought to have been a warning to Guizot; what has now happened to Guizot ought to be a warning to Italy. Guizot thought that by a packed Parliament and a corruptly-obtained majority he could control the will of the nation, and the result has been that the will of the Crown has been controlled by an armed popular force. People have long gone on crying up Louis Philippe as the wisest of men. I always have thought him one of the most cunning, and therefore not one of the wisest. Recent events have shown that he must rank among the cunning who outwit themselves, and not among the wise, who master events by foresight and prudence. This surrender of the King of the Barricades to the summons of the National Guard is, however, a curious example of political and poetical justice.

After much discussion with the King and his Ministers, Lord Minto was authorised to propose an arrangement which, in his opinion, the Sicilians might reasonably and probably accept. He then sailed for Palermo. Meanwhile, however, arrived the news of the French Revolution. This was a spark that set fire to all that was combustible in Italy. The news turned the heads of the Sicilians, and they suddenly determined no longer to acknowledge the King of Naples as their sovereign. This was what Lord Minto found to be the state of affairs on his arrival. He refused to land unless the Sicilians consented to the union of the two crowns, and he found it eventually impossible to carry out his mediation, owing to the ferment caused by events in France. Lord Palmerston writes pro-

[1] M. Guizot's resignation.

...turned out, ten years were to ...ment.

Foreign Office: March 28, 1848.

...—Was there ever such a scene of confusion ... all over Europe? Fortunate, however, ... that you crossed the Alps last autumn. ... had not been urged by you to move ... subjects were kept back, there would ... been nothing but Republics from the Alps to

... have been able to settle matters between ... the Government of Naples without a separa... though your last accounts, written just after ... Palermo, inspired us with some doubts on that

...more in addition to the numberless proofs of the ... If Bozzelli had not been so obstinate, you ...een able to settle it all before the news of the ...tion reached Sicily.

...st and most important event of these last few ...aps the retirement of Metternich. Happy would ...or the continent of Europe if this had happened ...go. But better now than later. We have just ...ntrance of Sardinian troops into Lombardy to help ... Northern Italy will henceforward be Italian, ...rian frontier will be at the Tyrol. This will be ... Austria. If North Italy had been well affected, ... been an element of strength. Discontented as it ...oved a source of weakness. Of course Parma and ...ollow the example, and in this way the King, no ...dinia, but of Northern Italy, will become a sove... importance in Europe. This will make a league ... and the other Italian rulers still more desirable ...re feasible. Italy ought to unite in a Confederacy ... of Germany, commercial and political, and now ... strike the iron while it is hot. Austria may ...Gallicia also. I hope her losses will go no further; ...ill even then remain to her to make her, if well ...ost powerful State. The question is, has she any ... of making any State a powerful one by good

...try is for the present quiet, though the Repealers ...ists meditate some movement. I think, however, that we shall be fully a match for them. The country is sound at heart, and there is a gallant public spirit which will show itself at the first intimation of real danger.

On the failure of Lord Minto's mediation the Sicilians proceeded to decree the separation of the crown of Naples and Sicily, and proposed to the Duke of Genoa to become their king, which he, however, declined. The King of Naples, on the arrival of this news, despatched ships and troops against Messina and Palermo. The bombardment of these towns was attended by such acts of violence and cruelty on both sides, that the English and French fleets interfered to procure an armistice. The period for cessation of hostilities expired, however, without any arrangement being arrived at. The fight was renewed; and the Sicilian revolt was finally put down by the middle of the year 1849.

CHAPTER III.

... IN ITALY — FRENCH REVOLUTION — ... IN LONDON—WAR BETWEEN AUSTRIA AND ... PEEL AT THE MANSION HOUSE—FRENCH ... OF ROME—DEBATES IN PARLIAMENT—CHOLERA—

... the Navigation Laws was one of the ... measures promised in the Queen's ... the opening of the new Parliament. The ... having thus pledged themselves to deal ... question, Lord Palmerston saw that such a ... advantageously affect our foreign relations ... powers, and especially with the United ... America. He desired that the obstacles which ... would remove from the way of our free ... with the latter country should be succeeded ... alliance. The following letter contains his ... it is interesting as showing how different ... spirit with which he approached these subjects ... usually ascribed to him both at home and ... Even as early as 1848, anticipating Cobden ... Declaration of Paris, he was suggesting the ... of arbitration, and advocated the abolition of ... marque :—

C. G.: January 20, 1848.

...ar John Russell,—If, as I hope, we shall succeed in ...ur Navigation Laws, and if, as a consequence, Great ... the United States shall place their commercial ... a footing of mutual equality, with the exception ... trade and some other special matters, might not ... afford us a good opportunity for endeavour- ... degree into execution the wish which Mr. ... in 1783, when he wished to substitute close alliance in the place of sovereignty and dependence as the connecting link between the United States and Great Britain?

A treaty for mutual defence would no longer be applicable to the condition of the two countries as independent Powers; but might they not, with mutual advantage, conclude a treaty containing something like the following conditions:—

1st. That in all cases of difference which may hereafter, unfortunately, arise between the contracting parties, they will, in the first place, have recourse to the (mediation / arbitration) of some friendly Power; and that hostilities shall not begin between them until every endeavour to settle their difference by such means shall have proved fruitless.

2nd. That if either of the two should at any time be at war with any other Power, no subject or citizen of the other contracting party shall be allowed to take out letters of marque from such other Power, under pain of being treated and dealt with as a pirate.

3rd. That in such case of war between either of the two parties and a third Power, no subject or citizen of the other contracting party shall be allowed to enter into the service, naval or military, of such third Power.

4th. That in such case of war as aforesaid, neither of the contracting parties should afford assistance to the enemies of the other, by sea or by land, unless war should break out between the two contracting parties themselves, after the failure of all endeavours to settle their differences in the manner specified in Article 1.

As to this arbitration question, however, he would in practice have tempered theory with prudence. In a debate in 1849 he spoke — I might almost say prophetically—of the disadvantages which England would probably have to encounter before such international tribunals. It was on the 12th of June, on a motion of Mr. Cobden's. Lord Palmerston combated vigorously the proposition that we should in any way pledge ourselves to submit to the arbitrament of a third party. He said:—

I confess also that I consider it would be a very dangerous course for this country to take, because there is no country which, from its political and commercial circumstances, from its maritime interests, and from its colonial possessions, excites

… feelings in different quarters than … is no country that would find it more … really disinterested and impartial arbiters. … country that would be more likely than England … important commercial interests from sub… arbiters not disinterested, not impartial, and … sense of their responsibility.

… that, in weighing our position, whenever … consider such a proposal, we must not forget … powerful nation can ever expect to be really … liked by any other. The interests and … perpetually clash, and men are apt to … those who stand between them and the … of their wishes.

… of the session a most violent onslaught … upon Lord Palmerston and his policy by … and Urquhart, and an impeachment be… of inquiry demanded in two speeches … occupied nearly the whole of a Wednesday's … had scarcely begun his reply when the … to an end by the six o'clock rule; and in … times that were coming on the House had … better to do than to listen to the outpour… men, who for many years would insist that … he was the secret agent of Russia.

… words, however, which he had time to say … the following manly and statesmanlike de…—

…conscious that during the time for which I have had … to direct the foreign relations of this country, I have … them all the energies which I possess. Other men … acted, no doubt, with more ability. None could … with a more entire devotion both of their time and … The principle on which I have thought the foreign … this country ought to be conducted is the principle of … peace and friendly understanding with all nations, … was possible to do so consistently with a due regard … the honour, and the dignity of this country. … have been to preserve peace. All the Govern ments of which I have had the honour to be a member have succeeded in accomplishing that object.

I hold, with respect to alliances, that England is a Power sufficiently strong to steer her own course, and not to tie herself as an unnecessary appendage to the policy of any other Government. I hold that the real policy of England is to be the champion of justice and right; pursuing that course with moderation and prudence, not becoming the Quixote of the world, but giving the weight of her moral sanction and support wherever she thinks justice is, and whenever she thinks that wrong has been done.

As long as she sympathises with right and justice, she will never find herself altogether alone. She is sure to find some other State of sufficient power, influence, and weight to support and aid her in the course she may think fit to pursue. Therefore I say that it is a narrow policy to suppose that this country or that is to be marked out as the eternal ally or the perpetual enemy of England. We have no eternal allies, and we have no perpetual enemies. Our interests are eternal and perpetual, and those interests it is our duty to follow. And if I might be allowed to express in one sentence the principle which I think ought to guide an English Minister, I would adopt the expression of Canning, and say that with every British Minister the interests of England ought to be the shibboleth of his policy.

He used also frequently to combat the romantic notion that nations or governments are much or permanently influenced by friendships, or that you could apply to the intercourse of nations the same general rules as to the intercourse of individuals. The only thing which makes one Government follow the advice or yield to the counsel of another is the hope of benefit to accrue from adopting it or the fear of the consequences of opposing it.

At the opening of 1848 Italy was agitated by the most violent heavings. To the thirst for social amelioration and political power were added aspirations for national unity. The reforms of Pio Nono, and the democratic concessions of Charles Albert and of the King of Naples, had so strongly stimulated the revolutionary passions, that it seemed only a question of [illegible] flames would break out in [illegible] Austria saw all this with [illegible] seemed inclined to interfere. [illegible] Palmerston's object, if possible, to

[illegible]

F. O.: February 11, 1848.

[illegible] I send you an important despatch to [illegible] Prince Metternich, and I wish you to re- [illegible] most anxious consideration. It is worded, I [illegible] so as not to be liable to give offence; but it [illegible] as meaning and implying more than it ex- [illegible] fact is, that upon Metternich's decision in [illegible] of Italy depends the question of peace or [illegible] If he remains quiet, and does not meddle with [illegible] the Austrian frontiers, peace will be maintained, [illegible] changes will be effected with as little dis- [illegible] consistent with the nature of things. If he takes [illegible] task of regulating by force of arms the internal [illegible] Italian States, there will infallibly be war, and it [illegible] principles which, beginning in Italy, will spread [illegible], and out of which the Austrian Empire will [illegible] issue unchanged. In that war England and [illegible] certainly not be on the same side—a circumstance [illegible] occasion to every Englishman the deepest regret. [illegible] whatever Louis Philippe and Guizot may promise, [illegible] champions contending against each other would be [illegible] France; and I would wish Metternich well and [illegible] consider what would be the effect on the internal [illegible] Germany which would be produced by a war be- [illegible] and France, in which Austria was engaged in [illegible] France in upholding constitutional liberty. It [illegible] for Prince Metternich to calculate beforehand, [illegible] portion of the *people* of Germany he could [illegible] allies in such a contest, but how many of the [illegible] would venture to take part with him in the [illegible] he wished to throw the greater part of Germany [illegible] with France, he could not take a better method

[illegible] knows the disposition of his own States; but I [illegible] doubt his receiving any support in such a struggle [illegible] or Bohemia; and he would of course have all the [illegible] subjects against him.

When one comes to reflect upon all the endless difficulties and embarrassments which such a course would involve, one cannot believe that a statesman so prudent and calculating, so long-sighted and so experienced, could fall into such an error; but the great accumulation of Austrian troops in the Lombard and Venetian provinces inspires one with apprehension.

The recent debates in the French Chambers will have shown to Prince Metternich how little he can count upon the support or even the neutrality of France; and he may depend upon it, that in defence of constitutional liberty in Italy the French nation would rush to arms, and a French army would again water their horses in the Danube.

Pray exert all your persuasion with the Prince to induce him to authorise you to send us some tranquillising assurances on this matter. We set too great a value upon the maintenance of Austria as the pivot of the balance of power in Europe to be able to see without the deepest concern any course of action begun by her Government which would produce fatal consequences to her, and which would place us probably, against our will, in the adverse scale.

At the same time he was consistently using his influence to keep the Italian Governments in the constitutional path on which they appeared to have entered. Mr. Abercromby was our Minister at the Sardinian Court.

F. O.: February 12, 1848.

My dear Abercromby,—I send you a despatch which I had prepared before I received yours, which reached me this morning, stating that the Cabinet at Turin were deliberating about the grant of a constitution. I hope their deliberation will have ended affirmatively, and in that case our exhortations will apply only to the method of carrying their assent into execution. If they should have refused, you will then have to exert your eloquence in trying to persuade them and the King to reconsider and to reverse their decision. Arguments will not be wanting. If the King resolves to oppose himself to the wishes and demands of his subjects, he must be prepared for one of two courses. He must either abdicate or call in foreign aid. The first alternative would be unwise and unnecessary, and would, moreover, be like a man shooting himself to avoid a danger which might threaten him with death.

As to calling in foreign aid, we cannot believe that, with his

... he would consent to hold his throne ... Austrian bayonets, and to become there... of Austria or of France. It is possible, ... have a more high-minded feeling on this ... committed himself in some way or ... , he may think it derogatory to his ... one. It is needless to point out how ... would be, and how futile any such ... former resolution ought to be deemed as an ... him from now performing a great and im... towards the nation which Providence ... to his charge.

... moment that one heard that the King of ... to a Constitution, it was easy to foresee ... Italy must have one too.

... George Hamilton, at Florence, he writes :—

... that before this reaches you the question whether ... to be a Constitution in Tuscany will have been ... do all you can to persuade the Government ... good grace to the wishes of the people, and upon ... to think of calling in or of letting in the ... coerce the subjects of the Grand Duke. The first ... national independence, and nothing can make up ... that.

... olution at Paris came, however, like a thun... scatter all the timid compromises and falter... of kings, emperors, and grand-dukes. ... the blind obstinacy of a self-willed King, the ... of the Government and governing classes, ... by the Cubières-Teste and Petit scandals, ... Praslin tragedy, the anti-Liberal and un... policy of the French Foreign Office, partly the ... estrangement from England caused by the ... Marriages;' these all had combined to bring ... discontent, which a long period of commer... financial distress had greatly fomented. The ... of malcontents agreed to unite on the ... demand for parliamentary reform. Banquets ... in different parts of France, when ex... were made, and complaints found audible expression. The Assembly met on the 28th of December. Upon the Address arose a debate, which lasted twenty days, and during which Guizot and Duchatel[1] had in vain tried to make head against the attacks of Thiers, Lamartine, Billault, and De Tocqueville. The Ministry kept a servile though a decreasing majority in the divisions which took place; but the victory lay with the others. The debate closed on the 7th of February. 'The war of words,' said the 'National,' on the 9th, 'is at an end. That of deeds is now to come.'

A political banquet, which had been originally fixed for the 19th of January in Paris itself, had been postponed in consequence of an interdiction by the police. On the day after the rejection of the amendment on the Address, the Liberal deputies met and determined to persevere in their design. The revived banquet was fixed for the 22nd, and was publicly announced. At this crisis Louis Philippe's obstinacy showed itself most disastrously. The death of his sister, the Princess Adelaide, a few weeks before, had removed his best counsellor. 'I never will consent to Reform,' he declared with cynical contempt for constitutional doctrine. 'Reform is another word for the advent of the Opposition!'

Vacillation, however, often hangs on the skirts of obstinacy. With Louis Philippe it was always so, and this occasion formed no exception. The Liberal chiefs were as anxious as the Government itself to avoid any violent collision. A compromise was agreed to, by which there was to be a procession, but no banquet. When it appeared likely that the multitude would be great, the authorities took alarm, again changed front, and, on the very morning of the 22nd, covered the walls of Paris with placards forbidding any assembly in the streets. The crowds, however, had collected, and all day thronged the central parts of the city. Their leaders had stayed away.

[1] Guizot was a brilliant orator, but neither a statesman nor a man of business. Duchatel had great aptitude, but was an idle man, and not an effective speaker, except on finance.

... Lord Palmerston the follow- ... personal observations during these ...

Paris: March 13, 1848.

... incidents in the last days of Louis ... Minister which came within my personal ... I should like to take this early opportunity ... recording, as they have their bearing upon ... to be derived from the astounding ...

... the middle of last year, to call your lordship's ... of political feeling in the country, and to ... could save the dynasty of July but an ... of men, and measures of reform at once ... Not one measure of a conciliatory descrip- ... time even contemplated by the Government, ... a moment when the very extent of the general ... to hold out hopes of a peaceful solution of ... The danger had always been that the King, ... packed majority of the Chamber, would persevere ... the popular will, but this will had latterly ... an irresistible impulse that it had even found its ... constitutional channels hitherto choked up by ... When one saw, in the course of the debates on the ... effect of public opinion in reducing even such a ... 120 to 30, one had even hopes that a vote of the ... upsetting the Ministry, might preserve the throne. ... personally every one of these sittings, which ... weeks, I could observe that the decline of the ... of the majority was not so strong an indication ... in its tone. There was still a disposition on the ... to prolong, for a short time, the existence of the ... order to avoid the probable dissolution of the ... during the whole of that discussion of unexampled ... was hardly an independent member, or one not ... office with the Government, who said one word in ... of their foreign or domestic policy; and it was ... that, often as M. Guizot had upon former ... himself from surrounding difficulties by the ... extraordinary talent in the tribune, he never ... debates on the Address, made a single effective

He heard, without an attempt at reply, the Spanish marriages stigmatised as a selfish and anti-national policy, amidst the cheers of his opponents, and without one dissenting murmur from that majority which had supported them last year. It was proved by the admission of his own Minister of War that at the time when he was proposing to Europe a mediation in Swiss affairs, he had smuggled, for the benefit of the Sonderbund, arms and ammunition out of the Royal Arsenal at Besançon, concealed in the shape of other merchandise, and with a false declaration to their own Customs. The only excuse he attempted of his Italian policy was to say that there could not be a thought of a Constitution in Italy for the next five or ten years, and this dictum was uttered on the very day the Constitution was proclaimed at Naples.

The miserable figure which the Government made during the whole of the debate was in no small degree caused by the profound sensation produced in the Chamber and in society by the incident with which it commenced. The personal integrity of M. Guizot had, next to his oratorical superiority, been the throne upon which his supporters had distinguished him from his fellows. That which was called 'l'affaire Petit' was, therefore, calculated to make a great sensation, not so much from its individual importance as from the system which it showed up. M. Guizot was not so much injured by his evident participation in it as by the callous audacity with which he treated the matter.

M. Bertin de Vaux, a peer of France, and a part proprietor of the 'Journal des Débats,' desired to procure a place for M. Petit, the husband of his mistress. As what M. Bertin desired was employment for M. Petit, and as M. Petit was not particular at what price his ambition was gratified, M. Guizot told M. Bertin de Vaux that, provided M. Petit would buy the resignation of a better place, he should himself possess a smaller one then vacant. This bargain was executed, but the exigencies of parliamentary corruption at that time pressing hard upon M. Guizot, he gave away, without reference to M. Petit, both the place he desired and that which he had bought, endeavouring to put him off with a promise of an early vacancy; but at this both M. Petit and his patron, M. Bertin de Vaux, were indignant, and the 60,000 francs which M. Guizot himself repaid M. Bertin de Vaux for M. Petit, as the price he had paid for the place, were obtained for that purpose out of the Secret Service Money. This was the real history of the first part of this affair, and yet M. Guizot had the effrontery to say from the tri-

[illegible] personally acquainted with any of the [illegible] there was not one of his majority who [illegible] this assertion, and how could they, as, [illegible] M. Bertin de Vaux came to assert in his [illegible] received the money *from him*, he was forced [illegible]

[illegible] general impression thus produced that the [illegible] arose.

[illegible] in former despatches, mentioned to your [illegible] caused by the hostile phrases in the [illegible] When, in addition to this, in assertion of the [illegible] banquets, the Minister of Justice made the [illegible] from the tribune that every act that was [illegible] permitted in the charter was thereby forbidden, [illegible] thought it necessary to make a striking demon- [illegible] of their rights.

[illegible] before that appointed for the banquet I went to [illegible] without knowing the decision of the Opposition [illegible] His Majesty had often volunteered to speak to [illegible] own affairs, I thought it possible he might do so [illegible] was prepared, if the occasion was thus offered, [illegible] to His Majesty the danger, in the then state [illegible] mind, unnecessarily to provoke a collision in the [illegible] I was told by one of the Government whom I met [illegible] that the Opposition had given up the banquet, and [illegible] whole Court in an ecstasy of delight, as if they had [illegible] victory. The King spoke to me for some time [illegible], but never once alluded to the passing [illegible] adverted to our proposed diplomatic intercourse [illegible] to the difficulty of receiving a priest at St. James's [illegible]; told a story of the Archbishop of Narbonne, [illegible] days of his emigration, had got over this difficulty [illegible] George the Third in a court dress with a sword. I [illegible] these trivial subjects of conversation because I [illegible] that the King had been studying effect to the [illegible] he had said to those to whom he spoke immediately [illegible] I am very well satisfied with Lord Normanby to- [illegible] he had been speaking to me of the pressing concerns [illegible], and that I had approved the course of his [illegible]

[illegible] of the King during the whole of the debates [illegible] was very remarkable. Several of the repre- [illegible] the smaller German Courts went to him with letters of condolence on Madame Adelaide's death, and to some he said, 'Tell your master not to mind having popular assemblies; let them only learn to manage them as I manage mine; see the noise they are making now; I shall soon have them in hand again; they want me to get rid of Guizot; I will not do it. Can I possibly give a stronger proof of my power?'

Although the Government had forbidden the meeting, they kept no troops to overawe the mob. Rioting, therefore, began towards the evening of the 22nd, and troops were sent for during the night. On the 23rd a collision took place in front of the Foreign Office between the soldiers and the people. Lives were lost, and the Revolution was started. During the following night the Guizot Ministry resigned, and was succeeded by Thiers and Odillon Barrot. Marshal Bugeaud and General Lamoricière were placed in command of the troops and National Guard. The Marshal lost no time in securing the control of Paris, and daybreak of the 24th found the whole city in possession of the army. Had he been allowed to act as he had arranged, the insurrection would have been easily suppressed; but an order from the Palace to cease the combat and withdraw the troops sealed the fate of the Monarchy. Sore and disheartened, those of his soldiers who retired on the Tuileries made but a feeble resistance to the mob which broke in, while the King, after signing his abdication, was escaping with his family by a back door. The Duchess of Orleans forced her way to the Chamber of Deputies, and made a courageous effort to secure the throne for her son, the Comte de Paris, but all in vain. Thus in two short days the Monarchy was swept away, and the Provisional Government of a Republic substituted in its stead.

The news of these startling events arrived in England on the night of the 25th. As they reached the lobby of the House of Commons the murmurs of conversation spreading from the door right through the crowded benches caused the unparalleled spectacle of a complete, although informal, suspension of business

...ings, every member being engaged in ... colloquy with his neighbour.

...merston acknowledged the news as follows ...manby:—

F. O.: February 26, 1848.

...d at half-past eleven last night in the House of ...r despatches of Thursday. What extraordinary ...us events you give me an account of. It is like ...f a play, and has not taken up much more time. ...a King who owed his crown to a revolution brought ...al blindness and obstinacy should have lost it by ...me means, and he a man who had gone through ...tudes of human existence, from the condition of a ... to the pomp of a throne; and still further that his ...ould have been assisted by a Minister deeply read ...s of history, and whose mind was not merely stored ...onology of historical facts, but had extracted from ...he reasons of events and the philosophy of their ...

...re you but provisional instructions. Continue at ... Keep up unofficial and useful communication with ...o from hour to hour (I say not even from day to ...ve the direction of events, but commit us to no ...ent of any men, nor of any things. Our principles ... to acknowledge whatever rule may be established ...t prospect of permanency, but none other. We ...ship and extended commercial intercourse with ...peace between France and the rest of Europe. We ...to prevent the rest of Europe from meddling with ...h indeed we are quite sure they have no intention ...e French rulers must engage to prevent France from ... part of the rest of Europe. Upon such a basis ...s with France may be placed on a footing more ...a they have been or were likely to be with Louis ... Guizot.

...cific intentions, however, of the Provisional ...t began to be doubted, and a report got ...t they were about to declare war against ...ence, and also to annex Belgium on the in... the Republican party in that country. The ...as making for the coast, hoping to reach

England, and the British Government was taking steps to assist him in his flight.

F. O.: February 27, 1848.

My dear Normanby,—I send you a hundred sovereigns by this messenger, and will send a hundred more by the next. You must use your discretion about going away or staying. It is desirable that you should stay as long as you can do so with safety both to yourself and to the dignity of the country, because your presence protects British subjects; and your coming away would be a measure of much import, and therefore of importance.

Your accounts of Friday night, received to-day, and the further reports that reach us, are fearfully ominous for the peace of Europe. A general war seems to be impending at the moment when we all were flattering ourselves that peace would last thirty years to come. One felt yesterday that the French army had till then counted for nothing in the events which had taken place in Paris, and that it was impossible that the French army should count for nothing in deciding the destinies of France. One therefore felt that it might be in the power of any popular general to march fifty or sixty thousand men into Paris, and decide matters according to his will, in spite of the armed mob or of the National Guard; this thought seems also to have occurred to those who are for the moment at the head of affairs, and they seem to propose to send the army to attack the neighbours of France instead of letting it come into Paris to upset them. It remains to be seen whether the army will take this bait. One fears that it may. If this should be, the British Government will have to come to a grave and serious determination. We cannot sit quiet and see Belgium overrun and Antwerp become a French port; and even a war in other directions will sooner or later draw us into its vortex.

We have taken such measures as are within our power to afford the means of coming over to such passengers as may come to the coast, including the persons to whom you alluded in your last.

Montebello says that he sent a message to the Duchess of Orleans on Thursday morning, which did not reach her, warning her not to rely on the Parliament, against whom, as much as against the King, the revolution was directed, but to take her son into the streets and throw herself on the National Guard. Perhaps if she had received this advice and acted upon it, things might have gone differently.

C. G.: February 28, 1848.

I received at 11 o'clock this evening despatches. All are important, but pre- note of yesterday reporting the pacific you from the Provisional Government, and not to accept the incorporation even a most wise resolve; for if they will look to the treaty finally concluded between the five and the Netherlands, they will see that there which would have a very awkward bearing by France to annex Belgium to its territory. Europe is now in the hands of the French with them rests the question of peace or war. received before this time my despatch desiring you are till you receive other instructions, you to hold such unofficial communications with as may be necessary for the public service. Of French Government cannot expect that we should credentials to a Government professedly pro- temporary, but we shall take no hostile step towards not bring you away as long as they continue to authority, and to use it with moderation and for order. Whenever a permanent Government shall established, then will be the time for deciding as to credentials; and you know that the invariable principle England acts is to acknowledge as the organ of every organ which each nation may deliberately choose to it must be an organ likely to be permanent, for it consistent with the dignity of England to be send- ambassador fresh credentials every ten days, according of the people of Paris might from time to time form and substance of French institutions. I grieve of a republic in France, for I fear that it must in Europe and fresh agitation in England. Large to be essentially and inherently aggressive, and of the French will be resisted by the rest of that is war; while, on the other hand, the example suffrage in France will set our non-voting population will create a demand for an inconvenient extension of ballot, and other mischievous things. However, for Lamartine!

fortunate for the peace of Europe that a

[illegible] Secretary were [illegible] been in London [illegible] imbued with [illegible] of Pitt, a [illegible] again have [illegible] England with [illegible] peace. No [illegible] Belgians bore [illegible] letter to Lord [illegible]

[illegible] my con[illegible] France has been [illegible] Government [illegible] difficulty [illegible] with

[illegible] this critical [illegible] any act [illegible] the Great [illegible] speedy re- [illegible] France to [illegible] bear upon [illegible] Berlin, and to

[illegible] 29, 1848.

[illegible] Lamartine [illegible] there [illegible] steps which [illegible] intention [illegible] is to wai[illegible] there is [illegible] our usual [illegible] to our am[illegible] with th[illegible] to wait fo[illegible] the pro[illegible] expedient to wai[illegible] All men [illegible]

... the Legitimists, are supporting ... as the only security at present against ... and massacre. It must be owned that ... republic in France is far from agreeable; for ... would naturally be more likely to place ... than a monarchy would be. But we must deal ... they are, and not as we would wish to have them. ... ought to serve, however, as a warning to the ... and should induce them to set to work ... to complete those constitutional institutions of ... last year laid the foundations.

F. O.: February 29, 1848.

... Ponsonby,—Here is a pretty to-do at Paris; it is ... the present at least, we shall have a republic in ... long it may last is another question. But, for ... the only chance for tranquillity and order in France, ... in Europe, is to give support to Lamartine. I am ... French Government will not be aggressive, if ... and it is to be hoped that Apponyi and others will ... remain in Paris till things take a decided turn. ... decidedly established, the other Powers of Europe ... give credentials addressed to that Government, ... have to give billets to its troops. I have no time ... but nothing can be more positive, or, as I believe, ... than Lamartine's declarations of a peace policy, ... observe that, by saying that France has not changed ... Europe, he virtually acknowledges the obligations ... treaties. He could not well have done so at present ... distinct terms.

... advise the Austrians to come to a good understand... Sardinia as to mutual defence if attacked, which, how... are not at present likely to be. But if the Austrian ... does not mitigate its system of coercion in Lom... grant liberal institutions, they will have a revolt ... if there shall be conflict in Lombardy between the ... the public, and much bloodshed, it is to be feared ... French nation will break loose in spite of Lamartine's ... restrain them.

... now issued a very able circular or mani... diplomatic agents of France. It deprecated ... the Republic of 1848 must necessarily follow the warlike principles of 1792, but went o[illegible] declare that, in the eyes of France, the treaties of [illegible] existed no longer as law, and that she would not [illegible] with indifference on any forcible attempt to repress [illegible] nascent aspirations of oppressed nationalities. L[illegible] Palmerston writes to Lord Clarendon on March 9;—

Any Government which wished to pick a quarrel w[illegible] France might find ample materials in this circular. But [illegible] seems to me that the true policy of Europe at present is, to [illegible] as little and do as little as possible, so as not to stir matters [illegible] France beyond their natural turbulence, and to watch events [illegible] be prepared for them. The circular is evidently a piece [illegible] patchwork put together by opposite parties in the Governm[illegible] the one warlike and disturbing, the other peaceful and concilia-tory. I should say that if you were to put the whole of it into a crucible, and evaporate the gaseous parts, and scum off the dross, you would find the regulus[1] to be peace and good-fellowship with other Governments.

There soon arose an occasion for testing the truth of this opinion. The Irish revolutionists, confident that they would get sympathy and aid from the French Republic, were sending over deputations to Paris; and at the interviews which they obtained Irish questions were very freely discussed. Lord Palmerston thought it well to speak out at once before much harm was done:—

F. O.: March 21, 1848.

My dear Normanby,—I have written you an official despatch about M. de Lamartine's allocutions to Irish deputations and his direct allusions therein to our internal affairs, such as Catholic Emancipation, Irish agitation, Repeal of the Union, and other matters, with which no foreign Government had any right to meddle. I wish you to convey to him, in terms as civil as you can use, that these speeches, and especially that to which my despatch refers, have given great offence in this country to many persons who very sincerely desire to see the most friendly relations maintained between England and France, and that if this practice of interfering in our affairs, and of giving in this

[1] The pure metal, which in the melting of ores falls to the bottom of the crucible.

[illegible] to political agitation within the [illegible] continue to be persevered in by the [illegible] will soon arise in this country for [illegible] embassy from Paris. This has already [illegible] by many of the supporters of the Govern- [illegible] mark of our disapprobation of the [illegible] French Government in these matters.

[illegible] was not without effect. A de- [illegible] by Smith O'Brien himself, received [illegible] an answer which must have dashed [illegible] He told them that it was not 'con- [illegible] French nation to intervene in the [illegible] with which they were and wished [illegible] peace. Lord Palmerston acknowledges [illegible] conduct of the French Foreign

F. O.: April 4, 1848.

[illegible] Normanby,—Pray tell Lamartine how very much [illegible] his handsome and friendly conduct about the [illegible] His answer was most honourable and gentle- [illegible] what might have been expected from a high- [illegible] like him.

[illegible] the hurry in which I have been living to tell you [illegible] and the Lievens to dinner on Sunday week [illegible] people to meet them; but I took care [illegible] not be put into the paper. Nobody, I imagine, [illegible] there is any political sympathy between Guizot [illegible] have been opposed to each other as public men, [illegible] adverse systems of general political prin- [illegible] acting upon conflicting views of international [illegible] Guizot and I were upon very good terms person- [illegible] was ambassador here; and he was particularly [illegible] when I was at Paris two years ago. He is now in [illegible] adversity; and though I may agree with most [illegible] in thinking that his own political errors have been [illegible] of his present condition, yet it would, I think, [illegible] in me if I had not shown myself as sen- [illegible] civility to me as I should have done if he [illegible] under circumstances more fortunate for himself. [illegible] no reasonable Frenchman can find fault with those [illegible] which are merely the expressions of personal feeling, and which have nothing whatever to do with any political matters. I shall, on the same principle, have the Duchess to dinner in a quiet and unostentatious manner; I saw a great deal of them on the Rhine, and they also gave us a very favourable reception when we were at Paris.

In Italy the news of the French Revolution had a prodigious effect. Everywhere the aristocratic had to yield to the democratic party. Venice broke away from Austria, and proclaimed a Republic. Milan revolted, and compelled the Austrian troops to commence a retreat which only ceased beyond the Mincio. Charles Albert, King of Sardinia, resolved to embrace the cause of Italian independence, and to bring the regular forces of the Piedmontese monarchy to the aid of insurgent Lombardy. On March 25 his army crossed the Ticino, and entered the Austrian territory. On March 31 Lord Palmerston writes to Lord Normanby:—

Our attitude with regard to what is passing in the north of Italy is that of passive spectators. Abercromby made no protest, though he urged all the arguments which suggested themselves to him against the advance of the Sardinian troops.

It may be questionable how far Charles Albert was justified by the rules of good neighbourhood in seizing an Austrian province; my own belief is that he could not help doing so, and as Europe is now undergoing great changes, I cannot myself regret that the establishment of a good state in Northern Italy should be one of them. As to your not always getting letters from me by every messenger who passes through Paris, never wonder at that nor think it extraordinary. Wonder rather when I am able to find time to write at all; I am sure you would if you saw the avalanche of despatches from every part of the world which come down upon me daily, and which must be read, and if you witnessed the number of interviews which I cannot avoid giving every day of the week. Every post sends me a lamenting Minister throwing himself and his country upon England for help, which I am obliged to tell him we cannot afford him. But Belgium is a case by itself, and both France and England are bound by treaty engagements in regard to that country, which it is most desirable for the repose of France and England that no events should call into active operation.

wished to be on good terms, as amid the general downfall; stated to the Government of the opinion of Her Majesty's Government, to a Constitution under the terms Vienna; so he says to Lord Bloomfield :—[1]

> Nesselrode that our feelings and sentiments exactly similar to those which he expresses England. We are at present the only two Europe (excepting always Belgium) that remain and we ought to look with confidence to each he must be aware that public feeling in this in favour of the Poles; but we, the Govern- do anything underhand or ungentlemanlike on I wish we could hope that the Emperor might settle the Polish question in some satisfactory

all these conflicts were surging in Europe, to wipe out almost every line of the Vienna, the British Foreign Office had, as posed, plenty of work to engage its atten- policy at this crisis may be thus sum-

peace as long as possible, but to main- asserting, and not by foregoing, English in- support the integrity and independence so long as the Belgians were themselves uphold it. To favour the development of —whether in the shape of one or two powers—strong enough to make head against from France or Russia. To advise Austria up a bloody struggle for the maintenance kingdom. Lastly, not to interfere in the form of government in France, but or part with any means of resistance French seek to relieve internal embarrass- aggression.

[1] to Lord Bloomfield. F. O., April 11, 1848.

England felt also in her home affairs the events in France, for they stirred up the revolutionary spirit, such as it was. The Chartists, with mad Feargus O'Connor at their head, prepared a demonstration for April 10, when they proposed, after meeting on Kennington Common, to march to the House of Commons with a monster petition. On the day named they were quietly informed by the police officers on the ground that they would not be allowed to cross the Thames. The whole affair ludicrously collapsed, although it had created serious alarm in London. Lord Palmerston reports the result as follows to our ambassador at Paris :—

F. O.: April 11, 1848.

Yesterday was a glorious day, the Waterloo of peace and order. They say there were upwards of one hundred thousand special constables—some put the number at two hundred and fifty thousand; but the streets were swarming with them, and men of all classes and ranks were blended together in defence of law and property. The Chartists made a poor figure, and did not muster more than fifteen thousand men on the Common. Feargus was frightened out of his wits, and was made the happiest man in England at being told that the procession could not pass the bridges. The Chartists have found that the great bulk of the inhabitants of London are against them, and they will probably lie by for the present and watch for some more favourable moment.

Meanwhile, the result of yesterday will produce a good and calming effect all over this and the sister island. The foreigners did not show; but the constables, regular and special, had sworn to make an example of any whiskered and bearded rioters whom they might meet with, and I am convinced would have mashed them to jelly.

Smith O'Brien surpassed himself last night in dulness, bad taste, and treason.

The speech here referred to was on the dis[illegible] of the 'Bill for the more effectual Repression of [illegible]sonable Proceedings,' and was the last occa[illegible] which Smith O'Brien appeared in the House [illegible]mons previous to taking the field! The con[illegible] indignation with which he was received by the [illegible]

[...] In the next letter we get a very [...] Sir Robert Peel's, which shows him [...] when occasion offered.

F. O.: April 18, 1848.

[...]manby,—Lamartine is really a wonderful [...] endowed with great qualities. It is much to be [...] should swim through the breakers and carry his [...] port. I conclude that he has escaped one dan[...] to naturalise Brougham; for it is evident [...]cellor meant, if he had got himself elected, to [...] being President of the Republic. It is woful [...] who is so near being a great man make himself so

[...] just been sending up to the Lords from the House [...] our Bill for the Security of the Crown. Peel made [...] the debate. Feargus O'Connor alluded to the pos[...] Beelzebub being sovereign, and Peel said that in [...] Feargus would certainly enjoy the confidence of the [...], at the close of the debate, blamed us for not [...] down the Convention,[1] which, he said, ought not to [...] to go on, and which, he contended (though erro[...] within the prohibitive provisions of our existing

[...] hear from Ireland tallies with what you wrote me [...]go, that there can be no decided and extensive out[...] potato and grain harvest is in, as men must eat to [...]ght. I trust we shall be able to keep them quiet

[...], King of the Belgians, was all through his [...]seful life one of Lord Palmerston's constant [...]ents. His sagacity and liberal views won [...] of the English Minister, who was always [...]kly to interchange ideas with him. Since [...] Paris had passed through a series of convul[...], at the moment when the following letter [...], the French Assembly, engaged in a struggle [...]ocialists, exhibited the strange spectacle of [...]ure elected by universal suffrage deliberating [...] protection of cannon pointed against its own

[1] Chartist Convention.

constituents. In Italy the tide had not yet turned in favour of the Austrians, and they were still entrenched in their lines beyond the Mincio. Lord Palmerston foresaw that their success, even if it did come, would be but temporary.

Carlton G.: June 15, 1848.

Sire,—I was much obliged to Your Majesty for the letter which I had the honour of receiving from Your Majesty some little time ago; and I am happy to have the opportunity which is thus afforded me of congratulating Your Majesty upon the continued tranquillity and stability of your kingdom. It would seem as if the storms which have shaken everything else all over the continent of Europe had only served to consolidate more firmly the foundations of Your Majesty's throne. As to France, no man nowadays can venture to prophesy from week to week the turn affairs may take in that unfortunate country. For many years past the persons in authority in France have worked at the superstructure of Monarchy without taking care of the foundation. Education and religion have been neglected, and power has now passed into the hands of a mob ignorant of the principles of government, of morality, and of justice; and it is a most remarkable fact in the history of society that in a nation of thirty-five millions of men, who have now for more than half a century been in a state of political agitation, which, in general, forms and brings out able men, and who have during that time been governed by three dynasties, there is no public political man to whom the country looks up with confidence and respect, on account of his statesmanlike qualities and personal character combined; and there is no prince whom any large portion of the nation would make any considerable effort to place as sovereign on the throne. The principle of equality seems to have been fully carried out in one respect, and that is that all public men are equally without respect, and all candidates for royalty equally without following.

As to poor Austria, every person who attaches value to the maintenance of a balance of power in Europe must lament her present helpless condition; and every man gifted with ever so little foresight must have seen, for a long time past, that feebleness and decay were the inevitable consequences of Prince Metternich's system of government; though certainly no one could have expected that the rottenness within would [illegible] and so completely have shown itself without. Lord [illegible]

[illegible] being the only figure among ciphers is [illegible] so it has been with Metternich. He [illegible] anything like talent or attainment in indi[illegible] like life in communities and nations. [illegible] time in damming up and arresting the [illegible] progress. The wonder is, not that the accu[illegible] should at last have broke the barrier and have [illegible], but that his artificial impediments should [illegible] so long.

[illegible] the expulsion of the Austrians from Italy. [illegible] Sire, that it will diminish the real strength nor [illegible] of Austria as a European Power. Her [illegible] to the Italians, and has long been maintained [illegible] expenditure of money and an exertion of military [illegible] Austria less able to maintain her interests else[illegible] to her the heel of Achilles, and not the shield [illegible] Alps are her natural barrier and her best de[illegible] wish to see the whole of Northern Italy united [illegible], comprehending Piedmont, Genoa, Lombardy, [illegible] and Modena; and Bologna would, in that case, [illegible] unite itself either to that State or to Tuscany. [illegible] arrangement of Northern Italy would be most condu[illegible] of Europe, by interposing between France and [illegible] State strong enough to make itself respected, [illegible] in its habits and character neither with France [illegible]; while, with reference to the progress of civi[illegible] a State would have great advantages, political, [illegible] and intellectual. Such an arrangement is now, in [illegible] Sire, inevitable; and the sooner the Austrian [illegible] makes up its mind to the necessity, the better con[illegible] be able to obtain. If Austria waits till she be [illegible]—which she will soon be—she will get no con[illegible]

I have the honour to be, Sire,
Your Majesty's most obedient humble Servant,
PALMERSTON.

[illegible] the first successes of the Italians the [illegible] Government asked for the 'good offices' of [illegible]

[illegible] came from Vienna instructed [illegible] the erection of Lombardy into a separate [illegible] Austrian prince, but under the suzerainty of the Emperor. Lord Palmerston told him that things had gone too far for that. He then said that he would recommend to his Government the abandonment of Lombardy on condition that she took on her shoulders part of the Austrian debt. Lord Palmerston replied that, with Venice already in Italian hands, neither Charles Albert nor his people would be satisfied with this, and suggested that a part at least of Venetia should be included. Baron Hummelauer then said that he would go back and submit this to his Government.

It was certainly a tribute to British influence that it should have been sought thus early by a Power which was not at any rate very well inclined to the man who represented England with foreign nations.

Prince Metternich had detested Canning, and nursed the greater part of his antipathy for the benefit of Canning's distinguished disciple. Prince Schwarzenberg, when he succeeded to Metternich's place, succeeded also to his prejudices, and brought at the same time a more passionate nature to bear. The consequence was that the spirit of Lord Palmerston's policy and proceedings towards Austria was entirely misunderstood by the Imperial Cabinet. The preservation of the Austrian empire was one of the leading considerations which bore upon his different projects for the settlement of the Italian question. Certainly, in 1848, he apprehended its downfall, but he only participated in the fears of every statesman in Europe, including the Austrians themselves. To concentrate her resources upon her own important territories appeared, in the summer of that year, the only way for Austria to extricate herself from her difficulties, and to save her Germanic crown.

In the following letters we find evidence of the general feeling at the time, shared by the Austrians themselves, that the independence of Lombardy was won. Lord Palmerston's suggestion as to the addition

Austrian empire, and has since
d patriotic ruler.

F. O.: April 21, 1848.

have, at the request of Dietrichstein,[1]
ecommend to the Sardinian Govern-
, in order to give Count Hartig an
tiation with the Milanese; but the
omby's application will depend en-
tary operations at the time when my
to say the truth, I have little expec-
will be successful, unless for the
of a few days. Of course, the Sar-
consider the armistice as a pretence
advance of Austrian reinforcements
ave received your note stating the
t which Hartig is authorised to pro-
I am quite sure, will not be listened
h too far to admit of the possibility
between the Italians and Austria.
angements might have been received
hs ago, but they now come too late.
agreed to or not, will probably de-
the war will have taken. If the
rong military position, from which
ithout much expense of time, blood,
y consent to buy them out; but even
likely be a wide difference between
at the other would give. If, on the
ould be evidently losing ground when
are that the Italians will not consent
ia, and will only agree to give the
ssare for their retreat to their own
agree with you and your Austrian
be much better out of Italy than in
be a useful possession for Austria.
n so powerfully excited that Lom-
the sword, and that tenure would,
circumstances, be very insecure, and
far more expensive than valuable.
trians would be right in trying to

[1] mbassador in London.

drive a good bargain with the Lombards, provided they do not stand out too long, nor for terms over-high: anything would be better than a prolonged contest; for that would infallibly bring the French into the conflict, and then Austria would have on her hands a war which every prudential reason should teach her not to provoke, though, of course, she would meet it stoutly if it came upon her unprovoked and without any reason.

On the whole, the conclusion to which I should come is, that the cheapest, best, and wisest thing which Austria can do, is to give up her Italian possessions quietly and at once, and to direct her attention and energy to organising the remainder of her coast territories, to cement them together, and to develop their abundant resources. But to do this there ought to be some able men at the head of affairs, and our doubt is whether there are any such now in office. First and foremost, what is the animal *implumis bipes* called Emperor? A perfect nullity; next thing to an idiot. What is the man who would succeed if the Emperor was to die? A brother scarcely a shade better than the Emperor. Who comes next? A lad of sixteen or twenty; and what else he is, nobody seems to know; but whatever he may become hereafter, he cannot now be competent to take any part in political affairs. If the next heir to the crown were a man of energy and capacity, I should say that the only way of saving Austria would be to persuade the Emperor to abdicate in favour of that successor; and I presume that if the Emperor was told that he must abdicate, he would do as he was bid. But to do any good in this way would require three successive abdications, so as to set aside the present, the next, and the next but one Emperor, and thus to pave the way for the accession of the Archduke John, though I do not know that even then we should be in the regular line of succession. But everybody seems to agree that he is the best man, if not the only man, among them all. Now, three abdications are not easily obtained without a revolution; even after the three glorious days of July there were only two, namely, that of Charles X. and that of the Duke of Angoulême. But the Archduke John might be brought forward and be placed in some situation of commanding influence. These are not times for standing upon ceremonies, and the Austrian empire is a thing worth saving. You cannot do amiss by suggesting this to any persons who may have influence in such matters.

And a few weeks later, in another letter, he says:—

[illegible] stand in these days without an emperor [illegible] an emperor I mean a man endowed with [illegible] suited to his high station. A mere man of [illegible] like the present Emperor, may do very well [illegible] a Metternich, who never leaves his study, [illegible] country by his unopposed will, and can draw [illegible] influence, various other Governments, de- [illegible] to pursue the same policy, to prevent all [illegible] to stifle all symptoms of life among nations, and [illegible] stillness of death, and to boast that such a state [illegible] it a proof of contentment and a guarantee for [illegible] But the present year has dashed Europe abruptly [illegible] condition. There is a general fight going on [illegible] Continent between governors and the governed, [illegible] and disorder, between those who have and those [illegible] have, between honest men and rogues; and as the [illegible] poor, and the rogues are in this world, though [illegible] always the most numerous, at all events the most [illegible] other classes require for their defence to be led and [illegible] intelligence, activity, and energy. But how can these [illegible] found in a Government where the sovereign is [illegible] Pray, then, tell Wessemberg from me, but in the [illegible] confidence, that I would entreat of him and his col- [illegible] consider, for the salvation of their country, whether [illegible] arrangement could not be made by which the Emperor [illegible] state, for which his bodily health might furnish a fair [illegible] while some more efficient successor might ascend the [illegible] his stead. I fear that his next brother is little better [illegible] but could not the son of that brother be called to [illegible] station? And though he is young, he yet could mount [illegible] and show himself to his troops and his people, could [illegible] enthusiasm for his person as well as for his official [illegible] and, by the aid of good Ministers and able generals, [illegible] re-establish the Austrian empire in its proper position at [illegible] abroad. I am sure that Wessemberg will forgive the [illegible] am taking, but the maintenance of the Austrian em- [illegible] object of general interest to all Europe, and to no [illegible] more than England.

Whatever chance, however, the Italians may have [illegible] being able to cope single-handed with the Aus- [illegible] thrown away by a want of cordial co-opera- [illegible] their different forces. They soon lost all the ground which they had gained. Complete victory crowned the efforts of Marshal Radetsky, and Milan surrendered on August 6.

The question of mediation between Austria and Sardinia had been under discussion between France and England previously to the great reverses sustained by the Sardinian troops. When their utter destruction seemed inevitable, and intelligence of the capture of Milan was daily expected, the French Government represented that nothing but an assurance that England would join in mediation could prevent them from marching to the assistance of the Sardinians;[1] and so urgent were they on this point, that Lord Normanby, before he received his instructions, found it indispensable, on the faith of a private letter from Lord Palmerston, to engage that England would concur. The instruction to this effect was sent to Lord Normanby on August 7, and with it were sent instructions to be forwarded to Lord Ponsonby and Mr. Abercromby in the event of the French Government agreeing to the basis of mediation laid down by Lord Palmerston. Even if the French Government had not concurred, the instructions were to be sent on, in order that those Ministers might tender the single mediation of England between the contending parties.

France, however, joined with England, and an armistice was concluded between the contending parties. Then ensued a long and infructuous negotiation. The object of Lord Palmerston was to persuade Austria, while retaining Venice, to give up Lombardy, and receive in money an equivalent for its loss.

F. O.: August 31, 1848.

My dear Ponsonby,—The real fact is that the Austrians have no business in Italy at all, and have no real right to be there. The right they claim is founded upon force of arms and the

[1] General Oudinot came to Paris for orders, and told Cavaignac that if he was not allowed to lead his army to Italy to assist Charles Albert, his army would go without him, and that many of his officers had already gone privately to offer their services.

Treaty of Vienna they themselves set took possession of Cracow, and they have engagement to give national institutions to their Polish subjects. They treaty when it suits their purpose, and at the suits their purpose, reject it. Moreover, in the Treaty of Vienna for any of its for those relating to Prussian Saxony and we offer them an equivalent for that which to give up, and they get, therefore, a sub- the treaty assigned them.

founded on force, force may be employed to just as much right.

at Vienna think, perhaps, that force will not If that is their opinion, the sooner they are better. I know very well that Metternich and up an active correspondence with Germany, amuse their correspondents at Vienna with all and expectations of the support which Austria this Italian question from hence, and of the want to go to war. Wessemberg knows Metter- well enough not to be misled by these tales of He well knows that private and personal intrigues nothing here; and he will easily understand that will do no more than was Zuylen able to accomplish, much. Pray request him not to be misled on this as to the interference of France, it will be given if stubborn; and if a French army enters Italy, the will be driven, not to the Mincio, or to the Adige, or but clean over the Alps. I do not wish to see the Italy; there are a great many strong and weighty I should dislike it; but I would rather that they than that the Austrians should retain Lombardy; eople at Vienna may depend upon it that if, owing to inacy, our mediation should fail, the French will enter with the consent of England, and we shall not then with Hummelauer's Memorandum.

meant mankind to be divided into separate for this purpose countries have been founded by and races of men have been distinguished by habits, manners, dispositions and characters. on the globe in which this intention is more that of the Italians and the Germans, kept apart by the Alps, and as unlike in everything as two races can be. Austria has never possessed Italy as part of her empire, but has always held it as a conquered territory. There has been no mixture of races. The only Austrians have been the troops and the civil officers. She has governed it as you govern a garrison town, and her rule has always been hateful. We do not wish to threaten; but it is the part of a friend to tell the truth, and the truth is that Austria *cannot*, and *must not*, retain Lombardy; and she ought to think herself well enough off by keeping Venetia, if, indeed, that province is really advantageous to her. They will twit you at Vienna with Ireland, and say what should we reply if they were to ask us to give up Ireland; but the cases are wholly different. In Ireland the races are mixed, and almost amalgamated; and, at all events, the Celts are in Scotland, and Wales, and Cornwall, as well as in Ireland. The language is the same; for English is spoken all over Ireland, and the land, and wealth, and intelligence of the country is for the connection. None of this can be said of Italy in regard to Austria.

Time presses. The French are growing very impatient. We are holding them back, because we wish these things to be settled amicably; but they cannot be withheld much longer; and if the mediation is refused, some energetic decision will infallibly be taken. Exert yourself to the utmost to prevent a crisis, which must end in the humiliation of Austria.

North of the Alps, we wish her all the prosperity and success in the world. Events have rendered it unavoidable that she should remain, in some shape or other, south of the Alps, and as far west as the Adige. Beyond that line, depend upon it, she cannot stay.

Brussels, after many *pourparlers*, was fixed upon as the place of meeting for the mediation Conference. But Lord Palmerston writes to point out that at such a conference nothing but matters of detail could be settled. The principles must be conceded beforehand.

Brocket: November 12, 1848.

My dear Ponsonby,—The true and real seat of the negotiations is Vienna, and, unless the Austrian Government agree to the proposed basis for an arrangement, I foresee no good to come out of the mediation; and as sure as fate Austria will find herself involved in a serious war before next Midsummer Day. It is totally and absolutely impossible that she can keep [illegible]

[illegible] provinces; and all you hear at Vienna [illegible] but the *bon à dire* of the Metternich [illegible] of the established practice of the dis[illegible] on asserting as facts that which they [illegible] wish to be true, under the absurd notion [illegible] falsehood may become truth. The [illegible] this system is, that those who act upon it [illegible] by it govern their conduct upon en[illegible]; and the results of such false policy are, [illegible] Metternich and Guizot meet in exile in London; [illegible] Louis Philippe drink unwholesome water [illegible] at Claremont, instead of champagne and [illegible]; and that ancient empires like Austria [illegible] anarchy and confusion, and are brought to the [illegible] dissolution.

[illegible] the drift and meaning of Prince Windisch[illegible] to our Queen; but pray make the Camarilla [illegible] in a constitutional country like England, these [illegible] answer; and that a foreign Government which [illegible] upon working upon the Court against the [illegible] of this country is sure to be disappointed.

[illegible], however, was not in a temper either for [illegible] conciliation.

Broadlands: December 28, 1848.

[illegible] Abercromby,—I have received your letter with the [illegible] enclosed in it. I am very glad that you pre[illegible] from taking any official notice of the attack [illegible] that paper contains. All I should wish is that [illegible] should be circulated and read from one end of Italy, [illegible] end of Europe to another. As regards the Aus[illegible] that our Austrian policy has excited the old[illegible] of some very small minds at Vienna; and the [illegible] us for our course by not sending an Archduke [illegible] to announce the accession of the Emperor is truly [illegible] of the State policy of European China; one should [illegible] to laugh at it outright if one did not feel grieved to [illegible] of a great empire in the hands of men who can [illegible] boast of such a childish revenge. Ponsonby wrote [illegible] Schwarzenberg had announced to him that no [illegible] be sent, because they would not place a member [illegible] family in contact with a person who had proved [illegible] an enemy as I have shown myself to be of

Austria. I told Ponsonby in reply, that I am sincerely grateful to the Austrian Government for having spared me the trouble and inconvenience which, amid a heavy pressure of business, such a mission would have occasioned to me. I am almost afraid, however, from what I have since heard, that they have thought worse of their first determination, and that some Archduke is coming to us. As to the abuse of me and my policy in the newspaper of Milan, I look upon all it says, considering whence it comes, as a compliment; and if there is any truth in the saying, *Noscitur a sociis*, I feel much obliged to the writers for classing me with three of the most enlightened statesmen of the present day—Espartero, Reshid Pasha, and Mavrocordato. As to the warlike announcements of the Italians, they must, I fear, end in smoke or in defeat. I heartily wish that Italy was *più forte*; but weak as she is, a contest single-handed with Austria would only lead to her more complete prostration, and I doubt whether France is as yet quite ready to take the field in her support. I do not wish to see Italy emancipated from the Austrian yoke by the help of French arms, but perhaps it would be better it should be so done than not done at all; and if it were so done at a time when England and France were well together, we might be able to prevent any permanently bad consequences from resulting from it. But the great object at present is to keep things quiet; to re-establish peace in Northern Italy, and to trust to future events for greater improvements.

Austria never sent a plenipotentiary to Brussels. The mediation and the Conference fell to the ground. In the spring of 1849 the armistice came to an end, and the disaster of Novara sealed the fate of Italian independence for another ten years. The British Government, however, did not cease its efforts to obtain better terms for the conquered. There was the question of payment for the expenses of the war. This still offered an opportunity of being of service to the Italians.

The following letter was in reply to one from the Premier finding fault with a despatch as being too 'dry and disparaging' to Austria. Admiral Cecille was French Minister in London. The Russians were occupying the Principalities, in consequence of their intervention in the revolt of Hungary.

Broadlands: April 9, 1849.

ell,—I merely repeat in my draft what
age. He said that, as a Frenchman and
ish interests, he could not object to the
nd payment, because it would necessarily
nt and drive her into the arms of France;
asure as cruel and oppressive as it was
mpolitic. I do not see why we should
de, and abandon our friends merely be-
unfortunate; and if it is said that the
r Charles Albert made war against our
of common sense, it ought to be borne in
arles Albert nor the late Turin Govern-
ontribution is to be paid, and that the
n will fall upon those who had no share
professes to be the punishment. General
deration will be of no avail; if we want
; Vienna, we must come to specific de-

that, as you say, the present moment is
I should hope that a firm attitude on
onjunction with France, may avert any
consequences. Austria seems to have
t to have sent troops as yet to Florence
is evidently a close connection between
ot closer, however, than has existed at
ich Revolution of 1830; and we are so
have hitherto been, that there are only
ther instead of three, as there used to be,
off and looks to be the leading Power of
instead of being the kettle tied to the
ilitary neighbours. When Minto was at
know the policy and views of Prussia
on, we used to be told that we must go
g and Vienna. That serfdom is now

ust either support France or court Aus-
r the first course we may restrain France,
ia and Russia; by the second course, if
and carried to the extent of any sacrifice
justice, we should lose France without
s we should lose our supporters at home
single Tory. Austria keeps hold on to

Austria. I told Ponsonby in reply, that I am sincerely grateful to the Austrian Government for having spared me the trouble and inconvenience which, amid a heavy pressure of business, such a mission would have occasioned to me. I am almost afraid, however, from what I have since heard, that they have thought worse of their first determination, and that some Archduke is coming to us. As to the abuse of me and my policy in the newspaper of Milan, I look upon all it says, considering whence it comes, as a compliment; and if there is any truth in the saying, *Noscitur a sociis*, I feel much obliged to the writers for classing me with three of the most enlightened statesmen of the present day—Espartero, Reshid Pasha, and Mavrocordato. As to the warlike announcements of the Italians, they must, I fear, end in smoke or in defeat. I heartily wish that Italy was *più forte*; but weak as she is, a contest single-handed with Austria would only lead to her more complete prostration, and I doubt whether France is as yet quite ready to take the field in her support. I do not wish to see Italy emancipated from the Austrian yoke by the help of French arms, but perhaps it would be better it should be so done than not done at all; and if it were so done at a time when England and France were well together, we might be able to prevent any permanently bad consequences from resulting from it. But the great object at present is to keep things quiet; to re-establish peace in Northern Italy, and to trust to future events for greater improvements.

Austria never sent a plenipotentiary to Brussels. The mediation and the Conference fell to the ground. In the spring of 1849 the armistice came to an end, and the disaster of Novara sealed the fate of Italian independence for another ten years. The British Government, however, did not cease its efforts to obtain better terms for the conquered. There was the question of payment for the expenses of the war. This still offered an opportunity of being of service to the Italians.

The following letter was in reply to one from the Premier finding fault with a despatch as being too '[illegible] and disparaging' to Austria. Admiral Cecille was French Minister in London. The Russians were occupying the Principalities, in consequence of their intervention in the revolt of Hungary.

Broadlands: April 9, 1849.

My dear John Russell,—I merely repeat in my draft what [illegible] said a few days ago. He said that, as a Frenchman and [illegible] merely to French interests, he could not object to the [illegible] of the proposed payment, because it would necessarily [illegible] weaken Piedmont and drive her into the arms of France; [illegible] thought it a measure as cruel and oppressive as it was [illegible] interests impolitic. I do not see why we should [illegible] the Tory example, and abandon our friends merely because [illegible] have been unfortunate; and if it is said that the [illegible] Government and Charles Albert made war against our [illegible] in defiance of common sense, it ought to be borne in [illegible] is not Charles Albert nor the late Turin Government [illegible] whom the contribution is to be paid, and that the [illegible] the infliction will fall upon those who had no share [illegible] of which it professes to be the punishment. General [illegible] of moderation will be of no avail; if we want [illegible] effect at Vienna, we must come to specific de[illegible]

[illegible] is no doubt that, as you say, the present moment is [illegible] danger; but I should hope that a firm attitude on [illegible] in conjunction with France, may avert any [illegible] permanent consequences. Austria seems to have [illegible] Italy, and not to have sent troops as yet to Florence [illegible] But there is evidently a close connection between [illegible] Russia, not closer, however, than has existed at [illegible] the French Revolution of 1830; and we are so [illegible] than we have hitherto been, that there are only [illegible] linked together instead of three, as there used to be, [illegible] broken off and looks to be the leading Power of [illegible] Germany instead of being the kettle tied to the [illegible] two great military neighbours. When Minto was at [illegible] wanted to know the policy and views of Prussia [illegible] great question, we used to be told that we must go [illegible] Petersburg and Vienna. That serfdom is now [illegible]

[illegible] that we must either support France or court Austria [illegible] that by the first course we may restrain France, [illegible] both Austria and Russia; by the second course, if [illegible] civility, and carried to the extent of any sacrifice [illegible], or justice, we should lose France without [illegible] just as we should lose our supporters at home [illegible] a single Tory. Austria keeps hold on to

Russia for the present, as a bad swimmer keeps cl[illegible]
one. She has hard and heavy work to do in Hun[illegible]
sylvania, and other provinces, and the Russian ar[illegible]
hand to help her if need be. We cannot outbid Ru[illegible]
matters; no fair words of ours can outweigh the fi[illegible]
of the Autocrat. It is unfortunate for Austria and
that the Austrian Government should place itself i[illegible]
of dependence upon Russia, because it disqualifies A[illegible]
being hereafter a check upon Russian ambition an[illegible]
ment. 'Hold your tongue,' the Russians will say, '[illegible]
ber that we saved you from dismemberment and r[illegible]
hope the Austrians may not, if they become strong[illegible]
reproaches; but still this sort of military assistan[illegible]
paid for one way or another. However, we must h[illegible]
best; and if England and France are steady, I ha[illegible]
we shall get the Russians out of the Principalities[illegible]
be she ever so subservient to Russia, cannot submi[illegible]
get possession of those military positions; and [illegible]
knowing the full extent of the moral prostration of [illegible]
a European Power, would not lightly encounter [illegible]
being opposed by England, France, and Turkey [illegible]
Turkey is now in a much more respectable cond[illegible]
her army and navy than she was in during the ca[illegible]
1828-29.

In August, Massimo D'Azeglio sent from [illegible]
acknowledgment of Lord Palmerston's aid t[illegible]
the negotiation.

Au moment où nous venons de conclure la pai[illegible]
triche, je manquerais à un de mes principaux devoi[illegible]
preuve des sentiments dont le Cabinet de S. M. est [illegible]
je m'empresse de faire parvenir à Votre Excellence [illegible]
notre vive gratitude pour le bienveillant appui q[illegible]
sincère intérêt qu'elle porte à l'Italie et surtout [illegible]
Votre Seigneurie a bien voulu nous prêter, durant [illegible]
une longue et difficile négociation. Le Roi et son [illegible]
ment, qui avaient invoqué cet appui avec une entiè[illegible]
se plaisent à reconnaître que c'est principalement à [illegible]
qu'ils doivent d'avoir obtenu des conditions meilleur[illegible]
[illegible]

…fondée que nous avions d'arriver avec … elle nous a donné une nouvelle preuve … franche et loyale amitié qui unit, depuis … Belgique et l'Angleterre, sa plus puissante et …

… of the session the leader of the Pro… in the Commons made a final effort to … of the House to the principles of com… which he had espoused. He accordingly … Select Committee on the state of the nation. … that distress and disgrace had been pro… the accession to power of the Whig … Sir Robert Peel warmly supported the …

O. G.: July 7, 1849.

… William,—Our session is drawing to a close, and … finish by the first week in August. After all the … of attacks that were to demolish first one and then … ber of the Government—first me, then Grey, then …—we have come triumphantly out of all debates …, and end the session stronger than we began it. … this morning, on Disraeli's motion 'On the State …,' was 296 to 156—a majority of 140! on a motion … a question of confidence or no confidence in the …

… ch are by this time in Rome.[1] I send you de… … ining our views on these matters. If you have an … of mentioning them to the Neapolitan Ministers, … spatches for your text, and say that it is impossible … can return to Rome—or even if he returned, … permanently maintain himself—unless he grants, … ather, to the Romans the Constitution which he … t year; and the Neapolitan Government would … ng usefully to the peace of Italy and would be … e interests of the Pope, if they were to concur … in strongly urging the Pope to pursue such a course. … eans certain that he would be taken back by the … on those conditions, but the probability is that

[1] …erston once said, when asked for an illustration of the … een 'business' and 'occupation,' 'The French undertook … of Rome, but they had no business there.'

be would; and it is almost a certainty that upon any [illegible]ditions he would be rejected.

If it should be impossible to bring the Pope and his [illegible] to terms, a very inconvenient state of things will arise. [illegible] French will never allow the Pope to be forced back [illegible]tionally on the Romans; some other independent Govern[illegible] must therefore be established at Rome, that would [illegible] a republic; and a republic at Rome would be an [illegible] neighbour for the King of Naples. But for my part, I [illegible] not see any insurmountable objection to acknowledging [illegible] Government, if the return of the Pope on the basis of a Consti[illegible]tution should be impossible. Colloredo has always said to [illegible] that the Austrians do not insist upon the unconditional [illegible] of the Pope. It seems quite clear that the Pope never [illegible] again be what he has been, and that his spiritual power will [illegible] much diminished by the curtailment or loss of his temporal authority. This is surely a good thing for Europe, both Ca[illegible]tholic and Protestant, and if it ends in very much nationalising and localising the Catholic Church in every country, that alone will be a great point gained, and will be a material step in the progress of human society.

Lord Brougham was this session in one of his harassing moods, and had given notice of a motion in the House of Lords, expressive of regret that the Government had shown in its conduct of foreign affairs a want of friendly feelings towards the allies of Great Britain. Lord Palmerston availed himself of the notice given to press on the French their questionable conduct at Rome.

F. O.: July 16, 1849.

My dear Normanby,—The debate on Brougham's motion on Friday will turn chiefly on Italian affairs, and of course Sicily, Lombardy, and Rome will be the main topics on which Brougham, Stanley, and Aberdeen—the three witches who have filled the cauldron—will dilate. As to Sicily and Lombardy, our Peers will be at no loss what to say; but the Roman affairs are not so clear, and it would be very useful—not only for us, but as it seems to me, for the French Government—if Lansdowne, and whoever else may speak on our side from the Ministerial bench, were able to say something positive and definitive as to the intentions of the French Government.

The questions which will naturally be asked are: Is [illegible] army taken possession of Rome?—is city to be added to France? Of course easily given. Is it then as friends of the of the Roman people? This question it is and for us, unaided by the French Govern-

that the priestly and Absolutist party is in the French Cabinet about the affairs of the French Government is preparing to re- Pope, leaving it to his generosity (which is like Shakespeare's knight) to grant *de novo* to his reforms of the Gregorian abuses as he may on re- think expedient; but that they, the French, and are to concur with the Cardinals, the priests, the Neapolitans, and the Spaniards in deeming all by the Pope last year as null and void. Now, would be well enough for Schwarzenberg, Nar- of Naples, and Lambruschini, but it would be creditable to the French Government.

ville may say, 'But if we propose conditions to the will refuse them, and what are we to do then?—are for ever at Rome; or are we to go out, and let Austrians or Garibaldi in?' My answer would be, who are in possession of Rome make the Pope and and the Austrian Government clearly understand cannot come back except upon the before-men- tions, the Pope will put his allocution of April 20 and will accept the conditions. But if he refuses: Why, if I was the French Government, I would I withdrew my interference, and should leave the Romans to settle their disputes as they could; would not allow Austria, or Naples, or Spain to exer- interference either; and that, in withdrawing my Rome, I would, if it was worth while, require from Municipality, or whatever the ruling authorities no foreigners—that is to say, no persons not Italians admitted to power within the city. I say not it is pedantry to call men belonging to other parts strangers' at Rome.

French would say, 'The result of this would be the of a republic at Rome.' Well, and what if it was? be the first time that an Italian adopted a repub- of government; and it cannot be feared that the

H

modern republic of Rome would conquer Europe, like its ancient predecessor.

My own belief is that sooner or later, Rome will become a republic, and that nothing but overruling and foreign military force can prevent such a result. There are mutually repelling properties between a reasoning people and an elective priestly Government. The Roman people have tasted too much of the spring of knowledge, both religious and political, during the last fourteen months—or, I may say, now nearly three years—not to be determined to 'drink deep,' and in the present state of Europe no human power can long prevent them from so doing. The Papal supremacy, both spiritual and political, has received an earthquake shake from which it never can recover, and all that can be done is to patch up the rent as well as circumstances permit, so that the fabric may last for a time; but there will be shock after shock, till it all crumbles to the ground. The Catholic Powers say to the Romans that they must submit to the worst and most anomalous Government in the civilised world, because they are Papists; the Roman people will ere long reply by saying, 'We are no longer Papists: take your Pope and give him as sovereign to those who are Papists still.'

The Reformation in Europe was as much a movement to shake off political oppression as it was to give freedom to religious conscience, and similar causes are apt to produce similar effects.

F. O.: July 24, 1849.

My dear William,—We are finishing our session; the prorogation will be next Tuesday or Wednesday. We end it triumphantly in the Lords as well as in the Commons; and I individually leave off, as I began, with a personal victory, for the motion by Brougham last week was in fact aimed at me specially.[1]

I had an opportunity on Saturday of paying off Aberdeen for his repeated and very ungentlemanlike attacks upon me. I just gave him enough to show him that, if I had thought it worth while, I could have given him more; and the House of Commons was quite with me, at least the members present.

This was in a debate on the Hungarian war. Several Liberal members took the opportunity of replying to speeches made in a reactionary spirit in the House of

[1] It was rejected by a majority of 12.

conduct of public affairs. Sir, there are men [illegible] their whole lives in adoring the Govern[illegible] they deemed it the great symbol of the [illegible] entertained, at last became fickle in their [illegible] transferred their allegiance to the Government [illegible] they thought that in that Government they [illegible] degree of leaning to the arbitrary principle, [illegible] forsooth, suspected the Government of designs [illegible] of freedom. We have heard of persons [illegible] use of the expression old women.[1] Public [illegible] deal in egotism, and I will not apply to them [illegible] has fallen from their own mouth. I will [illegible]he conduct of such men is an example of anti[illegible]

[illegible] letter to Mr. Charles Murray, the Con[illegible] Alexandria—though stating what is well [illegible] Englishmen as the rule of our public [illegible] astonish the great men of some other [illegible]ere presents are regarded as a considerable [illegible] remuneration:—

F. O.: August 30, 1849.

[illegible]urray,—In working up the chaotic arrear which [illegible]ring a session of Parliament, I have come upon [illegible] 10th May, in which you say that Ahmed Bey, [illegible] Ibrahim Pasha, had intimated an intention of [illegible]ne horses as a present. I hope no inconvenience [illegible]en from my not having answered your letter [illegible] he should mention his intentions to you again, I

[1] [illegible] a few days before, in a laboured attack upon Lord [illegible] had said that Lord Minto had only been received [illegible] for the same reason that the 'old woman' of [illegible] in the tyranny of Dionysius—lest the devil should [illegible]

wish you to say that you will make known to me his kind intention, and that you are sure that I shall be much flattered by the intended compliment, and much gratified by the friendly feeling of which it is a proof; but that you know that it is a positive and invariable rule for British Ministers not to accept presents of any kind from anybody, and that, consequently, although there is nobody from whom I should be more gratified by receiving such a mark of goodwill, I should be obliged, as a matter of duty, to decline the present, and it is better, therefore, that he should let the matter drop.[1]

There was one form of present, however, which his position did not forbid him to accept, and which, under the circumstances, was even more gratifying than a horse from a Pasha. Just before the end of the session he received a deputation of members of the House of Commons, who asked him to sit for a full-length portrait, to be given by them to Lady Palmerston, 'as a small memento of his great abilities, high honour, noble-minded independent policy, warm-heartedness, and worth.'

As soon as he gets out of town he sends his brother the local news, and an account of his country pursuits.

Brocket: September 23, 1849.

The present moment is the moment of reaction in Europe. The Revolutionists have had their swing; the tide is turned, and the Absolutists are for the time in the ascendant. But this state of things cannot last, and the Governments of Europe cannot finally settle down into the same practice of abuses and oppressions which was the real cause of the outbreaks of last year.

Here in England everything is quiet. Our harvest is good, and the potatoes not much diseased; trade and manufactures are rallying, and all interests tolerably well off. Cholera has been very active, and has been so spread over the country that hardly any place or town has been exempt from it. But it may almost everywhere be traceable to noxious effluvia, arising from accumulations of dirt and of animal and vegetable matter,

[1] The same rule applies to foreign 'orders.' Queen Elizabeth used to say that she would not allow 'her sheep to be tarred by another shepherd.'

towers, and things of that kind; and have been attacked by it who have not operating causes. There were several the end of July and in the beginning of and they were almost all in Banning hundred, where bad drainage, or rather no occasioned the presence of bad exhalations. other ladies, is nervous about these things, had to go to Broadlands till cholera shall be quite detained in London till the end of August by confinement, and since then we have been at here. It does not much matter to me where I make almost all places equal. I am, however, yesterday managed to take four hours' partridge-

Broadlands: January 1, 1850.

has been but indifferent, owing to a bad breed- following upon two previous years of the same kind, a good poaching season at Romsey; but I have get out three or four times with the hounds, which me more good than anything else.

will begin the last day of this month. We shall, have a sharp fire from the Protectionists at starting; make no permanent or material impression either or the country; and they are wholly unable to government, even if the offer to do so could be made to

you get on with your demands on the Neapolitan for compensation for the merchants for losses civil war? We have given Parker instructions to when he leaves the seas of the Levant, and to in enforcing certain demands, which have been before the Greek Government, for compensation subjects for various wrongs at different times done When the account of Parker's visit to Athens reaches may as well confidentially, and not in pursuance but as the result of your own good wishes to events from Naples, suggest to the Neapolitan possibility that Parker might receive orders to visit to Naples for a like purpose; and that well for the Neapolitan Government to prevent

[1] Lady Palmerston.

this by doing with a good grace that which, in such a case, they might find it best policy to do, although with a bad grace, and with some derogation to the dignity of the King.

We shall come later on to the history of these demands upon the Greek Government, but the foregoing passage shows that the strong measures which Lord Palmerston felt himself bound to take at Athens were prompted not merely by wrongs endured there, but also by his conviction that, at many other points, the prestige of England would suffer, and difficulties would arise, if she allowed herself to be baffled in the East by a Power whose weakness was its strength, and duplicity its weapon.

CHAPTER IV.

...—QUESTION OF THE HUNGARIAN REFUGEES.

ition at Vienna had been quickly followed by Hungary. The civil war raged for many d. success had attended the Magyars, so far ns in the field were concerned. In her dire tria had called in the aid of Russia. The icholas quickly responded with 150,000 men, justify his act in the face of Europe by con- of safety for his own possessions. This n decided the contest, and Hungary lay t the feet of the two great military empires. thies of men like Lord Palmerston were with rians, because, if they were revolutionists, so in the same sense as the men to whose close of the seventeenth century, it is owing resent Royal Family of England, happily for , are seated on the throne of these realms. ad long had its separate Constitution, Par- d laws. The crowns of Austria and Hungary ed upon one head, because the same person ferent and separate titles become, in order on, Sovereign of each of the two countries. ror of Austria became King of Hungary f his coronation at Pesth, on which occasion oath to observe and maintain its Constitu- Austrian Cabinet wished entirely to destroy itution, and incorporate Hungary with the mass of the empire. Whether this was a good arrangement for the parties, the

Imperial Government had no right to impose it by force without endeavouring to obtain the consent of the Hungarian Diet. This is, however, what they did, and the Hungarians were fully justified in resisting force by force. Supposing that at the time of the union of Scotland and England, the English Government, instead of proposing a Treaty of Union and obtaining the legal consent of the Scotch Parliament, had issued an Order in Council summarily terminating their separate existence and functions. The Scotch would have resisted. If then the King of England had sent his army over the Border to subdue the Scotch, and, finding the task too hard for him, had ended by calling in the French to help him, the parallel would have been complete.

In the earlier part of the year Lord Palmerston had vainly attempted to mediate between the contending parties in Hungary, so as to avert the Russian intervention, of which he here chronicles the result:—

F. O.: August 22, 1849.

My dear Ponsonby,—We heard yesterday from Warsaw that which must be considered the conclusion of the war in Hungary. I must own I am glad that it is over, for though all our sympathies in this country are with the Hungarians, yet it was scarcely in the nature of things that they should be able, against such superior forces, to hold out long enough to compel the allies to treat with them on equal terms, and a prolongation of the war would therefore only have led to the same result after the slaughter of many more thousands of brave men on both sides, and after still greater devastation of the country, than has already taken place. Now is the time for the Austrian Government to redeem itself in the opinion of Europe: a just and generous use of the success which has been gained would re-establish Austria in public estimation, and would again place her in the front rank among the great Powers of Europe. If the Austrian Government listens to passion, resentment, and political prejudice, they will enlist against them every generous and just mind in the civilised world, and will lay the foundation for permanent weakness and decrepitude in the Austrian empire. I shall write to you officially in this sense in a day or

while, shape your language to this effect. to be done is to re-establish the ancient ary, with the improvements made in it abolition of feudal service, and exemption of public burthens, and to publish a real y. If Austria wishes for a legislative y, it should be proposed in a legal way, like Scotland and Ireland, but I much fear that are not in favour at present at Vienna; assemblies founded upon election by intelligence and not by universal suffrage, are the only sure public order and permanent monarchy. It will the Emperor of Russia should take the Hungarians protection as against the Austrians, just as he pro- the Principalities against the Turks.

between the master and the revolted sub- not merely been a calm and strategical r: it had been a war of passion, bitter and I quote the following letter to illustrate the and strong sympathy of Lord Palmerston's He bounded like a boy at any cruelty or Many years later, during his second Pre- at the time when the Federal General Butler public opinion by proclaiming at New Orleans who showed discontent either by their dress nour would be treated like women of the town, to the American Minister an indignant letter nstrance so strong and outspoken that Mr. refused to receive it, and ran off with it to ign Office in the utmost consternation. The impulse of indignation against a cowardly er died out with him. It survived even in his the advent of which is too often accompanied al indifference to the sufferings of others:—

Panshanger: September 9, 1849.

ians are really the greatest brutes that ever called the undeserved name of civilised men. Their Galicia, in Italy, in Hungary, in Transylvania are equalled by the proceedings of the negro race in

Africa and Haiti. Their late exploit of flogging forty odd people, including two women at Milan, some of the victims being gentlemen, is really too blackguard and disgusting a proceeding. As to working upon their feelings of generosity and gentlemanlikeness that is out of the question, because such feelings exist not in a set of officials who have been trained up in the school of Metternich, and the men in whose minds such inborn feelings have not been crushed by court and office power have been studiously excluded from public affairs, and can only blush in private for the disgrace which such things throw upon their country. But I do hope that *you* will not fail constantly to bear in mind the country and the Government which you represent, and that you will maintain the dignity and honour of England by expressing *openly* and *decidedly* the disgust which such proceedings excite in the public mind in this country; and that you will not allow the Austrians to imagine that the public opinion of England is to be gathered from articles put into the 'Times' by Austrian agents in London, nor from the purchased support of the 'Chronicle,' nor from the servile language of Tory lords and ladies in London, nor from the courtly notions of royal dukes and duchesses. I have no great opinion of Schwarzenberg's statesmanlike qualities unless he is very much altered from what he was when I knew him; but, at least, he has lived in England, and must know something of English feelings and ideas, and he must be capable of understanding the kind of injury which all these barbarities must do to the character of Austria in public opinion here; and I think that, in spite of his great reliance upon and fondness for Russia, he must see that the good opinion of England is of some value to Austria; if for nothing else, at least to act as a check upon the illwill towards Austria, which he supposes, or affects to suppose, is the great actuating motive of the revolutionary firebrand who now presides at the Foreign Office in Downing Street.

You might surely find an opportunity of drawing Schwarzenberg's attention to these matters, which may be made intelligible to him, and which a British ambassador has a right to submit to his consideration. There is another view of the matter which Schwarzenberg, with his personal hatred of the Italians, would not choose to comprehend, but which, nevertheless, is well deserving of attention, and that is the obvious tendency of these barbarous proceedings to perpetuate in the minds of the Italians indelible hatred of Austria; and as the

...not hope to govern Italy always by ... hatred is not an evil altogether

... I call them not statesmen or states- ... brought their country to this remarkable ... Emperor holds his various territories at the ... of three external Powers. He holds ... and no longer than France chooses to let ... first quarrel between Austria and France ... out of Lombardy and Venice. He holds ... just as long as and no longer than Russia ... them. The first quarrel with Russia will ... from the Austrian crown. He holds his ... a tenure dependent, in a great degree, upon ... which it will be very difficult for him and ... to combine with or to stand out against. ... against these various dangers which are ... the Austrian empire would be generous ... instead of that, the Austrian Government ... of administration but what consists in flog- ... and shooting. 'The *Austrians* know no force.'

... Hungary was subdued, a joint demand ... the Porte by Russia and Austria to ... fugitives who had sought safety at ... the Turkish frontier. Prince Radzivil ... Titoff for Russia, and Count Stürmer for ... ed at Constantinople the surrender of these ... ong whom were Kossuth and Zamoyski. ... however, firmly resisted this attempt to ... to violate the laws of humanity by giving ... ngeance of the conquerors those who had ... erritory for refuge. As no threats could ... solution of the Ottoman Government, the ... notified to the Porte the suspension of all ... ntercourse between their own Courts and ... Sultan. Lord Palmerston determined to ... Sultan.

Carlton Gardens: September 29, 1849.

... Normanby,—I received yesterday afternoon, at ... letter from Drouyn de Lhuys, the telegraphic message announcing the breaking off of diplomatic relations by the Austrian and Russian Ministers at Constantinople. I am unable at present to send you anything but my own opinion on the matter. I am much inclined to think that this step of the two Imperialist Ministers is only an attempt to bully, and that if it fails, as it seems hitherto to have done, it will be disavowed or retracted by their Governments. But then it seems to me that the only way of bringing about that result is to give the Sultan the cordial and firm support of England and France, and to let the two Governments of Russia and Austria see that the Turk has friends who will back him and defend him in time of need. This might be done, first, by firm though friendly representations at Vienna and St. Petersburg, pointing out that the Sultan is not bound by treaty to do what has been required, and that, not being so bound, he could not have done it without dishonour. Secondly, we might order our respective squadrons in the Mediterranean to take post at the Dardanelles, and to be ready to go up to Constantinople if invited by the Sultan, either to defend Constantinople from actual or threatened attack, or to give him that moral support which their presence in the Bosphorus would afford. I feel the most perfect conviction that Austria and Russia would not, in the present state of Germany, Poland, and Northern Italy, to say nothing of only half-pacified Hungary, venture upon a rupture with England, France, and Turkey upon such a question as this. But all this is only my own personal opinion, and I cannot answer for the Broadbrims of the Cabinet; therefore do not, before you hear from me again, commit the Government to any opinion or to any course of action.

The Russian ambassador in London lost no time in calling on the Foreign Secretary. What took place is told in the following Memorandum :—

Carlton Gardens: October 2, 1849.

I had a conversation of some length this afternoon with Baron Brunnow. His object at first was to show that the best course for England and France to pursue was to remain perfectly quiet, to wait for events, and to trust to the moderation and good feeling of the Emperor to settle the matter amicably with the Sultan, without any injury to the independence of the Porte. In other words, to leave the Emperor time to frighten the Sultan into acquiescence.

... that the affair is in itself of very ... I could not but believe with him ... feeling of the two Imperial Govern- ... respect the Sultan's repugnance to ... thrown themselves on his protection; ... Russia would be satisfied with that secu- ... right to ask, and which the Sultan is ready ... would be given by sending into the ... of the refugees as may have no means of ... and by requiring those who are better off ... some to France or England. With regard ... I said we could not take that course, be- ... Government had officially asked us for help in ... and we had determined to address a friendly ... favour of the Sultan to the Austrian and Rus- ... He said he hoped our representation would ... in order that it might not do harm instead ... all men have their faults as well as their merits. ... his Emperor is that he is very sensitive, and ... the language of menace might prevent him ... he might otherwise be disposed to do. I said ... that kind would be sent; that we should express ... the French Government would probably do the ... two Emperors would be satisfied with the removal ... their frontiers, and would not insist on the sur- ... whom they would not know what to do with ... them. For it would not be supposed, for in- ... Emperor of Russia could take any pleasure in ... like Bem. Brunnow said it would be a pity ... representations should be made by England and France ... concurrently; that the joint action of the two would ... the appearance of something like menace. I said ... the unavoidable result of the fact that the Porte ... application to the two Powers; but he should remem- ... system of duality did not begin with us; that the ... Governments have been jointly pressing and ... Constantinople, and the Sultan being hard driven ... great, strapping neighbours, naturally looked about ... he could find two friends to come and take his ... the two Imperial Ministers, no doubt from over- ... wish to carry their point by a *coup de main*, and ... their Governments, had gone probably further ... instructed to do, and had not only held very high and threatening language, but [illegible] matic intercourse, a thing of no real [illegible] a means of intimidation. I said that the two [illegible] ments were no doubt entitled to ask for the [illegible] respective subjects, though the Russian demand, [illegible] upon the events of the Polish war of 1832, and [illegible] Hungarian war of 1849, was somewhat out of [illegible] on the other hand, the Sultan was entitled by [illegible] decline to surrender, and to prefer the other [illegible] either sending the refugees into the interior of his [illegible] requiring them to leave Turkey. Brunnow entirely [illegible] me in this interpretation of the treaty between [illegible] Turkey. He said the Treaty of Kainardgi had, like all [illegible] between Russia and Turkey, been drawn up by the [illegible] negotiators, and that they had purposely and [illegible] a choice, because it was much more likely that Turks [illegible] to Russia than that Russians would fly to Turkey; [illegible] Russian Government did not wish to be obliged to [illegible] political refugees to be handed over to the bowstring. [illegible] men guilty of ordinary criminal offences the case was [illegible] and the obligation more strict to give such persons up. [illegible] fully and distinctly admitted that the treaty, while it [illegible] rised the Emperor to demand surrender, equally authorised [illegible] Sultan to decline surrender, and to prefer the sending out [illegible] country. And Brunnow's own opinion seemed to be that [illegible] Emperor would, or at least ought to, acquiesce in the [illegible] decision. But it must be borne in mind that his [illegible] avowedly to persuade us to do nothing, and that he [illegible] himself to be without communications from his own [illegible] ment.

There was considerable opposition in high [illegible] to any interference on the part of England, but [illegible] Palmerston's colleagues acquiesced in his [illegible] he sends to Paris the decision arrived at.

F. O.: October 2, [illegible]

My dear Normanby,—The Cabinet met to-day, and [illegible] mined that the Sultan must be supported, and by all [illegible] to all extent that may be necessary, and that for this [illegible] the co-operation of France must be sought. What we [illegible] to do is that which I stated in my private letter a [illegible] namely, that a friendly and civil representation [illegible]

...at Vienna and Petersburg, to express ... will not press the Sultan to do ... his honour and for the laws of hos... dictates of humanity forbid him to do, ... treaty binds him to do; and, that, at ... squadrons should move up to the Darda... go up to Constantinople if invited so to do ... his immediate defence, or to afford him ... presence. Of course this decision in... to go all further lengths that circum... necessary; and we trust confidently that we ... upon the co-operation of France, ... willing to be as moderate in the manner ... steps as she may be firm and determined as ... I have seen the Turkish ambassador, who ... asking the moral and material assistance ... have told him the decision of the Cabinet, and ... to enter into communication with the French ... the matter. He says that the Turkish squadron ... and the Turkish military force round Con... quite sufficient to secure Constantinople against ... the fleet from Sebastopol.

...seen Brunnow, who professes to have heard ... Petersburg, and to know only what the papers ...he seems uneasy. He endeavours to represent the ... of small real importance. His object was to per... we ought to take no step, but wait to see what ... would do, or at all events to delay; that is to say, to give the Emperor full time to bully the Sultan ...stion, as we let him do some months ago about the ...ccupation. I told him that the Cabinet has deter... representations should be made at Vienna and Peters... that we should take care to make them in such a ...t to justify any *mauvaise réponse*. I said that the language and deportment of Radzivil, Titoff, and compelled the Porte to ask us for support, and that ... under such circumstances abstain from friendly ... to the two Imperial Governments. I of course ... saying anything about squadrons or material ... joined with him in considering it impossible that ... should not be satisfied with the departure of his ...bassy, observing that they must be very unreason... did not prefer France or England to Turkey as

He also communicates the decision to t
Minister at Constantinople, who had stru
the Turkish Government to remain firm.[1]

Foreign Office: Octo

My dear Canning,—As it is of importance to r
soon as possible from anxiety in regard to the r
which you may think you have incurred by the
you have given the Porte, and as it is also essenti
an hour unnecessarily in relieving the Porte from
to whether it will find aid and support from its fri
you this private letter by a special messenger, to
Cabinet has to-day decided to give an affirmative a
application for moral and material support which
ambassador, by order of his Government, has pr
We are, therefore, going to enter immediately into
tion with the Government of France, in order t
course of proceedings, assuming that which we c
namely, that the French Government is willing an
co-operate with us. What we mean to propose is,
Governments should make friendly and courteou
tions at Vienna and Petersburg to induce the Imp
ment to desist from their demands, urging that t
not bound by treaty to do what is asked of him, a
so would be dishonourable and disgraceful. We n
pose, at the same time, that the two Mediterranea
should proceed at once to the Dardanelles, with os
to the Bosphorus, if invited to do so by the Sult
defend Constantinople from actual or imminent
give him the moral support which their presence
I think it possible, however, that the admirals
have gone up to the neighbourhood of the Dardan
sequence of the letters they will have received fr

[1] 'If I had suspended my support for a moment, the
no doubt, would have given way; and on almost any qu
involving such obvious considerations of humanity, hon
manent policy, I might have been inclined, while left
counsel a less dangerous course, in spite of reason and
is, I have felt that there was no alternative unattende
credit and character. The dishonour would have been
knows that even Reschid himself, with all his spirit
would not withstand the torrent without us, and Fra
every subject here follows in our wake, from the nec

however, much better that the Porte ... for the squadrons to enter the ... necessity. The example might be ... by the Russians hereafter; and it would ... menace, and the way to deal with the ... him on his mettle by open and public ... we are trying to catch two great fish, ... the reel very gently and dexterously, not to ... Government have indeed resolved to sup- ... all events, but we must be able to show to ... we have used all civility and forbearance, and ... issue, they have not been brought on by any ... of ours. The presence of the squadrons at the Dardanelles, or in their neighbourhood, would ... sufficient to keep the Sebastopol squadron at ...; and the Turks have besides some naval and ... and about Constantinople sufficient to make a ... our squadrons could get up. We have steamers ... the line-of-battle ships. We have, I believe, six ...; the French about the same number. The ... believe, twelve or fourteen.

... wish you to impress upon the Turks is that this ... is confidential, to keep up their spirits and ... that they must not swagger upon it, nor make it ... hear it officially. From Brunnow's language, ... seen him since the Cabinet, I should infer the ... be amicably settled.

... Austria understand no less clearly and ... that England is going to stand by the

F. O.: October 6, 1849.

... Ponsonby,—I send you a despatch to be communi- ... Schwarzenberg. We have endeavoured to make it as ..., so as not to leave him any ground for saying ... not yield to threats. We make none; and in my ... communications with Brunnow and Colloredo I have ... about our squadron being ordered up to the Dar- ... it is right that *you* should know and understand ... Government have come unanimously to the deter- ... taking this matter up in earnest, and of carrying ... We have resolved to support Turkey, let who will ... in this matter. It is painful to see the Austrian

Government led on in its blindness, its folly, and its passionate violence into a course utterly at variance with the established policy of Austria. If there is one thing more than another which Austria ought to do, it is to support Turkey against Russia; and here is Schwarzenberg, in his fondness for bullying the weak, co-operating with the Russian Government to insult Turkey, and to lay her at the feet of Russia.

But you understand these questions so thoroughly that you will no doubt have been able to lay before the Austrian Government and Camarilla the full extent of the mistake they are making. They are besides uniting England and France in joint action, which is not what Austrian Government has hitherto been particularly anxious to do. I cannot believe the two Governments will push this matter further, as the rights of the case are clearly against them. Both Colloredo and Brunnow, though I beg they may not be quoted, acknowledge that the Sultan is not bound by treaty to do what is required of him. Metternich, I am told, says it is a great mistake.

What could Austria hope to gain by a war with Turkey, supported, as she would be, by England and France? Austria would lose her Italian provinces, to which she seems to attach such undue value, and she never would see them again. What she might gain to the eastward I know not; but perhaps Russia might not end by extending herself in that direction. At all events, I cannot conceive that, in the present state of Germany, it would suit Austria to provoke a war with England and France; and I do not think that such a war would be of much advantage even to Russia. Pray do what you can to persuade the Austrian Government to allow these Hungarians either to leave Turkey, if they are able to do so, or to remain in Turkey quietly. The leaders would of course pass on to other parts of Europe; the bulk of the emigrants might be settled somewhere in the interior of Turkey, and would make a useful colony.

There is a notion that Austria means to try to turn a penny by this transaction, and to call on the Turks to pay a large sum, which it suits the Austrian Government to say that the emigrants have carried away with them; but this dodge will not do, so pray try to persuade them not to attempt it.

The bold attitude of England and France soon produced its legitimate effect.

[illegible] F. O., October 22, 1849.

[illegible] I have a private letter to-day from [illegible] says that the Austrian Government has [illegible] it does not mean to insist on the sur- [illegible] refugees, and that the Russian Govern- [illegible] to this decision of Austria. But he says [illegible] officially announce this decision. We [illegible] that the Russians are indignant at the [illegible] Hungarians who had given themselves up to [illegible] that this feeling will probably make it more [illegible] desist from a demand which was made chiefly [illegible]

[illegible] has not altered. From the first he [illegible] although the treaty of Kainardgi gave Russia a [illegible] the surrender, it equally gave Turkey a right [illegible] other alternative. He asked me the other day, [illegible] intention, and within what limits, our squadrons [illegible] I said within the Mediterranean as at present [illegible] with the intention of giving comfort and support [illegible], who had been so vehemently threatened by their [illegible] Constantinople. That our sending one squadron [illegible] Mediterranean was, for the Sultan, like holding a bottle [illegible] nose of a lady who had been frightened.

[illegible] whether it would not have been better to have [illegible] the answer from Petersburg. I said that in that [illegible] might perhaps have been too late to prevent accidents [illegible] have happened before our fleets had arrived. But [illegible] as long as our squadrons were in that part of the [illegible] they could threaten nobody. If England and [illegible] sent large fleets into the Baltic, then, indeed, Russia [illegible] said, This must be intended for me; what does it [illegible] I have desired Ponsonby to say that if our [illegible] gone up the Adriatic, it might have been a threat [illegible] Austria. But our ships, where they are, threaten [illegible] only hold out to the Sultan assistance at hand in [illegible]

[illegible] indirect benefit accrued from the action of our [illegible] in this matter. The unanimity of public [illegible] in its support, as soon as it had declared [illegible] of supporting Turkey to the full extent of [illegible] war, had a great and excellent effect in Europe, as showing that we were not quite so incapable of being moved to manly action as some speeches in Parliament and at peace congresses might have led people to suppose.

A doubt was now raised that we had violated the terms of a treaty by the presence of our fleet in the Dardanelles. Lord Palmerston answered this.

F. O., [illegible] 22, 1849.

My dear [illegible],—We are quite aware that the treaty of [illegible] ships of war from entering within the Dardanelles or Bosphorus while the Porte is at peace. But that treaty does not prevent succour from [illegible] the Sultan in case war should [illegible] upon him. [illegible] the two Imperial Governments [illegible] the Porte [illegible] single man of the [illegible]

[illegible] have been authorised [illegible] despatches [illegible] communicated [illegible] think it was [illegible] having been made [illegible] governments [illegible] Turkey against the two Imperial and [illegible]

Lord Palmerston, when he had undertaken the task, was not the man to leave it half-way to take care of itself. Even to please an ally he was not disposed to run the risk, however small, of having to begin all over again. He felt sure that he had won, but would leave nothing to chance.

F. O., November [illegible], 1849.

My dear Canning,—I can, I think, now communicate you upon the peaceful termination of the question about the refugees. [illegible] has just been with me, and says very quaintly, that it has from the first been raised to undue proportions, and that it ought to have been treated as an 'affaire de police, et non pas comme une affaire de politique.'

as we understand them, now are, 1st, the Poles from the Turkish territory; 2nd, the converted Poles to Diarbekir; 3rd, an the Porte should apply to foreign Govern- to England and France, to consent that who may become naturalised or denizens in should not thereby be exempted from being according to their original nationality. The is just what the Sultan proposed to do. The as a temporary arrangement unobjectionable, it understood to be only temporary, and that these to be kept for the rest of their lives at Diarbekir. we shall probably not be found willing to consent: acquires by naturalisation the character, and with of a British subject; he acquires these by law, see how the English Government could undertake from any man the protection to which he has entitled. Naturalisation would not give a Rus- British rights in Russia, but it would do so in er country; but this is a question to talk about, and fought about. I therefore look on peace as secure, oon as we get the next despatches from you we shall ers to Parker to return to his usual station. The re impatient to get their ships back, in case they should against Morocco, where a petulant and self-sufficient has been trying to get up a quarrel with the I am glad their squadron has been out of reach; this time to settle the dispute peaceably. Buchanan, who ome from Petersburg, says that the Russians in general settled at the check which their Emperor has received policy, and that they say he will take some to pay us off; and the way in which they anticipate will be done, is by fomenting insurrections in Bosnia among the Christian subjects of the Porte; and cannot refrain from adverting to this, as a way Russia holds in her hands the good and evil destinies empire. The Turkish Government ought to be ll aware of this, and should lose no time in preparing to remove from the Christian subjects of the Porte of discontent, and should thus place the Sultan's a broad and solid foundation.

changes of Ministers in France will make no in the foreign policy of the country except to render it more conformable with the personal [illegible] of the President, and he is more disposed [illegible] Ministers were (though we have no great [illegible] them) to follow a course of foreign policy [illegible] community of views and action between England [illegible]

Broadlands: November [illegible]

My dear Canning,—The French are in a [illegible] to get their fleet back from the neighbourhood of the [illegible] nelles. But yesterday I received from Normanby [illegible] from the President that we should give you and [illegible] cretionary power to send away the squadron [illegible] soon as you should think their presence no longer [illegible] and this was so reasonable a proposal that we at once [illegible] with it.

Our own view is that it is desirable that our [illegible] should return towards Malta whenever its presence [illegible] Dardanelles is no longer wanted; but that it should stay [illegible] it is as long as its presence is of importance as a moral [illegible] for the Sultan. Whenever the Porte and the two [illegible] Courts have come to an agreement upon the main [illegible] squadron might well come away; but it would not do [illegible] bring it away while any material point was unsettled, [illegible] we should thus have the appearance of leaving the Sultan [illegible] the lurch.

Moreover, it would not do that the Russian agents at Constantinople should have a pretence for saying that Russia had ordered our fleets off, and that as we had thus yielded [illegible] demands of Russia, the Porte had better do so too, [illegible] experience in this instance would show her that though [illegible] might swagger at first, yet when it came to the point, [illegible] sure to knock under, and that thus Turkey would always [illegible] us ready to urge her on to resistance, but backing out [illegible] when Russia began to hold high language to us and to [illegible] a bold front.

They would represent us as a barking cur that runs [illegible] its tail between its legs when faced and threatened. We [illegible] thus lose all we have gained and most of what we had before.

You will, of course, not fail to bear all this in mind [illegible] using the discretionary authority now sent to you; and [illegible] we shall be glad to find the presence of the fleet [illegible] necessary, it is better that it should stay there a week or a [illegible] night too long than that it should come away too soon [illegible] the continuance of our fleet for a further ... and Aupick should, under his ... of opinion that the fleets are no ... if he should make a great difficulty in ... opinion, there would be no great harm ... the difference, and if the French fleet ... ordered to keep separate from ours ... towards Toulon, while ours remained a ... or anchoring in the Archipelago.

Broadlands: November 14, 1849.

...,—It would have been quite ridiculous ... ordered back our ships at the bidding of ... upon her assertion of what she had sent as ... Porte. Great countries ought not to act with ... levity, and should put some degree of method ... in their conduct. We sent our fleet up to the ... be ready to support the Sultan in case of attack, ... his knowledge that our fleet was there for ... might give him courage to hold his own in his ... Russia. That negotiation had not yet reached ... when our last accounts came away; it would ... some of which the Porte might object to; ... system might again be resorted to, if our ships ... everything was settled, and their departure ... negotiation would be represented by the Russian ... Constantinople as an abandonment of Turkey in defer- ... remonstrances of Russia. We ought either never ... our fleet, or to keep it there till matters are settled. ... however, are of course at liberty to do what they ... their own; but they ought to have pointed out to ... hasty retreat of their squadron will be represented ... at Constantinople as a concession by France to ...

... you say, disappointed ambition will try to turn ... against an English alliance which thwarts per- ...; but we must deal with this as best we can. ... some difficulty or other to be striven against in ..., 'For the current of politics doth seldom run ...

... reference to our alleged infraction of treaty ... Lord Palmerston writes:—

Broadlands: Novem[illegible]

My dear Canning,—Do not let Parker again [illegible] enter within the outer castles of the Dardanelles; [illegible] has a very bad effect; it is difficult to argue that [illegible] entering the Straits of the Dardanelles, and that [illegible] not a violation of the Treaty of July, 1841.[1] Neverthe[illegible] to have taken the matter quietly, and no wonder, [illegible] nibbling at our Dardanelles Treaty is just what the R[illegible] would like to see us establish as a precedent, and they [illegible] not be slow to follow our example. The port regulation [illegible] Turkish Government by which the anchorage within the [illegible] castles is allotted for ships-of-war of all nations to wait [illegible] they know whether they can be permitted to go up to Con[illegible]tinople, can fairly and logically be applied only to such [illegible]-of-war as may by permission go up to Constantinople; [illegible] those are only light vessels for the use of the embassies [illegible] missions, and that port regulation cannot be deemed to [illegible] to a squadron of line-of-battle ships, which cannot, accordin[illegible] treaty, go up to Constantinople while the Porte is at peace [illegible] all events, it is close shaving and nice steerage, and exposes [illegible] to a disagreeable discussion about words, and puts us to pro[illegible] that being within the Straits is not entering the Straits; [illegible] that is not an easy demonstration to make good. If Parker [illegible] blown away from Besika Bay, let him go to Enos, or Jaros, [illegible] anywhere else where he may find shelter, never mind how far off; for wherever he goes he can always be back in time, and any attack of the Turkish territory by a Russian fleet [illegible] is at present quite out of the question. We shall send you [illegible] in a few days our decision about the demands of the two Empe[illegible]rors. I should guess, from Brunnow's language to me to-d[illegible] that the Russian Government would be content to have [illegible] renegade Poles *eloignés* from the frontier, and made to reside [illegible] but not as prisoners—in Asia Minor; and Brunnow affected [illegible] treat very lightly the Austrian demand, representing that [illegible] matter the Porte could easily dispose of if she had settled [illegible]factorily with Russia.

[1] The words of the treaty were: 'All ships-of-war of all [illegible] coming to the Dardanelles are to stop and wait at the [illegible] between the outer and inner castles till they know from Consta[illegible] whether a firman will or will not be granted to allow them [illegible] further on.'

Powers were baffled in their demand of the fugitive Poles and Hungarians, a request that Turkey should keep and not allow them to emigrate y. The Sultan indeed had originally of the sort when their extradition demanded, although he had never his captives at the good pleasure of a ment, but only for a time, and at his n. In the following letter Lord Palmer- against the Austrian demand.

F. O.: November 27, 1849.

Ponsonby,—I have only time to write two lines goes. You say you do not understand what the which Canning alludes to as liable to be urged demand now made by Austria upon Turkey about Those objections are, that it is unreasonable and with the dignity and independence of the Sultan be made the gaoler of the Emperor of Austria, to of persons whom the Austrian Government may itically dangerous; and that the performance of his gaoler should be subject to the superintend- agents of a foreign Power, and should continue foreign Power should consent to the cessation of duties. The Treaty of Bucharest does not give right to exact this servitude from the Sultan, and the good neighbourhood do not require it at his hands. the Sultan is bound to do, is to prevent his terri- being made a place of shelter from whence machina- be carried on to disturb the internal tranquillity of States; but this obligation would be fully per- the Sultan sends out of his dominions those subjects Powers who may justly be suspected of having in- to abuse his hospitality. All, therefore, that Austria on the score of good neighbourhood—and this is an by treaty she can demand—is that the Hungarian should be sent out of Turkey; but to require that they be detained and kept under restraint in Turkey is an able demand, and one which if Turkey were to com- it would do more harm to Austria in public opinion than could be counterbalanced by any conceivable advantage to be derived from it. As to publications which these Hungarians might make in France or England, there are Hungarians enough come away to publish everything that can be said or revealed; and as to the sympathy which Kossuth would excite here or in France, they may depend upon it that he will be a much greater object of interest while unjustly detained in Turkey than if he was living at a lodging in Paris or London. It is bad policy in the Austrian Government, as well as injustice. Pray endeavour to persuade them of this, and to prevail upon them to be content with the expulsion of these Hungarians.

I write you this, and desire you to do your best, though I hear from many quarters that you oppose instead of furthering the policy of your Government, and that you openly declare that you disapprove of our course. No diplomatist ought to hold such language as long as he holds his appointment. It is idle trash to say that we are hostile to Austria because we may disapprove of the policy of a Metternich or the cruelties of the Manning Administration which now governs Austria; you might as well say that a man is the enemy of his friend because he tells that friend of errors and faults which are sinking him in the esteem of men whose good opinion is worth having.

And three days after to the same:—

F. O.: November 30, 1849.

The requirement of Austria about the Hungarian refugees is preposterous, and quite inconsistent with a due regard to the dignity and independence of the Sultan. It is as incompatible with the dignity of an independent Sovereign to make himself the gaoler for the State offenders of his neighbours as it would be for him to make himself purveyor for the executioner of that neighbour. Schwarzenberg, in his note of reply to Musurus, in pretending to quote what Musurus had said, put words into Musurus's mouth which Musurus did not use, and which materially alter the sense of the offered engagement. Musurus did not use the word 'Dorenavant;' and he said nothing about the arrangement lasting as long as the Austrian Government might choose. But what a childish, silly fear this is of Kossuth. What great harm could he do to Austria while in France or England? He would be the hero of half-a-dozen dinners in England, at which would be made speeches not more violent than those which have been made on platforms here within the last four months, and he would soon sink into comparative obscurity;

...; so long as he is a State détenu in ... and the object of never-ceasing interest. ... which he might be able to make of the mis... Government, generals, and troops, there ... to England to lay bare to the public ... of that kind, and the detention of Kos... greater bitterness into the feelings with ... will be made. The Austrian Govern... do well, for its own sake and with a view ... to consent to the expulsion of the Hun... But whether it consents or not, you may ... get away they will, by hook or by crook, and ... will then cut a silly figure by being ...

...ntents of the following letter illustrate the ... sensitive character of the Emperor ... later on, came out so forcibly and ...uring the Crimean War. The audience, how... given to the English ambassador a few days ... it is probable that when Prince Menschikoff ... Constantinople in 1853, his Imperial master ...gotten the mortification of 1849.

Broadlands: November 27, 1849.

... Bloomfield,—I have received your letter of the ... you say that the Emperor has not given you ...dience on your return to your post, and that ... privately informed that he means to see you ...blic occasions. I am sorry for this, because ... these late Turkish affairs should have pro... an effect upon the Emperor's conduct towards the ...sentative at his Court, but still I scarcely think ...d be useful that the Queen should retaliate upon ... But, indeed, the habits of our Court scarcely leave ...taliation. The Queen sees the foreign Ministers ... concerts, and at balls, when all, or nearly all, are ...sent, and about once a year she has the representa... principal Courts to dinner; but that would be later ... and by that time the Emperor may have altered his ...rds you. We must make great allowances for the ... great political check must have produced upon ... mind; and his annoyance at so public a thwarting is probably increased by the circumstance that it has been in some degree brought upon him by the injudicious zeal of Titow and Radzivil, who probably went beyond their instructions, and committed the Emperor further than he intended.

The mortification also is the greater because it has followed so quickly upon his great successes in Hungary, and has entirely dimmed the lustre of those successes; and, moreover, it must be galling to the lord and master of so many hundred thousand men and of near fifty sail of the line to be baffled by a squadron of seven sail of the line and by the time of the year. Our best course is not to take much notice of his ill-humour, and to try to bring him right again.

But though the Emperor will probably long remember what has happened, and will be long ready to take advantage of any opportunity to pay us off, yet when the Constantinople business is settled he will probably resume his usual cordiality, at all events in outward manner; and it may be some good long time before he may find an opportunity of giving us any serious embarrassment.

Nearly two years elapsed, however, before the Turkish Government could muster up courage to fly in the face of its powerful neighbour and liberate Kossuth with his companions. During this interval they were kept in honourable captivity at Kutayah. Much interest was taken in their fate, both in the United States and in England. Lord Palmerston writes to urge their release.

C. G.: February 10, 1851.

My dear Canning,—I have written you a despatch about Kossuth and his fellow exiles. I have made it as gentle as was possible; but pray let Reschid and Aali know privately that it is but a faint expression of the public feeling in this country on that subject.

You will have seen how the matter was noticed in the House of Commons in the debate on the Address; and I have representations coming in from large towns and small—from England, Scotland, and Wales.

There was last year great enthusiasm throughout the whole country in favour of the Sultan, because people here [illegible] that the Turkish Government was animated by a [illegible] manly determination not to be the executioner of the [illegible]

[illegible]; and it was that belief which led the [illegible] end of it to the other—Whigs, Tories, [illegible] and back up the defiance which, by our [illegible] squadron, we flung in the teeth of the two [illegible]. But the ground on which we took our [illegible] under our feet, and the bright hopes which [illegible] are rapidly fading away. The Sultan [illegible] the Poles and Hungarians from the rope [illegible]; but he is making himself the degraded slave of [illegible] the Hungarians to the lingering but not less [illegible] of the prison.

[illegible] of our protégés, the Sultan and his white-[illegible]; and you may tell the Ministers, confidentially [illegible], that if they go on in this way, not only not a [illegible] not a cockboat would we, or could we, send in any [illegible] assistance, and the enthusiasm of last year is rapidly [illegible] to contemptuous disgust at their servile consent [illegible] the most degrading office of turnkey for Prince [illegible]berg.

[illegible]ptember the men were freed. Shortly after-[illegible] deputation from Islington that went to the [illegible]ffice, to congratulate Lord Palmerston on the [illegible] some stir, owing to the language of the [illegible] and the tone of Lord Palmerston's reply. [illegible]ther things, he said that to gain the day [illegible]neralship and judgment had been required, during the struggle a good deal of judicious [illegible]lding was obliged to be brought into play.' [illegible]le, borrowed from the prize-ring, tickled the the public, and for many a day after, Lord [illegible]on, drawn with a sprig in his mouth, figured [illegible]ages of 'Punch' as the 'judicious bottle-

CHAPTER V.

GREEK AFFAIRS AND 'DON PACIFICO' DEBATE.

JUST as some unsightly knoll or insignificant stream has won imperishable fame by the accident of its crest or banks being the scene of a great battle, so did the name of a paltry adventurer become famous, in 1850, by its connection with a memorable debate. The fate of the Ministry as well as that of a Minister was involved, for the wrongs of Don Pacifico and the manner of their redress were only the battle-field on which a policy was attacked and bitter antagonisms fought out. The allied troops who led the attack were English Protectionists and foreign Absolutists. Victorious in their first onset among the Lords, they met with signal defeat in the House of Commons, after one of the most remarkable displays of eloquence and feeling that the walls of Parliament have witnessed.

Although the matters at issue were far wider than the narrow boundaries of Greece, it was round that centre that the contest principally raged; and it will be necessary, therefore, briefly to scan the ground-plan of the fight, and to recall the course of events which at last led the British Government to employ force.

Of all the races of Europe, none is more interesting than the Greek. It is singular to observe how many of its ancient characteristics have remained immutable amongst the varying misfortunes with which two thousand years have afflicted it. The same enterprising, speculative, and brilliant intellect which causes us to linger over the records of those three hundred years

[…] of the world is still alive, though
[…] counting-houses and dispersed
[…] national celebrities of Europe. It can
[…] that, amongst the men engaged in
[…] in Greece itself, have appeared gentle-
[…] distinguished for their manners and
[…] might take place amongst the accomplished
[…] their time. In the people are still found
[…] industry and hospitality. But by a sin-
[…] whilst the Greek nation might be es-
[…] admired, the Greek Government never,
[…] varying vicissitudes, obtained or merited
[…] or admiration. The assassination of the
[…] who had dedicated his life to her
[…] refusal to acknowledge as a debt the money
[…] her most desperate need, was advanced to
[…] from despair, commenced a series of events
[…] the lustre of a revolution which an un-
[…] had sanctioned and an unquestioned
[…] achieved. From the moment, in short, in
[…] agony of her glorious struggle was passed,
[…] it in her power to realise the generous
[…] those whose hearts and hopes had accom-
[…] throughout it, Greece, or at least, the rulers
[…] seemed bent on converting expectation into
[…] ment.

[…] seen that, when the question of establish-
[…] independencc was being agitated, Lord
[…] was amongst the first to feel the generous
[…] which animated the last days of Canning
[…]. Nor did his interest in the cause cease
[…] appeared triumphant. Although he did not
[…] young Bavarian prince as a desirable candi-
[…] still entertained hopes that, aided by the
[…] of Europe, he would be able to establish a
[…] sufficiently just and stable to permit the
[…] of the country to grow up gradually under it.
[…], as a compliment to his patronage that

[1] Capo d'Istria.

it was determined that the newly-elected sovereign (aged 18) should land in his dominions from an English ship of war; and the vessel selected was the 'Bellerophon,' commanded by Captain Lyons. The naval profession at that time did not seem likely to offer those chances of distinction which the heroic in Captain Lyons' character would have preferred to any other. It struck him, then, that to be British Minister at a Court which was certain to concentrate on itself much of the attention of Europe, would be a desirable post; and with this idea before his mind, it is easy to conceive how he insinuated into the mind of King Otho the idea that he was precisely the man who, in such a situation, would be most agreeable and useful to him. A request was made in his behalf, and complied with.

By this transaction the King expected he had got a staunch supporter, and Captain Lyons a docile pupil. Both were soon disappointed, and very angry at being so.

It is no use disguising the fact, Captain Lyons, though a very good officer, and a very clever as well as agreeable man, was not a very good diplomatist.

The position was a false one, since each was likely to expect too much from the other. It was rendered more false by the character of the King being slow and cautions to a fault, and that of Captain Lyons being in the same degree hasty and impetuous. The King's natural counsellers were, moreover, Germans; and German statesmen could not be expected to entertain the same views of government that were likely to be entertained by English statesmen. Add to this, that as all Greeks who had the slightest pretension to places, expected to have them, there was certain, whatever party was in power, to be a strong party in opposition.

It has been the fashion of late years to consider, in the Foreign Office, that the country is made for the diplomacy, and not the diplomacy for the country; and that a Minister's duty is to see that so many thousands a year are divided with as much impartial indifference as possible, between so many gentlemen, who are pre-

passed certain examinations, to have the fund.

of State for Foreign Affairs being once did not appoint a very able and ex-, then receiving a pension, to an that was then vacant, instead of another inferior, replied, 'Your man has had his another man's turn now!' It never Minister that the question was not which employed, but which was best for the to employ. So an unthinking cry has as to what is called 'a block in the service;' to pushing some men out of their places, and them, with a more rapid movement; and a of the House of Commons once recommended Minister or Ambassador should be left more than in his post.

anyone who has reflected on these subjects the knowledge of most value in any pro- especially in diplomacy, is that which you daily, hourly, without being sensible that you by practice and experience. It is quite true clever man is more useful with a year's than a very stupid one with twenty years', are, men so stupid that experience is thrown them. But take two men of equal ability, and who has been five years Minister or Ambassador place, is at least twenty times more fit for it than who has been wishing five years to be Minister Ambassador at that place. It is not merely that to do things better by habit in a particular one learns what not to do.

exercise but a little common sense. Would banking or mercantile house lay down, as a be always shifting its agents, and remove an who had been doing his business well at a par- to put another man, who perhaps had the place, in his stead?

of such a system is too apparent to need

K

proof; but if it were wanted, Captain Lyons was a capital instance of it. Captain Lyons was an active, able, ambitious, astute man; a man of the world, too but he wanted experience in the business he had been plunged into, and consequently he was often firing off very big guns at very small affairs. Nevertheless, that his language and conduct in the main, as the representative of a State which had bestowed its countenance, given its assistance, and lent its money to Greece, were no more violent in their reprobation than circumstances fully justified, may be amply proved by the following exposition of the Finance Minister at Athens in 1846.

Gentlemen,—Some days ago you sent for me to give you some account of the state of our finances; and I excused myself on the plea of having just taken office. I now come down to this House to tell you that the finance department is in a complete state of disorganisation and paralysis: that no accounts exist either as to the revenue or the expenditure, and that it will be utterly impossible to furnish you with anything in the shape of a correct budget. In consequence of the dishonesty and incapacity of the public functionaries, the public accounts are in a state of chaos. All that M. Provilegio and others have told you respecting every honest man having been dismissed, and of the spoliation of the public money at Syra and elsewhere, is perfectly true. Millions are due to the State; and we do not know our debtors, as the revenue books have disappeared. This is the financial statement I have to make.[1]

This was surely enough to account for all that could be thought of or said to the Government of Greece by the British Minister. But a diplomatist is frequently perched on the horns of a double dilemma. He strives by the courtesy and amiability of his personal relations to soften the character of official communications; and it is said of him, 'You will never do anything with that man: he is too polite: they don't believe him in earnest;' or, on the other hand, he seeks, by a somewhat stern and severe manner, to give additional weight to the observations he is charged to make use of; and

[1] *Annual Register*, 1846, p. 303.

critic of the Foreign Office ... and says, 'That fellow renders ... disagreeable; who would do any- ... if he could help it?' However, ... in Greek affairs took place not under ... of the naval captain, but under the ... philosopher.[1]

... France, and Russia had brought ... acknowledge the independence of Greece, the ... settled that the form of Government for ... should be a Monarchy; but England ... her assent as an indispensable condition that ... Constitutional Monarchy. Consequently, ... Otho of Bavaria, then a minor, was called ... the three Powers, on announcing the ... made, declared at the same time that ... institutions would be given by Otho as ... of age. This declaration was ratified ... of Bavaria, in the name and on behalf of ... young King of Greece.

... promise was not kept. The despotic Courts of ... and Austria, naturally averse to consti- ... availed themselves of the plea that the ... not yet ripe for representative government, ... avoid pressing on Otho the fulfilment of his ... France kept aloof on the same ground, Guizot ... the while with his favourite simile, that ... hundred horse-power engine is placed in a small ... tear it to pieces instead of moving it for- ... England, therefore, stood alone in her remon- ... and naturally incurred the dislike of those ... considered that it was her invidious duty to ... In other matters, also, she was on the un- ... while France, for her own objects, took the ... side. Monsieur Guizot, in his Memoirs,[2] tries ... in the following words between their ... attitudes :—

[1] ... Thomas Wyse, who succeeded Lord Lyons.

[2] ... Vol. xii. p. 324.

Tandis qu'à Londres on acceptait l'indépendance de comme une malencontreuse nécessité, nous n'acception que comme une nécessité fâcheuse les étroites limi lesquelles on resserrait cette indépendance.

But then he points the moral of his reflecti very significant remark:—

Mais en repoussant toute tentative d'extension Turquie, nous n'entendîmes point interdire aux grandes espérances.

Thus, while England saw well enough the di which the Greeks would find in self-governm considered the important matter was to urge learn the habits and practice of a Constitution archy, France, in order to retain a special influe secretly fostering hopes of future conquests and glories.

On England, therefore, fell the burden of strance against the evils of a constitution with government, the fruit of which was licence liberty. In the words of Lord Palmerston, th system grew to be full of every kind of abuse. could not be expected where the judges were at th of the advisers of the Crown. The finances co be in any order where there was no public respo on the part of those who were to collect or to sp revenue. Every sort of abuse was practised, fr gandage in the country to 'compulsory approp in the capital itself, and the tyranny of the pol almost unbearable. To recall such a state of t to provide some excuse for the English Min Athens, for the fact that a chronic ill-feeling between the two Governments, and prepared the an explosion. That explosion, as usually hap such cases, was lighted at last by a very small

There were in every town of Greece a persons whom England was bound to protect Ionians, and others. It became the practice Greek police to make no distinction between

...ts. Compensation was from time ... for many acts of violence to Ionians, ... at length an outrage on the boat's ... jesty's ship *Fantôme*, and the cases of ... Don Pacifico, exhausted Lord Palmer- ... and determined him to insist on an ... compliance with his just demands. Mr. ... Scotchman, whose land was taken to round ... gardens at Athens, and no payment could ... from the appropriators. Unlike Frederick ... who pointed with pride to the mill in his ... Sans Souci as a proof that in his empire the ... ry subject, however humble, were respected, ... only show a heap of diplomatic notes and ... itions seeking justice, as a proof that in his ... could nowhere be found.

...cifico was a Jew, a native of Gibraltar, whose ... pillaged and gutted, in open day, by a mob ... the sons of the Minister of War. While it ... ing no attempt was made by the authorities ... to protect him. During three years Sir E. ... Mr. Wyse had pressed his claims for com- ... without success. That some of his demands ... rtionate there can be little doubt; but there ... less doubt that he had been most grossly ... and had a right to redress.

... not without giving notice that Lord Palmer- ... mined to act. As long before as August 1847, ... written to Lord Bloomfield, our ambassador at ...:—

... have as yet been sent to Parker to compel the ... ernment to comply with our various demands; but ... not conceal from Nesselrode and the Emperor that ... must soon be sent, if Coletti does not render them ... by voluntary compliance. There is not the slight- ... that Joinville should give Parker the trouble of ... a passage to Portsmouth, because we are too palpably ... to make it possible for France to oppose us by force ... we are stronger than she is in the Mediterranean, and therefore there is the best possible security for her good behaviour. Tell Nesselrode and the Emperor that if they think the enforcement of our demands would be injurious to the stability of Greece, an opinion which we in no degree share, the only way of preventing it is to persuade Coletti to do what we require, as the Greeks have ample means to pay us if they choose.

Monsieur Coletti, 'chef de Pallicares,' the crafty physician of Ali Pacha, and erewhile the adventurous chief of half-savage insurgents in Epirus, having been for eight years Greek Minister at Paris, had returned to Athens after the constitutional revolution in 1843, and was now Prime Minister. He was a fit subject for a pen such as Monsieur About's. His character is thus traced by Lord Palmerston:[1]—

I have no doubt that Coletti would, as Wallenstein says, prefer France to the gallows, but I do not see why he should be reduced to that alternative. To be sure, St. Aulaire said to me the other day that Coletti was a necessary Minister, for that he is the chief and leader of all the robbers and scamps of Greece, and that if he was turned out of office, he would put himself at their head, and either make incursions into Turkey or ravage the provinces of Greece. To this I replied that it seemed an odd qualification for a Minister that a man was a robber by profession, but that I did not share St. Aulaire's apprehension of what might happen if Coletti was turned out, because if in that case he invaded Turkey he would probably be shot, and if he plundered Greece he would no doubt be hanged. But he will not be turned out; Otho loves him as a second self, because he is as despotic as Otho himself; and as long as a majority can be had for Coletti in the Chambers, by corruption and intimidation, by the personal influence of the King, and by money from France, Coletti will remain Minister. With this we cannot meddle; all we can insist upon is justice for our subjects and payment of the interest on that part of the debt which we have guaranteed. If we cannot get these things, we must have recourse to compulsion. If we do get them, we cannot interfere further; and I daresay Coletti will be wise enough to satisfy our demands, and not to drive us to extreme measures.

[1] To Lord Normanby, F. O., April 20, 1847.

[illegible] been a standing conspiracy against [illegible] among all his diplomatic colleagues, [illegible] Government. Lyons has been looked [illegible] of constitutional government. Otho [illegible] at the devil. Piscatory detests it, because [illegible] think they can exercise more influence [illegible] Courts than over popular assemblies; the [illegible] has, like his King, been hitherto all for [illegible], obeying Metternich, goes into convul- [illegible] notion of popular institutions; the Prussian [illegible] told implicitly to follow the Austrian; and [illegible] dares support the Constitutional party when [illegible] chance of Otho being frightened away and of his [illegible] the Grand Duke of Oldenburg. All these [illegible]fore, combined to suppress all information as [illegible] and abuses going on in Greece, and united to [illegible] Lyons.

[illegible]Palmerston at last notified formally to the [illegible]inister at Athens that the end of British for- [illegible] arrived.

F. O.: December 3, 1849.

[illegible] Wyse,—I have desired the Admiralty to instruct [illegible] Parker to take Athens on his way back from the [illegible], and to support you in bringing at last to a satis- [illegible] the settlement of our various claims upon the [illegible]ment. You will of course, in conjunction with [illegible] in the *suaviter in modo* as long as is consistent [illegible] dignity and honour, and I measure that time by days [illegible] by some very small number of hours. If, however, [illegible] Government does not strike, Parker must do so. In [illegible] should embark on board his fleet before he begins [illegible] hostile steps, in order that you and your mission [illegible] against insult. He should, of course, begin by [illegible] that is, by taking possession of some Greek property; [illegible] would probably not much care for our taking [illegible] merchant property, and the best thing, therefore, [illegible] seize hold of his little fleet, if that can be done [illegible] The next thing would be a blockade of any or all of [illegible] if that does not do, then you and Parker must [illegible] steps as may be requisite, whatever those steps [illegible] remember that at one time it was thought that a landing of marines and sailors at some town might ... seize and carry off public treasure of sufficient ... course, Pacifico's claim must be fully satisfied.

You should intimate to the Greek Government that ... we do not this time come to levy the amount due ... account of the Greek loan, yet we abstain from doing ... order to give them an opportunity of doing the right ... their own accord; but that we cannot go on requiring ... people of this country to pay fifty thousand a year to ... King Otho to corrupt his Parliament, bribe his electors, ... palaces, and lay up a stock purse for evil times, which his policy may bring upon him.

The fleet arrived at Athens, but the demands ... upon the Greek Government were not complied with. The French and Russian Ministers were furious at ... prompt action, and did their best to spirit up the King of Greece to resistance.

F. O.: February 1, 18[illegible].

My dear Normanby,—An agricultural speech of ... enables me to leave the House and add a few lines to what I have already written to you about Greek affairs. I think you may put to Lahitte what a contrast there is between the conduct of English agents towards France and that of French agents towards England. The French representative in Morocco, partly out of his own head, and partly by instructions from home, made demands on the Morocco Government, some of which were unusual and some exaggerated, and which the Moorish Government was most unwilling to accede to. Our Consul-General, Mr. Hay, first spontaneously, and then by instructions from me, bestirred himself with as much zeal and activity as if the case had been one in which his own Government had been concerned, and by an infinity of trouble persuaded the Morocco Government to comply with the French demands, and thus saved France from the necessity of employing force to obtain redress. In Greece we have demands for redress which have been pending for years, and the neglect or refusal of which we have borne with most exemplary patience; and when at last we find it necessary either to abandon or enforce them, and not being able consistently with our ... give them up, we send our fleet to support the demands of our diplomatic agent, we find the French Minister, ...

[illegible] have for years past pursued in [illegible] Government to refuse, and thus [illegible] the necessity of employing force [illegible] say that we have good ground for [illegible] return which we receive for our [illegible]

[illegible] which you talk of, it seems to me to [illegible] course. Our squadron arrived, and [illegible] been justified in assuming beforehand [illegible] which Wyse was to repeat, would be refused. [illegible] his arrival saluted as usual, and with his [illegible] to the King before Wyse repeated his [illegible] in good taste and well judged, because it [illegible] arrival the public appearance of a menace, [illegible] Government at liberty to yield without the [illegible]

[illegible] blamed Parker if he had come in with a [illegible] threatening preparation, with his tompions [illegible] at their quarters, so as to have made it impos[illegible] to appear to be passing under the Caudine [illegible] French diplomacy has ever been bitterly hostile [illegible] and as the French Government has chosen to [illegible] former diplomatic agent, the same spirit of [illegible] and national enmity prevails in the French [illegible] which we have had to lament and to cope [illegible] whole reign of Louis Philippe.

[illegible] the French object to as to our proceedings? We [illegible] redress for wrongs committed towards our [illegible] demands have been long treated with neglect, [illegible]. We send at last our squadron to enforce [illegible] France act in a similar way in similar cases, [illegible] more violence and less justice? Witness her [illegible] and Sandwich Islands, where she, on false [illegible] the Queen of the first into a surrender of her [illegible] plundered the King of the other because he [illegible] his tariffs on brandy and compel his Custom-[illegible] learn French.

[illegible] all along been thwarted in Greece by the [illegible] of French agents, who have encouraged [illegible] to ill-use our subjects and to refuse us [illegible] course Thouvenel is frantic that we have at [illegible]

[illegible] of the Greek Government to accede

to our demands, the British admiral proceeded, acting to his instructions, to lay an embargo upon
vessels at the Piræus. Lord Palmerston thus commu-
cates these proceedings to Drouyn de Lhuys,
Minister in London:—

C. O.: February

Mon cher Ambassadeur,—Voici un extrait d'une dépê
l'amiral Parker au Chevalier Baring, en date du 22 jan
The Greek vessels herein referred to (as having
tained) include, I believe, all that the Greek Government
in commission. The whole are of little value, and in
sent temper of the Greek Government, supported, as
by the counsels of the French Minister and of the
chargé d'affaires, the mild measures hitherto adopted, I
not likely to produce the desired compliance with our
Je suis peiné de voir que l'action de la mission
Athènes continue à nous être si hostile, mais du moins
nous forcent à des mesures de sévérité ne doivent pas
faire un sujet de reproches.

Mille amitiés,

PALMERSTON.

Je viens d'apprendre que M. de Thouvenel a appelé
française à Athènes; nous souhaitons rester bons
cela pourrait devenir sérieux.

Monsieur Thouvenel had called upon the
fleet to come to Athens. The admiral had,
sufficient discretion to wait for further
from home. Lord Palmerston writes to Lord
manby:—

F. O.: February

I have had despatches and letters from Wyse up
30. Thouvenel was continuing to pursue his system
hostility, and doing all the mischief he could by
Persiani to join him in improper notes to Wyse,
couraging Otho to refuse compliance with our
Thouvenel had written to the French admiral
Athens, of course to oppose our proceedings; but
having more sense than the diplomatist, declined
out orders from home.

Some of the notes written by Thouvenel

laughably absurd and ridiculously of the latter, he expresses his should have presumed to detain a of the commander of a French lying in the Piræus at the time; of the former, he protests against our get- wrongs done to British subjects, because Government is bound to apply the first pro- to the interest and sinking fund of the arrangement which the Greek Government which we should be glad if France would King Otho to fulfil, and which, if fulfilled, funds out of which our demands could protest is really a burlesque. In the mean- were beginning to understand the rights of they saw us detaining the *Otho*, they said the wrong one.

obliged to begin reprisals on merchant expected to have in that way sufficient value to

of Lahitte[1] that we were going on with repri- exclamation of the Neapolitans about the 'Ma cè canone!' or the reply of the aide-de- when our troops first landed in Portugal, to see firing was, who came back and said, 'Why, firing ball cartridge.' I think it not unlikely it all depends on him) may have given way negotiation begins, but we cannot suspend more than such time as may be reasonable to negotiator a fair opportunity to persuade

good; our right indisputable; Greece is an and responsible for the acts and misdeeds of and redress must be had. If the French are angry, I am sorry for it; but justice to our a paramount consideration.

ch Government, finding we were in earnest, were not to be intimidated by any action Athens, began to fear lest the matter without their having any share in it.

[1] Lahitte, French Minister for Foreign Affairs.

They had, accordingly, offered their good [illegible] Palmerston had accepted their offer, but only [illegible] understanding that there was to be no [illegible] the principle of our demands, and even on this [illegible] only as to some of them.

Baron Gros was ordered to Athens by the [illegible] Cabinet as mediator. The blockade and [illegible] to be suspended during the continuance of his [illegible] to accommodate matters. Lord Palmerston w[illegible] his brother:—

F. O.: February 15, [illegible]

We accept the good offices of France in regard to G[illegible] the same way in which we did so in the case of Naples [illegible] to obtain for us satisfaction, but not to arbitrate [illegible] claims. King Otho is the *enfant gâté de l'absolutism[illegible]* therefore all the arbitrary Courts are in convulsions at w[illegible] have been doing; but it is our long forbearance, and [illegible] precipitation, that deserves remark. The papers to [illegible] before Parliament will be ready in a day or two, and wi[illegible] this. What has happened may serve as a hint to other G[illegible] ments who turn a deaf ear to our remarks, and think [illegible] us out by refusals or evasions.

I conclude that by this time Parker will have got to[illegible] Greek vessels enough belonging to the Government and [illegible] vate individuals to be a sufficient security for payment of [illegible] is claimed. And, of course, we shall not let this securi[illegible] of our hands till the money we claim is actually paid t[illegible] persons for whom it is demanded.

Political matters are looking well here. Our majori[illegible] the two Houses have been decisive, and the measures w[illegible] brought in and announced seem to give satisfaction. Th[illegible] be no change of Government this year, nor probably [illegible] Peel finds it impossible to discover a party who will acc[illegible] as leader to form a Government; and Stanley, though [illegible] party as Opposition leader, is judged by them as by [illegible] son, who says, 'My father is a very clever man, but he [illegible] judgment, and would not do for a Minister of this co[illegible]

And the same day to Mr. Wyse at Athens:—

Nothing could be better than the manner in [illegible] and Sir William Parker have conducted the affair [illegible]

[illegible] You have both of you combined [illegible] with all the moderation, [illegible] compatible with the execution of your [illegible] give you full instructions for the [illegible] I believe, as good a choice as the French [illegible] he is a Frenchman, and of course an [illegible] purposely fixed no time for the duration of [illegible], but you will put him on his honour [illegible] he has failed, if fail he should. Perhaps, [illegible] succeed. All depends on his instructions. [illegible] offices to procure a settlement of our demands, [illegible] as to the amount of them. In fact, the [illegible] should admit of discussion in regard to its [illegible] Pacifico; but if his documents are right, as [illegible] be, his claim is as clear as the rest. We must [illegible] *sonante*, and not promises to pay. Those [illegible] infallibly be broken, and we should have to [illegible] again. The word of the Greek Government is [illegible] bond, and the bondholders can tell us what that [illegible], after the systematic violation of the article [illegible] of 1832, as to applying the first proceeds of the [illegible] payment of the interest and sinking fund of the [illegible] can be placed, even in a treaty engagement, [illegible] be offered to us. The plea of poverty cannot [illegible] at a moment when fresh expenses, diplomatic and [illegible] without any necessity incurred.

[illegible]ur Thouvenel, however, did not cease from [illegible] though secret opposition to the action of the [illegible]vernment. Such an old diplomatist as Lord [illegible] should hardly have required such a hint as [illegible]ing :—

F. O.: February 22, 1850.

[illegible] Normanby,—One word more about Thouvenel and [illegible] with him. In your private letters and public [illegible] you argue that Thouvenel cannot have done certain [illegible] *you are told* by the French Ministers that he [illegible] having done so; or because you have had [illegible] despatches in which he makes no mention of having [illegible]; or because you have seen or have heard of [illegible] written by him to his friends implying that he [illegible] different line of conduct. All I can say in reply [illegible] these negative inferences I place the positive assertions of the Minister and Admiral and the tone and substance of Thouvenel's own notes, which latter are quite inconsistent with the statements in his private letters. But you are surely too good a diplomatist not to be aware that there are such things as private letters and public despatches written expressly that they may be shown, and you must, moreover, be aware that the mere fact that a foreign agent is said by his employer not to have mentioned that he did a particular thing is no proof that he did not do it. Nesselrode stoutly asserts that Titow had never told the Turkish Government that the escape of any of the refugees would be tantamount to a declaration of war against Russia and Austria, but we are morally certain that such a declaration was made both by Titow and Stürmer. Thouvenel may be a very gentlemanlike man in private society, but that does not prevent his being a reckless intriguer in a political crisis, and there is nothing in the political habits of French diplomatists, especially of those of the Guizot school, that can render it improbable that he should be so.

A fortnight later, the same accounts arrive:—

F. O.: March 12, 1850.

I am somewhat afraid that when Gros gets to Athens, he will find France so engaged in support of the Greek Government that he will scarcely be able to disentangle himself from the meshes spread for him by Thouvenel; but if he does not do so, his mission will be a failure. We have got, I imagine, vessels enough to make good our demands, and we shall certainly not let one of them go till we, or those on whose behalf we make our demands, have been paid in hard cash the amount of their just claims.

The Russian Government was not less hostile than France, although more decorous in its hostility. It had expressed its disapproval in a strongly-worded despatch. Lord Palmerston writes to the English Minister at St. Petersburg:—

C. G.: March 27, 1850.

We do not mind the Russian swagger and attempt to bully about Greece. We shall pursue our own course steadily and firmly, and we must and shall obtain the satisfaction we require. The amount of money which we demand is really so small that the bottleholders of Greece ought to be ashamed the [illegible] they [illegible] [illegible] the [illegible] Greek [illegible] we shall remain there till we get [illegible] Portuguese claims of Pacifico, [illegible] the number of [illegible] fifty.

The Russian ambassador having written to complain of the language of the "Times" and "Morning Post" about the Emperor's acts and policy, Lord Palmerston's answer is as follows:—

[illegible] May [illegible]

My dear John Russell,—I return you Brunnow's letter. Any articles in the newspapers to which he alludes were drawn upon the Russian Government by the unprecedented publication of Nesselrode's despatch of the 17th March, and by the boastful threats made by the "Times" newspaper as to what Russia would do to put a stop to our proceedings in Greece. This war of words is, no doubt, much to be deprecated, but the responsibility for any evils which it may produce must rest with those by whom it is begun. With regard to the Russian despatch, the feeling in this country has been but one, and that one universal; and I happen to know that a leading man among our opponents in Parliament said lately that he must withhold his approval of our conduct with regard to Greece until he knew whether we had answered it in a manner befitting the dignity of England.

Baron Gros was very dilatory, and by his conduct gave colour to the suspicion that he meant to fail in his good offices, trusting that the English Government would not venture to renew the embargo, [illegible] that thus the whole matter would be transferred [illegible] consideration to London or Paris. It was gall [illegible] wormwood to the French and Russians that the [illegible] tiations should be going on at Athens, with the [illegible] the British fleet on the spot ready to support [illegible] Minister, and to coerce if all proposals were refused.

F. O.: May 7, [illegible]

My dear Wyse,—Gros had, up to the date of your [illegible] received despatches, been perpetually trying to slide out [illegible] character of organ of good offices, and to place himself [illegible] position of arbiter. He was sent, under our acceptance [illegible] good offices of France, to endeavour to prevail upon the [illegible] Government to agree to our demands, and his whole [illegible] and exertions seem to have been directed to prevail [illegible] to give up, or greatly to modify, those demands. In [illegible] has acted as the avowed advocate of Greece; and [illegible] admire the coolness with which, when asked by you [illegible] if you agreed to his required abatements, he could [illegible] the consent of the Greek Government, he replied that [illegible] do no such thing. His game was first to beat you down [illegible] as he could, and then to come back and to say that [illegible] not bring the Greek Government up to that point, [illegible] you must therefore come down lower still, or else he [illegible] away. When Drouyn[1] has held this sort of language, [illegible] that Gros would be obliged to renounce his task, I have said, 'Well, what of it? so much the worse for [illegible] that's all.' Drouyn, however, has behaved very well [illegible]

As to the claims of foreigners, Prussians or [illegible] account of the detention of their cargoes in Greek [illegible] answer would be, that a man who chooses to put [illegible] on board a vessel belonging to another country [illegible] chance as to any difficulties into which that country [illegible] with other Powers, and all the remedy which he [illegible] have is to get his cargo back again on proof [illegible] belongs to him. Last year, during the Danish [illegible] against Germany, many of our merchants had [illegible] German ships. Those ships were captured by [illegible] the only remedy our merchants had was to [illegible] before the Prize Court at Copenhagen, and [illegible] goods delivered up to them.

[1] French ambassador in London.

...with the French Government ... the basis of their exercise of good ... settled in London, matters were ... Athens. Baron Gros, after long and ...tions, threw up his office as mediator, ... Mr. Wyse renewed the embargo and ... several vessels. This at length brought ... terms, and they finally agreed to send a ... for the affair of the *Fantôme*, to pay ...,000 drachmas for Finlay and Pacifico, and ... put forward any claims for compensation ... that had been detained, which were, in ... immediately released. This was a great ... Lord Palmerston. His resolution and calm ... had attained the desired end, in spite of ... and opposition which might well have daunted ... man. But his troubles were not yet over. ...h were beyond measure annoyed that the ...should at last have been settled by our own ... not by their good offices. They tried to ...rrel upon England on the ground of breach ... in recurring to the employment of force with...ing for the result of their intervention. As ...os had notified both to Mr. Wyse and to the Government, two days before the renewal of ..., that his mission was at an end, this was an ... baseless charge. M. Drouyn de Lhuys, how... recalled from London; and General Lahitte, ... Foreign Minister, read a despatch in the ... in which he openly charged the British ...ment with duplicity. Anxious questions were ... both Houses of Parliament, and many thought ... on the verge of war.

... Palmerston knew better, and writes to Lord ...by:—

F. O.: May 17, 1850.

... clear that the French Government think a quarrel ... would be useful to them at home. In my answer in ... yesterday I purposely abstained from stating that

Drouyn was ordered back to Paris as a mark o because it would have been very improper in n difference which I hoped might be adjusted. O was at liberty, if he thought fit, to announce t own instructions to his own ambassador. It w do so unless I had intended to widen the breac

C. G.:

Drouyn came to me on Tuesday, and I s half hours in going through the papers wi explaining our course. On Wednesday he ca and began by reading to me Lahitte's despatch we went on for a couple of hours going throu papers which we had not gone through suff before. As he was leaving me he said he sl evening, as the next day his Government w before the Assembly, and it was important th able to communicate with his Government bef met. I said I thought he was quite right, an to give the substance of the explanations I had

I further assured him that we never had i respect to the French Government, and did n could be justly charged with having broken a and I said that, considering the many great interests, not merely English and French, but which require that a good understanding shoul and a close connection kept up between Englan did earnestly hope that his Government wou *querelle d'Allemand* between the two countri decision rested with them, as there were certa we could not do, and which they ought not t We parted with many friendly personal assu exchanged; though I by no means pretend to the points at issue I succeeded in satisfying hir

The best and shortest account of the ma recall was given by the Duke of Wellington, at Lord Anglesey's, on Thursday evening, t Lord Anglesey's, birthday. When the Duke people flocked round him and asked him wha the matter. His reply was, 'Oh, oh, it's a nonsense!' I see clearly that there was a co joint operation, and that it was preconcerted [illegible] himself send excuses and not attend my [illegible] All this was what the Americans would [illegible] and savours much of the strategy of the [illegible] of Paris, as I am told our old friend the [illegible] The Duke of Devonshire, when he heard, [illegible] Wednesday evening, that Brunnow and Cetto [illegible] from the dinner, said it was a proof [illegible] principles and feelings had spread, for that [illegible] diplomatists would have been guilty of so [illegible] I have seen neither of them since.

[illegible] has missed its aim, however, and people here [illegible] understand the whole affair. I suppose that by [illegible] also begin to see through the millstone. [illegible] who meant to punish me have in one respect [illegible] object, for I cannot, in the present state of things, [illegible] for the four days of Whitsuntide.

[illegible] Palmerston had now to exercise his diplomatic [illegible] order to smooth over French susceptibility. [illegible] therefore, some means of putting France [illegible] a successful mediator, and he managed it [illegible] were some further claims of Pacifico's [illegible] based upon the loss of papers which were [illegible] for certain demands upon the Portuguese [illegible]. In the agreement with Mr. Wyse it had [illegible] that a joint inquiry of the two Govern- [illegible] ascertain whether they were well founded [illegible] that meanwhile a deposit should be paid by [illegible] Government. Lord Palmerston wished to [illegible] France, that, instead of a joint inquiry by [illegible] Governments concerned, there should be arbiters [illegible] umpire, to be named by the joint concurrence [illegible] British, French, and Greek plenipotentiaries. [illegible] besides, as we have seen above, an engage- [illegible] into with Mr. Wyse that the Greek [illegible] should not put forward or support any [illegible] compensation for the detention of ships. [illegible] suggested that there should be sub- [illegible] engagement the good offices of France,

[illegible] Lieven, whose husband had been Russian ambassador in who should advise the King of Greece neit[illegible] nor to aid any such claims. The French For[illegible] ter was, however, in no humour to be appeas[illegible]

C. O.: Ma[illegible]

My dear John Russell,—You will see that La[illegible] take it, is pretty nearly the mere organ of Piscator[illegible] simply refuses our proposal, without giving reasons [illegible] anything else. His view of the matter seems to [illegible] quarrel is a mighty pretty quarrel as it stands, and [illegible] a pity to spoil it by explanation.'

But Normanby's conversation with the Pres[illegible] another question under the consideration of the Cab[illegible] Napoleon would be satisfied, as I infer, if to the ar[illegible] added the restitution of the deposit, and this the [illegible] have to consider to-morrow. The reasons for and [illegible] to me to be much as follows. In favour of it, may [illegible] the Parliament and the public would be glad of a [illegible] the dispute, and would not examine very minut[illegible] ditions of the arrangement; that they would not [illegible] prolonged estrangement between England and Fr[illegible] on account of the question as to the manner of [illegible] very doubtful claims of Pacifico in regard to hi[illegible] documents, and they might not easily understa[illegible] should face a quarrel with France rather than a[illegible] diplomatic security which we were willing to think [illegible] the 19th of last month. This would, probably, [illegible] view of the matter taken by those who look only [illegible] of things, and they are the majority here as well a[illegible]

On the other hand, it must be owned that i[illegible] appease the anger of the French Government ([illegible] France, for I do not believe the French people [illegible] about the matter), we return to Otho the deposit [illegible] compelled to place in our hands, the [illegible] from the British steamer in the Piraeus will be [illegible] Greece and in Europe generally as an act of [illegible] England to France, as a baisse de pavillon, and [illegible] much affect our moral position among the [illegible]

[illegible] twenty pounds which he had compelled [illegible] against his will.

[illegible] was, however, equal to the occasion. [illegible] this objection would be obviated if [illegible] of the deposit was accompanied by an [illegible] adhere to their promises on the part of [illegible] in the form of a convention to [illegible] presence of the French plenipotentiaries, [illegible] indirectly act as guarantors of the [illegible]. This ingenious device to save English [illegible] soothing French susceptibilities is a fair [illegible] branch of the 'art of diplomacy.' It [illegible] successful, but the next letter to St. [illegible] shows that there were meanwhile various [illegible] work trying hard to keep the two nations [illegible]

F. O.: May 24, 1850.

[illegible] Bloomfield,—I have been so busy fighting my [illegible] France that I have been obliged to put off for a [illegible] up again my skirmish with Russia, but I have [illegible] short answer to Nesselrode's last long despatch about [illegible] and a reply to Brunnow's protest, and you shall [illegible] both by the next opportunity. I think we shall be [illegible] to an understanding with France, unless the [illegible] Government want to pick a quarrel with us, and if that [illegible] intention, of course they can carry it into effect. This [illegible] up at Paris has had, however, a double object, first [illegible] over, next to sever the connection between England [illegible]. The Orleanist clique and Madame Lieven aimed [illegible] result; the Russian party, led and aided by Madame [illegible] calculated upon the second. There have been in [illegible] within the last week letters from Madame Lieven to [illegible] here, abusing me like a pickpocket, and full [illegible] and disappointment that we did not send for [illegible] the moment the French Government sent for [illegible]. She was unable to suppress her mortification that [illegible] succeeded in producing a decided rupture between [illegible] countries. Of course, she and Kisseleff[1] hunt in [illegible] we well know that Kisseleff's language at Paris

[1] Russian ambassador in Paris.

and Brunnow's at London are both of them [illegible] purposes of the Russian Government at each place [illegible]

All the accounts which come from Greece state [illegible] Greeks complain, not of what we have done, but [illegible] have not done; they say the English brought Otho, [illegible] ought to have taken him away.

The French were delaying coming to a [illegible] knowing that the Opposition were stirring [illegible] land, and hoping to get some aid from the [illegible] Parliament. On June 17, Lord Stanley moved [illegible] House of Lords the following resolution:—

That while the House fully recognises the right [illegible] of the Government to secure to Her Majesty's subjects [illegible] in foreign States the full protection of the laws of [illegible] it regrets to find, by the correspondence recently laid [illegible] table by Her Majesty's command, that various claims [illegible] the Greek Government, doubtful in point of j[illegible] exaggerated in amount, have been enforced by [illegible] measures directed against the commerce and people [illegible] and calculated to endanger the continuance of our [illegible] relations with other Powers.

Lord Stanley's fervid attack upon the [illegible] the Foreign Secretary was supported [illegible] energy by Lord Aberdeen and Lord Brou[illegible] motion was carried by a majority of [illegible] and Lord Palmerston wrote next morning [illegible] follows:—

F. O.: [illegible]

We were beaten last night in the Lords by a [illegible] than we had up to the last moment expected [illegible] took office we knew that our opponents [illegible] the Lords than we had, and that [illegible] to be fully [illegible] [illegible]

... brought up all their men, even the

... may do remains to be seen, but I ... party there venturing to propose ... of the Lords. If they do, I think ... well what the result would be.

... no adverse motion made in the House ... on June 24, Mr. Roebuck moved, ... vote of the Lords, the following resolu-

... principles on which the foreign policy of Her ... have been regulated have been such as ... to maintain the honour and dignity of this ... in times of unexampled difficulty to preserve peace ... and the various nations of the world.

... of four nights' duration followed. On ... night Lord Palmerston rose, and in a speech ... ours long, which was a masterpiece of argu- ... of detailed reasoning, vindicated his whole

... by expressing his opinion that those by ... the question had been brought under the ... of Parliament had not conducted themselves ... fficient sense of the gravity and importance of ... involved.

... party in this country imagine that they are ... to carry the Government by storm, and to take ... the citadel of office, or if, without intending to ... strength with that of their opponents, they con- ... are matters of such gravity connected with the ... the Government, that it becomes their duty to call ... ament solemnly to record its disapprobation of what ..., I think that either in the one case or in the other ... ought not to have been contented with obtaining the ... the opinion of the House of Lords, but they ought ... down their resolution for the consent and con- ... House; or, at least, those who act with them ... operation here should themselves have proposed to this House to come to a similar resolution. [illegible] what it may, we have come to the same end; [illegible] substantially considering whether they will [illegible] of the House of Lords or the resolution which [illegible] mitted to them by my hon. friend the member [illegible]

Now, the resolution of the House of Lords [illegible] future as well as the past. It lays down for [illegible] principle of national policy which I consider [illegible] patible with the interests, with the rights, with [illegible] and with the dignity of the country, and at [illegible] practice, not only of this, but of all other civilised [illegible] the world. The country is told that British subjects [illegible] lands are entitled to nothing but the protection of [illegible] the tribunals of the land in which they happen to [illegible] country is told that British subjects abroad must [illegible] their own country for protection, but must trust [illegible] different justice which they may happen to receive at [illegible] of the Government and tribunals of the country in [illegible] may be.

Now I deny that proposition, and I say it is a [illegible] which no British Minister ever yet has acted, and [illegible] people of England never will suffer any British Mini[illegible] Do I mean to say that British subjects abroad are [illegible] the law, or are to be taken out of the scope of the [illegible] land in which they live? I mean no such thing. [illegible] for no such principle. Undoubtedly, in the [illegible] British subjects are bound to have recourse for [illegible] means which the law of the land affords them [illegible] available for such purpose. . . . . . It is only [illegible] justice or upon decisions manifestly unjust [illegible] Government should be called upon to interfere. [illegible] be cases in which no confidence can be placed in [illegible] those tribunals being, from their composition [illegible] a character to inspire any hope of obtaining [illegible]

I will take a transaction that [illegible] instance of a case in which, I say, the [illegible] not [illegible] British subject to be [illegible]

[illegible] be brought before a court-martial, and, [illegible] be shot. Now, this happened. An [illegible] brought before a court-martial, accused [illegible] police officers, who stated that they had [illegible] him, in an open stable in his inn-yard, a [illegible] denounced as a concealed weapon. Witnesses [illegible], the counsel for the prosecution stated [illegible] case, as it was evident there was no proof [illegible] belonged to the man, or that he was aware it was [illegible] it was found. The counsel for the defendant [illegible] the opinion of the counsel for the prosecu[illegible] necessary for him to go into the defence, and he [illegible] in the hands of the court. The court, however, [illegible] pronounced the man guilty of the charge brought [illegible] the next morning the man was shot. [illegible] would the English people have said if this had [illegible] a British subject! and yet everything done was [illegible] a law, and the man was found guilty of an offence [illegible] of the country.

[illegible], that our doctrine is that, in the first instance, [illegible] be sought from the law courts of the country; [illegible] cases where redress cannot be so had—and those [illegible]—to confine a British subject to that remedy [illegible] be to deprive him of the protection which he is [illegible] receive.

[illegible] proceeded with a short sketch of English [illegible] with the Greek kingdom and of the deplorable [illegible] law, justice, and police in that country, and [illegible]:—

[illegible] be told, perhaps, as we have already been told, that [illegible] of the country are liable to have heavy stones [illegible] their breasts and police-officers to dance upon [illegible] they are liable to have their heads tied to their [illegible] to be left for hours in that state; or to be swung [illegible], and to be bastinadoed as they swing, foreigners [illegible] to be better treated than the natives, and have no [illegible] complain if the same things are practised upon them. [illegible] told this, but that is not my opinion, nor do I be[illegible] the opinion of any reasonable man. Then, I say, that [illegible] the cases of the Ionians, for whom we demanded [illegible] House must look at and consider what was the [illegible] in this respect in Greece; they must consider the practices that were going on, and the necessity of [illegible] to the extension of these abuses to British and [illegible] by demanding compensation, scarcely indeed [illegible] in some cases, but the granting of which would be [illegible] ledgment that such things should not be done [illegible] future.

In discussing these cases, I am concerned to [illegible] that they appear to me to have been dealt with [illegible] spirit and in a tone which I think was neither [illegible] persons concerning whom, nor the persons by [illegible] persons before whom, the discussion took place. [illegible] more convenient to treat matters with ridicule than [illegible] argument, and we have had serious things treated [illegible] grave men kept in a roar of laughter for an hour [illegible] poverty of one sufferer, or at the miserable habitation [illegible] at the nationality of one injured man, or the religion [illegible] as if because a man was poor he might be [illegible] tortured with impunity, as if a man who was born in [illegible] might be robbed without redress, or because a man [illegible] Jewish persuasion he is fair game for any outrage. [illegible] true saying, and has often been repeated, that a very [illegible] share of human wisdom is sufficient for the guidance [illegible] affairs. But there is another truth, equally indisputable [illegible] is, that a man who aspires to govern mankind ought [illegible] the task generous sentiments, compassionate [illegible] noble and elevated thoughts.

After relating the story of Finlay and [illegible] some detail, he proceeded :—

M. Pacifico having, from year to year, been [illegible] with answers wholly unsatisfactory, or with a [illegible] or with pertinacious silence, it came at last to [illegible] his demand was to be abandoned altogether, or [illegible] ance of the notice we had given the Greek Govern[illegible] or two before, we were to proceed to use our [illegible] enforcing the claim. 'Oh! but,' it is said, 'what [illegible] proceeding to employ so large a force against so [illegible] Does the smallness of a country justify the [illegible] acts? Is it to be held that if your subjects [illegible] rage, plunder in a country which is small and [illegible] tell them when they apply for redress that [illegible] weak and so small that we cannot ask [illegible] Their answer would be that the [illegible]

...the more easy to obtain redress. 'No,' ...to be the rule. We are to be generous ...ungenerous to you; and we cannot give ...have such ample and easy means of pro-...

...urged, Pacifico is such a notorious ...

...who have before had occasion to advert to ...I do not care what M. Pacifico's character is. ...admit, that because a man may have acted ...other occasion, and in some other matter, he is to ...ith impunity by others.

...s of a man depend on the merits of the particular ...s an abuse of argument to say that you are not to ...o a man because in some former transaction he ...e something which is questionable. Punish him ...unish him if he is guilty, but do not pursue him as ...gh life.

...entered on a long and lucid history of the ...actions already recounted, justifying both ...wards the Greek and his negotiation with ...Government.

...thus disposed of the matter of Greece, he ...e affairs of Portugal and Spain, about which ...attacked by Sir James Graham, then mem-...n. He pointed out that 'his little experi-...ium monarchy,' as it had been sneeringly ...een constituted by British intervention not ...kind from that employed in the former ...hat it had proved a secure and beneficial ...d that he hoped for Portugal the same ...d happiness. He then went on:—

...s now in the enjoyment of a Constitution, and ...working as well as under all circumstances, and ...w recently it has been established, could perhaps ...ected. 'Oh, but,' said the right hon. Baronet, ...ta Cabral as Minister, and your object was to get ...Now, the fault I find with those who are so fond ...e either here or elsewhere, in this country or in others, is, that they try to bring down every question to a per-sonal bearing. If they want to oppose the policy of a they say, 'Let us get rid of the man who happens to be the organ of that policy.' Why, it is like shooting a (Laughter, and cries of 'Hear, hear.') As long as England, as long as the English people are animated by the feelings, and spirit, and opinions which they possess, knock down twenty foreign Ministers one after another; depend upon it no one will keep his place who does not the same principles. When it falls to my duty, in my functions, to oppose the policy of any Government, the immediate cry is, 'Oh, it's all spite against this man, man, Count this, or Prince that, that makes you do this.'

After reciting the events in Spain which induced the British Government to interfere under the Quadruple Treaty, he added :—

If England has any interest more than another with reference to Spain, it is that Spain should be independent, Spain should be Spanish. Spain for the Spaniards is the upon which we proceed in our policy with regard to Much evil must ever come to this country from Spain being under the direction of other Powers. nently for our interest that when we have the misfortune in dispute or at war with any other Power, we merely on that account, and without any offence to Spain herself, be at war with Spain also. We consider the independence of Spain was more likely to be Government controlled by a representative and sembly than by a Government purely arbitrary, and merely of the members who might form the Admin- Therefore, on grounds of strict policy, independent general sympathy which animated the people as well Government of this country towards Spain at the thought it our interest to take part with Isabella, the pretensions of Don Carlos. That policy was Carlist cause failed ; the cause of the Constitution

Very dexterous was the next part of which, while apparently talking of France, he drew an unmistakable picture of

House caught the portrayal at appreciation by loud applause.

hon. Baronet (Sir J. Graham) says were of long duration, and produced because they were followed by events as regards another country, namely, out of those Spanish quarrels and Spanish differences between England and France catastrophe than the overthrow of the This is another instance of the fondness for great and national question to the smallness It was my dislike to M. Guizot, for- of these Spanish marriages, which overthrew and with it the throne of France! Why, French nation say when they hear this? They and high-spirited nation, full of a sense of and honour—what will they say when they that it was in the power of a British Minister to Government and their monarchy? (Much Why, sir, it is a calumny on the French nation to the personal hatred of any foreigner to their have this effect. They are a brave, a generous, minded people; and if they had thought that a had been formed against one of their ministers and prolonged cheering, which prevented the from concluding the sentence)—I say, that if people had thought that a knot of foreign conspira- against one of their Ministers, and caballing than that he had upheld, as he conceived, interests of his own country, and if they had such a knot of foreign conspirators had coadjutors land, why, I say that the French people, that spirited nation, would have scorned the in- a cabal, and would have clung the closer to, and the more, the man against whom such a plot If, then, the French people had thought that foreign Minister, was seeking to overthrow M. knowledge of such a design, so far from assisting would have rendered him stronger than ever in the occupied. No, sir, the French Minister and the were overthrown by far different causes. both in this country and elsewhere, would have done well to have read a letter [illegible] which then took place.

Leaving, to use his own words, the [illegible] Castille and the gay vineyards of France, [illegible] himself to the mountains of Switzerland [illegible] an elaborate justification of the charges [illegible] him in connection with the civil war [illegible] cantons. After that, in his own language [illegible] ling from the rugged Alps into the [illegible] Lombardy, he pleaded his cause as follows:—

With regard to our policy with respect to Italy [illegible] deny the charges that have been brought against [illegible] been the advocates, supporters, and encouragers of [illegible] It has always been the fate of advocates of [illegible] and of constitutional improvement to be run at as the [illegible] of revolution. It is the easiest mode of putting [illegible] it is the received *formula*. It is the established [illegible] those who are the advocates of arbitrary government [illegible] 'Never mind real revolutionists; we know how to [illegible] them; your dangerous man is the moderate reformer; [illegible] a plausible man; the only way of getting rid of him [illegible] the world at him by calling him a revolutionist.

Now, there are revolutionists of two kinds in this [illegible] In the first place, there are those violent, hot-headed [illegible] thinking men who fly to arms, who overthrow [illegible] Governments, and who recklessly, without regard [illegible] quences, and without measuring difficulties and [illegible] strength, deluge their country with blood, and draw [illegible] greatest calamities on their fellow-countrymen. These [illegible] revolutionists of one class. But there are revolutionists of another kind: blind-minded men, who, animated by [illegible] prejudices, and daunted by ignorant apprehensions, [illegible] current of human improvement until the irresistible [illegible] accumulated discontent breaks down the opposing [illegible] overthrows and levels to the earth those very institutions [illegible] a timely application of renovating means would have [illegible] strong and lasting. Such revolutionists as these [illegible] who call us revolutionists. It was not to make [illegible] that Lord Minto went to Italy, or that we, at the [illegible] Governments of Austria and Naples, offered [illegible] tween contending parties.

[illegible] successively with Lord Minto's mis-[illegible] with the events in Sicily, and with the [illegible] in Turkey in the matter of the Hungarian [illegible] as follows :—

"I have now gone through all the heads of the [illegible] have been brought against me in this debate. [illegible] shown that the foreign policy of the Govern-[illegible] the transactions with respect to which its conduct [illegible] has throughout been guided by those prin-[illegible]cording to the resolution of the honourable and [illegible], ought to regulate the conduct of the [illegible] England in the management of our foreign [illegible] that the principles on which we have acted are [illegible] held by the great mass of the people of this [illegible] convinced these principles are calculated, so far [illegible] of England may properly be exercised with [illegible] destinies of other countries, to conduce to the [illegible] peace, to the advancement of civilisation, to [illegible] happiness of mankind.

[illegible] complain of the conduct of those who have made [illegible] means of attack upon Her Majesty's Ministers. [illegible] of a great country like this is, undoubtedly, [illegible] and legitimate ambition to men of all shades of [illegible] a noble thing to be allowed to guide the policy [illegible] the destiny of such a country; and if ever it [illegible] honourable ambition, more than ever must it [illegible] moment at which I am speaking. For while we [illegible] stated by the right hon. Baronet, the political [illegible] Europe from side to side—while we have [illegible], shattered, levelled, institutions overthrown [illegible] while in almost every country of Europe the [illegible] war has deluged the land with blood, from the [illegible] Black Sea, from the Baltic to the Mediterranean, [illegible] presented a spectacle honourable to the people [illegible] worthy of the admiration of mankind.

[illegible] liberty is compatible with order; that [illegible] is reconcilable with obedience to the law. [illegible] example of a nation in which every class [illegible] cheerfulness the lot which Providence [illegible] at the same time every individual of [illegible] striving to raise himself in the social [illegible] wrong, not by violence and illegality,

but by persevering good conduct, and by the steady [illegible]
getic exertion of the moral and intellectual faculties [illegible]
his Creator has endowed him. To govern such a people [illegible]
is indeed an object worthy of the ambition of the [illegible]
who lives in the land, and, therefore, I find no fault [illegible]
who may think any opportunity a fair one for endeavour[illegible]
place themselves in so distinguished and honourable a [illegible]
but I contend that we have not in our foreign policy [illegible]
thing to forfeit the confidence of the country. W[illegible]
perhaps, in this matter or in that, have acted [illegible]
the opinions of one person or of another; and hard [illegible]
as we all know by our individual and private experie[illegible]
any number of men agreeing entirely in any matter [illegible]
they may not be equally possessed of the details of the
circumstances, reasons, and conditions which led to [illegible]
But, making allowance for those differences of opinion [illegible]
may fairly and honourably arise among those who [illegible]
general views, I maintain that the principles which [illegible]
traced through all our foreign transactions, as the gui[illegible]
and directing spirit of our proceedings, are such [illegible]
approbation. I therefore fearlessly challenge the verd[illegible]
this House, as representing a political, a commercial, [illegible]
tutional country, is to give on the question now brou[illegible]
it—whether the principles on which the foreign policy [illegible]
Majesty's Government has been conducted, and the [illegible]
duty which has led us to think ourselves bound to a[illegible]
tection to our fellow-subjects abroad, are proper [illegible]
guides for those who are charged with the governme[illegible]
land; and whether, as the Roman in days of old [illegible]
self free from indignity when he could say, '*Civis* [illegible]
sum,' so also a British subject, in whatever land he [illegible]
shall feel confident that the watchful eye and the st[illegible]
England will protect him against injustice and wro[illegible]

As Lord Palmerston sat down the Hou[illegible]
him with loud and prolonged cheers, echo[illegible]
seemed, by anticipation, the words extorted [illegible]
the debate from his generous antagonist, [illegible]
Peel, when he declared, 'It has made [illegible]
him.' This, as is well known, was Peel's [illegible]
ance in the House. He was killed [illegible]
from his horse.

[illegible] of the fifth day of discussion [illegible] against 264 gave a majority of 46 [illegible] conduct of foreign affairs. In the [illegible] announces the result to his corre-[illegible]

F. O.: June 29, 1850.

[illegible],—Our debate in the House of Commons [illegible] four o'clock this morning, and we had about [illegible] which we had reckoned upon; our calculation [illegible] forty and fifty. Our triumph has been com-[illegible] as well as in the division; and, all things [illegible] scarcely ever remember a debate which, as a dis-[illegible], oratory, and high and dignified feeling, was [illegible] to the House of Commons.

[illegible] speech last night was admirable and first-rate; [illegible] Cockburn's,[1] I do not know that I ever, in the course [illegible] heard a better speech from anybody, without any [illegible]

[illegible] was also a first-rate performance, and Peel and [illegible] spoke with great judgment and talent with refer-[illegible] respective positions.

[illegible] degree of public feeling which has been excited out [illegible] upon the matters on which the debate and division [illegible] most remarkable, and would have led to very strong [illegible] if the result of the division had been to throw [illegible] into the hands of our opponents.

C. G.: July 8, 1850.

[illegible] William,—You will have seen before this time how [illegible] the House of Commons have reversed the petulant [illegible] and foolish vote of the House of Lords, but you can-[illegible] from newspaper reports, nor know from newspaper [illegible] the admirable and enthusiastic spirit displayed on this [illegible] by the majority of the House of Commons, and by all [illegible] county papers, and by the nation at large. The [illegible] our foreign policy has been rightly understood by [illegible], as the shot fired by a foreign conspiracy, aided and [illegible] a domestic intrigue; and the parties have so entirely [illegible] purpose, that instead of expelling and overthrowing [illegible] disgrace, as they intended and hoped to do, they have [illegible] for the present the most popular Minister that for [illegible] course of time has held my office.

[1] Now Lord Chief Justice of England.

The speech I had to make, which could [illegible] within a shorter time than from a quarter [illegible] minutes past two, was listened to very patiently [illegible] by the House, and has had great success with everybody. [illegible]

Two hundred and fifty members of the Reform [illegible] invited me to a dinner next Saturday to celebrate my [illegible] and if we had not thought it better to limit the [illegible] to a small scale, the dinner would have been given in [illegible] Garden Theatre, and would have been attended by a [illegible] people.

I myself, the Government, and the country are [illegible] indebted to the Burgraves and to Stanley. But the H[illegible] Lords has been placed in an unfortunate position, and [illegible] has not raised his reputation as a statesman.

Peel's death is a great calamity, and one that seems to have had no adequate cause. He was a very bad and awkward rider, and his horse might have been sat by any better equestrian; but he seems, somehow or other, to have been entangled in the bridle, and to have pulled the horse to step or kneel upon him. The injury to the shoulder was severe but curable; that which killed him was a broken rib, forced by great violence inwards into the lungs.

Immediately after this successful combat the portrait of Lord Palmerston, by Partridge, which was so well known in later years to the frequenters of Cambridge House, where it hung on the staircase, was presented to Lady Palmerston by a hundred and twenty members of the House of Commons. They added to it a written address, expressive of 'their high sense of his public and private character, and of the independent policy by which he maintained the honour and interests of his country.'

It was altogether a great triumph for Lord Palmerston. 'His speech,' according to the testimony of Sir George Lewis,[1] 'was an extraordinary effort. He defeated the whole Conservative party, Protectionists and Peelites, supported by the extreme Radicals, and backed by the "Times," and all the organised forces of foreign diplomacy.'

[1] Sir G. Lewis to Sir E. Head, page 327 of 'Letters.'

Every element of hostility and of pent-up animosity which had been long gathering against him were on this occasion brought into one focus, but he only expanded the more instead of shrivelling under the burning-glass. He vindicated both with courage and, as we have seen, with eloquence all his actions at the Foreign Office, as being dictated solely by his care for the position and well-being of his country, and stamped himself upon the minds of the English people, according to Lord John Russell's long-remembered words, as emphatically and in a special sense, a *Minister of England.*

CHAPTER VI.

LETTERS—GENERAL HAYNAU AT BARCLAY'S BREWERY—ECCLESIASTICAL TITLES BILL—NATIONAL DEFENCES—MR. GLADSTONE'S LETTERS ABOUT NEAPOLITAN PRISONS—IONIAN ISLANDS—DEFENCE IN PARLIAMENT—QUESTION OF 'HOLY PLACES.'

WHILE still detained in town by the arrears of the session of 1850, he sends to his brother a report of his own position and of the state of parties. His estimate of Lord Aberdeen's capacity for the Premiership was destined to be tested within two years.

C. G.: September 1, 1850.

I have been more entirely swamped by business during the whole of this last session of Parliament than I ever was at any former time, and I have not even yet been able to work up the arrear of various matters which has accumulated by the regular overflowing of almost every day. But I have no reason to find fault with the session, for it has left me at its close in a very satisfactory and gratifying position. I have beaten and put down and silenced, at least for a time, one of the most widespread and malignant and active confederacies that ever conspired against one man without crushing him. But I was in the right, and I was able to fight my battle; and John Russell and my colleagues behaved most handsomely and honourably, and my triumph has been in proportion to the magnitude of the struggle. The death of Louis Philippe delivers me from my most artful and inveterate enemy, whose position gave him in many ways the power to injure me; and though I am very sorry for the death of Peel, from personal regard, and because it is no doubt a great loss to the country, yet as far as my [illegible] political position is concerned, I do not think that he was [illegible] disposed to do me any good turn. It is difficult to say [illegible] effect his death will have on the state of parties in [illegible] He had not much of a following latterly, though [illegible]

... such as Goulbourn, Robert Clive, Cardwell ... the like, were the most respectable of the ... Sidney Herbert, or Aberdeen, or Gladstone ... leader of the Conservative Free Traders, or the ... Conservatives; and perhaps Stanley may invite a ... him by some compromise about putting off Pro- ... have been told by a person who had it from Stanley ... during the time when a change of Government ... Aberdeen said to Stanley that in that case he, ... would be commissioned by the Queen to form a ...! This would have been a curious dish to set ... seen! On the whole, I rather am inclined to think ... overnment is made stronger by the events of last ... that we may look forward to getting successfully ... session of next year.

... acquaintance lately with a Sicilian Princess— ... I think, she calls herself—a widow, and one of ... f the Queen of Naples. She spoke highly of you; ... must add she spoke also highly of the King of ... ich makes her praise of less value.

... Lord Palmerston, a wise friend to Turkey, ... nd said about it, is still of so much interest ... re quote three or four letters on its affairs ... out this time. They at any rate show that ... t continued to sink for want of warning. She ... time contemplating her first loan, and Lord ... n's prognostications addressed to Sir Stratford ... proved very correct.

C. G.: August 7, 1850.

... r Canning,—I am sorry to hear so indifferent an ... 'progress' in Turkey as that which your letter ... contains. I will exhort through the ambassador ... how is it supposed that a foreign loan would help ... Would not such a loan add, by the amount of its ... d sinking fund, to the burthens of the State? and ... re not be a danger that a large part of it would ... r other find its way into the pockets of private ...? As to Douad Pasha, or Douad Effendi, he has, I ... all power of doing mischief here, and perhaps that ... reason why he tarries in the East; or maybe he ..., as the wise men are said to have come from thence, ... up there some of that wisdom which he so much lacks. But the Arabs have a proverb which [illegible] send a jackass to Mecca, and he will come [illegible]

Lord Palmerston's 'exhortation' was [illegible]

Broadlands: September [illegible]

Mon cher Ambassadeur,—Permettez que je vous [illegible] par écrit la prière que je vous ai faite verbalement [illegible] engager à tirer l'attention la plus sérieuse de votre [illegible] ment au mémorandum que Sir S. Canning a présenté [illegible] je voudrais y ajouter la demande que votre Gouv[illegible] veuille bien prendre en considération des observations [illegible] Colonel Rose[1] a faites au sujet de votre armée, et que [illegible] Canning aura déjà soumises au grand vizier.

Pardonnez-moi si j'ai l'air de m'ingérer dans des [illegible] ne me regardent pas, et croyez bien que ce que je dis, [illegible] uniquement dans l'intérêt du Sultan et de son Empire. L'[illegible] pire Ottoman n'est pas encore en état de maintenir son [illegible] pendance, et de défendre son vaste territoire contre les [illegible] qui le menacent sans l'aide et l'appui de temps en temps [illegible] Grande-Bretagne. Le Gouvernement Anglais a le sincère [illegible] et la ferme intention de vous donner toujours dans des [illegible] de difficulté l'appui dont vous aurez besoin. Mais le Gouverne[illegible] ment anglais le peut agir qu'en autant qu'il est soutenu [illegible] Parlement et par l'opinion publique; et ces soutiens [illegible] manqueraient si nous ne pouvions pas démontrer que le Gou[illegible] vernement Ottoman a fait tous les efforts en son pouvoir pour mettre toutes les branches de l'administration de la Turquie dans le meilleur état possible, et n'a rien omis qui pourrait contribuer à mettre la Turquie en état de se défendre en déve[illegible] loppant toutes les grandes ressources naturelles dont la Provi- dence l'a douée.

Jusqu'à présent il faut l'avouer ceci ne peut pas se [illegible] Votre Gouvernement a eu sans doute à lutter contre [illegible] obstacles; mais pour accomplir de grands résultats il [illegible] grands efforts, et de la détermination, et de la persévérance [illegible]

A Constantinople on chancelle, on hésite, on s'arrête [illegible] le moment actuel est favorable pour faire des réformes [illegible] améliorations. Le proverbe anglais dit qu'il faut faire [illegible] pendant que le soleil luit. Il faut réparer sa maison [illegible] qu'il fait calme, afin d'être en mesure contre l'ouragan.

Les points principaux que je voudrais signaler [illegible] demandant l'attention *pratique* de votre Gouvernement [illegible]

[1] Now Lord Stratheairn.

… fixe revenu, sans exiger de qui
… payer ; et cessation du système par
… des impôts.
… dépenses, choisissant d'abord les dépenses
… ce qui ne l'est pas.
… pendant pas de temps à construire des
… des fortifications pour le Bosphore, à
… sur la frontière, à établir des ouvrages
… capitale.

… de la justice devrait être sans reproche ;
… maintenant cet état de choses n'existe pas, et
… sont nombreuses.

… distinction politique et civile entre les différentes
… du Sultan par raison de différence de religion
… afin que le Sultan puisse devenir également
… toutes les populations qui habitent son Empire.

… l'armée il paraît que l'artillerie est excellente,
… admirables ; mais que l'infanterie est susceptible
… tions, et que la cavalerie en a grand besoin. Que
… ne sont pas bien armés, ayant quitté une excellente
… autrefois pour en prendre une assez mauvaise,
… ils ne sont pas fort adroits dans le maniement
… de la lance.

… Je vous souhaite personellement tout le
… ble, et je fais des vœux pour que votre pays
… prospérité rapide et avec cela solide.

Mille complimens,

PALMERSTON.

… et Pasha.

Broadlands : September 24, 1850.

… Canning,—I have just taken leave of the Turkish
…, who starts on Thursday for Constantinople. I
… opportunity of requesting him to impress upon his
… the necessity of improvement and reforms, and of
… to the prevalent system of corruption and in-
… I begged him to recommend strongly to the
… his Government the Memorandum which you had
… Sultan. There is obviously a great deal wanting
… every way and in every branch of administration
… into line with other Powers, and to put her
… to defend herself. But much has already been
… perhaps more than ever yet was done in the
… in any country in which there was so much

room for improvement; and I am not [illegible] by the apparent slowness of progress, but only [illegible] urge them on to further advance. It may be [illegible] of what has hitherto been done exists more in [illegible] orders than in actual execution; but one ought [illegible] value the worth of rules, and laws, and institutions, [illegible] they are not practically acted upon to the extent of [illegible] and spirit. As long as forms remain they are a [illegible] to refer to; and as men improve and opinion grows [illegible] ful, those forms become more and more the guide for [illegible] and events, and that which at first is only theory in [illegible] time is converted into practice.

As to foreign officers in the Turkish service, such men [illegible] necessarily impart to the Turkish officers notions and [illegible] that would be very useful; and the mere fact of [illegible] serving in this way in the Turkish army would have its [illegible] in breaking down that exclusive and fanatical feeling [illegible] represented as a bar to the admission of Christian [illegible] the Porte to situations of military command.

Why does the Turkish Government not get some [illegible] instructors for their cavalry? The Prussian cavalry is [illegible] lent, and, indeed, the Turkish infantry could not be [illegible] organised upon a better model than that of the Prussian [illegible]

I remember at the reviews in 1817 or 1818 of the [illegible] occupation in France, the Duke of Wellington being [illegible] which he thought the best army, the Austrian, the [illegible] the Prussian. His reply was: 'To say which are the best [illegible] is to say a great deal more than I will take on myself to [illegible] but I will tell you which of the three I should like [illegible] command in action. I should decidedly prefer the [illegible] they are the handiest, the best organised, and the most [illegible] telligent.'

Lord Palmerston was always especially [illegible] in his declarations that it was necessary for the [illegible] perity of Turkey that her Christian population [illegible] be placed and treated on a footing of absolute [illegible] with the Mussulman. He urges it in the [illegible] communication to Mehemet Pasha, and a year [illegible] repeats it to M. Musurus, in reply to a note [illegible] the ambassador's regret at the events which [illegible] Lord Palmerston's retirement from the [illegible] The letter is dated December 30, 1851, [illegible] follows:—

[illegible], mes remerciments les plus sincères [illegible] et soyez persuadé que, quelle que soit la [illegible] laquelle je pourrai me trouver, je serai [illegible] principes qui me font voir un intérêt non-[illegible] Européen dans l'indépendance et le [illegible] Ottoman, et vous connaissez bien mon [illegible] que la prospérité de cet empire ne reposera [illegible] vraiment solide tant que les sujets chrétiens [illegible] pas placés sur un pied d'égalité devant la loi [illegible] la religion Musulmane.

[illegible] a passage from a letter to Sir Stratford

[illegible] this consideration to show the Turkish Govern-[illegible] important it is that they should lose no time in [illegible] civil and political distinctions between Mussulmen [illegible] I pressed this yesterday on the Turkish ambas-[illegible] represented that, at present, the Sultan not only [illegible] himself of the use of his left arm, but runs constantly [illegible] being himself belaboured by it. Mehemet Pasha [illegible] the justice of the remark.[1]

[illegible] attack upon General Haynau by the men of [illegible] brewery gave Lord Palmerston some trouble [illegible] autumn of this year. General Haynau, an [illegible] general, who had won an evil reputation in [illegible] war for great cruelties and alleged flog-[illegible] women, came to London and went to visit the [illegible] of Barclay and Perkins. As soon as his [illegible] was known, a number of draymen came out [illegible] brooms and dirt, shouting out, 'Down with the [illegible] butcher!' He fled with the mob at his heels, [illegible] refuge in a public-house by the river-side, till [illegible] came to his rescue and took him away in a [illegible] to a place of safety. The following letter [illegible] to Sir George Grey, who was then Home [illegible]:—

Broadlands: October 1, 1850.

[illegible] Grey,—Koller[2] is very reasonable about the [illegible], and I believe that Schwarzenberg makes his

[1] [illegible] Sir Stratford Canning, F. O., October 11, 1849.

[2] Austrian ambassador.

move more to satisfy the feelings of the Austrian from any interest he himself takes about Haynau disgrace with the Austrian Government, and blamed in Austrian society at Vienna for his
I told Koller that it is much better that no should take place, because the defence of the necessarily be a minute recapitulation of all the committed by Haynau in Italy and Hungary, and be more injurious to him and to Austria than obtained against the draymen could be satisfactory.
I must own that I think Haynau's coming rhyme or reason, so soon after his Italian and exploits, was a wanton insult to the people of whose opinion of him had been so loudly proclaim meetings and in all the newspapers. But the wrong in the particular course they adopted. striking him, which, however, by Koller's accou not do much, they ought to have tossed him in a him in the kennel, and then sent him home in a his fare to the hotel.
Metternich and Neumann strongly advised passed through Brussels, not to come to England and Koller tried to persuade him to cut off his moustaches. But he would not shave, and he think that his presence in England could turn pu in his favour.
I explained to Koller that the people of this with respect, and even with kindness, their bitter enemies when duty or necessity brings them here. received no insult at Plymouth, Soult was re enthusiasm, Metternich, Louis Philippe, and courteous and kind hospitality; but Haynau was no matter wrongly or rightly, in the same Mannings and Tawell, and he ought to have had policemen to go about with him to protect him fro indignation of the mob. The Austrian Governm think that the proceedings at Barclay's were got Trencke, formerly editor of a Liberal paper at Vi exile here, and employed as a clerk in Barclay's

The rivalry between Austria and Prus leadership of Germany was complica that country. On the question of [illegible] German confederation, France and [illegible] understanding. Both Govern- [illegible] that might be produced on the [illegible] Powers by the carrying out of [illegible]

[illegible] had been engaged during the year [illegible] mediation between Denmark and [illegible] interminable Sleswig-Holstein dis- [illegible] of all these events are no longer of [illegible] contents of the following letter fore- [illegible] of 1866:—

F. O.: November 22, 1850.

[illegible]—German affairs are indeed come to a [illegible] The only thing that seems pretty clear is, that [illegible] or less in the wrong. But Prussia seems [illegible] the palm in this respect. Her course has been, [illegible] inconsistent, and irresolute and weak. In [illegible] Sleswig-Holstein question, she has throughout [illegible] the greatest duplicity and bad faith; in regard to [illegible], her only object from beginning to end seems to [illegible] own aggrandisement, which, at moments when [illegible] within her grasp, she had not courage or steadi- [illegible] to pursue. Her partisans try to make out [illegible] between her and Austria is a struggle between [illegible] and arbitrary government; but it is no such [illegible] a conflict between the two leading Powers in [illegible] which should be politically preponderant. We [illegible] had no objection to see Prussia take the first [illegible] contrary, a German Union, embracing all the [illegible], with Prussia at its head, and in alliance with [illegible] separate Power, would have been a very good arrangement; but when the empire was offered to [illegible] King shrank from the hazardous position thus [illegible], and declined to accept it till he should be [illegible] by the Sovereigns. That decided the question, [illegible] certain that the Sovereigns would never [illegible] with such a request. But the empire having [illegible], Prussia ought to have taken at once the [illegible] course, and to have come to an agreement [illegible] reconstructing the German confederation on [illegible] the treaty of 1815, with such modifications as [illegible] of parliaments in Prussia and Austria and all the other States might render necessary. In[illegible] Prussia went on pottering about an Erfurth Union [illegible] never could end in anything but smoke, and then [illegible] deliberately to expose herself to the humiliation [illegible] obliged by military threats to retreat step by step from [illegible] positions she had taken up in regard to almost all [illegible] affairs. All this is lamentable, and is a fresh [illegible] honesty is the best policy. What Austria means to do [illegible] to be seen. The Austrians declare that they mean to [illegible] Parliament of their own, and not to put down constit[illegible] government in any other country. We shall see. [illegible] meanwhile enormous armies have been put into the [illegible] both sides just as winter is setting in, and without any [illegible] gible question to fight about. The only thing that [illegible] ought immediately to do is to send these useless soldiers [illegible] to their stoves and provision stores. In the meanwhile [illegible] on one side and France on the other, notwithstanding [illegible] fair professions, must be inwardly chuckling at seeing [illegible] come down in so short a time from *Einheit* to [illegible] peration and to the brink of civil war.

The Papal aggression and the passing [illegible] Ecclesiastical Titles Bill was now occupying [illegible] attention. Lord Palmerston expounds his views [illegible] question to his brother.

C. G.: January [illegible]

During the month at Christmas that we spent [illegible] lands I broke loose, and, instead of working all day [illegible] my north room and only rushing out at sunset, [illegible] September and October, I took a fling, and went [illegible] days hunting and shooting in the fine of the early [illegible] home, of course, for work earlier than if I had [illegible] sportsman.

Public affairs are going on as well as they can [illegible] time be expected to do. Food has been abundant and [illegible] labouring classes fully employed, and in all respects [illegible] than they have been for a very long period of time [illegible] are greatly reduced, and though farmers complain [illegible] have been generally lowered, yet, all things considered [illegible] the owners nor the occupiers of land have [illegible] to complain. The cheapness of all things [illegible] degree for small diminutions of income [illegible] things are looking better, and rent [illegible] which it has been for some years past. The ... productive, and we shall have a surplus of ... This will not, however, enable us to take ... which will expire this year, and which we ... renewal of. This will produce some trouble- ... I have no doubt of its being carried; we ... in carrying it by many who want particular ... which cannot be repealed or modified if the ... not renewed, because in that case, instead of a ... for, there would be a deficit to provide for. ... produces upwards of five millions.

... aggression question will give us some trouble ... to stormy debates. Our difficulty will be to find ... which shall satisfy reasonable Protestants, ... those principles of liberal toleration which ... to. I think we shall succeed. But all the ... stories of divisions in the Cabinet on this or any ... are pure inventions, wholly devoid of any foun- ... Pope, I hear, and the people about him by whom ... he is guided, affect to treat lightly the excitement ... measures have produced in this country, and they ... the clamour as a thing got up by the Church—a ... They deceive themselves; the feeling is ... intense all through the nation, and the sensible ... themselves lament what has been done.

... itself, in truth, is little or nothing, and does not ... irritation. What has goaded the nation is the ... insolent and ostentatious, in which it has been done. ... have a right to organise their church as they ... If staff officers called Bishops were thought better ... officers called Vicars Apostolic, nobody would have ... or objected to the change if it had been made quietly ... in the bosom of the Church. But what offended— ... all England was the Pope's published Allocution ... announcement of his new dignities. The first ... England as a land of benighted heathens; the ... that the Pope had parcelled out England ... —a thing that only a Sovereign has a right to do ... he, Wiseman, and others were sent, and to be sent, ... those territorial districts, with titles belonging ... could not and would not have been done or ... any other country without the consent of the

... his advisers pretended at first that they had

the consent of the English Government [illegible] November, 1847—*three years ago*; but [illegible] out of that assertion; and then Wiseman [illegible] a mere statement that the intention was [illegible] in 1847, and that he said nothing and made no [illegible]

Now even this did not take place; and if [illegible] of such importance, silence cannot be construed [illegible] Moreover, Minto was at Rome upon quite another [illegible] had no instructions on this subject; and if the Pope [illegible] the consent of the English Government, he should [illegible] for it; and not having asked for it or obtained it, [illegible] not quote it as a justification of his course. He [illegible] three years have asked the question; and there was [illegible] tunity specially of doing so, for in August, when Wiseman [illegible] on the point of setting out for Rome to settle all [illegible] he wrote to ask an interview with John Russell, and [illegible] him more than half an hour; that was the time to [illegible] tained from the head of the Government himself what [illegible] be thought of the cut-and-dry measure; but not a [illegible] Wiseman say on the matter, and his excuse for his silence [illegible] is that he did not then think the measure likely to be [illegible] mediate. But he must have thought it as near as the [illegible] supposed to have thought it in November 1847, when he [illegible] tends to have spoken to Minto about it (which, however, [illegible] did not); and so far from Wiseman not supposing the [illegible] to be near, we know full well that the Pope's excuse, [illegible] forward, is that Wiseman pressed the measure upon him, [illegible] he knew England and the English people, and would [illegible] answerable that it would go off smoothly.

We must bring in a measure; the country would [illegible] satisfied without some legislative enactment. We shall [illegible] it as gentle as possible. The violent Protestant party [illegible] object to it for its mildness, and will endeavour to [illegible] further. The Pope might help us to resist that pressure [illegible] would do certain things that would allay public feeling, [illegible] instance, if he would disclaim any pretension to govern [illegible] bishops any but the Catholics in the districts to which [illegible] bishops are appointed. It sounds almost childish to [illegible] such a truism; but many people, forgetting that he [illegible] more claim jurisdiction or authority over Protestants [illegible] the winds and waves or the tides of the ocean, and [illegible] the words of the Allocution and of Wiseman's [illegible] imagine that he does, and some public disclaimer [illegible] useful. Again, offence has been taken at the [illegible]

...instead of appointing an Archbishop ... Bishops of this or that place, the Pope ... Archbishops and Bishops for the gover... Catholics (the word *Roman* is essential) in ..., &c., as the case might be, their epis... continuing to be places in *partibus infi*... measures, if adopted by the Pope, would ... storm, and restore harmony between Protes... But what would complete the calm would ... Wiseman to say that he would not go on ... advice at Rome. The departure of the ... the pledge of restored peace. If you should ... by chance of meeting the nuncio, you ... these suggestions; not as demands made by ... Government; not as a commission given you from ..., but as what you know to be, and what ... consequence of communications made to you from ... may say that what you tell him is quite pri... ..., to be made known by him to his Court ... may think best, but that you throw out the sug... most friendly spirit, and that you know that the ...ernment are most desirous of maintaining for the ...olics in the Queen's dominions all the freedom and ... rights which existing laws have conferred

...almerston was always very earnest in his view ...essity for England being strong in her home ... land as well as by sea. Sir John Burgoyne ...ay, 1850, written a Memorandum which called ... to our deficiencies in this respect. Lord ...n sends it to the Premier with the following ...ons:—

... you, to keep and ponder over at your leisure, a copy ...randum on our want of national defence, drawn up ...n Burgoyne, and lent to me some months ago by ...esey. It is worth reading, though it is only a repe... ...e opinions entertained and expressed by all men who ... war is, either by sea or by land. But I am well ... it is almost as difficult to persuade the people of this ... provide themselves with the means of defence as it ... them to defend themselves without those means, and that although our internal condition may still be of surrounding nations,' yet we have neither

> 'Hearts resolved nor hands prepared,
> The blessings we enjoy to guard.'

He also writes to Sir Charles Wood, then C of the Exchequer, about fortifications:—

C. G.: January

My dear Wood,—I am glad to hear that you me £8,000 for going on with the fortifications at Pen addition to what is to be taken for the detached ou Portsmouth; but could you not take a sum, howeve make a beginning, for similar defences at Plymout goyne will tell you that Plymouth Dockyard is, if po more exposed than the Portsmouth yard to be de shells from a small force landed in its neighbourhood. or 10,000 men were landed at Whitesand Bay, or thereabouts, they might establish mortar batteries opposite Plymouth yard without, I believe, being from any existing work. Cronstadt, Sebastopol, C Brest, and Toulon bristle with guns, and are secure a attack by sea or land. Our yards, full of valuable and containing the elements of our naval defence indeed pretty safe from any attack by sea, but st mercy of an enemy on the land. The French pro 'C'est l'occasion qui fait le larron;' and the more th shall see that our most important points are safe aga prise, the greater will be our chances of continued session of Parliament is always full of unforeseen an seeable accidents; and it would be a good thing, in of our official life being unexpectedly cut short, that leave behind us indisputable proofs that we had ma beginnings for the full protection of all our great dock

C. G.: January

As to Head's[1] book, I own I think it [illegible] deserving of the most serious consideration of every man, and more especially of all those who are charged destinies of the country. I mean those parts of his detail the aggressive means of Powers who may [illegible] and the slenderness of our own means of defence [illegible] the ruinous effects of even the temporary [illegible]

[1] Sir Francis Head.

As to his remedy, the amount of he proposes is not to be attained; but I will have done its full duty to the organised some dormant but partially nature of a militia or *landwehr*, which under arms in a fortnight or three weeks to of one hundred thousand in the two breaking out of a war. Every other to be called a Power has this kind of Austria, Prussia, the United States. but merely because she keeps up a war estab- of peace; though she, too, has in time of regular army on furlough. England alone, establishment inadequate for the defence of the invasion, has no means of increasing her defen- the outbreak of a war except by the tardy enlistment into the line, or the equally of passing a Bill to repeal the Act suspending through the tedious and complicated operation of assembling, clothing, arming, officering, and army of men who never handled a musket or fixed Then we are told that in a moment of crisis the rise *like one man*—a mere bitterly sarcastic a nation armed, as the English would be, with and pitchforks, would be against a disciplined army formidable as *one man* would be.

May 1 the Great Exhibition of all Nations was Hyde Park. Lord Palmerston went to the and gives an account of the scene. England full of refugees, cast upon her shores by con- revolutions, and their presence had inspired who were responsible for the maintenance of order anxiety.

C. G.: May 2, 1851.

Normanby,—Many thanks for your friendly good 'La Patrie.' Such articles, however intrinsically certainly not to appear in newspapers known to be communication with the Government; but Léon I know, always had a dislike to me, or at least to doings; and as to Guizot, I make allowances for the rancour of his feelings toward me. Winners laugh, but pardon.

N

But yesterday is the topic of thought and [illegible] everybody in London. It was indeed a [illegible] England; and the way in which the royal [illegible] was calculated to inspire humility into the [illegible] sentatives of foreign Governments and to strike [illegible] breasts of those, if any such there be, who may [illegible] confusion in this country. There must have [illegible] million than any other number of people who [illegible] post themselves as they could to see some part of [illegible] and Mayne, the head of the police, told me he [illegible] were about thirty-four thousand in the glass buildi[illegible] Queen, her husband, her eldest son and daughter, [illegible] selves in full confidence to this multitude, with no [illegible] than one of honour and the accustomed supply of [illegible] constables, to assist the crowd in keeping order [illegible] selves. Of course there were in reserve, in prope[illegible] ample means of repressing any disorder if any [illegible] attempted; but nothing was brought out and [illegible] what I have mentioned; and it was impossible for [illegible] guests of a lady's drawing-room to have conducted [illegible] with more perfect propriety than did this sea of huma[illegible]

The royal party were received with continued [illegible] as they passed through the parks and round the [illegible] House; and it was also very interesting to witness [illegible] greeting given to the Duke of Wellington. I was [illegible] him and Anglesey, within two of them, during the [illegible] round the building, and he was accompanied by an [illegible] running fire of applause from the men and waving of [illegible] chiefs and kissing of hands from the women, who [illegible] pathway of march during the three-quarters of an hour [illegible] took us to march round.

The building itself is far more worth seeing than [illegible] in it, though many of its contents are worthy of [illegible] You ought to contrive to run over to take a look [illegible] its final close.

Though this first day of the campaign has passed [illegible] of course we shall have to keep a watchful eye during [illegible] four months upon those who might be disposed to [illegible] tage, for purposes of mischief, of the congregation [illegible] in London; but with the means we have of making [illegible] pay dearly for any such attempt, I do not [illegible] hension as to the result of any schemes they [illegible]

The Ministry had been in rather [illegible]

the last twelvemonth. Lord Palmerston's the Greek debate had acted as a decided health was feeble. On February 18, of only eleven against a Protectionist Mr. Disraeli's; and a week later it was n a motion for the extension of the county Accordingly, on February 22, Lord John igned. Lord Stanley tried in vain to form Lord John in vain tried to form a the Peelites; so it ended in the Whig back just as it was before, though for one more year—the usual fate of come back after a defeat. Lord Palmer- brother :—

C. G.: April 3, 1851.

politically, are looking tolerably well, and I reckon ourselves pretty secure of remaining in year. It would be ridiculous for us to resign failures to form another Government, unless Commons were to pass a vote of censure or a confidence, and that they are not likely to do. some changes forced upon us in our financial for the Budget; but that will not much signify. papers exulted greatly at our fall; they will afterwards the melancholy news of our re- and Molesworth are full of the abominable by the Neapolitan and Roman Governments. the Neapolitan is a *Governo infernale*, and that, and a Christian, he feels it his duty to make has seen of its proceedings. Both of them say wrong last year in their attacks on my foreign did not know the truth. This is satisfactory concerned, though very unsatisfactory as regards

Bill will be carried in spite of the members, who are driven on by the over the Irish electors. But the feeling the Catholics is deep, strong, and general, and his priests have lately done has Catholic cause. All these exposures, moreover, about Miss Talbot and Mr. Connelly, [illegible] throw great discredit on the Catholic priesthood.[1]

I went one day to hear Gavazzi's harangue [illegible] abuses of the Catholic Church. He spoke in [illegible] hour and a half to several hundred hearers, with [illegible] and effect.

Soon after this, two letters, addressed to [illegible] Aberdeen by Mr. Gladstone on the subject of the [illegible] prosecutions and the State prisons of the Neapolitan Government, were published in the form of a pamphlet. The effect produced by these letters was very great. The high character and position of the author gave authority to his narrative of facts, attested as they were by personal observation. He asserted that [illegible] numbers of innocent and untried men were confined in the prisons of Naples for alleged political offences under circumstances of great barbarity. Lord Palmerston, in the House of Commons, paid an emphatic tribute to the course taken by Mr. Gladstone. He added that, concurring with the author of these letters that the influence of public opinion in Europe might have some effect in setting such matters right, he had sent copies of the publication to the British Ministers at the various Courts of Europe, directing them to give copies to each Government.

When the Neapolitan envoy in London saw the account of what Lord Palmerston had said in the House about the Gladstone letters, he wrote forwarding a pamphlet which had been written to order by a [illegible] Macfarlane, in reply to Mr. Gladstone, and requested Lord Palmerston to send it round also to the several

[1] 'The feeling is more political than religious. The people of [illegible] country bear with great composure mere differences in [illegible] opinions. They are too much accustomed to such differences among Protestants themselves to look with any hatred on such differences when exhibited between Protestants and Catholics; but the [illegible] nation are deeply impressed with the feeling that Catholic [illegible] and civil and political freedom are incompatible. The history of [illegible] country teaches them that opinion, and it is that chord which [illegible] made to vibrate from one end of the land to the other.'—*Lord Palmerston to Mr. Shiel, April* 3, 1851.

[illegible] Lord Palmerston declined being [illegible] circulation to a document which he [illegible] only a tissue of bare assertion and [illegible] mixed up with coarse ribaldry and [illegible] of public men and political parties.' [illegible], that as Prince Castelcicala had ad- [illegible] on the subject, he felt compelled to say

[illegible]'s letters to Lord Aberdeen present an afflict- [illegible] a system of illegality, injustice, and cruelty, [illegible] the officers and agents of the Government in the [illegible] Naples, such as might have been hoped would not [illegible] in any European country at the present day; and [illegible] which has been received upon these matters [illegible] other sources leads, unfortunately, to the conclusion [illegible] Gladstone by no means overstated the various evils [illegible] describes. But Mr. Gladstone's letters were evidently [illegible] published not, as the pamphlet which you have sent [illegible], in a spirit of hostility to the King of Naples, or [illegible] adverse to the parliamentary and monarchical [illegible] which his Sicilian Majesty has granted to his sub- [illegible] has confirmed by his royal oath. Mr. Gladstone's [illegible], on the contrary, to have been the friendly purpose [illegible] public attention to, and of directing the force of [illegible] upon, abuses which, if allowed to continue, [illegible] necessarily sap the foundations of the Neapolitan [illegible], and prepare the way for those violent revulsions [illegible] resentments produced by a deep sense of long-con- [illegible] and wide-spread injustice are sure sooner or later to [illegible]. It might have been hoped that the Neapolitan [illegible] would have received those letters in the spirit in [illegible] they manifestly were written, and would have set to [illegible] earnestly and effectually to correct those manifold and [illegible] abuses to which their attention has thus been drawn. It [illegible] that, by such a course, the Neapolitan Government [illegible] more to frustrate the designs of revolutionists, and to [illegible] the monarchical institutions of their country, than [illegible] effected by the most vigorous proceedings of the most [illegible] Minister of Police.

[illegible] he thus addressed the Neapolitan Minister, [illegible] follows to his brother:—

Broadlands: September 7, 1851.

Your account of the effect produced by Gladstone's pamphlet is highly interesting and curious. The Neapolitan Government will not have been much pleased and edified by my answer to Castelcicala about Macfarlane's pamphlet, nor would they be much gratified if they were to receive a collection of all the articles which have appeared on this subject in the various newspapers in England and in Germany.

I still hope that the discussion may do some good and excite some shame in their minds; one might almost hope it would work some change in their conduct.

The French, as you say, defend as well as they can the Neapolitan Government; but they every now and then let out things which undermine their defence. Walewski told Milnes the other day, as a proof of the goodness of heart of the King of Naples, that at his, Walewski's, request the King had at one time promised to set free three hundred prisoners against whom no charge or no proof had been established. 'How grateful [said Milnes] these men must have been; did they not come to thank you for their release?' 'Why [said Walewski], you see, after the King had made the promise, the chief of the police came to him and said that if the men were set free, he could not answer for the King's life; and so you see the men were not set free.'

I sent you a copy of my answer to Castelcicala to be given to the Neapolitan Government, because I thought that my friend the Prince would probably not send them exactly a correct copy, but would probably leave out the words about the King's oath.

This 'answer to Castelcicala' was kept back from the King by his Ministers. Lord Holland, writing from Naples, about two months afterwards, says:—[1]

The Ministers keep back from the King any despatches that are disagreeable. He had only heard of your answer to Castelcicala, but had never seen it till last Wednesday. It had only been described to him as 'une della solite impertinenze di Lord Palmerston'—one of his usual impertinences! Sabatelli read it to him; it made a deep impression on him, and he said that it was a most important and 'bien redigé' document.

To his brother, still British Minister at Naples, he again writes about Neapolitan affairs.

[1] Lord Holland to Lord Palmerston, October 13, 1851.

Brocket: November 6, 1851.

... you give of the state of things in Naples! ... of things last! But the French—at least ...—are all for the Neapolitan Government, ... general spite and hatred to us; and a cousin of ... blackballed the other day at a club in Paris ... the same name as the writer of the letters to ...

...'s recall, I am neither glad nor sorry. He ... mannered man; but I do not suspect him of ... beyond a certain average amount, and he gave ... As to Casini, we shall probably be able to ... ; and I believe it is rather useful than not ... of other countries should be sent here; it ... the effect of somewhat modifying their violence.

...'s reception must have been gall and wormwood to ... and to the Absolutists generally. His reception ... have been much better if he had not published ... that absurdly violent production at Marseilles. But ... remarked that at none of the meetings which have ... to greet him have any gentlemen appeared except ..., and, on one occasion, John Abel Smith. He is ... the United States on the 14th; and I believe that, ... there some little time, he intends to return here. ... he may stay there longer than he now proposes to ... avowed Republican theories of government will find ... there than here.

... unpleasant accounts from the Cape; but these are ... and partial checks, and Sir Henry Smith, when he ... said that as soon as the reinforcements then on their ... have reached him, he should be quite able to deal ... the Caffres, and he would get a battalion more than he ... Still, however, this war costs us some valuable lives, ... absorb a large part of our surplus revenue.

... see any rock ahead which is likely to wreck the ...; we shall have some difficulty, perhaps, about the ... of suffrage next session, but I understand, privately, ... Derby finds himself so liable to repeated attacks of ... he begins to be less desirous than he used to be to ... Prime Minister. Perhaps also the possession of a large ... him as much employment as he wants, and he may ... to be able to make flashy speeches now and then ... of Lords.

I fear that Panizzi will not have been able, even with the assistance of Aumale, to persuade the King of Naples to change his system towards his wretched subjects. Really, such sovereigns as those who rule over Naples and Greece are enough to make men Republicans.[1]

The Ionian Islands had recently received a new and more liberal constitution. With the enlarged opportunities for agitation thereby acquired the Ionian Parliament had become unmanageable, and attempted to pass a resolution in favour of annexation to Greece. Sir Henry Ward, the British Commissioner, had much trouble in keeping matters quiet. Lord Palmerston corresponds with him on the subject, and favours the retention of Corfu, whatever might be done with the other islands. He naturally saw that it would be useless to hand over Corfu to any great Power that was not a great maritime Power. Hence, when on one occasion the question was raised of giving it to Austria, he summarised his opinion by saying, 'To give Corfu to Austria would be like entrusting a duckling to a respectable old hen.'

Broadlands: December 26, 1850.

My dear Ward,—I have received yours of the 13th, with the co of the resolution for union with Greece. If we wished reall py punish the Ionians, we should grant this request and handy them over to the constitutional Government of King Otho. But this would be too severe a chastisement upon a nation for the sins of a few. There is, as you probably well know, a foolish and pedantic notion among some of the clerks in the Colonial Office that it would be better to *get rid* (as they term it) of the Ionian Islands. This notion was, I believe, first taken up by Stephen,[2] an excellent and very learned, but exceedingly wrong-headed, man. My opinion is very different. I consider Corfu as a very important position for Mediterranean interests, in the event of a war, and I hold that it would be a great act of folly for us to give it up. It could not be held permanently by any Power that was not strong at sea, and

[1] This reminds one of Madame de Coigny, who, when asked by the Prince of Wales (afterwards George IV.), 'Pourquoi donc êtes-vous démocrate?' replied, 'Mais c'est que j'ai vécu tant avec des [illegible]'

[2] Sir James Stephen.

...or later, fall into the hands of Russia ... of which it could belong without much

... later on, to the same:—

F. O.: February 18, 1851.

...have no visit from a Russian fleet this year. We ... possible terms with Russia, and she will do ... to disoblige us. I should even doubt her being ... of the disturbances which give you trouble, though ... quite in keeping with her standing policy to have ... by money and intrigues. But just at the present ... Austria is more likely to have done us an ill turn. ...berg and the Vienna Camarilla, Archduchess So... hate us with the bitterest hatred for the part ... English Government, Parliament, and people have ... the last three years about Italy, Hungary, and ... these worthies would be glad to revenge them... sympathy in favour of their insurgents, by creat... ...tion anywhere and anyhow against British authority; ... the Austrian Government is nearly bankrupt, yet, ...spendthrifts, it can always bring out money for its ...

... the plots which were going on, he says to the ...missioner:—

C. G.: November 19, 1851.

...nspirators may be confident—as all conspirators are ... that the day of their triumph is approaching; so say ... Red Republicans in England; but those days of ... ll recede as time advances, just as the mirage of the ...es before the slow march of the caravan. It is well, ... be on our guard, for it is only over-confidence and ...overnors than can give such ragamuffins a chance of ... am amused at the notion that I am to be accused of ...ted and paid for the recently attempted inroad upon ... Islands. I remember to have heard that, in former ...mbridge, it was the fashion for the young men to ...her's rooms, that is, to turn everything topsy-turvy; ...lish fellow got drunk and mobbed his own rooms, ...ble to get at a friend's. I am still, however, sober ... to play such pranks with our own house. I daresay ...Government is very angry with me for having shown them up about robbery to all the Go[illegible] no doubt they have had admonitions ever [illegible] ments which pretended to us that they would [illegible] meddle in the matter. The more angry they feel, [illegible] more likely it is that they will bestir themselves [illegible] matters; still, I fear that as long as Otho sits like [illegible] on the Greek throne, no Greek progress will be [illegible] career of improvement which the Greek nation is [illegible] mately to run.

For my part, I should not object to an [illegible] which Corfu should be annexed to the British [illegible] other islands added to Greece. Corfu is an important [illegible] and naval post, and ought never to be abandoned by [illegible] other islands might go to Greece without inconve[illegible] should think, to us, though at present such a transfer [illegible] attended with much inconvenience to them. No such [illegible] ment, however, could be made without the formal [illegible] of all the Powers who were parties to the Treaty of [illegible] which the Seven Island State was placed under our [illegible] and it is not very likely that France, Austria, and [illegible] would consent to give us Corfu; and perhaps Russia [illegible] fancy any addition to the Greek State, though she may [illegible] keep up a disturbing agitation in the Ionian Islands. [illegible] however, is a speculation in the clouds; but whenever you [illegible] to me again, let me know what you think of it.

Lord Palmerston, however, modified his views [illegible] on, and, in 1862, cordially agreed to hand over all [illegible] Ionian Islands to the new kingdom of Greece [illegible] Greeks would choose a king approved of by [illegible] which they accordingly did. The neutrality [illegible] islands was, however, to be declared by the Great [illegible] and the fortifications of Corfu demolished, both [illegible] conditions were observed.

Meanwhile things in France were hurrying [illegible] crisis: Lord Palmerston watching the game, [illegible] concealing his preference for the cause of the [illegible]

C. G.: November [illegible]

My dear Normanby,—Your accounts of what [illegible] Paris are very full and satisfactory as conve[illegible] Satisfactory as to details which they announce [illegible] But it seems to me that Louis Napoleon is [illegible] day. I have always thought that the best thing both for France and for person at present competent to be at France; and if Louis Napoleon should end by do not see that we need regret it, as far are concerned. The family of Bourbon hostile to England, and those members have owed us the greatest personal and poli- have, perhaps, in their hearts hated us the we gain by substituting Henry V. or the the race of Buonaparte? At all events, I *laudo manentem.* If he should fall, we endeavour to be on equally good terms with might be the official organs of the French have no wish to see him fall. If success is any he has not as yet played his cards ill; and which he has done, and which have been repre- have perhaps contributed to his success. *Je* was certainly a good declaration, and showed the faintness of heart of those who were trying to If the Bourgraves would fairly say they want a monarchy, one might wish them success; but seem to be ready for that, and yet they want to which, in the present state of affairs, seems the to a monarchy, and the only thing calculated to of order.

the session of 1851 Mr. Cobden renewed his for its object a pacific understanding by a mutual reduction of armaments. took occasion in this debate to vindi- from the charge of being a promoter of war to peace.

that, however little he might think the which Mr. Cobden endeavoured to give effect the best calculated to attain the end he subscribed implicitly to the general ten- views. He first, however, claimed some results of his own policy.

part it has been my lot to take in administering the affairs of this country has shown that in my conduct in any degree inconsistent with the opinions I am now professing; for [illegible] may be the fashion with some persons, in that easy [illegible] jaunty style in which they dismiss public matters [illegible] against modern diplomatic and international [illegible] yet at least I can appeal to facts. I can appeal to [illegible] during the considerable period for which I have been [illegible] for the conduct of the foreign relations of this country, events have happened in Europe of the most [illegible] and attended with great commotions of public feeling [illegible] agitation in the social and political system of the [illegible] although during that period events have happened [illegible] brought the interests of England, I will not say [illegible] but into opposition to the interests of other great and [illegible] nations, yet, at least, the fact is that we have been [illegible] and that not only has peace been preserved [illegible] country and other nations, but there has been no [illegible] war of magnitude between any of the other great [illegible] Europe. If, then, on the one hand, we are taunted [illegible] petually interfering and meddling in the relations [illegible] countries, we ought at least, on the other hand, to [illegible] credit of the fact that that interference and [illegible] been accompanied by the continuance of peace. It is [illegible] that we should be accused, on the one hand, of [illegible] stantly in the transactions of other countries, and at [illegible] time that we should be denied the credit of those [illegible] accompanied that course of policy.

But now a cloud, no bigger at first than [illegible] hand, was growing on the horizon; but, small [illegible] it was fated to burst eventually into the [illegible] So fully recorded are all the details of the [illegible] which Lord Palmerston notes the [illegible] following letter, that they need not be [illegible] but it may be well just to recall their [illegible] had in 1740 obtained from the Sultan '[illegible] securing to the Latin Church in Palestine [illegible] leges in connection with the Holy Shrines. [illegible] date the Greeks, supported by Russia, [illegible] firmans granting them advantages in [illegible] the Latin capitulations. These firmans [illegible] acquiesced in. Suddenly, for no [illegible] French ambassador at Constantinople [illegible] mand that the grants to the Latin ly executed. This was impossible, some of the privileges of the Greek lachrymæ!—Which of the two sets salem should have the keys of certain ther the Latins might have a cupboard the tomb of the Virgin! Such were the convulsed diplomacy on the Bosphorus, nion of the French ambassador, justified force. It is thus clear that the first step France.

merston tries a little oil for the troubled

C. G.: November 25, 1851.

Normanby,—I was in hopes, from the manner in ski had spoken of this Church question between and Russians in Turkey, that the French Govern- quieter view of it than seems to be the case. agreed with me that *le jeu ne vaut pas la chandelle,* would be very unwise for France in the present unsettled state of affairs all over Europe to get rel with Russia and Turkey about a matter in itself very trifling importance; and he quite admitted that had gone much too far, and he seemed to agree with is a discussion which might prudently be adjourned, allowed, in the Turkish fashion, to sleep till a fitter As to the merits of the case, I am not able to state or opinion, for Stratford Canning has kept studiously the discussion, and has only from time to time the general outline of the points at issue. But the in which you put it to the President is the just way it. Here are a few Catholics in Turkey, and many Greeks; here is a colossal power close on the Sultan's here is France a long way off; here are fourteen or istian churches in Asia Minor, of which the greater in the possession of Greek Christians and the mber in the hands of the Catholics; and the French insists that the Sultan shall, by making a half-and- ision of these holy places between Greeks and give a division unequal as with reference to the of the two Christian communities, disgust a his own subjects, and offend a powerful neighbour who can plague and annoy him in a hundred ways beyond the reach of France to protect him. This unreasonable course to pursue, unless really the obj were of essential national importance; but if I there can be but very few Frenchmen locally inter matter; the few who are in the Levant must be in some convents—men who have abandoned their and never think of returning to it. The real object President has in view must of course be to get favo Catholic clergy in France; but he should serious whether he is not paying too dear for that addition from them by engaging France in a great quarre small a thing. But suppose he goes on and sends a Dardanelles, what is that fleet to do? It must eithe the Dardanelles or force them and make its way stantinople, in order to give the law at the cannon's the Seraglio point. Now a blockade of the Dardan course, a very easily accomplished thing. The F would take up its position within the outer castles Bay, where Parker anchored, and it could there prevent any vessel from going up or coming down maritime trade up and down those straits communic the Danube, with Odessa, with Taganrog, and with is a matter of most important interest to many Europe, and especially to us English; and an inter that trade, without any real and adequate necess raise an immense outcry against France all over even in America, for it must be borne in mind blockade would differ essentially from blockades In ordinary cases, when you blockade a port, you bl port, and that port or country only; but here th would apply, not merely to Constantinople and Tur but to the southern ports of Russia and to the Danub countries; and if the French should find themselv as probably in point of justice and international would be—to let the Russian flag pass and repass blockade of the Turkish ports would of course to a nullity. But, supposing they were to try Dardanelles, that would be an operation not to without much loss if attempted by ships alone. have been greatly strengthened of late years, current downward to the Mediterranean going upwards to long-continued fire from

ed force to disembark and take the
would make the operation one of time.
the Russians would not be idle, and
they would probably contrive to send succour
if it should so happen that, by reason of
and resistances the attempt should fail,
nt would have lost caste in Europe and
itself ridiculous; and, moreover, the French
would have done more than Russia unaided could
to counteract and upset the policy which
have hitherto pursued in regard to Turkey
great object of which has been to foster the
of Turkey and to get her out of the hands and
Russian Government.

proceeded to offer the mediation of Eng-
the quarrel—not as a partisan of either
a sincere well-wisher to all three powers,
earnest promoter of peace on earth. But a
he finds that Russia was not in a humour
offices.'[1]

despatches lately received from Stratford Canning,
estion about the churches in the Levant is still under
and consideration at Constantinople, and that there
o pretence at present for any violent proceeding on
f France. But from a little conversation I have had
bject with Brunnow, I am inclined to think that
uld not be disposed to accept our good offices if they
red. The Turkish Government, Canning says, seems
an to the side of France. But really and truly this
l fitter for times long gone by than for the days in
live.

ugh after the *coup d'état* at Paris the French
was violently renewed, in the meanwhile, on
f the blow and in the uncertainty of its result,
was left free to act for himself by the tem-
moval of the instrument of coercion.

C. G.: December 1, 1851.

ar Canning,—Lavallette may represent his going away
f absence as a mark of the displeasure of the French

[1] To Lord Normanby, November 28.

Government at the conduct of the Porte on the question about the holy buildings, but I happen to know that he has had leave of absence sent him because the French Government thought he had gone too far, and they considered his temporary absence on leave as likely to be the best way of letting the question drop down into its proper proportions. Say nothing about this unless you find Reshid frightened, and then you may whisper it gently and secretly into his ear.

But official mediation, though it may frequently succeed in modifying public demands and political objects, cannot equally influence personal aims and ambitions. After the crisis at Paris an Emperor in France confronted an Emperor in Russia. The first had to vindicate his newly-won position in the eyes of Europe and of his own country. The second had a long score of checks to wipe out, which to his violent temperament had been most galling. It was not likely that under such circumstances the questions at issue would be allowed to drop. Before, however, they had ripened into a war in which England was involved, Lord Palmerston, as we shall now see, had been driven from the direction of our external affairs.

CHAPTER VII.

GOVERNMENT—EXPLANATIONS IN THE HOUSE OF COMMONS.

Cassio, I love thee,
... be officer of mine—*Othello*, Act. II. Sc. 3.

... arrive at a critical period in the lives of two ... eminent statesmen of their day. Lord John ... from the traditional recollections of his family, ... course of his own studies, and from the ten- ... his own opinions, was the statesman whom the ... party of his own time most trusted in domestic ... Lord Palmerston, on the other hand, from ... experience, decided character, and enlarged views, ... the confidence of the same party in foreign ...

... statesmen were said to have their faults; and ... then a portion of their general followers broke ... one or from the other. But, on the whole, ... each in his own specialty, there were no men in ... country to match them; and they had hitherto, ... not always agreeing, stood firmly together. ... circumstances had of late tended to dissolve this ... Lord John Russell, not only as Prime Minister, ... leader of the Liberal party, felt himself to be ... not only with great authority, but great re- ... , and was not unfrequently reproached by ... of his colleagues, who, without considering our ... policy in its general aspect, were prone to criti- ... , for allowing the Foreign Office too much

[1] To Lord Normanby, November 28.

independence. On the other hand, Lord Palmerston, who had acquired a complete mastery over the business of his department, who always acted on a thorough conviction that his views were undeniably right, and who refrained from any interference in the internal policy of the country, was disposed to think that very great latitude within the sphere of his own attributes should be allowed to him. His notion was that a Foreign Minister ought to be strictly bound to pursue the policy of the Cabinet he belonged to, but that he ought to be left free to follow out that policy in the ordinary details of his office, without having every despatch he wrote submitted to criticism and comment. There is this, moreover, to be said, that whereas in home affairs nothing important is done without the decision of a Cabinet, and the leader in Parliament has only to explain the resolutions of the Cabinet, in foreign affairs a Minister is called upon every day of the week and at any time to write and speak to foreign Governments, or their representatives, on current business. If he could not do this with a certain degree of promptitude and freedom, he would lose all weight and influence with his own agents and with the agents of other Powers.

If, then, there is to be a Minister of Foreign [illegible] fit for his post, he must have the thorough con[illegible] of the Premier, and act as if he had it.

Lord Palmerston especially required this; [illegible] because he held an important post in a Whig [illegible] not being a Whig; and, second, because his [illegible] that of constantly maintaining the dignity, po[illegible] prestige of England unimpaired—was not only [illegible] constant attention, but, necessarily, of constant [illegible]

Nor was this all: Lord Palmerston had no[illegible] to satisfy Lord John Russell, he had also to [illegible] Sovereign under whom Lord John held his [illegible] Foreign policy is that policy in which Sove[illegible] are thus brought into competition with [illegible] take the most interest. The Prince Consor[illegible] Her Majesty lived on such terms of [illegible] dered her application to him on questions of importance a matter of course, was not only a Prince of considerable ability, but one who gave a minute and scrupulous attention to any business on which he was consulted. He was naturally slow and cautious of judgment; and although his opinions were conscientiously and entirely directed towards English objects, he had not entirely an English mind; and in a German gentleman (Baron Stockmar) much in his confidence, and who deserved, from his great knowledge and abilities, to be so, he had for adviser a man who, though well qualified to have taken a place amongst the first statesmen in Europe, was clearly no admirer of popular or Parliamentary control over foreign affairs, which he regarded as the special concerns of royal and imperial minds.

Sufficient has thus been said to show that the royal authority was likely to be exercised in our foreign relations, and that the decided views which Lord Palmerston was accustomed to form or be disposed at times to carry out, and the strength of the language in which he often embodied those views, jarred at times with the disposition towards more consideration and [illegible]ation at Windsor. More caution, more deliberation was required of him; and, in fact, Lord John Russell, with a double view, I am quite ready to suppose, of paying due deference to the Crown and of [illegible] his colleague, made Lord Palmerston a communication in 1850 to this effect. Such restrictions [illegible] not be agreeable to the person on whom they were imposed, and, though conformable with the spirit [illegible] Constitution, were hardly compatible with the [illegible] and practical despatch of business which every [illegible] complicating and increasing, and which fre[illegible] required for a successful issue the transmitting [illegible] immediate reply. During the discussions about [illegible] marriages Lord Palmerston lost three weeks [illegible] a communication from Guizot, by having [illegible] backwards and forwards while the Court [illegible] engaged in a cruise on the Western Coast.

Guizot, in his subsequent notes and despatch always throwing this delay in his face; but his was tied, and he was obliged to accept the re silence.

It is not necessary to discuss here the exact tutional position of the Crown in these matters, that was not really at issue on the occasion to reference is about to be made. It will suffice phatically repudiate the doctrine which has be cently approved in certain anonymous quarter the Head of the State is entrusted in a special with the decisions upon foreign affairs, and to for a free people a voice in their foreign equ in their domestic concerns. But much has als said and written lately about the share whi Sovereign takes, or ought to take, in the daily of our foreign negotiations. The truth is that, pliant minister and under ordinary circumstan Crown has very great opportunities for impressin foreign affairs that tone and direction which the moment, desires. Even when an importan ence between Crown and Cabinet on a ques general policy has disappeared, by the former y to the representations of the latter, there still to the Sovereign many ways of influencing the of negotiations in accordance with his original Draft despatches, embodying the Cabinet policy be sent to him for approval. They may be r accompanied by objections to such and such pa as not fairly representing the decisions arrive by complaints of one paragraph as being too st while another is pronounced too weak. The C may be scattered, as, indeed, it always is during tion of the year; or, if all its members are at ha the occasion may not be deemed by the Prime M and the Foreign Secretary sufficiently grave to w the issue of a summons. The peccant paragrap accordingly recast and a doubtful instead of a cl strong expression of opinion or intention is trans to the foreign Court. Nor is this all: the Secretary of State, in such a supposed case, knows when preparing his draft that it is about to be submitted to a hostile critic—hostile, I mean, in the sense of being adverse to the policy of which he is the exponent—a critic moreover who must be heard and answered, not one who can be met by real or simulated indifference. He begins, therefore, insensibly by a compromise, and prepares, subject to further modification, an already modified version of the views of his Government. How great an influence may be exercised by means of this censorship will be evident to any person conversant with diplomatic language, and therefore aware of the important difference which even a slight alteration may imply.

Now, it is not contended that, on the whole, within its proper limits, the existence of this warning and criticising power, outside of party ranks, is otherwise than beneficial—especially as a good Secretary of State for Foreign Affairs is one of the rarest of our various political species. It is, however, certain that to Lord Palmerston, conscious of his knowledge and patriotism, [illegible] and eager in his aims, and thoroughly confident [illegible] his ways of attaining the end proposed were the [illegible], the delays and obstacles not unfrequently thus [illegible] in his way were most irksome; and in the ardour [illegible] chase he was too often tempted to leap the gate [illegible] than lose the time necessary to stop and open [illegible] It must also be remembered that he had, off and [illegible] the seals of the Foreign Office for a long term [illegible], during the greater part of which he had been [illegible] to be left very much alone. He was, in[illegible] already a veteran in foreign administration at the [illegible] his two able German critics first appeared [illegible] scene. But, whatever opinion may be formed [illegible] independence and promptness of action, his [illegible] rate must he admired, and it is not pos[illegible] who was acquainted with his character [illegible] any colour of disrespect for the Crown.

There had, however, been friction—and its [illegible] effects, though as yet latent, were undoubtedly at work, when there suddenly occurred a [illegible] important phase in the neighbouring kingdom. [illegible] Louis Napoleon, who had been elected President [illegible] French Republic, was in a position that threaten[illegible] and serious complications in that country, [illegible] during the last hundred years, for its vicissitudes [illegible] Prince, at the time of his election, did not pass [illegible] land, where he then resided, for having any [illegible] ability, nor, as it has been said, had he acquired [illegible] a reputation with leading men in France. He [illegible] been willing to connect their fates with his. M. [illegible] Barrot and M. de Tocqueville were the only two [illegible] any reputation who had served under him, and [illegible] these told their friends that it would be impossi[illegible] serve him long, because they knew they co[illegible] satisfy his ambition. M. de Tocqueville ha[illegible] willing to make a compromise, and would have co[illegible] the presidency for life, and a revenue, say, [illegible] position, though inferior, doubtless, to the civi[illegible] an emperor.

The Prince himself had, possibly, at first n[illegible] idea but that of governing France with as much [illegible] as it would accord him. That which, according to [illegible] was said of him by his cousin at the time of his [illegible] prestige is probably near the truth. 'For a [illegible] world thought my cousin an idiot; now they th[illegible] a genius. He was not an idiot, and is not a [illegible] He was not a great man, but he had a fair idea [illegible] a great man should be; and he could in certa[illegible] tions play the part of one. But, at all eve[illegible] talents, whatever they were, had no clear de[illegible] in any visible direction. His conversation, [illegible] natural, was in no wise striking. He could [illegible] an argument; and his written composition[illegible] certainly remarkable, appeared so [illegible] capacity he had otherwise evinced that [illegible] credit for it. His unsuccessful attemp[illegible]

the reign of Louis Philippe had
an opinion of his spirit of enterprise,
of his intellect.
of the thinking classes then either in
considered his reign otherwise than
the longer his power continued, the
those who thought they could cut it
pleased became of it. This impatience
increased. The Assembly had boldly
as his rival, and he had at last found it
name a Parliamentary Ministry.
Palmerston, as far back as January 24, in a
ord Normanby, had given his views of what
oleon's course should be in such a contingency.

s the President I should not trouble myself as to
Assembly supported my Ministers or not, whether
or approved them. I should say to the Assembly
rid of you and you cannot get rid of me, and your
not change my opinions of my own conduct. For
t I am not answerable to you (as long as I keep
law), but to France. My Ministers are acting by
ions, and they are responsible to me and not to you.
t good laws which I propose to you, yours be the
you will not vote money to keep up an army, navy,
overnment, let the nation call you to account for
ing your country; but that which I will not do is
Ministers who shall be your instruments and not

logy of our Constitution in regard to the relation of
Parliament and to the Crown does not hold good
sition of the French Ministers. The Constitutions
ountries are wholly different.

sembly met after the recess in November of
e crisis arrived on December 2, when the
embers of the Opposition were arrested in
, and a purely military rule was established
n appeal to universal suffrage as to the future
t of France.

On December 3, Count Walewski, the French bassador, called upon Lord Palmerston to inform of what had taken place, and in the course of sation Lord Palmerston expressed the view held as to the necessity and advantage for France Europe of the bold and decisive step taken by President.

The following Memorandum, written several later, shows that he was well aware what was on at this moment in England as well as in among those who were seeking to cut short Napo term of power:—

Memorandum of certain Circumstances connected with Coup d'état.

The *coup d'état* took place on Tuesday, December and was known in London by the next day. On We the 3rd, Mr. and Mrs. —— dined with us in Carlton and told me that they had been down to Claremont preceding Friday to visit the Queen Amelie; that they the ladies of the French Court in a great bustle; and told Mrs. —— as a great secret that they were making paquets, as they expected to have to go to Paris at the then next week, that is to say, at the end of the which the *coup d'état* took place.

On the Sunday following, that is to say, on Mr. Borthwick, editor of the 'Morning Post,' came to said he had a communication to make to me which important for me to receive, and which he conside at liberty to make. He said that the day before, Saturday the 6th, General de Rumigny, attached to Court, had come to him and said that as he, Mr. had been civil and attentive to the ex-Royal Family, Rumigny) had been desired to say to him that, useful to his paper, he should have daily accounts tary operations that were about to commence France; that the Prince de Joinville and the were gone to Lille to take the command of troops the President; that the Royal Family had suade the Prince de Joinville from this step, that, finding him determined on doing so, had said, 'My brother is a sailor, he knows [illegible]; I am a soldier, I will go with him and share his [illegible] fortune.' Mr. Borthwick said he had declined the [illegible] communications, as he did not wish his paper to be considered the organ of the Orleans family; and as the communication had not been made to him under the condition of [illegible], he came at once to tell me of it.

I immediately wrote to Sir George Grey, then Home Secretary, to ask him to make inquiry through the detachment of police stationed at Claremont for the protection of the [illegible] Family, to know whether all the French princes were [illegible], that is to say, those who were in England. I said that General de Rumigny or Borthwick must have made a mistake in [illegible] D'Aumale, because he was then at Naples, and it [illegible] the Duc de Nemours who had gone with Joinville.

In the course of the afternoon I received from Sir G. Grey a [illegible] that both Nemours and Joinville were still at Claremont. That Joinville had been several times in London in the [illegible] of this week, and was that day at Claremont. That [illegible] had been very ill for several days, and had been confined to his room, and nobody had seen him but his medical [illegible], who visited him twice a day. This report at once [illegible] that Joinville was off, as I afterwards heard was the [illegible]. He went as far as Ostend, but found that the attempt [illegible] succeed, and he came back again. I believe the [illegible] of Lille had been changed. This confirmed the story [illegible] Joinville, but left unexplained the statement as to [illegible]. But some days afterwards I received a letter [illegible] brother, Minister at Naples, written before the news [illegible] d'état had reached Naples, saying that the Duc and [illegible] d'Aumale had received alarming accounts of the [illegible] of the ex-Queen of France, and that in consequence [illegible] the Duke had suddenly set off for England. That two [illegible] afterwards the Duchesse d'Aumale had received better [illegible], and she regretted that her husband had not waited a [illegible] longer, as he would then have been spared a fatiguing [illegible] in the depth of winter.

[illegible] statement confirmed the whole of General de Rumigny's [illegible] D'Aumale had evidently, by preconcerted arrange[illegible] Naples to meet Joinville on a given day at a given [illegible] proved that there had been a plot long proposed [illegible] the President.

[illegible] fortnight or three weeks afterwards Count Lav[illegible] Minister in London, went to Claremont.

to visit the Princesse de Joinville, who is a Bra
said he found her *toute eplorée* at the turn of affai
and that she said it was most afflicting: *et pour n
être à Paris le* 20!

All this clearly proves that if the President h
when he did, he would himself have been knocked

P.,

On the same day as his conversation
Walewski Lord Palmerston wrote privat
Normanby as follows:—

C. G.: Decem

Even we here, who cannot be supposed to know
people at Paris did about what was going on am
bonists, cannot be surprised that Louis Napoleo
blow at the time which he chose for it; for it
known here that the Duchess of Orleans was p
called to Paris this week with her younger son to
new period of Orleans dynasty. Of course the
an inkling of what was passing, and, if it is true
our newspapers, that Changarnier was arrested a
in the morning in council with Thiers and others
good reason to believe, what is also asserted, that th
had a stroke prepared which was to be struck
President that very day, and that, consequently,
the principle that a good thrust is often the b
have reason to think, because I have heard it
quarters, that the President has been sometimes
from your social intimacy with the Burgrave p
political sympathies were more directed toward
towards him. Of course a Minister or Ambassad
expected to adapt his social relations to the par
the Government to which he is accredited, but if
that personal friendships and private and social
him into frequent communication with persons
to the Government, it is the more necessary fo
care to destroy in the mind of the Government
hension which this circumstance might give
have no doubt that you have been careful

[illegible] Constitution, which you say in your [illegible] is habitual to Englishmen, that respect [illegible] equitable laws framed under a Constitution [illegible], and consecrated by its antiquity and by [illegible] long years of happiness which the nation [illegible] it; but it is scarcely a proper application of [illegible] require them to be directed to the day-before-[illegible] which the scatter-brained heads of Marrast [illegible] invented for the torment and perplexity of the [illegible] and I must say that that Constitution was [illegible] by the breach than the observance.

[illegible] time to get rid of such childish nonsense; and [illegible] seemed to be resolved that it should not be [illegible] and by deliberate alteration and amendment, [illegible] that the President determined to get rid of [illegible] to all rational arrangement.

[illegible], as we suppose, they meant to strike a sudden [illegible] he was quite right on that ground also to knock [illegible] first.

[illegible] have written on two sheets by mistake; the blank [illegible] appropriate emblem of the present state of the French [illegible]. It is curious that such a nation as the French, [illegible] than sixty years of political struggle and five revo-[illegible] ting the assumption of power by Napoleon as [illegible] at last have arrived at a point where all Constitu-[illegible] away, and where they are going to give a practical [illegible] that original compact between the people and the [illegible] is generally considered as an imaginary illustration [illegible] al theory.

[illegible] of Lord Palmerston's difficulties was the ill-[illegible] hostility of the British ambassador to the President, which Lord Palmerston had to re-[illegible] which were naturally distasteful to Lord [illegible]y. The Government, indeed, at the request [illegible] President, were obliged to recall him shortly

[illegible] Walewski very naturally communicated at [illegible] the French Foreign Office the tenor of what [illegible]merston had said to him. Meanwhile Lord [illegible] had applied for instructions as to his future [illegible] received the following official reply :—

Foreign Office [illegible]

My Lord,—I have received and laid [illegible] Excellency's despatch of the 3rd instant, [illegible] nished with instructions for your guidance [illegible] of affairs in France.

I am commanded by Her Majesty to [illegible] cellency to make no change in your relations [illegible] Government.

It is Her Majesty's desire that nothing should [illegible] her Ambassador at Paris which could wear the [illegible] an interference of any kind in the internal affairs [illegible]

I am, &c.,

PALM[illegible]

Lord Normanby hastened to the French [illegible] for Foreign Affairs in order to communicate to [illegible] tenor of this despatch. M. Turgot, who had [illegible] piqued, as Louis Napoleon himself had been, [illegible] hostile language held by the English representa[illegible] replied tartly that such a communication was [illegible] sary, as M. Walewski had already informed him [illegible] Lord Palmerston entirely approved of what the [illegible] dent had done. This statement Lord Norman[illegible] ported home in the following despatches, to w[illegible] append two side-notes which appear in Lord Pa[illegible] ston's handwriting, and his despatch of Decem[illegible] pointing out the unreasonable character of Lord [illegible] manby's complaints:—

Paris: December 6, [illegible]

My Lord,—I this morning received your Lordship's [illegible] of yesterday's date, and I afterwards called on M. T[illegible] informed him that I had received Her Majesty's comm[illegible] *say* that I need make no change in my [illegible] with the French Government in conse[illegible] what had passed. I added that if there had been [illegible] delay in making this communication, it arose from [illegible] rial circumstances not connected with any doubt on [illegible]

Not so.

M. Turgot said that delay had been of less [illegible] as he had two days since heard from M. Walew[illegible] lordship had expressed to him your entire appro[illegible] act of the President, and your conviction [illegible] have acted otherwise than he had done. . . [illegible]

[illegible] communication, and no instructions [illegible] rule to do nothing which should have [illegible] interfering in any way in the internal affairs [illegible] I had often had an opportunity of showing, [illegible] circumstances, that whatever might be the [illegible] I attached the utmost importance to main[illegible] amicable relations between the two countries. [illegible] was sure, had the Government known of the [illegible] the insurrection of the Rouges at the time I had [illegible] I should have been commissioned to add their [illegible] to mine.

[illegible] thought it necessary to mention what was stated [illegible] Walewski's despatch because two of my colleagues [illegible] to me that the despatch containing expressions [illegible] that effect had been read to them in order to show [illegible] opinion which England had pronounced.

I have, &c.,

NORMANBY.

Paris: December 15, 1851.

[illegible]—In my despatch of the 6th instant, notifying my [illegible] of my instructions to M. Turgot, I reported [illegible] Excellency had mentioned that M. Walewski had [illegible] despatch in which he stated that your Lordship had expressed your complete approbation of the course taken by the President in the recent *coup d'état*. *I also reported* that I had conveyed to M. Turgot my belief *that there must be some mistake in this* [illegible] *and my reasons for that belief*.

[illegible] a week has now elapsed without any explanation [illegible] Lordship on this point, I must conclude M. Walew[illegible] to have been substantially correct.

[illegible] being the case, I am perfectly aware that it is beyond [illegible] of my present duties to make any remark upon [illegible] of your Lordship, except inasmuch as they affect my [illegible]. But within these limits I must, with due [illegible] be permitted to observe, that if your Lordship, as [illegible] Minister, holds one language on such a delicate point [illegible] Street, without giving me any intimation you had [illegible] prescribing afterwards a different course to me, [illegible] avoidance of any appearance of interference of [illegible] the internal affairs of France—I am placed thereby [illegible] awkward position.

If the language held in Downing Street ... to the existing order of things in France ... on which I am directed to guide myself upon ... be obvious that by that act of your Lordship's I ... to misrepresentation and suspicion in merely ... according to the official orders received through ... from Her Majesty.

All this is of more importance to me, because ... before, several of my diplomatic colleagues had had ... read to them, and had derived from it the conv... accurately reported, your expressions had been ... qualified satisfaction.

I have ...

Foreign Office: December ...

My Lord,—I have received your Excellency's ... the 15th instant, referring to the statement made ... French Minister for Foreign Affairs on the occa... communicating to his Excellency the instructions ... you have been furnished by Her Majesty's Gov... your guidance in the present state of affairs in F... have to state to your Excellency that there has ... in the language which I have held, nor in the opini... have at any time expressed on the recent events ... which has been in any way inconsistent with the ... addressed to your Excellency, to abstain from any ... could bear the appearance of any interference in ... affairs of France. The instructions contained in ... of the 5th instant, to which your Excellency refer... to you, not in reply to a question as to what ... Excellency should express, but in reply to a quest... understood to be, whether your Excellency shou... your usual diplomatic relations with the Presiden... interval which was to elapse between the date of ... lency's despatch of the 3rd instant and the ... French nation on the question to be proposed ... President.

As to approving or condemning the ... President in dissolving the Assembly, I ... for the French nation, and not for the ... State or for the British Ambassador, to ... upon that event; but if your Excellency ...

[illegible] which has taken place in France, it [illegible] antagonism had arisen between the [illegible] that it was becoming every day [illegible] could not be of long duration; [illegible] better for the interests of France, and, [illegible] interests of the rest of Europe, that the [illegible] should prevail, inasmuch as the con- [illegible] might afford a prospect of the main- [illegible] order in France, whereas the divisions of [illegible] in the Assembly appeared to betoken that [illegible] the President would only be the starting- [illegible] civil strife.

[illegible] opinion was right or wrong, it seems to be [illegible] interested in property in France, as far at [illegible] and sudden rise in the Funds and in other [illegible] be assumed to be indications of increasing [illegible] the improved prospect of internal tranquillity in

I am, &c.,
PALMERSTON.

[illegible] despatches, however, of the English am- [illegible] in due course before the Queen and the [illegible] and Lord John Russell, on the 14th, called [illegible] Secretary to account for what he appeared [illegible] in the matter. Lord Palmerston answered [illegible] exposition of his view of the whole [illegible] gave the grounds on which he had formed [illegible]

Carlton Gardens: December 16, 1851.

[illegible] John Russell,—I return you the Queen's Memo- [illegible] the despatch from Normanby to which it relates. [illegible] I expressed entire approbation of what the Presi- [illegible], and that I stated my conviction that he could [illegible] otherwise than he had done, is giving a high [illegible] anything that I may have said to Count Walewski [illegible] instant, the date, apparently, of his despatch to [illegible]; but it must be borne in mind that Normanby [illegible] recollections of what Mons. Turgot said to him; [illegible] Turgot spoke to him, apparently somewhat piqued [illegible] his communication, and also from recollection, [illegible] natural that Count Walewski in writing his despatch should colour highly what anybody ... wrote had said to him on the events of the ... But the opinion which I entertain of this grave ... matter, and which, no doubt, I expressed in, ... an antagonism had grown up between the President ... Assembly that it was to be foreseen that they could ... coexist, and that each was planning the overthrow ... —either meaning aggression or believing that their ... only self-defence: there are circumstances which ... countenance the supposition that the Assembly int... the course of that very week to have struck a blow ... President, and to have deprived him of his position. ... between the President and the Assembly it seems to ... the interests of France, and, through them, the interests ... rest of Europe, were better consulted by the prevalence ... President than they would have been by the prevalence ... Assembly; and the great rise which had taken place ... French Funds from 91 to 102, together with the sudden ... which has been made by commerce in general, seem to ... that the French people in general are of the same opinion ... that what has happened has inspired the nation with a ... of confidence which they had not before.

Indeed, to account for this we have only to look at ... each of the two parties offered to France as the result of ... victory over the other party. The President had to offer ... of authority and of purpose and the support of the whole ... against the anarchists for the maintenance of order. ... Assembly had to offer immediate division among them... a division in the army, and, in all probability, civil war, ... which the anarchists would have had immense opport... and facilities for carrying their desolating schemes into ... tion. If the Assembly had had any acceptable ruler to ... to the nation instead of Louis Napoleon they might, with ... opinions and preferences, have been acting as true patri... overthrowing the President. But there were scarcely ... than three alternatives which they could have proposed; ... Henry V., who represents the principle of Legitimacy, ... has a devoted and a considerable party in France; but ... is still a minority of the nation, and a minority cannot ... the majority. Secondly, they might have proposed the ... de Paris, but he is only about twelve years old; ... years' minority with a regency, and with Thiers ... Minister, was not a proposition which a nation ...

was at all likely to accept. Thirdly, the Prince de Joinville as a President, erals as a commission of government, but arrangements would have been acceptable to The success, then, of the Assembly would, ability, have been civil war, while the success promised the re-establishment of order.

antagonism between the President and the partly the consequence of the arrangements of partly the result of faults on both sides, but chiefly the Assembly.

be affirmed that a long duration of a cen- distinguished from a Federal Republic, in a like France, with a large standing army, and the ment not in an unimportant place like Washing- a great capital which exercises almost paramount over the whole country, is a political impossibility, ngement of such a Republic be ever so well or so structed.

arrangements of 1848 greatly increased that general y, and, indeed, the work of Messrs. Marrast and would more properly be called a dissolution than a on, for they brought the political organisation of the very brink of anarchy.

more than mention, among other defects, that there great Powers, each deriving its existence from the almost sure to disagree, but with no umpire to between them, and neither able by any legal means to the other—not to dwell upon that, the question in which the rupture took place was sure to bring about later collision, and probably violence.

stitution contained a regulation that the same per- not be twice running elected as President; that is at the end of the first and of each successive term ship the French nation should not be allowed to person whom they might prefer and think fittest to head of their Government. Now, there seemed every prospect that the vast majority of the nation would re- Napoleon, and the great majority of the Conseils petitioned that the Constitution might be altered, specifically in this respect. But another regulation of red. A certain proportion of the Assembly was give validity to a resolution that the Constitution should be revised, and this majority the Assembly did [illegible] It had been generally expected that the actual conflict [illegible] put off till May of next year, but the measures of both [illegible] brought it on sooner.

The proposal of the President to restore universal [illegible] was evidently intended for the purpose of securing for [illegible] an overwhelming number of votes, that the Assembly [illegible] not have set his election aside. The Assembly tried [illegible] this by various schemes, either projected or actually [illegible] ward. One plan was a law attaching punishment to any [illegible] who might vote for an ineligible candidate; but this [illegible] was not actually brought forward. Another was [illegible] called the Questeur proposal, which went to place a [illegible] the army under the orders of the Assembly. This, [illegible] negatived, but it showed what its proposers intended. [illegible] came the proposal to declare it high treason in [illegible] President to take any steps to procure his re-election [illegible] which, if it had passed, would obviously have placed the [illegible] dent at the mercy of the Assembly, unless he could [illegible] a sufficient portion of the army to fight against that [illegible] which might go over to the Assembly. It is said, [illegible] truth I cannot tell, that it was the intention of the [illegible] the majority of the Assembly, if that law had been [illegible] immediately to have arrested within the walls and [illegible] such of the Ministers as were members, among whom [illegible] Minister of War, and to have also endeavoured to [illegible] President to Vincennes, so far as I know; at least [illegible] to me on the Tuesday or Wednesday that those who [illegible] the Royal Family at Claremont expected something [illegible] considered favourable to their interests to happen [illegible] before the end of that week. I mean that this [illegible] been expressed in the course of the week preceding [illegible] this month.

It seems to me, then, it is fair to suppose that L[illegible] leon may have acted from mixed motives. There [illegible] that he was impelled by ambition, and by a rooted [illegible] he is well known to have entertained from a very [illegible] that he was destined to govern France. But he [illegible] felt that, in the present deplorable state of [illegible] he was much more capable of promoting the [illegible] country than his antagonists were; and a man [illegible] personal ambition might, in his situation, [illegible] *Reipublicæ suprema lex.*

[illegible] no doubt, very much depend upon the [illegible] he may be able to adduce that he was [illegible] in self-defence, and was only anticipating [illegible] and also upon the use which he may make [illegible] which he has acquired.

[illegible] with the opinion which I understand Macau[illegible] in a letter to Lord Mahon, that the French [illegible] for military despotism; nor can I believe [illegible] which is not what we mean by the term [illegible] have a long duration in France.

[illegible] of the events of Thursday and Friday, [illegible] but one feeling as to the wanton destruction [illegible] the soldiers appeared to have inflicted on the [illegible]

[illegible] a reply that the question at issue was [illegible] for the judgment he had formed, but [illegible] ought to have given any opinion without [illegible] consulting the Cabinet and taking the orders [illegible] Sovereign. Lord Palmerston rejoined that the [illegible] by him was given as his own and in an [illegible] conversation, and that it in no way fettered [illegible] of the Government; that if it were laid [illegible] a Secretary of State was to express no [illegible] on passing events in conversing with foreign [illegible] except as the organ of a previously-consulted [illegible] there would be an end of that easy and familiar [illegible] intercourse which is so useful for the mainte[illegible] friendly relations with foreign Governments. [illegible] not satisfy the Premier, who, in the following [illegible] the debate by a very summary decision:—

Woburn Abbey: Dec. 19, 1851.

[illegible] Palmerston,—I have just received your letter of [illegible] No other course is left to me than to submit the [illegible] to the Queen, and to ask Her Majesty to appoint [illegible] to you in the Foreign Office.

[illegible] I have often had the misfortune to differ from [illegible] questions, I am deeply convinced that the policy [illegible] pursued has maintained the interests and the [illegible] the country.

I remain, yours truly,

J. Russell.

To soften the blow, however, he [illegible] wards made a proposal almost com[illegible] and offered to Lord Palmerston the [illegible] the Court across the Irish Channel. [illegible] civilly declined, but the retort which [illegible] cation afforded to one who had been [illegible] duct both imprudent and indecorous [illegible] be neglected.

Broadlands: [illegible]

My dear John Russell,—I have received you[illegible] terday; I cannot, however, allow our correspo[illegible] matter to close without saying that I do not [illegible] of violations of prudence and decorum, and I [illegible] that that charge is refuted by the offer which [illegible] the Lord Lieutenancy of Ireland, because I [illegible] be an office for the due performance of the duties [illegible] dence and decorum are qualities which cannot well [illegible] with.

That the dismissal of Lord Palmerston [illegible] later was an event which had been long co[illegible] is evident from the following letter of the Prin[illegible] to the Prime Minister published in Martin's '[illegible] Prince Consort,' vol. ii. p. 418:—

Windsor Castle: Dec. [illegible]

My dear Lord John,—. . . It was quite clear to [illegible] that we were entering upon most dangerous time[illegible] military despotism and red republicanism will for [illegible] the only powers on the Continent, to both of which [illegible] tional monarchy of England will be equally hateful. [illegible] calm influence of our institutions, however, should [illegible] suaging the contest abroad must be the anxious wi[illegible] Englishman, and of every friend of liberty and [illegible] civilisation. This influence has been rendered [illegible] Palmerston's personal manner of conducting the [illegible] and by the universal hatred which he has excited [illegible] nent. That you could hope to control him [illegible] doubted by us, and its impossibility is clea[illegible] last proceedings. *I can therefore only* [illegible] *the opportunity of the rupture should have* [illegible] *the right is on your side.*

[illegible] was summoned on the 22nd to receive [illegible] Lord Palmerston's dismissal and the [illegible] of Lord Granville in his stead. Lord [illegible] meanwhile, was silent except to his most [illegible], for, as he said to Lord Broughton, [illegible] resigns, he is expected to say why; when [illegible], it is for others to assign reasons.'

[illegible] reason was assigned and the public had to [illegible] the meeting of Parliament. Meanwhile the [illegible] hostility of certain foreign Courts and [illegible] found vent in notes of exultation at the [illegible] man who had so long occupied a position of [illegible] towards them. All over Europe the result [illegible] as a triumph for the absolute and a blow [illegible] Liberal cause.

[illegible] the British embassy at Vienna, Mr. Murray [illegible] a friend:—

> [illegible] Palmerston's retirement is received with the most [illegible] regret by the Liberal party in Austria, who look [illegible] the utter annihilation of their hopes. It will hardly [illegible] that these arrogant fools here actually think that [illegible] overthrown Lord Palmerston; and the vulgar triumph [illegible] Schwarzenberg knows no bounds. Not content with pla-[illegible] the news with lying comments of all sorts, and des-[illegible] couriers into the provinces to circulate the most mon-[illegible] about the 'Victory of Austrian Policy,' his bad [illegible] actually gone far enough to make him give a ball in [illegible]. I believe if an earthquake had swallowed up [illegible] Queen, Lords and Commons, Constitution, Free Press [illegible] it would not have created more sensation than this [illegible] strange change in the English Cabinet.

[illegible] must recall the German doggrel, in vogue at [illegible], if we wish to understand the excited feelings [illegible] moment:—

> Hat der Teufel einen Sohn,
> So ist er sicher Palmerston.

[illegible] enthusiasm might be forgiven at the pro-[illegible] getting rid of the devil's son!

From Madrid Lord Howden at once [illegible] resignation to Lord Granville, alleging [illegible] no longer be of any use there, as 'the [illegible] Lord Palmerston either actually is, or most [illegible] will be, believed to be a direct concession to [illegible] actionary spirit which is riding rough-shod [illegible] world, and which is nowhere more to be [illegible] than in Spain.'

It was the same everywhere abroad.

At home the feeling of astonishment [illegible] the moment every other feeling: an [illegible] confined to the general public, but extending [illegible] some of his colleagues. Lord Palmerston [illegible] letters from all sides expressing regret and [illegible] explanation. He contented himself with [illegible] ing their sympathetic communications. I [illegible] quote one letter addressed to him on the [illegible] that is one from Lord Lansdowne:—

Bowood: [illegible]

My dear Palmerston,—I cannot resist the [illegible] write to you, and give some expression to the deep [illegible] feel at the event which has just occurred, of the [illegible] which I was only made aware the day before the [illegible] by two letters from J. Russell, which, owing to [illegible] my being absent from home, reached me at the same [illegible] there appeared to be no reason left for further and [illegible] factory explanation.

I have felt this concern the more deeply [illegible] fectly convinced there was and is no difference in [illegible] with respect to the neutral position to be [illegible] affairs, and because I have felt inclined from the [illegible] same individual opinion, the grounds of which [illegible] your letter to J. Russell, as to the necessity of a [illegible] *one* person to give France any chance of a [illegible] though I wish such opinions had not been [illegible] ambassador, apparently not very well disposed to [illegible] without having been previously communicated [illegible] and to the Queen, knowing as I long have [illegible] susceptibility which prevailed in that quarter [illegible] and greatly lamented, and which I have [illegible] to combat.

[illegible] however, to say to you on this occa-
[illegible] have I approved of every essential act
[illegible] of foreign affairs at the time, but
[illegible] with respect to which upon subsequent
[illegible] to recall my approbation. Your policy
[illegible] you live, want the ablest of all defenders, but
[illegible] office (and J. Russell is well apprised upon
[illegible] my own tenure of office now hangs), I
[illegible] it impugned in public or in private without
[illegible] conviction and admiration of its great ability,
[illegible] with the interests, and, above all, the
[illegible] country.

Yours sincerely,
LANSDOWNE.

[illegible] letter to his brother gives, in Lord
[illegible] own words, a full story of the whole
[illegible]

Broadlands: Jan. 22, 1852.

[illegible] not been able to write to you sooner except by the
[illegible] post, and I did not like to send you details by that
[illegible]. The history of my dismissal is short and simple.
[illegible] all the rest of the world, long considered the French
[illegible] of 1848 as one that would not long work, and as
[illegible] which approached to the very verge of anarchy.
[illegible] pursued by the Assembly—and more especially after
[illegible] in the beginning of November—showed that a con-
[illegible] that body and the President was inevitable; that
[illegible] no way out of the difficulty in which France was
[illegible] by some act of violence against the law and Con-
[illegible] and it seemed to me better that in such a conflict
[illegible] should prevail over the Assembly, than that the
[illegible] should prevail over the President. Therefore when
[illegible] took place, and Walewsky came to me on the
[illegible] (December 3) to tell me of it, I expressed to him
[illegible]. The President could offer to France settled
[illegible], with order and internal tranquillity; the Assembly
[illegible] candidate to offer in the room of the President.
[illegible] had only a minority with him, and could not with
[illegible] the majority of the nation. The Comte de Paris
[illegible] twelve years old, and France could not now accept
[illegible] six or eight years' duration, with a foreign
[illegible] princess as Regent, and Thiers as Prime

Minister. The Triumvirate of the Generals Cavaignac, Changarnier, and Lamoricière would be military despotism; and Joinville as President would be a political solecism. Any one of these arrangements would have been civil war and local and temporary anarchy; and the Assembly had nothing else to offer. Walewsky wrote on the 3rd a private letter to Turgot, giving him an account of what I had said, the sum and substance of which was, that I thought that what the President had done the day before was the best thing for France, and, through France, for the rest of Europe. On the 3rd, Normanby, who had for some time been on very bad personal terms with the President, wrote a despatch to ask whether in consequence of what had happened, he should alter in any way his relations with the French Government. On the 5th I sent him a despatch, saying that he was to make no change in his relations with the French Government, nor to do anything which would wear the appearance of any interference in the internal affairs of France. He received this despatch on the 6th, and went immediately to Turgot to tell him of it—a step wholly unnecessary, because all he was told to do was to make no change in his relations with the French Government. Turgot, who was nettled at the existence of any doubt on the subject, said that the communication was unnecessary, as he had two days before received an account from Walewsky, saying that I had entirely approved what the President had done, and thought he could not have acted otherwise. This despatch having been read by the Queen and John Russell, the latter wrote to me to say that he hoped I should be able to contradict that report of what I had said. To this I replied that the particular expressions ascribed to me were rather a highly-coloured version of what I had said, but that it must be remembered that Normanby reported what Turgot had said to him verbally; that Turgot stated from memory what Walewsky had written in a despatch or letter received two days before; and that Walewsky gave the impression which he had derived from our conversation, but not the particular words which I had used. But I stated to John Russell, at considerable length, my reasons for thinking that what had been done was the best thing for France and for Europe.

To this John Russell replied that I mistook the point at issue between us. That the question was not whether the President was or was not justified in doing what he has done, but whether I was justified in expressing any opinion thereupon [illegible] having first taken the opinion of the [illegible]. To this I answed that his doctrine so [illegible] and not practical. That there is a well-[illegible] understood distinction in diplomatic [illegible] conversations which are official and which [illegible] and conversations which are unofficial and [illegible] Governments That my conversation with [illegible] of the latter description, and that I said nothing [illegible] would in any degree or way fetter the action of [illegible]; and that if it was to be held that a Secretary [illegible] never express any opinion to a foreign Minister [illegible], except as the organ of a previously-consulted [illegible] would be an end of that easy and familiar inter-[illegible] tends essentially to promote good understanding [illegible] Ministers and Governments.

[illegible] Russell replied to this that my letter left him no [illegible] but to advise the Queen to place the Foreign Office in [illegible]; but he offered me the Lord Lieutenancy of Ireland, [illegible] arrangement which I might prefer. Of course, [illegible] so cavalierly sent to the right-about, I told him [illegible] obvious reasons which prevented me from availing [illegible] his offers, and that I only waited to learn the name [illegible] to give up the seals. John Russell distinctly [illegible] down the ground of my dismissal to the fact of my [illegible] expressed an opinion on the *coup d'état* without refer-[illegible] the nature of that opinion, Johnny saying that that [illegible] the question. Now, that opinion of mine was expressed [illegible] on Tuesday, the 3rd; but on Wednesday, the [illegible] had a small evening party at our house. At that party [illegible] Russell and Walewsky were, and they had a conversation [illegible] *coup d'état*, in which Johnny expressed his opinion, [illegible] Walewsky tells me was in substance and result pretty [illegible] same as what I had said the day before, though, as [illegible], John Russell is not so *expansif* as I am; but, [illegible] Friday, the 6th, Walewsky dined at John Russell's, [illegible] met Lansdowne and Charles Wood; and in the course [illegible] evening John Russell, Lansdowne, and Charles Wood [illegible] their opinions on the *coup d'état*, and those [illegible], if anything, rather more strongly favourable [illegible] had been. Moreover, Walewsky met Lord Grey [illegible] the Park, and Grey's opinion was likewise expressed, [illegible] to the same effect. It is obvious that the reason [illegible] for my dismissal was a mere pretext, eagerly caught at for want of any good reason. The real [illegible] truckling to the hostile intrigues of the Orleans [illegible] Russia, Saxony, and Bavaria, and in some degree [illegible] present Prussian Government. All these parties [illegible] respective views and systems of policy thwarted by [illegible] pursued by the British Government, and they thought [illegible] they could remove the Minister they would change [illegible] They had for a long time past effectually poisoned the [illegible] the Queen and the Prince against me, and John Russell [illegible] way, rather encouraged than discountenanced the desire [illegible] Queen to remove me from the Foreign Office.

In the meanwhile the papers, having but little to [illegible] have all over the country—both London and provincial [illegible] —been full of my removal; and the general tone has [illegible] highly complimentary to me, and far from agreeable to [illegible] Russell. This, of course, has much annoyed him; and I [illegible] if known by the Court, must afford them matter for [illegible]

The general opinion is that the Ministry will not stand [illegible] after the meeting of Parliament. Indeed, it is likely that [illegible] will be wrecked upon the Reform Bill. At all events, [illegible] scarcely probable that they should get through the [illegible] without some defeat which would lead to their resignation. [illegible] that case the Queen would send for Lord Derby, who [illegible] probably be able to form a Government even without [illegible] Peelites; but they would most likely join him. However, [illegible] these things are matters of speculation.

Parliament met on February 3. Immediately after the speeches of the mover and seconder of the Address were concluded, the Prime Minister was asked to explain the reason for Lord Palmerston's removal from office. Lord John Russell began by saying:—

It will be right that I should first state to the House [illegible] I conceive to be the position which a Secretary of State [illegible] as regards the Crown in the administration of foreign [illegible] and as regards the Prime Minister of this country. [illegible] respect to the first, I should state that when the Crown, [illegible] sequence of a vote of the House of Commons, places [illegible] stitutional confidence in a Minister, that Minister [illegible] other hand, bound to afford to the Crown the most [illegible] full detail of every measure that is taken, or to [illegible] Crown its full liberty, a liberty which the Crown [illegible]

...Minister no longer possesses its confidence ... general doctrine. But as regards the noble ... appear that in August, 1850, the precise terms ... communication on the part of Her Majesty ... the transaction of business between the Crown ... of State. I became the organ of making ... to my noble friend, and thus became re... the document I am about to read from.

... only to that part of the document which has ... the immediate subject :—

... requires, first, that Lord Palmerston will dis... what he proposes in a given case, in order that the ... know as distinctly to what she is giving her royal ...

... having once given her sanction to a measure, that ... arbitrarily altered or modified by the Minister. Such ... must consider as failing in sincerity towards the ... justly to be visited by the exercise of her constitu... of dismissing that Minister. She expects to be kept ... of what passes between him and the foreign Ministers ... important decisions are taken based upon that intercourse; ... the foreign despatches in good time, and to have the ... her approval sent to her in sufficient time to make ... acquainted with their contents before they must be ... The Queen thinks it best that Lord John Russell ... this letter to Lord Palmerston.'

... that accordingly, and received a letter in which the ... said :—

... have taken a copy of this Memorandum of the Queen, ... not fail to attend to the directions which it contains.'

... John Russell then proceeded to remark that—

... first important transaction in which Lord Palmerston ... part since the end of the last session of Parliament ... reception of a deputation of delegates from certain ... parishes respecting the treatment of the Hungarian ... by the Turkish Government. On this occasion he ... Russell) thought that his noble friend had exhibited ... of due caution; but he gave him the credit of sup... this was through an oversight.

... next occasion to which he thought it necessary to refer ... the events which had taken place on December 2,

The instructions conveyed to our [illegible] Queen's Government were to abstain from all [illegible] the internal affairs of that country. Being [illegible] alleged conversation between Lord Palmerston and [illegible] ambassador repugnant to these instructions, he (Lord [illegible] had written to that noble lord; but his inquiries [illegible] days met with a disdainful silence, Lord Palmerston [illegible] meanwhile, without the knowledge of his colleagues, [illegible] despatch to Lord Normanby, in which he, however, [illegible] question whether he had approved the act of the [illegible] The noble lord's course of proceeding in this matter he [illegible] sidered to be putting himself in the place of the Crown [illegible] passing by the Crown, while he gave the moral [illegible] England to the acts of the President of the Republic of [illegible] in direct opposition to the policy which the Government [illegible] hitherto pursued.

Under these circumstances, he (Lord John Russell) [illegible] alternative but to declare that, while he was Prime [illegible] Lord Palmerston could not hold the seals of office; and [illegible] assumed the sole and entire responsibility of advising the [illegible] to require the resignation of his noble friend, who, [illegible] had forgotten and neglected what was due to the Crown [illegible] his colleagues, had not, he was convinced, intended any [illegible] disrespect.

Lord Palmerston then rose, and the following [illegible] report of what he said:—

He should be sorry if the House and the country [illegible] run away with the notion which Lord John Russell [illegible] entertain, that he had abandoned principles. He [illegible] Lord John's definition of the relations between the [illegible] Minister and the Crown, and he contended that he [illegible] nothing inconsistent with these relations. With [illegible] the deputation on the subject of the release of the [illegible] refugees, he had thought it to be his duty to receive [illegible] had repudiated certain expressions contained in the [illegible] he had said nothing upon that occasion which he [illegible] uttered in that House and elsewhere. He then [illegible] lengthened statement of the transactions in [illegible] *coup d'état* in France, which had been represented by [illegible] Russell as forming the groundwork of his [illegible] After recounting the interview with Count Wa[illegible] he said that on that same day Her Majesty's ambassador wrote a despatch to ask what instructions he should for his guidance in France during the interval before the the French people on the question that was to be pro- them, and whether in that interval he should infuse relations with the French Government any greater reserve than usual.

[Lord Palmerston proceeded to say] the opinion of on that question, and a draft of that opinion was and sent for Her Majesty's approbation. The answer be one in consistence with the course we had pursued beginning of the events alluded to, and was such as lord has read. Her Majesty's ambassador was in- to make no change in his relations with the French and to do nothing that should wear the appear- interference with the internal affairs of France. no instruction to communicate that document to the Government; it simply contained instructions, not in the English ambassador was to do, but what he was from doing. The noble lord, however (the Marquis thought it right to communicate to the French Foreign Affairs the substance of that document, his communication with certain excuses for the however, did not rest with that noble marquis, as to the English Government was dated December 3. Minister stated that he had nothing to com- with respect to the delay, and the less, indeed, because before he had received from the French ambassador in statement which the noble lord (Lord John Russell) that I entirely approved of what had been done, and President of the French fully justified. That was a highly-coloured explanation of the result of the long we held together. Those particular words I never probably the French ambassador never would have consistent with the dignity due to his country to of a Foreign Secretary of State. Consequently was not given, and was not asked. When the Normanby's despatch reached my noble friend (Lord he wrote to say he trusted that I could contra- There was, as he has stated, an interval of the noble lord's letter and my answer. letter was dated the 14th, and my answer the the time labouring under a heavy pressure of business, and wishing fully to explain the [illegible] it was not until the evening of the 16th [illegible] write my answer. The noble lord got it early [illegible] on the 17th.

This letter has already been given above [illegible] the history of the correspondence which [illegible] Lord Palmerston's claim for the unfettered [illegible] foreign secretary. He then continued:—

Now, I expressed this opinion to which the no[illegible] referred to the French ambassador on December [illegible] I the only member of the Cabinet who did thus [illegible] opinion on passing events? I am informed that on [illegible] of that very day, and under the same roof as I ex[illegible] opinion, the noble lord at the head of the Governme[illegible] versation with the same ambassador, expressed h[illegible] (Hear, hear, and laughter.) I cannot tell what th[illegible] was, but from what has fallen from the noble lord th[illegible] it may be assumed that that opinion was not ver[illegible] even from the reported opinion which I am suppo[illegible] expressed. Was that all? On the 5th, and in the [illegible] own house, I have been informed that the French [illegible] met the noble lord, the President of the Council, and [illegible] cellor of the Exchequer. The noble lord again ex[illegible] opinion, and the President of the Council and the [illegible] of the Exchequer also expressed an opinion. (C[illegible] laughter.) And be it remembered that the charge [illegible] nature of the opinion, for the noble lord distinctly [illegible] 'You mistake the question between us. It was n[illegible] the President was justified or not, but whether [illegible] justified in expressing an opinion on the matter at all.' [illegible] that the noble lord, the Secretary of State for the C[illegible] also, in those few days, express an opinion on those ev[illegible] I have been informed also that the then Vice-Presid[illegible] Board of Trade, and now the Secretary of State f[illegible] Affairs, also expressed his opinion. Then it follows [illegible] member of the Cabinet, whatever his political a[illegible] have been, however much his attention may have be[illegible] to other matters, is at liberty to express an opinion [illegible] events abroad; but the Secretary of State for F[illegible] whose peculiar duty it is to watch those events [illegible] for his office if he has not an opinion on them [illegible] an opinion; and when a foreign that he has news, he is to remain or the mute of some Eastern pacha.) Now I am told, 'It is not your con- Walewsky that is complained of, but your of Normanby.' What had I stated in reference to which a great parade has been been guilty of breach of duty to the Crown to the Prime Minister, in sending it communicating with the noble lord? No the matter more strongly than I have in obligations of the Secretary of State for Foreign always admitted, that if the Secretary of State Affairs sends a despatch of importance to an am- without ascertaining the opinion of the Prime Crown, he is guilty of a breach of duty. But cases in which it is perfectly well known that the opinion of the Government, and in- might arise from delay.

Palmerston then concluded his statement by that it was a misrepresentation of the fact he had given instructions to Lord Normanby with the relations of general intercourse England and France. It was no instruction He did not profess to give the opinion of the or that of England. It was his own opinion, right or wrong, it was shared by numbers Therefore the charge made against him by Russell, founded on this despatch, had no either in justice or in facts.

his seat with the House only partially The attack had been very vigorous: his been incomplete. The motives that actuated comparative reserve may be gathered from details as to these events, which he gave to Lord Lansdowne,[1] relating a conversation Duke of Bedford in October, 1852.

assigned by John Russell, in his letters to me, dismissal of me, was an opinion which I had ex-

[1] Dated Broadlands, October 1852.

pressed to Walewsky about the President's coup d'
morning conversation at my house, the day after that
happened—that opinion being to the effect that the
had acted in self-defence, and that what he had done w
circumstances of the case, the best thing for France.
said to the Duke, in regard to the validity of that
have only to repeat to you what Count Walewsky
either the day (or two days) before the matter was di
the House of Commons.

Count Walewsky then said to me that he had the
had with John Russell a conversation which concerne
which he thought it right to report to me. He said t
John had sent for him, and had said he wished to a
question. He had been told that Count Walewsky had
he, Lord John, had expressed to him, Count Walews
gard to the *coup d'état*, opinions similar in substance
to those which had been expressed to him by me, and
to know if that report was true. Count Walewsky
his reply to Lord John was, that that report was perfe
that it was true that he had said so, and that what he
was true. He told Lord John that he, Lord John, h
two occasions expressed such opinions. The first occ
on the evening of Wednesday, the 3rd of December,
day in the morning of which I had expressed to hi
Walewsky, the opinion which he, Lord John, had fo
with. That he, Count Walewsky, had that evening
John at a party at Lady Palmerston's, and that then
Lord John had spoken of the event of the day before
similar to those used by me in the morning. The sec
sion was the Friday following, when he, Count Walew
with Lord John, and met there some other memb
Cabinet, and that evening, said Count Walewsky to L
'upon that very sofa' (pointing to one in the room)
pressed opinions if anything stronger than what Lo
ston had said to me on the Wednesday; and wh
contented myself with reporting what Lord Palmers
in a private letter to Monsieur Turgot, I made wh
said the subject of an official despatch.' Count W
to me that after this Lord John asked him whethe
all this to me; and Count Walewsky said that, h
passed a day at Broadlands, he had talked
circumstances connected with my dismissal from
he had stated to me all that he had then

[illegible] does Lord Palmerston mean to say all [illegible] of Commons?' 'Of that,' said Count [illegible] nothing.'

[illegible] that I stated in my speech in the House of [illegible] result of this communication made to me [illegible] I did not like to be too precise, or to go [illegible] of delicacy to Count Walewsky, though he [illegible] no objection to my making the assertion on his [illegible]

[illegible] to the Duke of Bedford that the ground on [illegible] John Russell had, in his letters to me, placed my [illegible] if it had had any intrinsic validity, which it had [illegible] by this statement, which showed that I had [illegible] no more than John Russell himself had said and [illegible] I went on to say to the Duke that I had still further [illegible] of the manner in which John Russell had made his [illegible] in the House of Commons; for that, finding his [illegible], as put forward in his letters to me, thus rendered [illegible] he had, in his speech, adopted another ground, and [illegible] dismissal partly on the ground—first, that I had [illegible] days more than I ought to have taken to answer a [illegible] explanation made to him by the Queen, and sent [illegible] and, secondly, on the ground that, by sending a de- [illegible] Normanby without previously sending the draft to the [illegible] incurred the penalty of dismissal, intimated by [illegible] Memorandum of August 1850, as likely to be the [illegible] an omission. I said to the Duke that the Queen's [illegible] explanation as to what I had said to Count Walewsky [illegible] from John Russell at a moment when I was over- [illegible] with pressing office business, thrown into arrear by [illegible] having been occupied by a succession of Cabinet meet- [illegible] the explanation to be given by me was necessarily a [illegible] that, in order to write it, I had to sit up one night [illegible] four in the morning, having put a messenger under [illegible] take it down to Woburn in an office-box by the first [illegible] next day; and that in the box which contained my [illegible] I put a short note, saying that it was then half-past [illegible] morning, that I could not sit up any longer to take [illegible] paper, and that I begged that John Russell would [illegible] either send me a copy of it or let me have it again, [illegible] copy it. 'Well,' said I to the Duke, 'if John Russell [illegible] the Queen would consider the two or three days' de- [illegible] transmission of my reply to her inquiry as disrespectful

Q

to her, what was it his duty to do when [illegible] him? Why, of course, to send it off imme[illegible] where the Queen then was. But what did [illegible] very afternoon he quietly sent my paper back [illegible] might take a copy of it; and he added that [illegible] to him he would transmit it to the Queen, with [illegible] answer which he intended to write to it. Thus [illegible] further delay of at least three days, in addition to the delay which he made the subject of complaint against [illegible]

Then I said to the Duke that I thought it was [illegible] by me, and very wrong by the Queen, for him, [illegible] to have read in the House of Commons the Queen's [illegible] dum of August 1850, hinting at dismissal. In regard [illegible] Queen, he was thus dragging her into the discussion, [illegible] ing her a party to a question which constitutionally [illegible] and before Parliament could only be, a question [illegible] and the responsible adviser of the Crown; and I [illegible] mention of the Queen as a party to the transaction [illegible] rise to newspaper remarks much to be regretted, and [illegible] Prime Minister ought not to have given an occasion [illegible]

I said that, as regards myself, the impression cre[illegible] reading that Memorandum was, that I had submi[illegible] affront which I ought not to have borne; and seve[illegible] friends told me, after the discussion, that they wonde[illegible] not sent in my resignation on receiving that paper [illegible] Queen through John Russell. My answer to those [illegible] said, had been, that the paper was written by a lady [illegible] by a Sovereign, and that the difference between a [illegible] man could not be forgotten even in the case of the [illegible] a throne; but I said that, in the first place, I had no [illegible] suppose that this Memorandum would ever be seen [illegible] known to, anybody but the Queen, John Russell, and [illegible] that, secondly, my position at that moment, namely, in [illegible] 1850, was peculiar. I had lately been the object of [illegible] political attack, and had gained a great and signal victory [illegible] House of Commons and in public opinion: to have [illegible] then would have been to have given the fruits of [illegible] adversaries whom I had defeated, and to have [illegible] political supporters at the very moment when by the[illegible] had triumphed. But, beyond all that, I had [illegible] my friends, by pursuing the course which they [illegible] to have followed, I should have been bringing [illegible] the bar of public opinion a personal quarrel [illegible]

[illegible] step which no subject ought to take, if [illegible] it; for the result of such a course must [illegible] or injurious to the country. If he should [illegible] wrong, he would be irretrievably condemned; [illegible] should be proved to be in the wrong, the [illegible] suffer.

[illegible] to the Memorandum of August 1850, [illegible] of debate in the House of Commons, [illegible] John Russell an unexpected success in the [illegible]. It was an unfair advantage, because, as we [illegible] the foregoing letter, Lord Palmerston con[illegible] tongue to be tied in the matter. In con[illegible] the general impression on the House was, no [illegible] the moment, unfavourable to Lord Palmerston. [illegible]iscence of this debate which Lord Dalling left [illegible], the scene is described as follows:—

[illegible] to be under the gallery on the night in which [illegible] made his explanations.

[illegible] certainly was one of the most powerful I ever [illegible]. It was evidently intended to crush an expected [illegible], and, by the details into which it went, took Lord [illegible] completely by surprise. I listened to his reply [illegible] more affectionate interest, since he was kind enough [illegible] my own name with praise; but I felt, and all his [illegible], that it was feeble as a retort to the tremendous [illegible] had been made on him.

[illegible] Mr. Bernal Osborne coming to the bench where [illegible], and expressing to me a regret similar to that which [illegible]; and I think it was the night after, in debate, [illegible] Mr. Disraeli on the staircase of Ashburnham [illegible] which was then the Russian embassy, he said in his [illegible] manner, 'There *was* a Palmerston!'

[illegible] is smashed,' was, indeed, the expression [illegible] at the clubs; but it did not in the least convey [illegible] Lord Palmerston had formed of his own position. [illegible], in truth, that I never admired him so much as [illegible]. He evidently thought he had been ill-treated; [illegible] heard him make an unfair or irritable remark, nor [illegible] in anywise stunned by the blow he had received, [illegible] by the isolated position in which he stood.

I should say that he seemed to consider that he had had a quarrel put upon him, which it was his wisest course to close by receiving the fire of his adversary and not returning it.

He could not, in fact, have gained a victory against the Premier on the ground which Lord John Russell had chosen for the combat which would not have been more permanently disadvantageous to him than a defeat. The faults of which he had been accused did not touch his own honour nor that of his country. Let them be admitted, and there was an end of the matter. By-and-by an occasion would probably arise in which he might choose an advantageous occasion for giving battle, and he was willing to wait calmly for that occasion.

It came soon enough.

CHAPTER VIII.

)F THE RUSSELL ADMINISTRATION—LORD DERBY'S GOVERN-
—DISSOLUTION—SPEECHES AT TIVERTON AND LEWES—
—DEFEAT OF THE DERBY CABINET.

> Your power and your command are taken off,
> And Cassio rules in Cyprus.—*Othello*, Act V. Sc. 1.

bruary Lord J. Russell brought in a Militia Bill was intended to develop a local militia for the e of the country. Lord Palmerston at once ex- d his dissatisfaction at the form of the measure, committee on the Bill moved as an amendment it the word 'local,' so as to constitute a regular , which should be legally transportable all over ngdom, and so be always ready for any emergency. e carried against the Government by a majority en, and the Russell Administration came to an The event created little wonder, as the progressive ness of the Cabinet, since one of its strongest ers left it, had for some time prepared the public for a change. We have, however, Sir George 's testimony[1] that the division on the amendment surprise, and that Lord Palmerston himself did ish to turn out the Government; but the cup full, a little movement was sufficient to make it ver. Lord Derby formed a Government, after invited the co-operation of Lord Palmerston, hus writes to his brother:—

[1] Sir G. Lewis to Sir E. Head. 'Letters,' p. 251.

C. G.: February [illegible]

I have had my tit-for-tat with John Russell, and [illegible] him out on Friday last. I certainly, however, did [illegible] to do so, nor did I intend to do anything more than [illegible] the House to reject his foolish plan and to adopt [illegible] sensible one. I have no doubt that two things [illegible] to resign. First, the almost insulting manner towards [illegible] which the House, by its cheers, went with me in the [illegible] and, secondly, the fear of being defeated on the vote of [illegible] about the Cape[1] affairs which was to have been moved [illegible] As it is, the late Government have gone out on a [illegible] which they have treated as a motion, merely [illegible] they had lost the confidence of the House, whereas if [illegible] gone out on a defeat upon the motion about the [illegible] would have carried with them the direct censure of the [illegible] of Commons. Lord Derby has formed his Government [illegible] out of his Protectionist party—none of any other party [illegible] join him. He made me on Sunday, immediately after [illegible] seen the Queen, a very civil and courteous offer to [illegible] but of course it was impossible for me to do so on [illegible] my entire difference with him on the question of [illegible] duty on the importation of corn even if there had been [illegible] reasons, but there are many other reasons against [illegible] House is adjourned till Friday, and then it will probably [illegible] again for ten days to allow time for the new Ministers [illegible] re-elected. They are not going to dissolve immediately [illegible] will do so as soon as the Estimates are voted and the M[illegible] passed. I cannot conceive that such a Government [illegible] long, or can even get a majority by a fresh general [illegible]

And to his brother-in-law, Mr. Laurence S[illegible] writes the same day:—

Lord Derby invited me to join him, but as he [illegible] adherence to or abandonment of protective duties [illegible] to depend on the result of the next general [illegible] announcement created a preliminary obstacle [illegible] all further discussion as to any other points [illegible] not, however, have joined him even if that [illegible] removed, because his Government was not [illegible] any broad principle of a general union of [illegible] me to come in singly; and the office of all [illegible]

[1] The Caffir war of 18[illegible]

...ary. I do not mean to say that, ...ation of Protection, I should have been ... him in any case; but if his Government ... comprehensive principle, and Protection ... overboard, the matter would have required

...ought in and carried their own Militia ... John Russell opposed, but which was ...ted by Lord Palmerston on the second ... the following letters he describes with an ... the position of affairs; but it is curious ... Lord Aberdeen, who was to be Prime ... eight months, is not even mentioned as ...choice:—

Carlton Gardens: April 30, 1852.

...William,—It is a long time since I wrote to you, ... one's time nearly as much occupied out of office ... are so many things one has been obliged to leave ... a five years' incessant Downing Street toil. But ...ly getting through a mass of accumulated confusion. ...ver, a member of a committee on ventilation, which ... much of my mornings, in addition to House of ... attendance in evenings.

...w Government gets on pretty well; Disraeli has ... made a good financial statement. His speech of ... was excellent, well arranged, clear, and well delivered, ...ade out the complete success of the financial and ...al measures of the last ten years, of the Peel and of ... Administrations, which, while they were in progress ...r discussion, he and Derby were the loudest to con-... He was vociferously cheered by Liberals and Peelites, ...ned to in sullen silence by the supporters of the ...ent. His only proposal is that the income tax, which ...n the 5th of this month, shall be continued for one ..., to give the Government time to consider what ... system they will propose; but he has entirely ... the idea of import duty on corn, or, in other ... principle of Protection. Opinions differ as to the ... of the session, but the chances are that the dissolution will not be till the end of June. I do not see that we need care much when it may be, now that by general consent it is agreed that the new Parliament is not to meet till November. The only inconvenience of delay is that people are put to trouble and expense by the measures necessary to guard against contests. In the meantime it is a real public advantage that the Tory party has come into office, and has had an opportunity of seeing and learning and judging as responsible Ministers many things of which in Opposition they had very imperfect knowledge and conceptions. They do better than was expected of them, but nevertheless it is scarcely possible that they should stand as they are, and if they do not get some material reinforcement, they will probably not live over next Christmas, notwithstanding any addition to the number of their supporters (and that will not be great) which a general election may bring them. The most natural reinforcement for them to look to would be the Peel party, not very numerous, counting about fifty or sixty, but containing a good many men of capacity. But as yet it seems to me that the Peelite leaders have not softened the bitter animosity they have hitherto felt for the Derby Protectionists. There is no knowing, however, how far a liberal offer of places in the Government might alter those feelings, still I think it unlikely. I believe the Derby Government rather calculate upon inducing me to join them when Protection has had its public funeral: on this point of course I am studiously silent, but I have no intention or inclination to enlist under Derby's banners. I do not think highly of him as a statesman, and I suspect that there are many matters on which he and I should not agree. Besides, after having acted for twenty-two years with the Whigs, and after having gained by, and while acting with them, any little political reputation I may have acquired, it would not answer nor be at all agreeable to me to go slap over to the opposite camp, and this merely on account of a freak of John Russell's which the whole Whig party regretted and condemned: moreover, I am in no great hurry to return to hard work, and should not dislike a little more holiday. On the other hand, I own that it would be a very pressing public emergency which would induce me to place myself again under John Russell, not on account of personal resentment, which I have ceased to feel, and he and I meet in private as good friends as ever, but he has shown on so many occasions such a want of sound judgment and discretion that I have lost all political confidence in him. This last frolic of his

President, or, as he will by that time perhaps be, th
My Tiverton friends are staunch, and I am not lik
any contest there. I have received many overtures
places, but had the offers been ever so plainly demo
success I should still have preferred keeping a go
seat when I have been lucky enough to get it.

There was to be a dissolution at the end o
sion, and speculation as to its result was afloa

C. G.: May

My dear William,—Those who have looked into
of the general election, like Tufnell,[1] for instance,
the next Parliament will in its subdivisions not
much from the present one, and that the Governm
have a majority. If that should so be, and it seem
this Government can scarcely long survive the mee
new Parliament unless it is kept alive by the
forming another Administration; but difficulties o
seldom prevent the overthrow of what is, though
embarrass those who have to build up something els
what they have thrown down. John Russell wou
be the person to be sent for to form a new Governm
has gone down wofully in public opinion of late, an
in the opinion of his own party. His talents
dispute, but the infirmity of his judgment seems
deniable. At the same time there he is, at all e
par droit de naissance, even though his title by
been somewhat shaken; and he is so circumstance
he cannot be dealt with as if he were not, and wi
always be an important man while his health a
lasts, yet he does not inspire that confidence wh
Minister ought to enjoy in order that he may be
he were again called upon to form a Government
difficult to rally round him such colleagues as
to have. However, all speculations as to the
present idle. Much will depend upon the result
election, and the present Government are [illegible]
the year at all events.

Young Stanley (Derby's son) is just [illegible]
promising young man, and, if he trains [illegible]

[1] Had been 'Whip.'

[illegible] Administration. My position in the [illegible] agreeable one. As I have no office which [illegible] nobody abuses me in order to knock me [illegible] the Government and the Liberals, wishing [illegible] side, are vying with each other in civilities. [illegible] as long as it lasts, and after five years and [illegible] labour, I find it not disagreeable to have [illegible] of my time.

[illegible] was here I called upon him, and took that [illegible] telling him what I thought about the system of [illegible] Naples. He asked me to put in writing what [illegible] him, and I did so.

[illegible] Palmerston, who spoke and wrote Italian [illegible] correctly, availed himself of his comparative [illegible] of office to pay Count Aquila the compliment [illegible] with him in his own language. When [illegible]manuel was made a Knight of the Garter at [illegible] Castle, the Queen wished that he should have [illegible] of the oath which he was about to take. [illegible]merston accordingly wrote out a translation in [illegible] handed it to the King. Cavour, when he [illegible] it, was so interested in the incident that he [illegible] the paper, and, having ascertained that it was [illegible] Palmerston's own handwriting, put it away, as [illegible] relic, among the archives under his control. [illegible] early part of June there was a debate in the [illegible] Commons on the general conduct of our foreign [illegible] by the Tory Government. The immediate oc[illegible] the question of compensation to a Mr. Mather, [illegible]man, who had been cut down in the streets of [illegible] by an Austrian officer. Lord Palmerston found [illegible] the faltering action of the Foreign Office; [illegible] next letter shows that he regarded the state of [illegible] as merely provisional:—

C. G.: June 20, 1852.

[illegible] William,—Poor Malmesbury has got into sad [illegible] his diplomatic mismanagement and his ungram[illegible] despatches; but every trade requires an apprenticeship,

[1] One of the Royal Princes of Naples.

and a man cannot expect to start at once into being a good Foreign Secretary any more than into being a good performer on the violin. He is, however, naturally a clever man, and, with practice, may become a good Minister; but it was a hard trial for a man who had never been in any office whatever to undertake at once the management of our foreign affairs.

We are now on the eve of our dissolution, which is expected to happen about Tuesday or Wednesday week. The House of Commons will have finished all its business by Friday week, and the Lords will wind up theirs in two or three days afterwards. Those who have studied the matter, and are able to judge, think that the general election will send us back a House of Commons divided into fractions, not very different in their relative proportions from those which exist in the present House. Some say the Derby party will gain from ten to twenty votes, some say it will lose from ten to twenty; but that gain, if they make it, will not give them a majority of their own, and it may fairly be assumed, therefore, that the Government, as it now is constituted, cannot long survive the meeting of the new Parliament, if, indeed, it shall continue to exist as it now is until then.

The fact is, that this Government has only two real men in its ranks—one in the Lords, and one in the Commons—Derby and Disraeli. The rest are all cyphers as to debate, though many of them are, I fancy, inconvenient entities in council.

There will, however, be great difficulty found in the improvement of this Government, or in the construction of a new one. The Peelites are the only party who could as a body join Derby, and they are at present very hostile to him, and seem to me to think more of forming a Government upon the ruins of his than of entering into a combination with him. Still a liberal offer of places might alter their feelings; and they must be conscious that they are not numerous enough as a party to make a Government by themselves. John Russell, on the other hand, still clings to the position of leader of the Whig and Liberal party; but a great number of the Whigs openly express their opinion that he has shown himself unfit to lead a large party or to be the head of a Government, and that he has in a great measure lost their confidence. He certainly has entirely lost mine. I feel no resentment towards him personally or privately; but it would require strong inducements to persuade me to become again a member of a Government of which he was the head. I could feel no confidence in his discretion [illegible] leader, and could place no trust in [illegible] colleague having my official position at [illegible] arrangement that could be made would [illegible] Lord Lansdowne as head of the Govern- [illegible] John Russell and myself with other [illegible] best of the Peelites might serve as col- [illegible]. But Lansdowne's friends and family [illegible] not undertake such a task. We shall see. [illegible] the Court does not like the present Govern- [illegible] believe it. All royal persons like acquiescence [illegible] of demeanour and conduct. Peel and his [illegible] Aberdeen as Foreign Secretary, spoilt them [illegible] but Derby has an off-hand and sarcastic way [illegible] is not the manner of a courtier, and has, I [illegible] and successfully on the Danish question.

[illegible] my position is as agreeable as it is possible for [illegible] position to be. The Court, indeed, are cold, [illegible] Either they are conscious of having made a [illegible] passionate hostility to me, and do not like to [illegible] it, or else they still dislike me, and only are just [illegible] to prevent remarks. But the public, the press, [illegible] and political parties are all well disposed and [illegible] free to act individually, I can express my own [illegible] without caring for others, and those opinions have [illegible] lucky enough to meet with concurrence. The [illegible] are civil to me, hoping I may join them. The [illegible] civil to me, hoping that I may not leave them.

[illegible] got a new gardener at Broadlands; our former [illegible] dwindled down into a smoking sot. It is a trial to a [illegible] left as much alone and unlooked after as the gar- [illegible] Secretary of State necessarily is.

[illegible] that Aquila has been told at Naples to hold his [illegible] anything he heard or saw in England, and not to [illegible] revolutionary doctrines of the northern barbarians [illegible] more civilised sages of the south of Europe.

[illegible] dissolution of Parliament Lord Palmerston [illegible] first week in July went down to Tiverton, and [illegible] elected without opposition. At the former [illegible] election the Chartists had brought down a [illegible] lecturer, Mr. Julian Harney, to oppose [illegible] on this occasion their hearts failed them [illegible] moment. The only opponent, therefore, that he had to encounter was his old [illegible] the Tiverton butcher, whom he dis[illegible] happiest manner, as will be seen by [illegible] characteristic extracts from his speech [illegible] Much speculation was afloat as to wh[illegible] would join the Conservatives, now that he [illegible] from his former leader. Reporters flock[illegible] parts to gather any stray indications of [illegible] conduct. These he dexterously baffled all [illegible] humorous speech; and when the Radical [illegible] patient of this evasion, boldly put the direct [illegible] he was no less successfully parried. After [illegible] the electors for the honour which they had [illegible] on him for the fifth time, Lord Palmerston proc[illegible]

We were told when we came to this place that [illegible] not only have hot weather and a warm reception, [illegible] hot contest. We were told, in mysterious language, [illegible] bills circulated throughout the town, that an unkn[illegible] date would appear—a gentleman of 'independent [illegible] I have heard, gentlemen, of an independent fortun[illegible] heard of independent conduct; I have heard of in[illegible] character; but the handbill does not condescend to ex[illegible] is meant by 'independent principles.' I presume th[illegible] is to principles wholly independent of common sense, [illegible] and of liberality. (Laughter.) I am glad, gentlemen, [illegible] of the constituency of Tiverton, that such a man has [illegible] found.* We have been told that the general election [illegible] this country is now engaged is to determine finally [illegible] one great question—I mean the question of Prot[illegible] Protection. It is my humble opinion that that que[illegible] been long since settled. I took the liberty of telling [illegible] autumn, when I had the pleasure of being here, that [illegible] saw the River Exe running up from the sea to [illegible] instead of running down from Tiverton to the sea, [illegible] then, and not until then, consider certainly that the [illegible] Protection was near at hand. I see no change in [illegible] of the Exe. I don't even see that in the constr[illegible] bridges you have taken any precautions to secure [illegible] a turn of the stream. What, gentlemen, after all [illegible] question which is called Protection? Why, [illegible] single word which represents a not very [illegible]

...something like that of 'independent princi... ...transferred; but Protection, stripped of its ...ically taxing the food of the many for the ... of the few. I have that notion of the good ... feeling of the British nation, that I am con... ... will consent to revert to a system which is ... and mistake. (Cheers.) If you wished to ... been accomplished by the Liberal commercial ... have marked for some years past the course of ... should give you an answer similar to that in... ... tablet which records the burial-place of the ... who built the magnificent cathedral of St. ... know very well that it is usual to adorn the ... of eminent persons with marble statues, or ... different ideas connected with them. The ... the architect of St. Paul's has no such ornaments. ...simple inscription of his name, and it is added, 'If ... his monument, look around you'—look around at ... structure which bears witness to the skill he ... in his profession. Well, gentlemen, if I am asked ... merit of those commercial measures which have of ... formed into laws, I answer, 'Look around you.' ...d you, beginning with the pros erity of the princely ...n his counting-house, and descending to the humble ... in his cottage. Ask the mother who carries ... her arms; ask the father whose children are ... him; ask them what has been the benefit of ...rcial relaxations of late years. They will tell you ... is felt both physically and morally, and they will ... not to revert to a system which would deprive ... enjoyments with which they have been blessed. ...nevertheless, told that there is one class which, amid ... prosperity, has suffered in some degree—namely, ... and occupiers of land. If I am asked what is the ... for them, I say their protection lies mainly in ... and contentment of the rest of their fellow... ...n. Is that a vain assertion? Why, look what hap... three or four years ago. In 1848, when all Europe ..., when thrones were overturned, when constitu... ... and modern, were alike levelled in the dust, what ... shown by this great country? There were a ... unjustly and unwisely dissatisfied with the con... ... country, wished for a violent change; but the moment that change was threatened you saw every man in the great city of London, from the highest peer down to the [illegible]blest labourer, mingling in honourable fellowship, and [illegible] forward to defend the laws and institutions of their [illegible] an array so formidable that it prevented even the [illegible] manifestation of disorder. Now, I believe that [illegible] happened if the people of this country had not [illegible] course of legislation had been directed towards the [illegible] good. Now, gentlemen, those persons and those [illegible] wish to improve the institutions of a great country [illegible] are bound to go slowly and deliberately, and they [illegible] meet with great resistance at every step which they [illegible] for one, do not complain of that resistance. It [illegible] character of the country, and it has this advantage, [illegible]vents sudden and ill-considered alterations, and that [illegible] proposed as improvements receive that due [illegible] discussion which renders them ultimately better [illegible] condition of the people to whom they apply. A [illegible]tion for ancient practices and institutions is an [illegible] peculiar characteristic of the people of this country, [illegible] the last to wish that that honourable and useful [illegible] should ever be discarded from their minds. There [illegible] the nations of the Continent who are more [illegible] apt to change, and national character is often [illegible]cumstances apparently trifling in themselves. [illegible] parts of the Continent if an innkeeper wishes to [illegible] his inn, he hangs up a sign of 'The New White [illegible] 'The New Golden Cross.' The last novelty is [illegible] considered the most attractive. Here, gentlemen, [illegible] course is pursued, and, if the owner of a [illegible] wishes to draw custom, he hangs up the sign of [illegible] Plough New Revived.' There is at a place [illegible] not far from London, an inn to which [illegible] fond of pigeon-shooting used to resort to [illegible] Well, what is the sign of that inn? It is the [illegible] Not that anybody was thought to prefer an old [illegible] one, but it was expected that gentlemen would [illegible] Old Hats' in preference to 'The New Hats.' [illegible] [illegible] up, and what was its sign? Why, 'The [illegible] [illegible] it prefixed by that superlative [illegible] [illegible] came down here, at the [illegible]

[illegible] attractions of national feeling with the [illegible] living, they add that it is the oldest turtle [illegible] The people of this country, too, when they [illegible] attachment to the land they live in, call [illegible] endearment, 'Old England;' but that does [illegible] from repairing what may have got into decay, [illegible] or ornamenting, or embellishing that which [illegible] may be made better.

[illegible] then turned to the Militia Bill [illegible] Government had just passed, and which he [illegible] though many of his constituents dis-[illegible]

[illegible] that no man in this country, except the few who [illegible] with the author of a pamphlet which I felt [illegible] to mention in the House of Commons, and who, [illegible] recommended that we should quietly submit to be [illegible] conquered, in the hope that the conqueror would [illegible] at our submission that he would grow ashamed [illegible] and would go away after having taken some [illegible] of our money—I presume, with this exception, [illegible] is no man who has an English heart in his bosom [illegible] feel that England is worth defending, and that he [illegible] make any sacrifice rather than allow his country to be [illegible] Why, I may say, gentlemen, that this country is [illegible] of civil and political liberty, and that the conquest of [illegible] would not only be one of the greatest calamities to [illegible] itself, but would be a misfortune to the whole of [illegible] world. A poet, Campbell, who died not long ago, [illegible] describing the fate of Poland, that—

> Hope for a season bade the world farewell,
> And Freedom shrieked when Kosciusko fell;

[illegible] would indeed for ever bid adieu to the world, and [illegible] would die and not shriek, if England were to be con-[illegible] You have for the last two days had bands of music [illegible] your streets, followed by all the healthy-looking chil-[illegible] place, some toddling along in the ranks who were [illegible] to keep their feet; but that peaceful display has [illegible] the joy and contentment of all the people of [illegible] What would you have said, however, if these bands [illegible] a hostile force—if the armed hosts following the [illegible] had come to occupy at free quarters every house of [illegible]

R

your town, and, having occupied every house, to [illegible] selves perfectly free with everything and every[illegible] contained? I may be told these are vain [illegible] appeals made to the fanciful fears of the country [illegible] purpose of obtaining the means of adding to the [illegible] ture. That reminds me of a story which I [illegible] heard of an elderly lady who lived near Henley-[illegible] and who, when an invasion was expected by Napoleon [illegible] parte, said she did not believe he would ever come, [illegible] had been told in her youth the Pretender was coming, [illegible] he never came to Henley, she believed Napoleon [illegible] never would come there either. Now, I do not quote this, gentlemen, to throw any reflection upon the intelligence [illegible] elderly portion of the fairer sex, because I remember [illegible] heard that the Duchess of Gordon, in the time of Mr. [illegible] talking to an elderly statesman, was told by him, with [illegible] something in which he thought he had acted unwisely, '[illegible] Madam, I feel that I am growing an old woman;' [illegible] the Duchess replied, 'I am glad to hear that that's all, [illegible] thought your Grace was growing an old man, and [illegible] worse thing.' (Great laughter.) Now, I say that [illegible] who tell you that because you have had no invasion [illegible] Norman Conquest you never will have one, and that [illegible] not guard against it, are old men. Though they [illegible] old in years, they are old in imbecility of intellect. [illegible] who are most able to judge of military and naval [illegible] tell you that an invasion is perfectly possible; that it [illegible] possible now than it ever was before, mainly on account [illegible] great change which has been made by the application [illegible] in naval and military operations; and to tell you that [illegible] safe from invasion now because you were able to [illegible] before, to tell you that you are safe from invasions now [illegible] precautions, because hitherto you have prevented it by [illegible] tions, is the greatest of all possible absurdities. Why, [illegible] happened it that you had no invasion at the time of [illegible] good old lady at Henley spoke? Because you had [illegible] standing army within the kingdom; you had your [illegible] militia organised, enrolled, and on permanent pay; [illegible] besides, four hundred thousand volunteers, the whole [illegible] was in arms, and the enemy could not have made [illegible] attempt; but even then, I believe, and I have [illegible] good authority, it was only in consequence of the [illegible] naval operation, by which the French fleets [illegible]

... that an attempt to invade you was not made. ... have been such as it always will be when ... armed and prepared; but I say that, if ... not armed, and are not prepared, they are ... themselves, and are not showing themselves ... great and inestimable blessings which it has ... Providence to bestow upon them.

... then came forward and put several ... the nature of which will be fully apparent ... Palmerston's reply.

... friend, Mr. Rowcliff, has reproached me for not ... among you. I must say that he does not ... to make my visits here particularly agreeable ... (Laughter.) I cannot say that the manner in which ... me affords much encouragement to cultivate the ... of his way of thinking. Whether Mr. Row... Radical, a Chartist, or a Tory, I really cannot say. I ... all parties may have some reason or other for ... him. Mr. Rowcliff says that I only told you of the ... Governments and Parliaments have done, and that I ... done, and that I have not told you of the bad. ... bless me! it was quite unnecessary for me to do ... he was here. (Loud laughter.) If there was a bad ... be recorded, to be invented, or to be imagined, I am ... Mr. Rowcliff would be the first man to tell you of it. ... which was increased when Mr. Rowcliff called out ...!") Well, Mr. Rowcliff is impatient under this ... I will hit lower or higher, just as he pleases; but ... allow me to hit somewhere. Mr. Rowcliff has asked me ... Government I mean to join. Now, that is a question ... depend upon the future; but I will tell him what ... I do not mean to join. I can assure you and him that ... will join a Government called a Rowcliff Administration. ... (Laughter and cheering.) Now, gentlemen, do not you ... because you deem it very absurd that there should be ... administration, that my friend Mr. Rowcliff is at all ... way of thinking; for I believe I am not far mistaken ... opinion that he will consider everything going wrong in ... and in this country until the Rowcliff Administra... govern the land. Mr. Rowcliff has raked up old and ... commonplaces about pensions. He ought to know—

because he has no right to talk upon the subject [illegible] forming himself about it—that pensions are now [illegible] limited in amount, and that they are only given for [illegible] ledged public services. All those abuses of sinecure [illegible] dinate pensions, and of misbestowed pensions, which [illegible] former times, have been corrected, and the pension list [illegible] enormously reduced. Mr. Rowcliff says I voted [illegible] Militia Bill. As I have already explained to you, the [illegible] difference between the Militia Bill which I opposed [illegible] Militia Bill which I supported was, that the former was [illegible] upon compulsory service as the rule, admitting [illegible] service as the exception, while the Bill of the present [illegible] ment, which I supported, was founded upon voluntary [illegible] as the rule, and admits of compulsory service as only the [illegible] and contingent exception. The militia now to be raised [illegible] raised by bounty, and, if I have any fault to find with [illegible] is that I think the bounty is rather too high. That, [illegible] I presume, can be no ground of objection to young [illegible] may be disposed to enlist. My belief is that you [illegible] no ballot, but that you will gain all your men from [illegible] taneous patriotism of the people, aided by the induce[illegible] the bounty. I do not think so ill of the young men of [illegible] as to believe that they will be afraid of twenty-[illegible] service during the year in the militia. I command[illegible] ment of local militia, which used to assemble for tw[illegible] days' training, and I knew only one instance of a [illegible] wished to go home before the twenty-eight days [illegible] He was one of the privates, who came to me and [illegible] lord, I wish you would let me go home.' I replied [illegible] You have only a week to serve now.' 'Well,' said [illegible] fact is that before I comed here I promised a young [illegible] my parish that I'd marry her, if so be as I surviv[illegible] paign.' (Great laughter.) I replied, 'Heaven for[illegible] young woman should be disappointed! Go home [illegible] her, and tell her the campaign has not been so dange[illegible] may have thought it.' (Laughter.) I am convinc[illegible] young men of England will not be afraid of [illegible] campaign in a militia regiment. Mr. Rowcliff [illegible] my notions of Parliamentary reform. Now, Mr. [illegible] Chartist, and is for the five or six or any [illegible] points of the Charter. I am not a Chartist, and [illegible] to become a Chartist. I am quite satisfied with [illegible] of the country under which I have been [illegible] lived, and under which I hope to die. I am for a limited constitutional monarchy; I am not for a republic. I have what republics are in other countries. I have seen that cannot maintain their ground, and that when you try to them you invariably lead the way to a military . I am for septennial Parliaments. A septennial , practically, is not a Parliament that lasts for seven for we all know that the average duration of the Parlia- during the last thirty or forty years has not been more three or four years. If you establish annual Parliaments will have the country in a perpetual commotion. Your of Parliament will not have time to learn their duties, business will be ill done. In the same way, if you nial Parliaments, during the first year the members rning their business, in the second year they will ginning useful measures, and in the third year they nking of the Rowcliffs of their respective consti- (laughter), and endeavouring to shape their course, good of their country, but in order to conciliate the of their constituents. With regard to vote by bal- voting—I object to it, because I think it at variance national character, and with the principle of our . I think a true Englishman hates doing a thing or in the dark. I do not believe that a majority of would consent to give their votes in secret, even permitted them to do so; and I think if the law them to do so, it would be a debasement of the character. But I have a higher objection. I hold right of voting is a trust reposed in the elector for good. I do not think that a vote is given for the the man who possesses it, and that he can take it to bidder and get £5, £10, or £20, as the case may be. is given as a trust for the public and for the nation; that any trust reposed in a man for the public good to perform in public. I say, that for men who are with the high and important duty of choosing the best the country in Parliament to go sneaking to , and, poking in a piece of paper, looking round no one could read it, is a course which is unconsti- unworthy the character of straightforward and men.

he went to Lewes to attend the Royal Agricultural Society. In his speech on this occasion occurred that definition of [illegible] which has become a household word. The toast w[illegible] he had to propose was, 'Prosperity to the Borough[illegible] after remarks on its antiquity and its history [illegible] from the time of the Romans, he spoke as follows[illegible]

Now, gentlemen, the Romans were great agricultur[illegible] drew great supplies of grain from this island. But [illegible] was closed that wonderful book of knowledge which the [illegible] investigations of the present day have opened to you [illegible] mysterious science of chemistry which was then unkn[illegible] ever there was a case in which it was true that know[illegible] power, that maxim is peculiarly true in reference to [illegible] which chemistry affords to agriculture. Allusion has [illegible] made to the question of guano, and it has been [illegible] what is perfectly true, that when I held an office which [illegible] have enabled me, if it had been possible, to assist the [illegible] with regard to guano, my endeavours proved fruitless. [illegible] the Peruvians were not more disposed to let us put [illegible] their guano than the British farmer would be to hav[illegible] put upon his corn. But, gentlemen, I cannot but [illegible] the progress of chemical science, and the applicati[illegible] science to practical agriculture, may lead you to [illegible] which will render you less anxious and solicitous [illegible] same guano, and that instead of sending to the other [illegible] world for more manure for our fields, we shall find [illegible] nearly, if not quite, as good within a few hundred [illegible] dwellings. Now, gentlemen, I have heard a defini[illegible] I have heard it said that dirt is nothing but a thin[illegible] place. Now, the dirt of our towns precisely corre[illegible] that definition. It ought to be upon our fields, [illegible] could be such a reciprocal community of interests [illegible] country and the towns, that the country should [illegible] towns, and the towns should fertilise the country, [illegible] disposed to think that the British farmer would [illegible] he does, though he still might care something, [illegible] guano. Now, we all acknowledge that there [illegible] of nature, and that those who violate these laws [illegible] for it. Well, it is a law of nature that n[illegible] Matter is decomposed, but only for the purpose [illegible] some new form useful for the purposes of [illegible] But we neglect that law. We allow decom[illegible] towns to pollute the atmosphere, to ruin [illegible]

[illegible] is so pestilent to life and destructive of [illegible] sustenance, if instead of that there could be [illegible] by which those substances which are noxious [illegible] should be transferred so as to fertilise the [illegible], I am persuaded that, not only would the [illegible] town populations be thereby greatly improved, [illegible] of the agricultural population would derive [illegible] benefit from the change. I therefore recommend [illegible] to ponder the maxim that 'Knowledge is power,' [illegible] diffusion of the most useful kind of knowledge is [illegible] main objects for which the Royal Agricultural [illegible] established, I am persuaded it will tend mainly [illegible] efficiently to the advancement of the interest and the [illegible] the agricultural class of the country.

[illegible] returns to town, and sends off a report to his [illegible] Naples of what he has been doing, and what [illegible] result of the general election.

C. G.: July 24, 1852.

[illegible] Tiverton election went off very well, and my little [illegible] there, as well as my speech at the Lewes Agricultural [illegible] afterwards, have had much more success and praise [illegible] really deserved. It is a comfort, however, when the [illegible] on the right side.

[illegible] only thing that everybody, except a few family ad- [illegible] now consider impossible is, that John Russell should [illegible] new Administration. He has lost immensely in public [illegible] and consideration. Some of the most sensible of [illegible] are trying to put Lord Lansdowne up as head of the [illegible] the man to form the next Administration. That [illegible], and it seems to me that John Russell as well as I [illegible] serve under Lord Lansdowne, but I would certainly not [illegible] under Johnny, and Johnny, I should think, would [illegible] serve under me, at least at present; and he is too [illegible] able a man, with all his faults and failings, to be put [illegible] shelf and entirely passed by. Lansdowne would, I [illegible] willing to undertake such a task if he was called [illegible] do so. The Government seem to have gained by the [illegible] just strength enough to make it impossible to carry, [illegible] beginning of the session, whether it be October, Novem- [illegible] January, or February, a vote of no confidence, and I [illegible] that no such vote will be attempted; but they have not gained strength enough to carry them thı measures in the session, and what I expect is, that tl beat upon some of their fanciful schemes for relieving and increasing nobody's burdens. This is too mou to be practicable.

Indirect overtures have lately been made to me members of the Government, but I at once made n saying, I am well content at present with my preser Many people, and more than might have been suppo me as the next Minister, but I do not think that there would be at once the difficulty about John Ru was Minister I should ask him to take the Foreign go to the House of Lords to assist Lansdowne, or Lansdowne should not choose to do so.

I have only one horse in training this year, and four races with him, two of which, however, were over. He is three years old, and likely to win me se races. He runs next week for the Goodwood Cup, b his winning, as he would have to meet some very g He is by Venison out of an Emilius mare that I some time.

We have lost some good men in this new I George Grey, Cardwell, Mahon, Grenfell, and seve but then we have got rid of some bad ones, George Urquhart, and the like. I do not reckon Anstey riddances, for though he came in to impeach me, he I become one of my warmest friends and supporters. is that Urquhart and Anstey were brought in at t of 1847 in order that they might be set at me an me if they could. Urquhart's seat at Stafford, and Youghal, cost many thousand pounds, and neither o any money to throw away.

Allusion is made in the foregoing letter to of political warfare which attracted much at the time. Lord Palmerston, in the earlier career, and especially about the time of his action, in 1840, against Mehemet Ali, in France, had to encounter attacks more more unscrupulous than often fall to the lot man, however eminent. There went about a knot of men, half of them fanatical [illegible] the Foreign Secretary as a [illegible]try, and as having sold himself to [illegible] money. If more recent instances of [illegible] were not too fresh in our minds to [illegible] excessive wonderment, we might well feel [illegible] even a small section of their hearers should [illegible] ear to their assertions. But so it was; and [illegible]merston, however imperturbable by nature, felt [illegible] counsel's opinion as to the propriety of [illegible] informations against the authors of these [illegible] course, however, was, on consideration, [illegible]; and, indeed, it would have been giving [illegible] an importance which they did not deserve. [illegible] time previously he had been obliged to take [illegible] Court of Queen's Bench the publisher of the [illegible] in the columns of which he had been accused [illegible] his official knowledge for stockjobbing pur[illegible] he obtained from another newspaper, without [illegible]edings, an apology for a suggestion that he [illegible]erned in a disreputable mining adventure [illegible] He received, therefore, his full share of the [illegible]rected by political malice during the years [illegible] was making his way to the unassailable position [illegible] latterly occupied.

[illegible] returning to 1852, we find him describing to [illegible] the state of parties during the pause be[illegible] the general election and the meeting of the new [illegible]ment:—

Brocket: September 17, 1852.

[illegible] seem generally disposed to wait to see what measures [illegible] propose, and to deal with those measures [illegible] to their merits, and I think the chances are that [illegible] these measures will be deemed objectionable, and [illegible]jected by Parliament. It will then remain to be [illegible] such rejection will be considered by the Go[illegible] a sufficient reason for resigning. The probability [illegible] Derby will not easily take such a hint, but will [illegible] ground until he is forced to retire. His language is that his is the last Conservative Government, [illegible] him comes the Deluge. But if he begins [illegible] find it hard to get any fresh troops to join him, [illegible] own corps he can draw little additional strength. [illegible] forced to retire great difficulties will arise. [illegible] clings pertinaciously to his former position of [illegible] and will not serve under any other chief. On [illegible] the Whig and Liberal party have greatly lost [illegible] capacity as a leader, and he would find it very [illegible] such a Government as would be strong enough to [illegible] not think the Peelites would join him. I certainly [illegible] serve under him again, though I might serve with [illegible] a third person. Thus he would be driven either to [illegible] his old clique of Greys and Barings, of whom the [illegible] tired, or to ally himself with Graham and the [illegible] whom the country is afraid, and against him he would [illegible] the supporters of the present Government, numbering [illegible] 290, the Peelites, about 50, and a certain number of [illegible] who would be disposed to look to me, perhaps 20. [illegible] make a majority against him, besides the general [illegible] the country that he has not the qualities required [illegible] Minister. The way of avoiding these embarrassments [illegible] be to place Lansdowne at the head of the Government [illegible] *present* Johnny will not hear of serving under anybody [illegible] probable, however, that somehow or other this [illegible] be got over, and that thus a Liberal Government [illegible] formed, supposing always that Derby should not be [illegible] maintain himself. However, time will show.

So we have at last lost our great Duke.[1] Old [illegible] and both bodily and mentally enfeebled by age, he [illegible] great loss to the country. His name was a tower of [illegible] abroad, and his opinions and counsel were valuable [illegible] No man ever lived or died in the possession of more [illegible] love, respect, and esteem from his countrymen.

I have been rather lucky this year on the turf, [illegible] only one horse (Buckthorn[2]) in training, and having [illegible] races with him. Some who have had six horses have [illegible] one race.

The Liberal party were now looking out [illegible] and a leader. Lord John Russell was [illegible]

[1] Duke of Wellington.

[2] Won the Ascot Stakes. He looked at one [illegible] race that, during the running, 100 to 1 was offered [illegible]

Palmerston had given too recent a blow. In a letter to which the following is a reply, Lord Fitzwilliam suggested the Marquis of Lansdowne as a leader, although he alluded to his age as being against him, and referred to declarations made in the House of Lords as to his wish for retirement.

Lord Palmerston, as we have seen, had already thought of him as the best man for the post.

C. G.: September 24, 1852.

My dear Lord Fitzwilliam,—Seventy-two is certainly, as you say, an advanced period of life, but if health and faculties are unimpaired, lapse of years can be no objection. Cardinal Fleury was seventy-three when made Prime Minister; and we are now lamenting the loss of a man who continued in the able administration of an important office till the age of eighty-three.[1]

Leave-takings, announced in Parliament, should be construed with reference to circumstances, and they sometimes only mean that the person who pronounces them does not intend again to place himself in the particular and relative position from which he has just been freed. But your previous question—unlike those which are moved in Parliament—is a very practical one. You ask whether 'it is desirable at present to overthrow the Derby Government.' To this I would add another doubt, namely, whether it is possible to do so? I apprehend that there are in the House of Commons many men who rank as Liberals, and who differ from the supposed principles of the present Government, who, nevertheless, would not join in any vote at the opening of the session, the avowed object of which would be to overthrow the present Government. Their motives, I conceive, would be: first, that there is no existing party or combination which would at once present the elements of a strong Government to succeed the present one; and, secondly, that in such a state of things, the best course to pursue is to allow the present Government to explain their intended policy, and to develop their proposed measures, and to deal with that policy and those measures according to their intrinsic merits. I own that such appears to me to be the best course. If the present Government propose good measures, why should not the country have the benefit of such measures? If the

[1] Duke of Wellington.

[illegible] are bad, let them be rejected, and [illegible] abide the consequences of their own [illegible]. It is indeed hard to imagine that [illegible] will be able to make good all the expectations [illegible] they have held out to various classes of the [illegible] the chances seem to be that they will [illegible] when those measures come to be discussed [illegible] the composition of the Government is not one [illegible] without material changes. The Govern[illegible] two men of first-rate abilities, one in one House [illegible] in the other—Derby and Disraeli; but it may [illegible] whether the other members of the Cabinet are [illegible] sustaining the rude shock of parliamentary [illegible] a difficult session. What you say about organic [illegible] is perfectly true. They ought not to be proposed [illegible] they are really needed for the public good, and [illegible] not be launched by a Government as a clap-trap [illegible] popularity without any fair prospect of their [illegible]

[illegible] do not myself see any reason why we may not go on [illegible] without any such organic changes. It would, I think, [illegible] improvement (if there would be no obstacle in the details [illegible] of such a measure) if the present system of [illegible] could be got rid of, and if the poor-rate register [illegible] made also the register for the right of voting; and if such [illegible] change were accompanied by some small diminution in the [illegible] qualification for electors, no harm would be done. I should [illegible] be surprised if the present Government were to propose [illegible] measures of this kind. It would not be out of character [illegible] a Government of which one member proposed to give every [illegible] a vote, and of which another member, on a motion [illegible] Parliamentary reform, talked very freely about the ex[illegible] of emancipating the labouring classes.

The great frankness of Lord Palmerston's charact[illegible] out in the next letter. He remained on perfect[illegible] friendly terms with Lord J. Russell, but, as will [illegible] he had not hesitated to tell him openly that [illegible] confidence in him, as a leader, was shaken, and that [illegible] would be unwilling, therefore, to serve under him agai[illegible] This was all received in good part by the ex-Premie[illegible] for offence can never be taken at an open expression [illegible] honest opinion, whether it be right or wrong.

Broadlands: October, 1852.

[illegible]sdowne,—The Duke and Duchess of Bedford [illegible] for a day while we were there; and as I found [illegible] that the Duke was desirous of knowing my [illegible] serving in any Government that might be formed [illegible] Russell, I sought an opportunity of a conversation [illegible] and as he led to the subject, I spoke my mind to him [illegible] detail. I said that my private and personal regard [illegible]ship for John Russell remain unaltered, and that I [illegible] entertain towards him individually those senti[illegible] kindness which one feels for a private friend with [illegible] has been acting in public life for more than twenty [illegible] But I said that my political confidence in him is gone, [illegible] I would not again act under him as a chief who [illegible] the arbiter of my official position or the guide of my [illegible] course. That as a political leader he is not to be [illegible] upon: is infirm of purpose, changeable in his views, [illegible]tually swayed by influences which are known and [illegible] by their results.

[illegible] I said as to my political confidence in John Russell [illegible] Minister. In regard to my own feelings as to a [illegible] my former official dependence upon him, I said that [illegible] and the longer I reflected upon his conduct towards [illegible] year, the more I felt those sentiments which induced [illegible] time to write him a note to beg that he would not [illegible] from the quiet manner in which I took what he had [illegible] I did not feel that just indignation which his con[illegible] necessarily inspire.

[illegible] letter here goes into details connected with his [illegible] in December, 1851, which have already been [illegible], and then continues:—

[illegible] to the Duke of Bedford that the upshot of all this [illegible] I could not again serve under John Russell, but that [illegible] not object to serve with him on equal terms under a [illegible]. But I said that indeed it seemed to me impos[illegible] in the event of the present Government falling John [illegible] should be able to form a Government; that I do not [illegible] Peelites would join him; and that he would therefore [illegible] him the two hundred and ninety who are reckoned [illegible] of the present Government, the forty or fifty [illegible] and a certain number, however small, who are likely

to ask what course I should under such circumstances [illegible] In conclusion, I said to the Duke that which indeed I [illegible] stated to him some weeks before—that in the present [illegible] up condition of parties it seems to me that you are the [illegible] the most likely to reconcile and reunite the sections [illegible] Liberal party, and also to receive support from some [illegible] men whose present tendencies would lead them to [illegible] adherents of the existing Government.

The Duke expressed himself pleased with my [illegible] feelings towards John Russell, and acknowledged [illegible] manner in which, according to my own view of the [illegible] had stated my own case.

I do not think, however, that he seemed to be [illegible] that John Russell shares my conviction as to the [illegible] of his now forming another Government.

Lord Lansdowne, however, pleaded age [illegible] for repose in reply to those sections of the Li[illegible] who called upon him to come forward and fill th[illegible] Upon this Lord Palmerston remarks:—

Broadlands: October [illegible]

I can easily understand that you should, after [illegible] of ministerial labour and confinement, prefer freed[illegible] straint, but—

> When Honour calls, where'er she points the way,
> The sons of Honour follow and obey;

and if the course of events should render a sacrifice [illegible] part necessary, that sacrifice will undoubtedly be [illegible]

I should not be surprised, however, if Derby's [illegible] were to have more life in it than people generally [illegible] Protection Derby will openly throw over, and if [illegible] which he proposes are tolerably good they will be [illegible] any proposal of a vote of no confidence would [illegible] and if Derby would recruit a little more debating [illegible] out of his own followers, which may not be [illegible] might be able to struggle on for some consider[illegible] there was an obvious prospect of forming [illegible] Government, all these resources would be too [illegible] but if there can be no Liberal Government [illegible] John Russell, Derby may have a longer [illegible] was at first imagined.[1]

[1] To Lord Lansdowne, October [illegible]

[illegible] met for business on November [illegible] had little altered the balance of [illegible] the Government were still in a minority. [illegible], as will be seen, had adjusted their [illegible], and were prepared to form a Cabinet,

C. G.: November 17, 1852.

[illegible] William,—I think the chances are that the [illegible] will fall by their measures if they are measures [illegible] and importance, because any such measures [illegible] changes in the distribution of taxes; and though [illegible] who are to be lightened may like such changes, [illegible] to be burthened will object, and the measures will [illegible] be thrown out. If the measures are very small [illegible] disappoint the expectation which has been excited; [illegible] seems likely that this Government will not last [illegible] now there is another formation ready to take their [illegible] Lansdowne would consent to be chief if asked [illegible] to do so. John Russell would take office under [illegible], and would, moreover, if it were wished, go up to [illegible] of Lords, and I should then be left to perform that [illegible] but irksome task of conducting the business of the [illegible] in the House of Commons. In that case I should [illegible] Home Office, and Johnny the Foreign. I should, in [illegible] much prefer the Home Office to going back to the [illegible] labour of the Foreign Office. *J'y ai été*, as the [illegible] said of fox-hunting. The Peelites would form [illegible] such a Government, and we should have the support [illegible] few of those who are now adherents of the present [illegible]. However, all this is as yet in the clouds; one [illegible] dispose of the bear till the bear is taken and slain, [illegible] ought not to make a Government for the Queen till [illegible] sure what her intentions are upon that matter. [illegible], however, that this Government will sink under its [illegible] before Easter.

[illegible] Austrians have distinguished themselves by declining [illegible] anybody to the funeral of the Duke, and I am told [illegible] Queen is very angry with them. The papers say it is [illegible] himself who took this decision; and I am told he [illegible] fanatic, sleeps on a hard mattress on the floor, stints [illegible] sleep, and mortifies the body in all ways. This is a [illegible] enlightened and sensible Emperor of Austria would

> be a great acquisition for Europe, though [illegible] be a novelty. But the Austrians hate [illegible] English nation, notwithstanding the civil [illegible] changed between the Austrian Government and [illegible] Administration when Derby came into office [illegible] we can do without them, and I hope they can [illegible] It is desirable for their own sakes that they should [illegible] do so, for help from England they are not very likely [illegible]

The Queen's Speech at the opening of Pa[illegible] had been very ambiguous on the subject of Fr[illegible] In the opinion of many it was studiously so; and [illegible] therefore considered necessary to elicit, without [illegible] a parliamentary declaration, in order to show [illegible] world that a free-trade policy had been irrev[illegible] adopted. Accordingly, on November 23, Mr. C[illegible] Villiers moved a resolution which was so worded [illegible] the Government could not possibly accept it, and, there-fore, had the House adopted it, the Ministry must [illegible] once have retired from office. It was, however, not the general wish to turn out the Government before they had proposed their Budget; so Lord Palmerston came to the rescue, and proposed an amended resolution worded with more regard to Tory susceptibilities. The difference between the two resolutions was, that while they both unequivocally affirmed the doctrine of Free Trade and its permanent establishment, Lord Palmerston's did not compel those who agreed to it publicly to recant the private opinions which, at a former period they may have honestly entertained. The Government accepted it, and it was carried by a large majority.

This debate finally closed the discussions on Free Trade, which had for so many years proved the subject of controversy in Parliament.

The result of the division in the House of Commons did not, however, deceive the Ministry as to the weakness of their position, and they naturally [illegible] round to see how they could strengthen it. [illegible] no time to lose; so on the following day, [illegible] made a formal proposal to Lord Palmerston [illegible]

Derby's Government. He declined; saying that he could not do so singly, and that the Peelites with whom he was then acting showed no disposition to approximate to the Government. The Ministry, therefore, had to face without any new allies the battle over their Budget which Mr. Disraeli, as Chancellor of the Exchequer, introduced on December 3. The principal features were, besides a diminution of the tea duties a reduction of the malt tax, which created a large deficit, and a doubling of the house tax, to supply the void. The farmers, expecting something better, did not care about the reduction made in their favour, while the townsfolk did care very decidedly about the increase made at their cost. The Budget was generally condemned, and, in spite of an energetic 'whip,' the Government were beaten by 19 in a very full House. They accordingly resigned.

CHAPTER IX.

GOES TO THE HOME OFFICE IN THE ABERDEEN ADMINISTRATION—WORK AT HOME OFFICE—TEMPORARY RESIGNATION.

Lord Aberdeen was charged with the formation of a new Government. He at once sought the co-operation of Lord Palmerston, who, at first, withheld it, being unwilling to share the responsibility of a Cabinet whose foreign policy, he anticipated, would be of a character to merit his disapproval. But he was indispensable. A general though undefined feeling among the public had already marked him out as the coming man. Lord Lansdowne therefore renewed Lord Aberdeen's solicitations, and induced Lord Palmerston to reconsider his decision. He selected the Home Office as his department, and gives to his brother the following account of his feelings and motives:—

C. G.: December 22, 1852.

I have accepted the Home Office in the new Government. When first Lansdowne and Aberdeen asked me to join the new Government I declined, giving as my reason that Aberdeen and I had differed so widely for twenty-five years on all questions of foreign policy that my joining an Administration of which he was to be the head would be liable to misconstruction both at home and abroad. But the next day Lansdowne came again and urged me strongly, and I found that the Foreign Office, which I had determined not myself in any case to take, would be held either by Clarendon or John Russell, whose well-established reputations for liberality would give a security in regard to our foreign relations.

Lansdowne's representations of the great importance, in the present state of things at home and abroad, that the new Government should be as strong in its fabric as the materials available

…it, determined me to yield to his advice … Home Office; and the more I have thought … the better satisfied I have felt that I have … Foreign Office will be taken by John Russell, … business too much for him, in addition to his … in the House of Commons, he will then … Clarendon. The Home Office was my own choice; … in my own mind that I would not go back to … Office, and that if I ever took any office it should … —It does not do for a man to pass his whole life … and the Home Office deals with the concerns … internally, and brings one in contact with one's … men, besides which it gives one more influence in … militia and the defences of the country.

…Government will combine almost all the men of talent … in the House of Commons except Disraeli; but … will be numerically strong, as they reckon about … many of these, however, will probably be disposed … Government a fair trial.

…o Mr. Sulivan, his brother-in-law, he writes:—

Carlton Gardens: December 24, 1852.

…sday I positively declined joining the new Government, …nsdowne, who was nearly an hour talking to me, and … to Aberdeen, who came and offered me *carte blanche* …artments; but on Wednesday morning Clarendon …ll me he had had the Foreign Office offered him, and …s disposed to accept it. That removed much of the …hich I had felt. When he left me, Lansdowne came …stly to press me to take office; and I at last con… …ake the Home Office, the department which I had … as the one I should have preferred if I had been …join the new regiment. Reflection has satisfied me …e acted rightly. The state of the country in all its …oreign and domestic, requires a Government as strong …e elements for making it; and if my aid is thought …wne and others likely to be useful, I ought not to let …elings stand in the way. As regards myself indi… …, must be borne in mind that when the Whigs and …ite to form a Government and to support it, I …had persisted in standing aloof, have been left in a … political solitude. I am glad, therefore, that I …hered to my first determination; and I am sure that the course which, on second thoughts, I ... the best for the public interest and for my own ...

There was a large body of men, however, ... have been only too glad to relieve Lord Pa... the 'political solitude,' which he here ... alternative to joining Lord Aberdeen's Gov...

The Tories were discontented with their ... Commons leader. They further had been ... ralised by recent party circumstances as to ... to doubt all political morality, and to regard ... as mere party swordsmen; when, therefore, ... of the year they saw the Foreign Secretary ... turned adrift by the Whig leader they began ... towards him with the same anxiety and yearning ... which an Italian little state in the Middle Ag... have looked for some *condottiere* of good repute ... about to be out of employment. They would ... have hailed him as their new chief had he been ... to join them. But between these three hund... odd gentlemen and Lord Palmerston there wa... common political creed; and the members of the ... sition who indulged in such a dream as this only ... thereby how completely they misunderstood his ... his character, and his political principles.

On December 27 the new Government ... their places in Parliament, when Lord Aberde... House of Lords, gave a sketch of its intend... With regard to foreign affairs, he said that ... 'adhere to the principles which had been pu... the last thirty years, and which consisted in ... the rights of all independent states, while, at ... time, we asserted our own rights and inte... above all, in an earnest desire to secure the ... peace of Europe.'

Considering that Lord Palmerston had ... Foreign Office during more than half the ... Lord Aberdeen was paying an indirect ... policy. As for Lord Palmerston him...

new duties, and writes thus to his

Carlton Gardens: January 31, 1853.

) are now preparing for the renewal 10th of this next month. We shall be bench, and I hope not weak in the It is clear that if we were to be turned out, that could be put in our stead would be has proved that his Government could may therefore expect that the moderate men him will not be disinclined to give us a fair will be our business to deserve it. Though the of men of various parties and shades of opinion, to unite, will, I doubt not, unite to agree, we shall go on very well.

labouring to place the country in a state of defence, limit is the purse of the Chancellor of the Ex- whatever may be at the bottom of the secret the French Emperor, into whose bosom no man can no reason to apprehend an immediate or even an with France; and if we have two years more of allowed us, we shall be in a good defensive position. meantime we do not allow that we are even now de- The increase of navy, artillery, marines, and the of the militia, have placed us in a very different from that in which we stood two or three years ago. marriage seems to me a most sensible one. He of a political alliance of any value, or of sufficient to counterbalance the annoyance of an ugly or epi- whom he had never seen till she was presented to bride; and he was quite right to take a wife whom and liked. I admire the frankness with which he himself a *parvenu*, and the assertion of that truth, it may shock the prejudices of Vienna and Petersburg, him to the bulk of the French nation.

Home Secretary Lord Palmerston astonished except those who knew him well, by the vigi- intelligence, and originality with which he his duties. No details were too small if only important to those concerned. He paid a Parkhurst Prison, and wrote a Memorandum on the ventilation of the cells with just as m[illegible] thoroughness as if he were conducting a measure in full view of the country. A sta[illegible] ment of this period of his career is the syst[illegible] ing tickets of leave to convicts. Hazar[illegible] experiment was at that time considere[illegible] successful, and solved the difficulty which the face when the Colonies declined any lo[illegible] us to shoot our refuse on their shores. It him to find a substitute for transportatio[illegible] become no longer available, and he carried House of Commons a Bill constituting the of secondary punishment, which, in its m[illegible] is still in force.

Many other useful measures owed their activity during the two years that he was [illegible] Office. The abatement of the smoke nui[illegible] metropolis, whereby to a great extent its was purified—the cessation of intramural i[illegible] which people could only have been induce[illegible] the evils by the influence of long custom—t[illegible] of the Factory Acts,[1] and the more genera[illegible] winter assizes for the trial of prisoners a[illegible] delivery, were among the most prominent doubted boons which his practical mind de[illegible] benefit of the country.

He was especially happy in his manner those numerous deputations which alwa[illegible] towards the Home Office. Deputation has defined as 'a noun of multitude which sig[illegible] but does not signify much.' However a[illegible] may be as a definition, it would be a gr[illegible] undervalue the importance to a minister o[illegible] the art of listening patiently, and giving

[1] The ten and a half hours of work were by [illegible] tween six a.m. and six p.m. This was a great [illegible] of the law. It was found, however, that the [illegible] not extend this limitation to children, but [illegible] Lord Palmerston warmly took up the cause [illegible] was brought to his notice, and rectified the law. [illegible]

civil 'No.' Lord Palmerston had it in degree. His prompt but cordial refusal was palatable than another man's cold and acquiescence.[1]

to some of his work in the following

C. G.: April 8, 1853.

William,—It is now a long while, I fear, since I you, but ever since the meeting of Parliament I as people do during a contested election, talked till night, and with no time to do anything. business of the Home Office, as far as that correspondence, is very far lighter than that of Office, but, during a session of Parliament, the the Secretary of State, up to the time when he the House of Commons, is taken up by deputa- and interviews with Members of Parliament, &c. But on the whole it is a much easier the Foreign, and, in truth, I really would not, on undertake again an office so unceasingly day of the year as that of Foreign Affairs. I to do some good in the Home Office. I am all the graveyards in London, a measure authorised session, and absolutely required for preserva- of the town. There is a company who are two great tunnels under London, fifty feet below north, the other south, of the Thames, running the river, beginning some way above the town, way below it. These tunnels are to be the which all the sewers and drains of London are so that nothing is to go into the Thames, and these tunnels are, at the point of termination, converted into manure to be sold to agricul- guano. I shall try to compel, at least, to burn their own smoke, and I should like shops, and to let shopkeepers sell beer like oil,

[1] certain inhabitants of Rugely, who wanted a new which had acquired an unenviable notoriety owing the residence of the poisoner Palmer, gives a which he could deal with requests that could He got rid of them by offering his own name would suit them.

and vinegar, and treacle, to be carried home and [illegible] wives and children.

Our session will be long but not dangerous. We [illegible] to renew the income tax and the East India Charter, and other matters will take time, but I do not see [illegible] other Government is, at present, possible. The last Cab[illegible] been too much discredited to be put back again, and Der[illegible]ing failed in his experiment to make a Cabinet out of [illegible] knew nothing of public business, would scarcely like [illegible] another trial with a new lot equally ignorant and [illegible] Besides, if we were beat by mere numbers, there [illegible] the resource of a dissolution, to which I conclude [illegible] have recourse rather than at once give up our posts. [illegible] have some difficulty next year about Parliamentary [illegible] but enough for the year are the troubles thereof. [illegible] nothing can be more harmonious than our Coalition [illegible]

I dare say you have heard at Naples much abo[illegible]bouring conspiring refugees. The answer I make to [illegible] complain of those matters here is, that a handful of [illegible] London cannot arrange a revolution in a foreign cou[illegible] send out the plan to be executed off-hand. They [illegible] first place, have associates and instruments many [illegible] number in the country to which the plan is to [illegible] because a revolution cannot be acted by a handful[illegible] They must have much local knowledge to make [illegible]ments, and this knowledge, bearing upon circumst[illegible] vary from day to day, is not possessed by men in [illegible] can only be furnished by men on the spot. The[illegible] London conspirators can do nothing without the co-[illegible] a great number of people in the foreign country, [illegible] they must have long and detailed communica[illegible] letters or by messengers. But what are the Gov[illegible] the foreign countries about if they cannot, by the[illegible] their passport system, find out the proceedings [illegible] mass of these conspirators who are in their own [illegible] they cannot intercept the letters or discover [illegible] messengers? It is plain that the real and [illegible] is worked out in the foreign country and not [illegible] these foreign Governments try to throw upon [illegible] really belongs to them, and if arms and [illegible] provided, it is the foreign Government that [illegible] find that out.

The country generally is highly pros[illegible]

[illegible] the emigration having gone just far [illegible] to a proper amount without making [illegible] scarce. The Irish emigration will, I [illegible] would be a good thing if a larger number [illegible]. The priests are, of course, furious, [illegible] so much out of their pocket.[1]

[illegible] that Clarendon[2] has got the Foreign Office. [illegible] business well, and keep up the character and [illegible] country.

[illegible] appeared this year in the United King- [illegible] the autumn the Presbytery of Edinburgh [illegible] their Moderator, to Lord Palmerston, [illegible] whether, under the circumstances, a national [illegible] be appointed on Royal authority. The Home [illegible] like Cromwell, who supplemented his exhor- [illegible] men to put their trust in God by a caution [illegible] powder dry, sent the following answer:—

Whitehall: October 19, 1853.

[illegible] am directed by Viscount Palmerston to acknowledge [illegible] of your letter of the 15th inst., requesting, on behalf [illegible] Presbytery of Edinburgh, to be informed whether it is [illegible] to appoint a day of national fast on account of the [illegible] of the cholera, and to state that there can be no doubt [illegible] manifestations of humble resignation to the Divine Will, [illegible] acknowledgments of human unworthiness, are [illegible] appropriate than when it has pleased Providence [illegible] mankind with some severe visitation; but it does not [illegible] Lord Palmerston that a national fast would be suit- [illegible] circumstances of the present moment.

[illegible] Maker of the Universe has established certain laws of [illegible] the planet in which we live, and the weal or woe of [illegible] depends upon the observance or the neglect of those [illegible] of those laws connects health with the absence of [illegible] exhalations which proceed from over-crowded [illegible] dwellings, or from decomposing substances, whether animal [illegible]; and those same laws render sickness the almost

[1] [illegible] Palmerston for many years spent a large portion of his [illegible] in enabling those of his tenants to emigrate who wished

[2] [illegible] succeeded Lord John Russell.

inevitable consequence of exposure to those noxiou
But it has at the same time pleased Providence
within the power of man to make such arrange
prevent or disperse such exhalations so as to rende
less, and it is the duty of man to attend to these la
and to exert the faculties which Providence has t
man for his own welfare.

The recent visitation of cholera, which has for
been mercifully checked, is an awful warning g
people of this realm that they have too much neg
duty in this respect, and that those persons with wh
to purify towns and cities, and to prevent or remov
of disease, have not been sufficiently active in reg
matters. Lord Palmerston would, therefore, sugg
best course which the people of this country ca
deserve that the further progress of the cholera
stayed, will be to employ the interval that will ela
the present time and the beginning of next spring
and executing measures by which those portions of
and cities which are inhabited by the poorest
which, from the nature of things, must most need
and improvement, may be freed from those causes
of contagion which, if allowed to remain, will inf
pestilence and be fruitful in death, in spite of all
and fastings of a united but inactive nation. Wh
done his utmost for his own safety, then is the tim
the blessing of Heaven to give effect to his exertions

I am, Sir, your obedient serv

HENRY I

This letter created a great stir, and some
tion among certain sections of the communi
was, after all, the embodiment of common
reminded those in authority that it was the
duty not to neglect the teachings of science
of practical Christianity. It suggested tha
had fulfilled their duty to their neighbour
not lift up clean hands in prayer and
lesson which it thus sought to inculcate on
pal authorities of Scotland was greatly
tary laws were at that time even less
cared for than now; and in the

[illegible] of this terrible disease, the fact [illegible] the conditions under which it was [illegible] were under human control, and [illegible] negligence and folly of individuals and [illegible] To substitute a national fast for the [illegible] of cleansing the drains and purifying [illegible] have been a strange misunderstand[illegible] the Will, as revealed in the operations of [illegible]

[illegible] of the day averred that Lord Palmer[illegible] into his new office the proclivities of [illegible] department, and that in his answer to the [illegible] he treated Heaven as a 'foreign power.' [illegible] was, however, wide of the mark, if it meant [illegible] any irreverence for sacred things on his [illegible] never either showed such a feeling himself, [illegible] its manifestation in others.

[illegible] was yet another occasion, about this time, [illegible] to a speech, he found himself made into a [illegible] target. In the winter of 1854, presiding [illegible] meeting at Romsey, he told them that [illegible] find that all children were born good, and [illegible] bad education and bad associations corrupted [illegible]. There might be exceptions, as there are [illegible] physically defective; but that the heart of [illegible] naturally good, and that it depended upon [illegible] whether that goodness, implanted at birth, [illegible] continue to display itself. This apparent piece [illegible] as to the doctrine of 'original sin' greatly [illegible] the clerical world, appearing as it did at the [illegible]. One leading organ had an amusing but [illegible] article, saying that if Lord Palmerston had [illegible] nurse he would have known better. 'If any[illegible] it continued, 'could teach a child to smile away [illegible] to bear abstinence with fortitude, rebukes [illegible], and inward commotions with grace, Lord [illegible] is the man to do it; nevertheless we feel [illegible] he would soon find he had as difficult subjects [illegible] as he ever found in perverse princes and the evil associations of Courts.' But [illegible] disposed to deal with it so lightly, and [illegible] gravely. The truth being all the time [illegible] had not the remotest idea of touching [illegible] abstruse topic as 'original sin,' but was [illegible] bouring men about those ordinary features [illegible] good or generally bad conduct which could [illegible] to every one of them.

One of the provisions of the Act forbidding [illegible] mural interment gave power to the Home Secretary [illegible] make exceptions in cases which he might deem [illegible] Lord Palmerston, however, appears to have deemed [illegible] fit, as may be gathered from the following answer [illegible] request for special permission in the case of a de[illegible] dignitary of the Church :—

Broadlands : January 2, 18[illegible]

My dear Stanley,[1]—I am sorry to say that I have [illegible] felt myself obliged to decline compliance with the request [illegible] tained in the enclosed letter. The practice of burying [illegible] bodies under buildings in which living people assemble [illegible] numbers is a barbarous one, and ought to be at once [illegible] ever put an end to, and I have made this a general rule [illegible] cases. But a rule is no rule if partial exceptions are [illegible] the rule then degenerates into an invidious selection of par[illegible] persons for its application, and other particular persons [illegible] relaxation.

And why, pray, should archbishops and bishops, and [illegible] and canons, be buried under churches if other persons [illegible] to be so? What special connection is there between [illegible] dignities and the privilege of being decomposed under the [illegible] of survivors? Do you seriously mean to imply that a [illegible] more likely to go to heaven because the body which it in[illegible] lies decomposing under the pavement of a church in[illegible] being placed in a churchyard?

If commemoration is what is wanted, a monument [illegible] placed in a church though the body is in the burial[illegible] but why cannot the monument be equally well erected [illegible] consecrated burial-ground?

As to what you say about pain to feelings by [illegible] burial-grounds, that is perfectly true. I am qui[illegible]

[1] Lord Stanley of Alderley.

[illegible]ly attended with pain to feelings which [illegible] to pressure upon pecuniary interests [illegible]serving of consideration. But no great [illegible] improvement can be effected without some [illegible]convenience to individuals, and the necessity [illegible] the demand for such sacrifices. To have [illegible] the application of the new system gradual [illegible] it to a nullity. England is, I believe, the [illegible] which, in these days, people accumulate putre[illegible] amid the dwellings of the living; and as to [illegible] under thronged churches, you might as well put [illegible], drawing-rooms, and dining-rooms.

[illegible] the first year of his renewed tenure of office [illegible] parted from his colleagues. In the [illegible]egister' for 1853 occurs this passage:—

[illegible] 16th of December an important ministerial crisis [illegible] by the announcement that Viscount Palmerston [illegible] his office. His resignation, however, was not [illegible], after an interval of some days' suspense, the [illegible] was prevailed upon to withdraw it. The opponents [illegible]vernment asserted that Lord Palmerston's secession [illegible]e was occasioned by a difference of opinion on his part [illegible] policy of the Cabinet upon the Eastern Question. On [illegible] hand, it was strenuously contradicted by the adherents [illegible]nistry; but as all explanation upon the subject was [illegible]n Parliament, the motive for a step so dangerous to [illegible]ity of the Earl of Aberdeen's Cabinet must remain [illegible]r conjecture.

[illegible]ote a letter to his brother-in-law, the Right [illegible]urence Sulivan, which states the case:—

C. G.: December 19, 1853.

[illegible]ate of the matter is plain and simple. I told Aberdeen [illegible]downe last year, when I joined the Government, that [illegible]at doubts as to my being able to concur in the plan of [illegible]ntary reform which John Russell might propose this

[illegible] day I was put on the Committee of Cabinet to [illegible] plan. John Russell stated his scheme. I wrote [illegible] day to state my objections. I re-stated them verbally in the Committee, and [illegible] Cabinet when John Russell [illegible] Cabinet. I stated them in a private [illegible] two occasions, to Aberdeen. I stated [illegible] in writing. In reply to that [illegible] by him that he would communicate with [illegible] colleagues. He then afterwards wrote [illegible] communicated with John Russell and [illegible] my objections were inadmissible; and [illegible] their decision. I had then nothing left for it [illegible] My office is too closely connected with [illegible] to allow me to sit silent during the whole [illegible] Bill through Parliament; and I could not take [illegible] contained material things of which I [illegible] fight it through the House of Commons, to [illegible] Lords, and to stand upon it at the hustings. [illegible] leave an office in which I took interest, and political [illegible] whom I like; but I could not do otherwise. [illegible]

The *Times* says there has been no difference in [illegible] about Eastern affairs. This is an untruth; but I felt [illegible] would have been silly to have gone out because I [illegible] have my own way about Turkish affairs, seeing that my [illegible] in the Cabinet did good, by modifying the views of [illegible] policy I thought bad. [illegible]

What were the 'differences' on Turkish [illegible] be seen later on, when we come to the Eastern [illegible] tion; but they concerned the moving of our [illegible] to the scene of conflict. However, Lord [illegible] withdrew his resignation, as is shown by [illegible] letter:—

C. G.: December 2[illegible]

I remain in the Government. I was much and [illegible] pressed to do so for several days by many of the [illegible] the Government, who declared that they were no [illegible] Aberdeen's answer to me, and that they [illegible] details of the intended Reform measure as still [illegible] cussion. Their earnest representations, and the [illegible] that the Cabinet had on Thursday taken a [illegible] affairs in entire accordance with opinions [illegible] unsuccessfully pressed upon them, decided me [illegible] resignation, which I did yesterday.

Of course, what I say to you about [illegible]

Turkish affairs is entirely for yourself, and not to be mentioned to anybody. But it is very important, and will give the allied squadrons the command of the Black Sea.

The French ambassador rejoiced at the return of the Home Secretary to the Cabinet. As soon as he heard that the resignation was withdrawn, he wrote to him :—

Au début de la campagne que nous allons faire ensemble, c'est un grand confort pour moi et une grande garantie pour l'Empereur que de vous savoir l'âme des conseils de notre allié. Votre concours d'ailleurs pèse d'un poids très-réel dans la balance, et on sait à Paris en apprécier toute la valeur.

Abroad as well as at home Lord Palmerston was regarded as the backbone of the Ministry.

CHAPTER X.

RUSSIAN POLICY—OCCUPATION OF PRINCIPALITIES; ENGLISH FLEET—LORD ABERDEEN—ACTIVE PREPA WAR—REFORM CLUB BANQUET—PROPOSES CRIMEA —1855—MOTION OF MR. ROEBUCK—RESIGNATION OF RUSSELL—DEFEAT OF THE GOVERNMENT.

IT can hardly be doubted that the prospects were darkened during the eventful prelim 1853 by the fact of Lord Palmerston's absence Foreign Office. He had won a character in being resolute, and was regarded as the embodi English pugnacity. That a statesman of his prestige should at this crisis in foreign affairs gated to the Home Office meant, in the opinion adversaries of England, that his policy was at a di and that the tide of national spirit was ebbing had formerly floated him through so many forei cultics. Lord Palmerston, all the same, was thoroughly engrossed by questions of health, po local administration as to view with any indiff dispute between Russia and Turkey. On the he watched every turn with the keenest inte held himself not only entitled but bound to active concern in the progress of the negotiati

Many a man, ousted from his old post, shown, or at any rate would have felt, some lousy towards the person who had been pref Lord Palmerston, so far from being influen such feeling or indulging in any carping frankly acknowledged that Lord Cl more fit Minister to be at the Foreign O ment. His reasons for saying so may [illegible] from a letter to the Foreign Secre-

[illegible] your writhing letter, but I did not like [illegible] its praise at the Cabinet, for fear that by so [illegible] others to think that it was too strong. I [illegible] it is a great comfort and satisfaction to me [illegible] of our foreign relations is in such able [illegible], and your administration of your important [illegible] attended with this great advantage to the [illegible], from a variety of circumstances, you can say [illegible] which could not so easily have been said or done

[illegible] war as much as any man, but he hated [illegible] more; and he thoroughly understood the [illegible] of the adversary against whom England and [illegible] entering the diplomatic lists in a struggle [illegible] very soon saw involved far more than the mere [illegible] immediately at issue. He thus describes the [illegible] adopted by Russia in any acts of aggres-

[illegible] and practice of the Russian Government has [illegible] to push forward its encroachments as fast and as [illegible] apathy or want of firmness of other Governments [illegible] it to go, but always to stop and retire when it was [illegible] decided resistance, and then to wait for the next [illegible] opportunity to make another spring on its intended [illegible] In furtherance of this policy, the Russian Govern- [illegible] always had two strings to its bow—moderate language [illegible] professions at Petersburg and at London; [illegible] by its agents on the scene of operations. If [illegible] succeed locally, the Petersburg Government [illegible] as a *fait accompli* which it did not intend, but [illegible] honour, recede from. If the local agents fail, they [illegible] and recalled, and the language previously held is [illegible] as a proof that the agents have overstepped their [illegible] This was exemplified in the Treaty of Unkiar- [illegible] in the exploits of Simonivitch and Vikovitch in [illegible] succeeded in extorting the Treaty of Unkiar-

[1] To Lord Clarendon, July 31, 1853.

T

[illegible] Turkey against attack, will continue [illegible] is over.

[illegible] would essentially tend to prevent any further [illegible] on Turkish territory in Europe or in Asia, and [illegible] manifest that any such further inroad would [illegible] increase the difficulties of a settlement.

[illegible] would act as a wholesome check upon the Em[illegible] and his advisers, and would stimulate Austria [illegible] Prussia to increased exertions to bring the Russian [illegible] to reason.

[illegible] would relieve England and France from the dis[illegible], and not very creditable, position of waiting [illegible] venturing to enter the back door as friends, [illegible] the Russians have taken forcible possession of [illegible] front hall as enemies.

[illegible] orders are to be given, I would suggest that it is [illegible] that they should be given without delay, so [illegible] able, when these matters are discussed this [illegible], to say that such orders have been sent off; [illegible] would at the same time be communicated to the [illegible].

[illegible] that this country expects that we should [illegible] course, and I cannot believe that we should [illegible] but support in pursuing it from the party now [illegible]

[illegible]rdeen replied, that although the invasion [illegible] was an indefensible act, and one [illegible] every European Power a right of inter[illegible] as the Emperor had made no declaration [illegible] the contrary, notified that he would not [illegible] became very doubtful how far it would be [illegible] our fleet to violate the treaty of 1841 by [illegible] Dardanelles. As to Lord Palmerston's [illegible] general approval which a bold course [illegible] Lord Aberdeen concluded his letter by a [illegible] paragraph to the effect that in a case of [illegible] popular support, just as on some [illegible] the Athenian assembly vehemently [illegible], he asked if he had said anything

Meanwhile the representatives of the [illegible] England, France, Austria, and Prussia, were [illegible] in the Austrian capital and drawing up a [illegible] which soon became known to Europe under [illegible] of the 'Vienna Note.' It was an abortive [illegible] reconcile conflicting views. The English Cabinet [illegible] busy on a similarly hopeless task:—

C. G. July [illegible]

My dear John Russell,—The Cabinet yesterday [illegible] visionally to an amended draft of Convention to be [illegible] for Russia and Turkey, simply renewing the engage[illegible] Kainardjy and Adrianople without any extension. [illegible] to be communicated first for approval to the French [illegible]ment, and, if finally agreed to, it was proposed that it [illegible] be sent by Vienna to Constantinople, and, if not [illegible] objected to by the Porte, to be returned to Vienna, and [illegible] sent on thence to Petersburg with any recommendation [illegible] the Austrian Government might be inclined to give. [illegible] Convention made no mention of the Holy Places, because [illegible] French would not agree to a Convention between Russia [illegible] Turkey on that matter. All this is very well for effect [illegible] a Blue Book, but, in my opinion, the course which the [illegible] has pursued on these matters from his first overtures [illegible] partition of Turkey, and especially the violent, abusive [illegible] menacing language of his last manifesto, seem to show [illegible] has taken his line, and that nothing will satisfy him but [illegible]plete submission on the part of Turkey; and we ought [illegible]fore, not to disguise from ourselves that he is bent [illegible] stand-up fight.

I tried again to persuade the Cabinet to send the [illegible] up to the Bosphorus, but failed; I was told that St[illegible] La Cour have powers to call for them. This is, [illegible] stated in public despatches, but we all know that he [illegible] privately desired not to do so. I think our position, [illegible] timidly and submissively at the back door while [illegible] violently, threateningly, and arrogantly forcing her [illegible] the house, is unwise with a view to a peaceful settle[illegible] derogatory to the character, and standing, and dig[illegible] two Powers. I think that when pressed on this [illegible] course we shall be in both Houses, we shall [illegible] answer or explanation to give. We cannot [illegible] vinces are not parts of the Turkish empire, [illegible]

[illegible] and it is as such that Nicholas seizes them, [illegible] the Porte to submit to his demands. [illegible] that Turkey is at peace, because no [illegible] when important parts of its territory are [illegible] of coercion, with a threat of further advance [illegible] and blindness should make such a step, in the [illegible] invader, necessary. We cannot deny that the [illegible] squadrons in the Bosphorus would greatly [illegible] Porte, greatly discourage insurrections in any part [illegible] greatly tend to make the Emperor pause. The [illegible] can give for our inactivity must be a yielding to [illegible] advice and a fear of displeasing the Emperor. But [illegible] ought to have led us to leave Turkey to her fate. [illegible] properly be answered by words, but acts should be [illegible] by acts; and the entrance of the Russians as invaders [illegible] territory ought to be followed and replied to by [illegible] of the squadrons into the Bosphorus as protectors. [illegible], of the effect of such a measure must depend [illegible] promptitude of its execution, and it would have this [illegible] that, while it indicated spirit and determination on [illegible] England and France, it could not by any perversion [illegible] as an act of hostility against Russia. We [illegible] relieved from much embarrassment in the approach- [illegible] if we could say that orders for this purpose had [illegible] sent, and the actual advance of the squadrons [illegible] to accompany any overtures made to Russia.

[illegible] Russian Government now addressed a despatch [illegible] diplomatic agents, the burden of which was to the [illegible] the occupation of the Principalities was in [illegible] to the presence of the British and French fleets [illegible] the Dardanelles, and would only cease when [illegible].

[illegible] following Memorandum, sent round by Lord [illegible] to the members of the Cabinet, he states [illegible] would wish to meet this declaration:—

C. G.: July 12, 1853.

[illegible] Circular of Count Nesselrode, dated July 2, and pub- [illegible] the newspapers of this morning, shows how imper- [illegible] have understood the character of the Russian Govern- [illegible] how entirely thrown away upon that Government has been the excessive forbearance with [illegible] France have acted. But the result might [illegible] It is in the nature of men whose influence [illegible] whose power over others are founded on [illegible] up by arrogant assumptions and pretensions, [illegible] bearance for irresolution, and to look upon [illegible] tion as symptoms of fear, and forerunners of [illegible]

Thus it has been with Russia on the one hand and [illegible] and France on the other. If the two Powers had [illegible] that energy, decision, and promptitude which the [illegible] required; if when Menschikoff began to threaten, the [illegible] rons had been sent to the neighbourhood of the [illegible] and if the Russian Government had been plainly told [illegible] moment a Russian soldier set foot on Turkish [illegible] soon as a Russian ship-of-war approached with hostile [illegible] the Turkish coast, the combined squadrons would [illegible] Bosphorus, and, if necessary, operate in the Black [illegible] can be little doubt that the Russian Government [illegible] paused in its course, and things would not have [illegible] pass at which they have now arrived. But the [illegible] Government has been led on step by step by the [illegible] timidity of the Government of England, and [illegible] propagated that the British Cabinet had declared that [illegible] have *la paix à tout prix* have not been sufficiently [illegible] by any overt acts. The result has now been that the [illegible] of St. Petersburg, not content with bullying Turkey, [illegible] and insults England and France, and arrogantly [illegible] forbid the ships-of-war of those Powers from frequ[illegible] waters of another Power over whose waters Russia [illegible] authority whatever, and who has invited those ships [illegible] waters specifically to protect it against Russian aggre[illegible]

It is the robber who declares that he will not [illegible] house until the policeman shall have first retired [illegible] courtyard.

The position of England and France was already [illegible] humiliating, but this insolent pretension, published to [illegible] even before it was communicated to us, seems to [illegible] that position no longer tenable consistently with a [illegible] to the honour and character of this country.

I would therefore beg to submit, and to place [illegible] thus on record, that orders should forthwith be [illegible] squadrons to go up to the Bosphorus, and that [illegible] Government should be informed that, altho[illegible] this move should have taken place without some ...some more urgent request from the Porte, yet ...nissible pretension put forward in Count Nessel- ...dictate to us as to the movements of our fleet, ...ernative left but to station that fleet at the heart ...e whose integrity and independence have been ...threatened by a Russian invasion of its terri-

PALMERSTON.

'7.

...erdeen, on the other hand, hoping and be- ...the form of Convention between Russia and ...h had been prepared by France and England, ...epted, and that peace would thus be main- ...idered that Count Nesselrode's Circular ...be met by a grave expostulation. 'When, ...he four Powers simultaneously advised the ...regard the entrance of the Russian troops ...ncipalities as a *casus belli*, it was not that ...ed any weight to the declaration of the ...at he did not intend to make war upon ...hat they entertained any doubt of an act of ...having been committed, but they wished ...declaration so far as to preserve in their ...he means of negotiating with greater hopes ...an if the utmost extremity of war had been ... Lord Clarendon also shared Lord Aber-

...lmerston acquiesced, with reservations, in ...'s decision. He said:—

...hink that we advised the Porte not to consider ...f the Principalities a *casus belli*. A *casus belli*, if ...he term, means a case which would justify war. ...the Porte that the invasion of the Princi- ...justify war on the part of Turkey against Russia, ...the Sultan, on grounds of prudence and as a ...not to exercise his right and to send an ...advantage beyond the Danube. It seems ...we have told the Sultan that the invasion ...a *casus belli*, but that he would do best by

standing on the defensive. As to the fleet, I acquiesce
reasoning, and, on consideration, I admit that, as
launched proposals for a peaceful arrangement, it
better not to endanger the negotiation by throwing
fresh element of difficulty; and I am, therefore,
share the responsibility of submitting even to insult
afford to the quibbling and pettifogging Government
which we have to deal any pretext arising out of
for refusing terms of accommodation unobjectionable
selves.[1]

Parliament was prorogued, with an express
hope, in the Speech from the Throne, that the
would yet be arranged without recourse to arms.
Palmerston, as soon as he was released from the
of Commons, went down to Derbyshire to
Melbourne Athenæum, on which occasion he
address on the educational facilities provided
institutions. This was very proper for a Home
retary, although, in his character of ex-Foreign
tary, it was abroad that his eyes were fixed,
was in close correspondence with his colleagues,
lating each in turn to adopt a bold tone as to the
then taking place. To Mr. Sidney Herbert,
at War, he writes, in September, from
whither he had gone in attendance on the Queen

Balmoral: September

The question between Russia and Turkey seems,
to be in an unsatisfactory and unpromising state, and
in a nutshell, and its solution depends upon honesty
and plain dealing on the part of Russia. What
Emperor wants? Why will he not plainly tell
Does he want merely what all of us want—
Christians in the Turkish empire shall be safe from
vexation, and injury? If that is what he wants,
by himself setting the example, and let him, by
Principalities, relieve the Christian inhabitants
the Turkish empire from the complicated and
which the occupation of their country by a
upon them. Beyond that, let him be

[1] To Lord Aberdeen, July 15,

[illegible] liberal system of Turkey, and let him [illegible] till some case and occasion arises which [illegible] present he has not been able even to allege [illegible] Christians, except that which he himself [illegible] I believe the real fact at the [illegible] unintelligible pretences is that what he really [illegible] Sultan should not, by liberal measures and [illegible], interfere with the arbitrary and [illegible] which the Greek clergy now too often [illegible] by right or by assumption, to the cruel [illegible] Greek communities. But if the Emperor [illegible] what I have said, he ought to be satisfied [illegible] which the Sultan is ready to make. If, [illegible] the Emperor wants to become acknowledged [illegible] Greek subjects of the Sultan, and to be allowed [illegible] between the Sultan and the Sultan's subjects, why [illegible] him manfully avow this pretension, and let us [illegible] Turkey in manfully resisting it, and let the [illegible] decide between the Emperor's wrong and the [illegible] cause. In my opinion Russia ought to be [illegible] give a categorical answer, and to be driven from [illegible] subterfuges behind which she has so long [illegible] aggressive intentions. I believe that what I have [illegible] is what the Emperor really means and wants, and [illegible] am coming reluctantly to the conclusion that war [illegible] and Turkey is becoming inevitable. If such war [illegible], upon his head be the responsibility of the conse-

[illegible] means think with you that he will have an easy [illegible] the Turks. On the contrary, if the betting is not [illegible] lay the odds on the Turks. All that the Turkish [illegible] are directory officers, and it would be strange [illegible] England, France, Poland, and Hungary could not [illegible] that deficiency. I do not believe in the dis- [illegible] the Turkish provinces; this is an oft-repeated tale [illegible] the Russians. The best refutation is, that for many [illegible] the Russian agents have been trying *per fas et nefas* [illegible] insurrection in Turkey, and have failed. The fact [illegible] Christian subjects in Turkey know too well what [illegible] is not to be aware that it is of all things the [illegible], and the oftener Russian troops enter Turkish [illegible] stronger this conviction is impressed upon the [illegible] ought not to forget that she has weak points— [illegible], Georgia. My wish is that England [illegible]

true that I may formerly have regarded the posi- between England and Russia with the utmost ; but for some time past I have seen the desire for so much as to lend me to think that it is but too At present, therefore, *vous prêches le converti.* As he is already frightened out of his wits at the and most assuredly he hears nothing from me to his alarm.

crisis was now rapidly culminating. On Octo- Porte issued a declaration making the further of peace depend upon the evacuation of within fifteen days; and on October and French fleets passed up to Constan- the request of the Sultan. Lord Palmerston something even more decisive on our part.

C. G.: October 7, 1853.

Aberdeen,—The state of Russo-Turkish affairs some statement on the part of England and of course, that war has been declared by that hostilities between Russia and Turkey are I should, therefore, wish to propose to the

that instructions should be sent to Constantinople of war having been declared, the two squad- the Black Sea, and should send word to the at Sebastopol that, in the existing state of ship-of-war found cruising in the Black Sea and be given over to the Turkish Govern-

that England and France should propose to the a convention to the effect that, whereas war broken out between Russia and Turkey, in created by unjust demands made upon and by an unwarrantable invasion of the by a Russian army; and whereas it is deemed to be an object of general European importance to them that the political territorial integrity of the Ottoman empire inviolate against Russian aggression, the furnish to the Sultan such naval assist- in existing circumstances for the defence of his empire; and they moreover engage of their respective subjects who may be willing to the military or naval service of the Sultan. In Sultan to engage that he will consult with England as to the terms and conditions of the new treaty determine, on the conclusion of hostilities, the future of Russia and Turkey.'

Such a convention would unquestionably have a useful effect on the course to be pursued by the Powers.

Lord Aberdeen, in reply, said: 'I cannot I think the present state of the Russo-Turkish would authorise such a proceeding on our part which you intend to propose.' Indeed, as the of peace appeared more and more likely, more hesitation was developed in high quarters. sentations were made that the fanatical party stantinople had become so clamorous for war, own purposes, that the Turk was thwarting assisting English efforts to come to a satisfacto derstanding with Russia. It began to be feared England was about to be dragged behind the man chariot in a campaign the real object of was to obtain more power for two millions of men to rule oppressively twelve millions of tians. Suggestions were thrown out that if, aside all Turkish considerations, it was thought England and Europe had such a strong in keeping Turkish territory out of the Russia as to be justified in going to war for pose, such a war ought to be carried on unshac any obligations to the Porte, and ought to such a peace as would provide other and better ments for the future than the 'recomposition ignorant, barbarian, and despotic rule of the man over the most favoured and fertile Europe.'

Lord Aberdeen had forwarded to Lord a Memorandum which he had received [illegible] Palmerston returned it with the follow-[illegible]

Broadlands: November 1, 1853.

[illegible] Memorandum, which states very clearly the [illegible], but which, towards its conclusion, points [illegible] not consistent with the policy laid down in its [illegible] not easy to be carried into execution.

[illegible] to my view of the matters in question, the case [illegible] our course is clear. The five great Powers have, [illegible], recorded their opinion that it is for the [illegible] of Europe that the integrity and independence [illegible] empire should be maintained; and it would be [illegible] that strong reasons, political and commercial, make [illegible] the interest of England that this integrity and inde-[illegible] should be maintained. But Russia has attacked the [illegible] and has violated the integrity of the Ottoman [illegible] Russia must, by fair means or foul, be brought to [illegible] pretensions and withdraw her aggression. England [illegible] urged by common interests to defend Turkey [illegible], have given Turkey physical assistance and [illegible] diplomatic support. They undertook to obtain for [illegible] negotiation, a satisfactory and honourable settlement [illegible] with Russia, and, failing that, to support [illegible] her defensive war.

[illegible] our efforts at negotiation have failed, because the [illegible] which we proposed was declared, both by Turkey [illegible], to be such as Turkey could not honourably nor [illegible]. The Turkish Government, seeing no apparent [illegible] of better results from negotiation, and aware that [illegible] was running to the disadvantage of Turkey, at [illegible] having for some considerable time yielded to our [illegible] remain passive, came to a determination not unnatural, [illegible], and issued that declaration of war which we [illegible] and publicly said that the Sultan would have been [illegible] in issuing the moment the Russians invaded his [illegible]

[illegible] declaration of war makes no change in the position of [illegible] and France in relation to Turkey. We may still try [illegible] Russia to do what she ought to do, but we are still [illegible] a regard for our own interests, to defend Turkey. [illegible] excellent thing, and war is a great misfortune; but [illegible] many things more valuable than peace, and many [illegible] worse than war.

[1] From the Prince Consort.

... of the Memorandum points to the ... from Europe, and the establishment of ... European Turkey. But such a scheme ... opposed to the principles of the policy ... hitherto acted. To carry such a system into ... join the Russians against the Turks, ... the Turks against the Russians; for how ... of Turkey become the result of a ... England and France in defence of Turkey? ... for the Turks as Mahometans, and should ... would be turned into Christians; but as to ... the Turkish Government in regard to its ... Christians, I am well convinced that there are a ... Christians under the Governments of Russia, ... and Naples who would be rejoiced to be as well ... enjoy as much security for person and property ... subjects of the Sultan.[1]

... from Europe the Sultan and his two millions of ... subjects, including the army and the bulk of the ... might not be an easy task; still, the five Powers ... it, and play the Polish drama over again. But ... find the building up still more difficult than the ... There are no sufficient Christian elements as ... Christian state in European Turkey capable of per... functions as a component part of the European ... The Greeks are a small minority, and could not be ... race. The Sclavonians, who are the majority, ... the conditions necessary for becoming the bones ... a new state. A reconstruction of Turkey means ... nor less than its subjection to Russia, direct or ... or for a time delayed.

... to me, then, that our course is plain, simple, and ... we must help Turkey out of her difficulties by ... if possible; and that if negotiation fails, we must, ... arms, carry her safely through her dangers.

... Palmerston was not confining his suggestions ... for mere acts of force. He enters, in the ... on a discussion as to the best way of pre... form of arrangement to the two contending ... to secure its favourable consideration. He

[1] ..., when this was written, had not achieved the liberty ... which they now enjoy.

agreed with Lord John Russell in thi[illegible]
able to present the note to the Turks w[illegible]
them any discretion as to alterations whi[illegible]
desire.

Broadlands: O[illegible]

My dear John Russell,—If we wish to prevail [illegible] to sign a note for presentation to the Emperor, we [illegible] the Turkish Government the power of proposing al[illegible] the draft we send them. We may hope that our d[illegible] accepted by them without alteration; but they may [illegible] reasons which have not occurred to us for d[illegible] changes, or they may have even bad reasons w[illegible] changes they propose would not increase our d[illegible] Petersburg, might, in spite of their badness, be allowed [illegible] vail. If we send them a draft which they must ei[illegible] it is or reject, we may have a rejection, and we ma[illegible] our pertinacity an invaluable chance of a peaceful a[illegible]

But further, if we are prepared to impose o[illegible] words on Turkey, we should thereby incur an [illegible] engagement to impose them equally on Russia; and a[illegible] are the French, or is Austria, or is Prussia prepared t[illegible] war against Russia, not for the defence of the Turkis[illegible] and the preservation of the balance of power in [illegible] in order to compel the Emperor of Russia to accept a [illegible] form of words put together in Downing Street. [illegible] surely be carrying the parental affection of author[illegible] reasonable extent. Then as to the way in which th[illegible] note should be sent to Constantinople. I agree wi[illegible] it would be inexpedient to revive the Vienna c[illegible] such a purpose, or, indeed, for any other. That c[illegible] dead—peace to its remains. No good can come out o[illegible] ence at Vienna on these matters, and at the pre[illegible] Vienna conference means Buol, and Buol means [illegible] and Meyendorf means Nicholas; and the Turks kno[illegible] so does all Europe.

Moreover, the very atmosphere of Vienna is [illegible] I doubt whether even you or I should not find o[illegible] lysed by the political miasma of the place. If th[illegible] of a conference is to be set up again, and it may [illegible]

[1] 'Vienna is a sad place for humbug, and X. [illegible] atmosphere as does the liveliest and sturdiest d[illegible] Cane.'—*Lord Palmerston to Lord Clarendon.*

You will say that this would be an act of [illegible] Russia; but so is the declaration already made, [illegible] ships shall be permitted to make any landing [illegible] part of the Turkish territory. The only [illegible] two declarations is, that the one already made [illegible] and insufficient for its purpose, and that the [illegible] pose would be complete and sufficient. If the [illegible] were shut up in Sebastopol, it is probable that the [illegible] be able to make in Asia an impression that would [illegible] facilitate the conclusion of peace.

With regard to the conditions of peace, it seems [illegible] the only arrangement which could afford to Europe [illegible] security against future dangers arising out of the [illegible] of Russia on Turkey, and the attempts of the Russian [illegible] ment to interfere in the internal affairs of the Turkish [illegible] would be that arrangement which I have often [illegible] namely, that the treaty to be concluded between [illegible] Turkey should be an ordinary treaty of peace and frie[ndship] [illegible] boundaries, commerce, and mutual protection of the [illegible] one party within the territories of the other; and the [illegible] stipulations which might be required for the privileg[es] [illegible] Principalities and of Servia, and for the protection [illegible] Christian religion and its churches in the Ottoman d[ominions] [illegible] by the Sultan should be contained in a treaty betw[een] [illegible] Sultan and the five Powers. By such a treaty Rus[sia] [illegible] be prevented from dealing single-handed with Turkey [illegible] to those matters on which she has, from time to time, [illegible] to fasten a quarrel on the Sultan.

Lord Aberdeen replied on the 13th: 'I conf[ess] [illegible] not prepared to adopt the mode which you th[ink] [illegible] likely to restore peace.' He went on to [illegible] should prefer an open declaration of war to [illegible] sure' which Lord Palmerston proposed; but [illegible] union of the four Powers had just been effected [illegible] declaration that the integrity of the Turkish [illegible] was an object of general interest, it was to be [illegible] that they would take measures to secure it [illegible] therefore, to direct hostility would be [illegible] although it might eventually come.

Lord Palmerston resigned on the [illegible]

[illegible] chapter what was the immediate reason [illegible]gned; but the fact is that, as Mr. King- [illegible] was gifted with the instinct which enables [illegible] the heart of a nation, and he felt that [illegible] people would never forgive the Ministry if [illegible] was done after the disaster at Sinope. [illegible] short absence of about ten days, the Cabinet [illegible] send the fleet into the Black Sea, with in- [illegible] to the admiral to prevent any Russian vessels [illegible] leaving port. Lord Aberdeen, in acknow- [illegible] withdrawal of Lord Palmerston's resignation, say[illegible]

[illegible] to find that you approve of a recent decision of [illegible] with respect to the British and French fleets adopted [illegible]. I feel sure you will have learnt with pleasure [illegible] you are absent or present, the Government are [illegible] to preserve from all injury the interests and dignity [illegible]ntry.

[illegible] session of 1854 began on January 31. On Feb- [illegible], the Russian ambassador was recalled, and [illegible] after the British Government sent a final ulti- [illegible] to the Russian Emperor, calling upon him to [illegible] the Principalities by April 30. Meanwhile [illegible] were despatched to the East, and active prepara- [illegible] were carried on at home. On March 7 Lord [illegible]ston presided over a banquet given at the Reform [illegible] Sir Charles Napier, previous to his departure [illegible] fleet for the Baltic. I give an extract from [illegible] Palmerston's speech on this occasion, both as [illegible] the temper of the time, and as a specimen [illegible] spirited ease and humour with which he could [illegible] an after-dinner audience. His enjoyment was [illegible], and the company laughed sympathetically [illegible] they heard the joke.

[illegible] the formal toasts had been duly drunk, Lord [illegible] rose and said :—

[illegible] was a very remarkable entertainer of dinner company, [illegible] R. Preston, who lived in the City, and who, when he gave dinners at Greenwich, after gorging his guests wi used to turn round to the waiters and say, 'Now bring Gentlemen, we have had the toasts which correspond turtle, and now let's go to dinner. Now let us drink which belongs to the real occasion of our assembling give you 'The health of my gallant friend Sir Charles who sits beside me. If, gentlemen, I were addressing shire audience, consisting of country gentlemen residin county, to which my gallant friend and myself belong, introduce him to your notice as an eminent agricultu has been my good fortune, when enjoying his hospi Merchistoun Hall, to receive most valuable instructi him while walking over his farm about stall-feeding, turnips, wire fencing, under-draining, and the like. M friend is a match for everything, and whatever he turns to he generally succeeds in it. However, gentlemen, he Cincinnatus, leaves his plough, puts on his armour, an pared to do that good service to his country which always perform whenever an opportunity is afforded to pass over those earlier exploits of his younger days, well known to the members of his profession; but, perl of the most remarkable exploits of his life is that performed in the same cause of liberty and justice in is now about to be engaged. In the year 1833, when volunteering to serve the cause of the Queen of against the encroachments and the usurpations of Dom —to defend constitutional rights and liberties against power—he took the command of a modest fleet of frig corvettes, and, at the head of that little squadron, he a squadron far superior in force, including two line ships, one of which my gallant friend was the first But on that occasion my gallant friend exhibited a char trait. When he had scrambled upon the deck of th line-of-battle ship, and was clearing the deck of those possession of it, a Portuguese officer ran at him full his drawn sword to run him through. My gallant frien parried the thrust, and, not giving himself the troubl in any other way with his Portuguese assailant, me him a hearty kick, and sent him down the hatchway gentlemen, that victory was a great event—I don't victory over the officer who went down, but the vi the fleet, which my gallant friend took into port; the tory decided a great cause then pending. It

… decided the question between constitutional … —a contest which began in Portugal, and … afterwards in Spain, when my gallant friend Sir … his powerful aid in the same cause, and with … My gallant friend Sir Charles Napier, how- … turn of fortune, and it was mainly owing to … that the Queen of Portugal afterwards occu- … to which she was rightfully entitled, and the … obtained that Constitution which they have … enjoyed. A noble friend of mine, now no more, … greatly lament, for he was equally distinguished as … soldier, and as a diplomatist, the late Lord William … an honour to his country, as to his family—told me … he heard that my gallant friend Sir Charles Napier … neighbourhood of the fortress of Valenza, a Portu- … some considerable distance from the squadron … commanded. Lord W. Russell and Colonel Hare … my gallant friend, and Lord W. Russell told me … met a man dressed in a very easy way, followed by a … two muskets on his shoulders. They took him at … Robinson Crusoe; but who should these men prove to … the gallant admiral on my right and a marine behind … 'Well, Napier,' said Lord W. Russell, 'what are you … here?' 'Why,' said my gallant friend, 'I am waiting to … Valenza.' 'But,' said Lord William, 'Valenza is a forti- … and you must know that we soldiers understand how … towns are taken. You must open trenches; you must … approaches; you must establish a battery in breach; and … takes a good deal of time, and must be done according …' 'Oh,' said my gallant friend, 'I have no time for all … I have got some of my blue-jackets up here and a few of … guns, and I mean to take the town with a letter.' … he did. He sent the governor a letter to tell him he … much better surrender at discretion. The governor was a … sensible man; and so surrender he did. So the trenches, the approaches, the battery, breach, and all that, were saved, the town of Valenza was handed over to the Queen of … Well, the next great occasion in which my gallant … took a prominent and distinguished part—a part for … I can assure you that I personally, in my official capacity, the Government to which I had the honour to belong, felt … indebted and obliged to him—was the occasion of the … Syria. There my gallant friend distinguished himself,

e possible should all fear be removed of Russia's esent hold upon the Danube. He was, therefore, rong advocate for leaving the Russians in undisbed enjoyment of the pestilent air of the Dobrudscha, for crossing over from Varna to the great Russian nal on the Black Sea.

The Cabinet unanimously acknowledged the force of arguments, though there were some few who wished a postponement of such an expedition until the ond year of the campaign. The difficulty was the repared state of the French army, which was still cient both in men and material. The French officers, eed, generally disliked this selection of the Crimea as r battle-field.

The following Memorandum on the measures to be pted against Russia was sent round to the Cabinet:—

C. G.: June 15, 1854.

Some conversation having passed on Wednesday evening ir Charles Wood's between some members of the Cabinet, t the objects to which our operations ought to be directed in war against Russia, I wish to submit the following observa- to the Cabinet.

ngland and France have entered into war with a great r, have made great exertions, at a great expense, and for a purpose. They would lose caste in the world if they con- the war with only a small result. The particular overt which Russia broke the peace was the invasion of the Principalities, but the purpose for which we took up ould be very imperfectly accomplished if the only result of was to be the evacuation of those provinces by the army, even if that evacuation were accompanied by a n the part of Russia of the demands she has made upon Such a result would be a triumph rather than a defeat a.

ould say that she had defied and withstood the naval tary strength of two of the greatest Powers of the t these Powers had been unable to hurt her, and that bstantially gained all that she had set out by demand- uch as the Sultan had done by his own act for his subjects that which she had required. We should no security for the future, and whenever a more

and precarious advantage for her. The of the Russian Black Sea fleet would important advantage to us. Such a success weight upon the fortunes of the war, and upon the negotiations for peace. We materially and at once to reduce our naval ex- Russian Black Sea fleet were destroyed or in and, holding the Crimea and Sebastopol, we conditions of peace in regard to the naval in the Black Sea.

not seem good reason to believe that the Rus- present more than 40,000 men in the Crimea, if ; and if 25,000 English and 35,000 French somewhere in the large bay to the north of there can be little doubt that they would be able to on the hill on the north side of the harbour of and they would then command the harbour, fleet,

enterprise need not prevent the capture of Anapa and year, but even if it did there can surely be no com- between the value of the capture of Sebastopol and the the forts on the coast of Circassia. The capture of and the capture or destruction of the Russian fleet course imply the surrender of the Russian troops the garrison of the place, or their evacuation of the by capitulation, and either of these results would be a feat of arms for the allied forces. Anapa and Poti taken at leisure afterwards, and with greater ease if had been mastered.

If the attack on the Crimea is put off till next year the Government will have time to strengthen the defences , and to increase the garrison to any amount which can hold, and we may find the undertaking far then than it would have been this year.

Emperor will, during the autumn, winter, and spring, train recruits enough to make good his losses during campaign, and next year we should have to deal with a and reorganised army, instead of with one worn and dispirited by the unsuccessful operations of this On the other hand, the allied troops are now fresh, ready for enterprise. If they are to remain inactive spring, their health may give way, their spirits may mutual cordiality and good understanding may be cooled down by intrigues, jealousies, and [illegible] opinion, which in England and France now [illegible] Governments, and bears up the people of the [illegible] make the sacrifices necessary for the war, [illegible] turn, and people may grow tired of burthens [illegible] duced no sufficient and satisfactory result.

It seems to me, then, that the French Gov[illegible] to be urged to press forward the complete [illegible] co-operating army in Turkey, and that we ought [illegible] to make arrangements with them for an attack [illegible] as soon as the combined army is in a state to unde[illegible]

We do not seem likely to accomplish anything [illegible] importance in the Baltic, and on that account it is [illegible] desirable that we should gain some real and signal [illegible] the Black Sea.

PAL[illegible]

And to the Minister of War he writes on [illegible] subject.

Brocket: June [illegible]

You said yesterday at the Cabinet that you wish[illegible] over what was to be written to Raglan by the mail wh[illegible] go before our next Cabinet, and as I was obliged to [illegible] Cabinet early to save my railway train to this place, I [illegible] my vote in writing.

It seems to me that to keep the allied army in [illegible] and to carry on operations on the banks of the Danube [illegible] be to throw away time, money, men, official and [illegible] putation.

Nothing that we could do there would have any [illegible] effect on the war, nor could it help us one step [illegible] attainment of that future security which our conv[illegible] France specifies as one of the main conditions of pe[illegible] if we were to drive the Russians across the Pruth, [illegible] what the French call a *coup d'epée dans l'eau*—a [illegible] advantage which would cease the moment we w[illegible] should, indeed, doubt the wisdom of an advance of [illegible] to the north of the Danube, nor ought they to attach [illegible] importance to the line of the Danube. Omar Pasha [illegible] right to defend the Danube and Silistria as long [illegible] but I should not have thought less well of him [illegible] he had retired at length to Schumla and Va[illegible]

... difficulties would increase with every ... southward, and the dangers of their position ... and more serious.

... of bringing Russia to terms is by offensive ... operations. We and the French ought to ... and take Sebastopol and the Russian fleet the ... armies are in a condition to go thither. Sixty ... and French troops, with the fleets co-operating, ... the object in six weeks after landing, and if ... accompanied by successful operations in Georgia ... we might have a merry Christmas and a happy

... not the slightest danger of the Russians getting to ... The Turks are able to prevent that; but even ... not, the Austrians would be compelled, by the ... circumstances, to do so. Austria has, as usual, been ... shabby game. When she thought the Russians likely ... and while she fancied England and France needed ... she bragged of her determination to be active against ... As soon as she found our troops at Varna, she changed ... and, according to a despatch which Clarendon had in ... yesterday, she now says she shall not enter the Prin... and the Russians must be driven out by the Turks ... English and French. She can hardly think us simple ... do her work for her; but the best way to force her ... would be to send our troops off to the Crimea. This is

... the 29th of June the Duke of Newcastle sent ... instructions to Lord Raglan to make an immediate ... on Sebastopol. Few persons at that time fore... delay and difficulties which would have to be ... before success crowned the enterprise. The ... of State for War himself, writing to Lord ... in the beginning of September, said that he ... enough to give the allied forces only three ... days after descending upon the Russian coast ... they would be in possession of Sebastopol. On ... of September the troops of France and England ... the Crimea, and a few days later they won the ... the Alma. On the 3rd of October the news ... of Sebastopol arrived. It was believed by most people for nearly twenty-[illegible] Emperor of the French himself [illegible] troops at the camp of Helfaut.

These reported successes [illegible] authority than Mr. Gladstone a [illegible] Palmerston's initiative in designat[illegible] the proper field for the allied armies. [illegible] the 4th October, he says:—

> My purpose is to offer you a congratulati[illegible] be especially due to you upon the great events [illegible] place in the Crimea. Much as we must all [illegible] grounds at these signal successes, and thankf[illegible] nation may justly feel to a Higher Power, yet [illegible] upon the instruments through which such [illegible] about, I for one cannot help repeating to yo[illegible] offered at an earlier period for the manner in wh[illegible] when we were amidst many temptations to fr[illegible] ing and less effective proceedings—the duty [illegible] our strokes upon the true heart and centre [illegible] Sebastopol.

In the month of November, 1854, Lo[illegible] went over to Paris with Lady Palmerston [illegible] the view of having an interview with [illegible] He writes to his brother:—

> Yesterday Emily and I dined at St. Cloud. [illegible] very handsome, and our hosts very agreeabl[illegible] was full of life, animation, and talk, and the [illegible] her the prettier one thinks her. I have found [illegible] Drouyn de Lhuys in very good opinions on th[illegible] war, and acting towards us with perfect fairnes[illegible]

[...] letter to the Prime Minister Lord John [...]ity of a change in the War Department, [...] out the 'necessity of having in that office a [...] from experience of military details, from in[...]our of mind, and from weight with the House [...], can be expected to guide the great opera[...] with authority and success. There is only [...],' he continued, 'belonging to the Govern[...] combines these advantages. My conclusion [...] Parliament meets Lord Palmerston should [...]sted with the seals of the War Department.' [...]berdeen, however, declined to recommend the [...] the Queen, alleging, with great fairness, that [...] on the first constitution of the office such an [...]ment might have been best, yet that the Duke [...]astle had discharged his duties too ably and [...]bly to afford any justification for his removal.

[...]er a short winter session, in which the Foreign [...]ent Bill was passed, Parliament reassembled on [...]d of January, 1855. Mr. Roebuck, on the first [...] gave notice that he intended to move for the ap[...]ent of a select committee 'to inquire into the [...]on of our army before Sebastopol, and into the [...]t of those departments of the Government whose [...] has been to minister to the wants of that army.' [...]ohn Russell immediately resigned. Writing to [...]berdeen, he said: 'I do not see how the motion [...] resisted: but as it involves a censure upon the [...]epartment, with which some of my colleagues are [...]ed, my only course is to tender my resignation.' [...]almerston's opinion on this event is contained in [...]owing letter:—

Piccadilly: January 24, 1855.

[...]ear John Russell,—I received your letter of this morn[...] much regret, and I feel bound in candour to say that [...] your decision ill-timed. Everybody foresaw that on the [...] of Parliament after Christmas some such motion as that [...]tice of by Roebuck was likely to be made; and if you [...]mined not to face such a motion, your announcement

> of such a decision a fortnight ago would have [illegible] easy for your colleagues to have taken whatever course the announcement might have led to, either to have met your [illegible] by a new arrangement of offices, or to have given up the Govern-ment in a manner creditable to all parties concerned. [illegible] you will have the appearance of having remained in office [illegible] ing in carrying on a system of which you disapproved [illegible] driven out by Roebuck's announced notice, and the Govern-ment will have the appearance of self-condemnation by [illegible] from a discussion which they dare not face; while as [illegible] the country, the action of the executive will be paralysed [illegible] time in a critical moment of a great war, with an [illegible] negotiation, and we shall exhibit to the world a [illegible] spectacle of disorganisation among our political men [illegible] similar to that which has prevailed among our military [illegible] abroad. My opinion is that, if you had simply renewed the proposal which you made before Christmas, such an arrange-ment might have been made; and there are constitutional and practical grounds on which such a motion as Roebuck's might have been resisted without violence to any opinions which you may entertain as to the past period.

The ministerial explanations which took place in the House of Commons were immediately followed by the Roebuck motion for a select committee. Left in the lurch by their recognised leader, the Aberdeen Cabinet found their best defender in the man for whom many of them had felt distrust. Lord Palmerston, coming gallantly forward to take upon himself the invidious duty of supporting an Administration over which he had little control, and which, before disaster came, had neglected his advice, said that he fully concurred that the responsibility for the conduct of the war fell not on the Duke of Newcastle alone, but on the whole Cabinet. He did not deny that there had been something calamitous in the condition of our army, but he traced it to the inexperience arising from a long peace. If the House thought the Government not deserving of confidence, the direct and manly course would have been to affirm that proposition. The course about to be pursued would be dangerous and inconvenient in its results, [illegible]

[H]e hoped that when the House had determined what [s]et of men should be entrusted with public affairs, they [w]ould give their support to that Government, and not [s]how to Europe that a nation could only meet a great crisis when it was deprived of representative institutions. When the House divided there appeared for Mr. Roebuck's motion, 305; against it, 148. Majority against the Government, 157. This startling result so amazed the House that they forgot to cheer, but laughed derisively.

On the 1st of February Lord Palmerston formally announced in the Commons the resignation of the Ministry. Thus fell the Coalition Cabinet of 1852, the victim of the war which it had itself declared.

CHAPTER XI.

BECOMES PRIME MINISTER—ATTENDS TO [illegible] NEGOTIATIONS AT VIENNA—REFORMS FOR [illegible] BREAKS UP.

LORD DERBY was sent for to form a [illegible] immediately sought the co-operation of [illegible] ston, offering him the leadership of the [illegible] Commons, which Mr. Disraeli was willing to [illegible] his favour. Offers were also made, through [illegible] Mr. Gladstone and Mr. Sidney Herbert. Lord [illegible] ston, however, in the following letter, declined [illegible] posals, having also expressed his great unwill[illegible] under existing circumstances, to belong to any [illegible] ment in which the management of foreign [illegible] not remain in Lord Clarendon's hands :—

144 Piccadilly: January [illegible]

My dear Derby,—Having well reflected upon the [illegible] which you made to me this morning, I have come [illegible] clusion that if I were to join your Government, as [illegible] you, I should not give to that Government that [illegible] you are good enough to think would accrue to [illegible] acceptance of office.

I shall, however, deem it my duty, in the [illegible] state of affairs, to give, out of office, my support to [illegible] ment that shall carry on the war with energy and [illegible] will, in the management of our foreign [illegible] dignity and interests of the country, and [illegible] the alliances which have been formed.

I have conveyed to Gladstone and [illegible] communication which you wished me to [illegible] seemed to me to be best that they [illegible] themselves.

[illegible] at once retired, and Lord John Russell [illegible] person sent for by the Queen, who signified [illegible] would give her particular satisfaction if Lord [illegible] would join in the formation. He expressed [illegible] to do so; but many of the Whigs posi-[illegible]declined, and notably Lord Clarendon. Lord [illegible] Russell therefore resigned the commission which [illegible] Queen had entrusted to him; and in his letter an-[illegible] this to Lord Palmerston he thanked him for [illegible] readiness with which he had consented to aid the [illegible] of a Government, and promised his support [illegible] event of Lord Palmerston being charged by the [illegible] with this difficult but honourable task.

[illegible] Palmerston replied:—

February 4, 1855.

[illegible] you for your letter, which I have just received. [illegible] the course which you have adopted was, under all cir-[illegible], the best. The events which led to the present [illegible] things were too recent to have allowed personal feelings [illegible] sufficiently to have enabled you to succeed in the [illegible] which the Queen had asked you to undertake; and to [illegible] an imperfect arrangement would not have been [illegible] either to yourself or to the country.

[illegible] feel very thankful to you for what you say with reference [illegible] possibility that the Queen might desire me to try to form [illegible]ment; and if this should be, I should, of course, lose [illegible] in communicating with you.

[illegible] 'possibility' was what everyone, during these [illegible]' negotiations, foresaw to be a necessity. Lord [illegible] was requested to take up the abandoned [illegible] and he successfully performed it. He thus writes [illegible] brother to announce the event:—

Downing Street: February 15, 1855.

> . . . . . . 'Quod nemo promittere Divum
> Auderet volvenda dies en attulit ultro.'

[illegible] month ago if any man had asked me to say what was one [illegible] most improbable events, I should have said my being [illegible] Minister. Aberdeen was there, Derby was head of one [illegible], John Russell of the other, and yet, in about ten days' time, they all gave way like straws before the wi so here am I, writing to you from Downing Street, Lord of the Treasury.

The fact was that Aberdeen and Newcastle had discredited in public estimation as statesmen equal emergency. Derby felt conscious of the incapacity greater portion of his party, and their unfitness to gov country, and John Russell, by the way in which he abandoned the Government, had so lost caste for the that I was the only one of his political friends who was to serve under him. I could not refuse to do so, bec told me that upon my answer depended his underta form a Government, and if I had refused, and he had the task, and the Queen had then sent for me, peopl have ascribed my refusal to personal ambition. Bes broke with the late Government because the War Dep was not given to me, and it would have been ungratefu to have refused to assist him. It is, however, curious same man who summarily dismissed me three years unfit to be Minister for Foreign Affairs, should no broken up a Government because I was not placed he conceived to be the most important post in the prese of things.

I think our Government will do very well. I am by the general opinion of the whole country, and I reason to complain of the least want of cordiality or co on the part of the Court.

As Aberdeen has become an impossibility, I am, moment *l'inévitable*. We are sending John Russell to n at Vienna. This will serve as a proof to show that w earnest in our wish for peace, and in our determination sufficiently satisfactory terms. I have no great faith sincerity of Russia, though it is said that the Emperor is much pressed by many around him to make peace as he can. But we must insist upon his having a ver number of ships-of-war in the Black Sea, probably than four, and it will be a great gulp for him to swall a condition, especially seeing that we have not been yet to take his fleet. We must also *ask* for the destru the works at Sebastopol, although we should not mak *sine quâ non*, unless we had taken the place and had the works ourselves. However, a short time will we are to have peace or war, and, in the mean [illegible] preparations for war as if peace was out of the [illegible]

[illegible] tolerably strong in Parliament for some little [illegible] and I think that when the session is over it will [illegible] dissolve.

[illegible] have many discontented men behind us, because the [illegible] Whigs are angry that the Peelites joined me, and [illegible] places which the Whigs hoped to have them- [illegible] if the Peelites had not joined me, we should have [illegible] numerous band of discontented, only with this [illegible] that they would have consisted of more able men. [illegible] and Newcastle behaved in the most friendly and [illegible] manner possible in persuading their friends to [illegible] the Government, but I see that the Peelite section [illegible] to endeavour to make itself a little separate [illegible]

[illegible] one of the leading Peelites hesitated to accept [illegible] made to him, Lord Palmerston, divining his [illegible], wrote openly to him as follows :—

[illegible] speak plainly and frankly, you distrust m views and [illegible], and you think that I should be disposed to continue [illegible] without necessity, for the attainment of objects either [illegible] in themselves or unattainable by the means at [illegible] command, or not worth the efforts necessary for their [illegible]. In this you misjudge me. If by a stroke of the [illegible] I could effect in the map of the world the changes which [illegible] wish, I am quite sure that I could make arrangements [illegible] more conducive than some of the present ones to the peace [illegible], to the progress of civilisation, to the happiness and [illegible] of mankind; but I am not so destitute of common [illegible] as not to be able to compare ends with means, and to see [illegible] the former must be given up when the latter are wanting; [illegible] when the means to be brought to bear for the attainment [illegible] ends consist in the blood and treasure of a great nation, [illegible] who are answerable to that nation for the expenditure of [illegible] blood and treasure must well weigh the value of the [illegible] which they pursue, and must remember that, if they [illegible] forget the just proportion between ends and means, the [illegible] of the people whose affairs they manage will soon [illegible] to correct their errors, and to call them to a severe [illegible] for the evils of which they would have been the cause.[1]

[1] February 6, 1855.

No time was lost by the [illegible] remedying some of the most [illegible] borne down our army in the Crimea. [illegible] in announcing to the House of Comm[illegible] of his Government, detailed also some [illegible] ministrative measures. The office of [illegible] was to be amalgamated with that of the [illegible] State in the person of Lord Panmure; [illegible] immediately to be introduced for the [illegible] older men on short service; the Admiralty [illegible] tablish a special Board to superintend the [illegible] service; lastly, a sanitary commission was to [illegible] the Crimea, and another, under Sir John [illegible] superintend the commissariat. I append [illegible] merston's letter to Lord Raglan accompa[illegible] Sanitary Commission:—

Downing Street: February [illegible]

This will be given to you by Dr. Sutherland, [illegible] Sanitary Commission, consisting of himself, Dr. Gav[illegible] Rawlinson, whom we have sent out to put the h[illegible] port, and the camp into a less unhealthy conditio[illegible] hitherto existed, and I request that you will give [illegible] assistance and support in your power. They will, [illegible] opposed and thwarted by the medical officers, by th[illegible] have charge of the port arrangements, and by those [illegible] the cleaning of the camp. Their mission will be ri[illegible] their recommendations and directions set aside, unl[illegible] by the peremptory exercise of your authority.

But that authority I must request you to exert [illegible] peremptory manner for the immediate and exact e[illegible] execution whatever changes of arrangement they [illegible] mend; for these are matters on which depend the [illegible] lives of many hundreds of men, I may indeed say [illegible] It is scarcely to be expected that officers, whether [illegible] medical, whose time is wholly occupied by the press[illegible] of each day, should be able to give their attention [illegible] to the matters to which these commissioners [illegible] years devoted their action and their thoughts. [illegible]

But the interposition of men skilled in [illegible] required. The hospital at Scutari is [illegible] pestilence, and if no proper precautions [illegible]

[illegible] to be felt, your camp will become one vast seat [illegible] virulent plague. I hope this commission will [illegible] time to prevent much evil, but I am very sure that [illegible] hour should be lost after their arrival in carrying into [illegible] precautionary and remedial measures which they may recommend.

The patriotic impatience, however, of a certain [illegible] of ambitious politicians was so great that they would not wait. Before five days had elapsed Mr. Layard again drew attention to the state of the army, and in a speech decidedly hostile to Lord Palmerston's administration, recommended that, in imitation of the French revolutionary Convention, the House should send out some of its own members to sit in judgment on the guilty. In reply to this, Lord Palmerston, amid general laughter, suggested that it might be satisfactory to the House to take the honourable member at his word, and to add to the direction that he and his colleagues should proceed instantly to the Crimea, the further instruction that they should remain there during the rest of the session.

As to Mr. Roebuck's committee, Lord Palmerston still retained his objection to it, as not in accordance with the Constitution or efficient for its purpose. He told the House that, as an English king once rode up to an insurrection and offered to be its leader,[1] so the Government offered to the House of Commons to be its committee, and would do of itself all that it was possible to do. As, however, Mr. Roebuck still persisted, 'aiming,' as he said, to 'assist the noble Lord in infusing new vigour into the Constitution of the country,' Lord Palmerston yielded, giving as his reason for so doing that the country asked for an inquiry, and that, whatever inconvenience there might be in such a course, there would be greater inconvenience and danger if the government of the country were again to be in abeyance. This concession, however, produced another ministerial crisis, which was, however, of short dura-

[1] Richard II. in Wat Tyler's insurrection.

tion. Sir James Graham, Mr. Gladstone, and Mr ney Herbert retired because the renewed motion not to be resisted; and Sir Charles Wood, Sir G Lewis, and Lord John Russell took the vacant pla

The death of the Emperor Nicholas and the alliance of Sardinia with the Western Powers were events which appeared likely to affect favourabl peace the negotiations which had now been renew Vienna. Lord John Russell, who went to the ference as English representative, was instructe the end to be held in view was the admission of T into the great European family, and that there certain points which must be insisted on as nec fully to attain this object. They lay under four pal heads, namely, the Principalities, the free navi of the Danube, Russian supremacy in the Black Se the independence of the Porte. Lord Palmerston to Lord John Russell private instructions:—

Piccadilly: March 28,

I fear from all you have said to Clarendon, private, that there is no chance of the new Emperor of agreeing to the only conditions which would afford us for the future, and though some few people here would us for making peace on almost any conditions, yet the nation would soon see through the flimsy veil w we should have endeavoured to disguise entire failure ing the objects for which we undertook the war, and receive the general condemnation which we should deserve.

The Austrians, the Prussians, and the Russian course trumpet forth the vast value of the conce Russia by her acceptance of the four points as a tion; but the whole value and practical effect must depend upon the manner in which they and, according to the schemes of Gortschakoff vaunted concessions would be reduced to abs two important points of the four are the the second lays down a principle not new, even by Russia herself, though in practic evade the carrying of it out. The fourth [illegible] ishment of a pretension which could not be [illegible] when England and France resolved to back [illegible] the admission involved in the Russian acceptance [illegible] point does not take from her one particle of her [illegible] aggression against Turkey, though it saves [illegible] a source of great internal weakness. But the [illegible] was one which Russia had yet to make good, and she [illegible] make it good against Turkey supported by England [illegible]

[illegible] point is very important, because the object the allies [illegible] view to be attained by it is to emancipate the Princi[illegible] from foreign interference and to tie them more closely [illegible] Sultan, while, at the same time, security should be given [illegible] the maintenance of local self-government, and for [illegible] privileges of religion, internal administration, and com[illegible] which are essential to their welfare and prosperity. For [illegible] purposes it is plain that their Constitution should be im[illegible] and liberalised, that their Prince should be appointed [illegible] Sultan, with the only condition that he should be one of [illegible] Sultan's Christian subjects. That the Constitution, which [illegible] to include a representative system, should be granted [illegible]) by the Sovereign, confirmed by him by the most [illegible] sanction, and communicated by him to the contracting [illegible] Such an arrangement would seem to be a sufficient [illegible], considering that there has been no complaint by the [illegible] provinces that the Sultan has endeavoured to infringe on [illegible] privileges or to curtail their liberties. The only evil to [illegible] guarded against is the recurrence of that intermeddling in [illegible] internal affairs of the provinces by a foreign Power, and [illegible] military occupations of those two provinces by foreign [illegible], which have led to the conflicts between the Powers of [illegible]

Now, the scheme of Gortschakoff and Prokesh, so far from [illegible] the objects we have in view, would have the effect of [illegible] the foreign shackles which Russia has sought to fasten [illegible] the Principalities, adding to their tightness and their weight, [illegible] fixing them down by the assistance and co-operation of [illegible], with the formal sanction and approval of England and [illegible]

The treacherous game of Austria and Russia is manifest [illegible] palpable. They propose to England and France the most [illegible] arrangements on the first, second, and fourth [illegible] They tell England and France, or, at least, Austria suggests to England and France, that it would be necessary for those two Powers to agree to these objectionable conditions, in order to secure the co-operation of Austria on the third point, the most important to the Western Powers. And what would be the result? Why that which follows all such bargains with his sable majesty: we should have paid the price without obtaining the thing we wanted to buy. Austria evidently means to throw us over on the third point; and if that is to happen, the sooner we are undeceived as to her intentions the better.

Her substitutes for a narrow limitation of the Russian Black Sea fleet, are, as you say, futile. The opening of the Straits would be a standing danger to the Sultan, with no compensating advantage, but, on the contrary, with probable inconvenience to England and France. The maintenance by us and the French of permanent fleets in the Black Sea to counterbalance the fleet of Russia, is simply a *mauvaise plaisanterie*. The stipulation that Russia should not have a larger fleet than she now has, even assuming that the sunken ships are not to count, would still leave her with too powerful a naval force; and it must be remembered that it is easy to build steamers which, though unarmed at first, may easily be strengthened and turned into ships-of-war. The neutrality scheme of Drouyn might do, if confined to the Black Sea and the Sea of Azoff, but it would probably be as distasteful to Russia as our own proposals. The truth is we are in the middle of a battle, and our adversary seems determined to try the fate of arms, though it is clearly for his interest not to do so. Possibly this Czar might find more difficulty in yielding than his father might have done. However, I presume a few days will now give a turn to affairs. Drouyn comes here to-morrow on his way to Vienna, whither he is going to stiffen Bourqueney.

We are getting on very fairly in the House of Commons, and people there are behaving very well towards the Government.

I am taking charge of the current business of the Colonial Office, in order to know a little about it, and because I thought it began to press a little too much on George Grey's health. I did not, however, state that latter reason to him, but put upon the first, my proposal to take charge.

Whilst there was a chance of peace issuing out of the doings at Vienna, Lord Palmerston was consider-

reforms which would have to be Sultan. Letters have been already how constantly he urged upon the equality between Christian and the only means whereby the Ottobe permanently strengthened; and letter he summarises what he was preon the Porte. He also advocated the of primary schools in which Christian children should receive elementary together:—

May 14, 1855.

Clarendon,—What remains to be done for the in Turkey would be, I apprehend, speaking

for military service by voluntary enlistment eligibility to rise to any rank in the army.

of non-Mussulman evidence in civil as well criminal cases.

of mixed courts of justice (with an equal number of Christian and Mussulman judges) for all in which Mahomedans and non-Mahomedans are parties.

of a Christian officer as assessor to every governor of a province when that governor is a Mussulman; such assessor to be of suitable rank and to have full liberty to appeal to Constantinople against any of the governor unjust, oppressive, or corrupt.

of Christians to all places in the administration, whether at Constantinople or in the provinces, a practical application of this rule by the appointof Christians at once to some places of trust, civil and military.

total abolition of the present system by which offices Constantinople and in the provinces are bought and and given to unfit and unworthy men for money or promised. Such men become tyrants in their either from incapacity or bad passions, or from desire to repay themselves the money paid for their appointments.

not only to be complete toleration of non-Mus- but all punishment on converts from Islam, or foreigners, ought to be abolished.

This would have been a very complete [illegible] of civil and religious emancipation, could [illegible] struments have been found to carry it out [illegible] and honestly. But thorough and honest [illegible] can never be found under such a blighting [illegible] despotism as that of the Sultan of Turkey. [illegible] of criminal recklessness and indifference to [illegible] habitually descends is illustrated by the [illegible] Memorandum of Lord Palmerston's, from [illegible] appears that the very first loan the Turkish [illegible] ment ever raised—a loan paid to them at [illegible] height of war, and for the purposes of their [illegible] national existence, was being deliberately squan[illegible] their sovereign on favourites and on personal [illegible] while the fortress of Kars and its gallant defende[illegible] being abandoned to their fate. We were pouring [illegible] into a cracked vase: no wonder that it was all [illegible] lessly spilt:—

Should we not be justified in saying to the Turkish Go[illegible] ment that we will not advance any more of the loan [illegible] have guaranteed until these extravagant prodigalities have [illegible] put an end to? We shall not be able to justify to Parli[illegible] our having incurred pecuniary responsibility to [illegible] Turkish Government in carrying on the war if it [illegible] that our guarantee has thus been made subservient to [illegible] expenditure for personal and private purposes. The T[illegible] troops are in arrear of their pay. We are told that [illegible] supplies are stopped for want of money. Kars and [illegible] army are lost because the Turkish Government has not [illegible] pay, provisions, and munitions of war to them; and [illegible] crisis, when a proper sense of duty would have led the [illegible] stint himself, in order to find money for the defence of [illegible] and empire, he launches into extravagance in [illegible] building palaces, and he nearly doubles the amount [illegible] applied to his personal expenses and to the allowance [illegible] bers of his family. This is scandalous.

P. [illegible]

[illegible] Sea. Lord Palmerston had some [illegible] these Conferences in keeping our ally [illegible]'s bugbear was a German Con- [illegible] France, and this inclined him to back [illegible] of Austria, with a view to remaining [illegible] with her, so as to secure her neutrality. [illegible] had never been so popular in France [illegible] England, and the French appeared too [illegible] terms which the English Government [illegible]cient. In the following letter the Em- [illegible] French is urged not to allow a subtle [illegible] to rob him of the fruits of victory. The [illegible] Ministry had just obtained a large majority in [illegible] of Commons on Mr. Disraeli's resolution [illegible] 'dissatisfaction with the ambiguous language [illegible] conduct of Her Majesty's Government.'

Londres: Mai 28, 1855.

[illegible] Votre Majesté a daigné me permettre de vous exprimer [illegible] de temps en temps dans des occasions importantes. [illegible] vous soumettre que la proposition que nous fait [illegible] de prononcer dans la Conférence de Vienne le mot [illegible],' n'est qu'un piége qu'on nous tend.

[illegible] de Limitation n'a aucune valeur pour nous, tout [illegible] Chiffre. La Russie pourrait bien accepter le principe [illegible] fussions pour cela plus près d'une paix sûre et [illegible] Mais par une telle acceptation, la Russie nous [illegible] dans un dédale de négociations qui amolliraient les [illegible] France, en Angleterre, en Allemagne, partout, et [illegible] armée; car ces négociations oisives et illusoires em- [illegible] de conduire énergiquement la guerre, et ne nous [illegible] à faire la paix. La position de la France et de [illegible] n'est-elle pas simple et claire? Nous avons fait [illegible] des propositions qu'on ne peut critiquer qu'en les [illegible] trop libérales envers notre ennemi; ces propositions, [illegible] a rejetées avec fierté, on pourrait même le dire, [illegible]. Qu'avons-nous à faire donc, excepté de nous [illegible] des succès par la guerre; pourquoi nous humi- [illegible] de nouvelles propositions à la Russie, et en quit- [illegible] où nous nous étions placés? Ce terrain n'est [illegible] de Limitation, mais une Limitation définie et [illegible] yeux pour parer aux dangers de l'avenir.

ulse was to resign, therein fol- Monsieur Drouyn de Lhuys, the iad also expressed his assent to a. Yielding, however, to the colleagues, he remained a mem- till July, when Sir E. Lytton, a motion in the House of Com- him and his conduct at Vienna, rnment of the embarrassment ck by retiring from the Adminis- the supporters of the Govern- s members out of the Cabinet, n that this step was necessary.
f this session the Opposition and a incessant fire on the Treasury eir artillery from very different itrating it in the same direction. the country to believe that the less of the honour and prestige too ready to make peace at any hester school, on the other hand, sell's attitude at Vienna as their folly and wickedness of the war. ough almost single-handed, met cess. He had the confidence of in his character that mixture mness which the circumstances the keynote of the public tone ugust 7, he referred to what had ssent of the Turkish ambassador he Vienna Conference which the binets had subsequently rejected, objects of the war were wider on the decision of the Turkish otection of Turkey was a means protection of Turkey was the ressing the grasping ambition of the extinction of political and The Governments of France and

England had as great, or even greater, [illegible] Turkey in the conditions of the future peace of [illegible]

Parliament was prorogued on August 14, [illegible] sage from the Lords interrupting Lord Pal[illegible] he was speaking in acquiescence with Sir D[illegible] Evans's exhortations for the vigorous prose[illegible] military measures.

The Prime Minister was indeed indefatigabl[illegible] attention to all the details of the campaign. [illegible] lowing letter, only one among many, illustrates [illegible] and knowledge which he showed :—

Piccadilly : June 1[illegible]

My dear Panmure,—This is capital news from [illegible] Azoff, and the extensive destruction of magazines and [illegible] in the towns attached must greatly cripple the Russians [illegible] the Crimea. I am very sorry, however, to see so sad [illegible] of the health of the Sardinians, and I strongly recomm[illegible] to urge Raglan, by telegraph to-day, to move the [illegible] camp to some other and healthier situation.

Such prevalence of disease as the telegraphic [illegible] tions *must* be the effect of some local cause; and I [illegible] as if I was on the spot that these Sardinians are [illegible] some unhealthy place, from which they ought without [illegible] of a day to be removed. Our quartermaster-general [illegible] bestow a thought about healthiness of situations, [illegible] they are in general wholly ignorant of the sanitary [illegible] upon which any given situation should be chosen [illegible] but if Raglan were to consult Dr. Sutherland on [illegible] am confident he would get a good opinion. At all [illegible] men ought to be removed from where they are [illegible] a day; and no excuse of military arrangements [illegible] accepted as a pretence for delay.

As the cholera seems to be increasing among [illegible] should advise you to send for the doctor I mention[illegible] would give you useful suggestions as to the [illegible] disease, and as to the best way of administering [illegible] which seems now to be the most effectual [illegible] if taken in time, seldom fails in stopping the [illegible]

We are 40,000 men short of the number [illegible] ment, and we shall be without the [illegible] do not resort to every possible means and [illegible]

[illegible] to the number which Parliament has [illegible] get as many Germans and Swiss as we can; [illegible] Halifax; let us enlist Italians; and let us [illegible] our bounty at home without raising the stan[illegible] departmental, or official, or professional pre[illegible] stand in our way. We must override all [illegible] and difficulties. The only answer to give to [illegible] such grounds is, the thing *must* be done; we *must* [illegible]. War cannot be carried on without troops. We [illegible] Parliament for a certain amount of force, and have [illegible] ourselves to the opinion that such a number is [illegible] and we shall disgrace ourselves if we do not make [illegible] to raise that amount. We are now getting on in [illegible] of June, and no time is to be lost.

[illegible] forget to suggest to our commissariat people in the [illegible] that large supplies of oxen to be eaten, and of horses [illegible] or to draw, may be derived from the country on [illegible] shore of the Sea of Azoff, from whence these animals [illegible] brought down to the port of Taman, near the Straits [illegible], and be from thence carried coastwise to Balaclava; [illegible] be well also to point their attention to the pro[illegible] of land or island called Krassnoi, in the Bay of [illegible], which is said to abound in sheep and hay. It lies [illegible] of the coast of the Crimea.

[illegible] good results of the new energy infused into the [illegible] authorities were soon evident. In a speech at [illegible] during the autumn, Lord Palmerston was [illegible] to say that the hospitals in the Crimea were, [illegible], 'in an admirable condition, and might, in [illegible] be regarded as models for the hospitals of [illegible]. The troops enjoyed every comfort compatible [illegible] military campaign, and were in as good a con[illegible] if they were on a peace establishment at [illegible].'

[illegible] was England, as is her wont, profiting by [illegible] experience, gradually strengthening through the [illegible], and slowly, but surely, outstripping her [illegible] development of her latent resources.

[illegible] the minor results of the evidence of her [illegible] military resources was an offer made, about [illegible] of a Spanish contingent of ten to twenty thousand men. It is not unreasonable to [illegible] if they had been really wanted we should [illegible] had the chance given to us of declining [illegible] their proffered services.

Lord Palmerston now foresaw, with the [illegible] crease of the dangers which accompany war, [illegible] approach of dangers from diplomacy. He [illegible] brother:—

Piccadilly: August [illegible]

I am kept in town for the present, but hope to [illegible] Broadlands in the first week of September, subject to [illegible] attendances here in London on matters connected with [illegible] duct of the war. Things in that matter are looking [illegible] bombardment of Sweabourg and our successes in [illegible] Russians in the Crimea will, I hope, be followed by the [illegible] of Sebastopol and the expulsion of the Russians from [illegible] Crimea. Our danger will then begin—a danger of [illegible] not a danger of war. Austria will try to draw us [illegible] negotiations for an insufficient peace, and we shall not yet [illegible] obtained those decisive successes which would entitle us [illegible] sist on such terms as will effectually curb the ambition of [illegible] for the future.

I must try to fight the battle of negotiation as well as [illegible] battle of war, and, fortunately, the spirit of the British [illegible] will support us. I wish I could reckon with equal [illegible] on the steady determination of the French.

King Bomba's insult to England, through the British [illegible] sion at Naples, must be properly atoned for. Clarendon [illegible] at Paris, nothing can be decided till he returns and the [illegible] can be assembled; but I have written to Clarendon [illegible] my opinion is that we ought to insist upon the [illegible] missal of Massa,[1] and upon a promise that he shall [illegible] be employed in any public capacity. I would [illegible] demand till our reserve squadron—now in [illegible] Queen, but which will return with her on Tuesday [illegible] consists of three line-of-battle ships—shall have [illegible] Bay of Naples, opposite the King's palace, and [illegible] on board the mission and the consul, and then [illegible] boat sent on shore with a demand that in two [illegible] should be sent by the King saying that [illegible] allowing half an hour for the letter to go, [illegible] answer to come back, and a whole hour [illegible]

[1] Minister of Police at [illegible]

f the time passed without a satisfactory reply, the place should hare the fate of Sweabourg; *e poi dopo*, if that should not be ufficient. However, we shall see what resolution may be come o when the Cabinet meets on the question.

The King of Naples had acted a very unfriendly part during our war with Russia. He had forbidden, within his territory, the sale of horses, mules, or other upplies to English agents. He gave way in this natter of the Minister of Police as soon as he heard of our success at Sebastopol, which happened very hortly afier the date of this letter.

CHAPTER XII.

RENEWAL OF NEGOTIATIONS—PEACE SIGNED—DECLA
PARIS—DISPUTES ABOUT EXECUTION OF TREATY—
STANDING WITH THE UNITED STATES—DEATH OF SI
TEMPLE—EGYPT—PERSIAN AFFAIRS.

In September came the news of the fall of Se Austria, who had never relaxed her efforts about an accommodation, now renewed her enc and found in France a much more pliable subje with than England. The French Emperor was on all sides by a 'feu d'enfer' of Russian and intrigue trying to shake his constancy and to c to some act of weakness. One such act that tated at this moment, and that it required weight of English persuasion to arrest, was t of a considerable number of his troops home Crimea.

The Austrian and French Cabinets, howe much mistook the intention of this country imagined that we were going to surrender blindly into the hands of our allies withc exercising our own rights and judgment. On ber 21, Lord Palmerston thus writes to the (Persigny, French ambassador in London:—

Piccadilly: 21 Novemb

Mon cher Comte,—D'après notre Constitution Régime Parlementaire, le pouvoir exécutif ne doit j une démarche aussi importante que celle dont il avoir des pièces officielles à produire au Parlement, même d'expliquer clairement ce qui a été proposé par quels motifs la proposition a été appuyée, les raisons qui ont conseillé son adoption.

nous n'avons rien de tout cela. Il y
à laquelle nous n'avons pas pris
paraphé, un protocole pour nous,
communique confidentiellement ce pro-
prendre ou à laisser, en nous disant qu'il faut
accepter immédiatement, bon ou mauvais, sans
et les détails.
d'agir dans une affaire tellement grave ne
Nous souhaitons nous conformer aux désirs
mais il faut que nous soyons en règle vis-à-vis
et nous ne pouvons pas souscrire à une
paix à être faite en notre nom, à la Russie, sans
entièrement d'accord et sur la forme et sur la
telle proposition. Il est donc indispensable que
proposition par écrit, dont nous puissions
la rédaction, avant de pouvoir donner à l'Autriche
qu'elle nous demande, de parler à la Russie en

parler en notre nom, parce que, malgré que l'Autriche
la démarche qu'elle voudrait faire à Péters-
propose de dire qu'elle sait d'avance que sa pro-
adoptée par la France et l'Angleterre, si elle
acceptée par la Russie.

anglaise serait enchantée d'une bonne paix qui
objets de la guerre; mais plutôt que d'être entraînée
paix à des conditions insuffisantes, elle préférerait
la guerre sans d'autres alliés que la Turquie, et elle
fait en état d'en soutenir le fardeau, et de se tirer
Soumettez, je vous prie, ces observations à

observations were not unnecessary, because had already persuaded France to favour that the Black Sea arrangements should in a separate treaty between Russia and Four days after this letter, Count Persigny at Downing Street, acquiescence in this but he met with a distinct refusal.

to stand firm,' said Lord Palmerston, 'as to stipulations about the Black Sea made parts of Russia and all the belligerents. I can fancy hooted in the House of Commons if I were to get up and say that we had agreed to an imperfect and unsatisfactory arrangement about one of the most important parts of the whole matter, as a personal favour to Count Buol, or to save the *amour-propre* of Russia. I had better beforehand take the Chiltern Hundreds.'[1]

Towards the end of the year, when winter had caused hostilities to cease, Count Buol put forward, in the name of Austria, four new points, which in substance were nearly the same as the four old points. The third, on which the former negotiations had broken off, proposed that no fleet and no naval station of any country should be permitted in the Black Sea. The Czar, on January 16, 1856, accepted these proposals as a basis for negotiating a treaty of peace; although, of course, there were other points, many and difficult, to be settled by subsequent negotiation. Sir Hamilton Seymour was now our ambassador at Vienna. He was one of the ablest members of our diplomacy, and Lord Palmerston felt that he could speak proudly to him in reply to Austrian pressure without leading him into imprudences.

94 Piccadilly: January 24, 1856.

My dear Seymour,—Buol's statement to you the night before last was what in plain English we should call impertinent. We are happily not yet in such a condition that an Austrian minister should bid us sign a treaty without hesitation or conditions. The Cabinet of Vienna, forsooth, must insist upon our doing so! Why, really our friend Buol must have had his head turned by his success at St. Petersburg, and quite forgot whom he was addressing such language to. He should remember that he is a self-constituted mediator, but that nobody has made him umpire, arbiter, or dictator. He may depend upon it we shall do no such thing. We shall not sign without knowing what it is that we are signing. We shall not sign unless we are satisfied with that which we may be asked to put our names to. Pray tell him so, and say to him privately from me, with my best regards and compliments, that we feel very sincerely obliged to him for his friendly and firm conduct in these recent transactions, that we accepted, with the addition

[1] To Lord Clarendon, November 28, 1855.

[illegible] conditions, the arrangement which [illegible] because we felt that it contained all that, [illegible] of things, we were entitled to exact from [illegible], to any further demands which the [illegible] and authorises us to make.

[illegible] rather than the allies who ought to feel [illegible] his good offices in these matters, because we [illegible] if the war goes on, the results of another [illegible] us this time twelvemonth to obtain from [illegible] conditions than those which we are now [illegible]

[illegible] the exhaustion, the internal pressure, difficulties, [illegible] of Russia quite as well as Buol does; but we know [illegible] he does our own resources and strength. He may [illegible], however, that we have no wish to continue the [illegible] prospect of what we may accomplish another year, [illegible] now obtain peace upon the conditions which we [illegible] necessary and essential; but we are quite [illegible] go on if such conditions cannot be obtained. The [illegible] is unanimous in this matter. I say unanimous, [illegible] reckon Cobden, Bright, and Co. for anything; and [illegible] Government were not kept straight by a sense of [illegible] duty, the strong feeling which prevails throughout [illegible] would make it impossible for us to swerve. So [illegible] Count Buol keep his *threats* for elsewhere, and not send [illegible] here.

[illegible] February 1 a protocol was signed at Vienna by [illegible] representatives of the five Powers, and the congress [illegible] final settlement of the terms of peace was ap[illegible] to meet in Paris.

[illegible] this Congress Lord Clarendon went as British [illegible] plenipotentiary, in concert with Lord Cowley. During [illegible] Lord Palmerston was in constant correspon[illegible] with him, and entered, with indefatigable in[illegible] into the smallest details. They had, however, [illegible] task in the negotiations. The Russians, [illegible] beaten, were not inclined to yield one inch, [illegible] absolute necessity, and the French were too [illegible] peace to be depended upon for much assist[illegible] The Emperor himself was swayed by Count [illegible] many Russian affinities; he was horrified by the daily accounts of the privations [illegible] army in the Crimea, and he was absorbed [illegible] event which had given him an heir, whom he [illegible] to christen amid the rejoicings for peace [illegible] therefore, only thinking of how to 'faire [illegible] towards the Czar, whom he would gladly [illegible] ciliated now that his position in Europe [illegible] Amid all such secret motives and tortuous [illegible] British Government had to hold on its [illegible] then yielding on minor matters, but adhering [illegible] the principal conditions of peace. In this [illegible] and on March 30 the Treaty of Paris was [illegible]

A few days later, the plenipotentiaries [illegible] scribed a declaration about maritime war.

At the beginning of hostilities Great [illegible] tacitly abandoned her ancient doctrines [illegible] neutrals, which she could only have [illegible] force under pain of having all mankind [illegible] It was evident that they could never be [illegible] that the concessions which she had [illegible] neutral rights could never be withdrawn [illegible] therefore, the President of the Congress [illegible] of his Government, suggested to the English [illegible] tentiary that it would be a 'benevolent [illegible] Congress to proclaim as permanent the principles [illegible] which the war had been carried on, with [illegible] that privateering should be abolished,'[1] [illegible]

[1] *Original Draft of Resolution handed by Lord* [illegible] congrès de Westphalie a consacré la liberté des [illegible] Vienne l'abolition de la traite des noirs et la liberté [illegible] des fleuves ; il appartiendrait au congrès de Paris [illegible] tion de la course et la franchise du commerce [illegible] ment aux principes appliqués dans la guerre actuelle [illegible]

'Ces principes sont d'après les déclarations [illegible] de l'Angleterre au début de la guerre ;

'Que le pavillon neutre couvre la marchandise [illegible] contrebande de guerre.

'Que la marchandise neutre, excepté la [illegible] pas saisissable sous pavillon ennemi.

'Et que les blocus doivent, être effectifs [illegible] une force navale suffisante.

The Americans had previously by [illegible]

[illegible] home, and, with the approval of the [illegible] entire Cabinet, conveyed the assent [illegible] plenipotentiaries to the proposal, point- [illegible] same time, as a necessary proviso, 'that [illegible] should not be binding except between [illegible] who have acceded or shall accede to it.' [illegible] was added, and certain other modifications [illegible] the declaration before it was finally settled. [illegible] is not a matter for discussion here; but the [illegible] having been deliberately adopted by the [illegible] Cabinet, for what they considered good and [illegible] reasons, is the point which it is desirable to [illegible] as many absurd tales have been from time to [illegible] current about it: as though the English plenipo- [illegible] had agreed to it without any authority from [illegible] consultation with the rest of the Ministry.

[illegible] May 5, an animated and prolonged debate took [illegible] in the House of Commons on the treaty of peace. [illegible] Palmerston spoke on the second night of the [illegible] from twelve o'clock till half-past two, and [illegible] defended the acts of the Government. The [illegible] day he moved a vote of thanks to the navy [illegible].

Thus ended the Crimean war—a war which, how- [illegible] some men may look back to it with regret, on [illegible] of the incapacity since shown by the Turks for [illegible] by the breathing-time afforded to them, was [illegible] just, and possibly necessary. It cost England [illegible],000 men, and fifty millions in money, but Rus- [illegible] overbearance and greed of dominion received a [illegible], if only temporary, check, and, had the war [illegible] a little longer, would have been still more [illegible] punished. The plans proposed to the Allies for [illegible] campaign embraced operations in Circassia

[illegible] Powers to the doctrine of 'free ships, free goods.' Most of [illegible] consulted England as to the answer they should give, and, [illegible] with our views, answered that they should not agree [illegible] United States at the same time gave up the system of [illegible]. This they declined to do; but by the Declaration of Paris [illegible] to stand alone in their anachronism.

and Finland; the English to have chief [illegible] the South, and the French in the North. [illegible] of Persia had promised certain facilities [illegible] in view of a campaign in Georgia, and [illegible] Sweden had already been signed the [illegible] It is not impossible that the result might have [illegible] restoration of Finland to Sweden, of her [illegible] to Persia, and the independence of Circassia. [illegible]

Only twenty years, however, elapsed before [illegible] and Turkey again found themselves in [illegible] conflict; but this time they fought [illegible] France nor England intervened, and the [illegible] maintain the struggle without allies. There [illegible] of reasons, both foreign and domestic, why [illegible] men in 1877 should be unwilling to fight [illegible] cause about which even in 1854 they were, [illegible] wholly indifferent. But, at first sight, it [illegible] many that Englishmen were, to say the [illegible] sistent when they successfully protested [illegible] a second time led to war with Russia [illegible] Turkey. This was a very superficial view [illegible] as the circumstances of the two periods [illegible] different. In 1877 the Russian Czar [illegible] free a nationality. This, at any rate, [illegible] sible object as well as the inevitable result [illegible] whatever secret aims and unavowed motives [illegible] also been at work. At the time of the [illegible] not only was there no such justification [illegible] forward, but had there been it would [illegible] value in England, because the Bulgarians [illegible] not deemed to be in a condition to [illegible] demands made in their behalf. But [illegible] which elapsed between the Congress [illegible] Conference at Constantinople educated [illegible] general civilisation had, by various [illegible] among the Slavs of Turkey, that [illegible] dictum, as to there being among [illegible] capable of self-government, [illegible] anachronism. He himself, [illegible] to recognise this; nor, if we may at the time of the establishment , would he have been among the action to endow them with whatever they were capable of receiving. of Czar Nicholas and of his son —in other words, the Russia of to the world a totally different aspect of 1877. The Emperor Nicholas in arrogance and imperious conduct was but and embodiment of what had been policy of his empire for many years. between him and Lord Palmerston, as the representative of British honour and interests, in the Crimean war. During earlier been fiercely maintained, while almost in its personal incidents. Persia, India, Po- and the outlying parts of Turkey had in the ground of contest. That a check to the encroachments of Russia was required had cardinal point in the creed of almost every statesman. The Emperor Alexander, on the was not only credited with a distaste for with a conciliatory disposition, but also had shown himself a disturber of the peace. His triumph—namely, the emancipation of the serfs at home. When at last he did proceed to arms abroad he had patiently waited till the voice of Europe at the Constantinople Con- pronounced that, in the actual controversy, he and his adversary wrong. Lastly, the Govern- the Turk stood before the eyes of the English in a very different light from that with which surrounded it in 1854. That Lord Palmer- most of the statesmen of that period believed probable reform and regeneration of Ottoman rule, an undoubted truth, but the only justifica- policy which they so long and so earnestly . But when Lord Russell, in 1860, in a letter to Lord Palmerston, stated his fears that 'not [illegible] but honesty and energy in a degree that [illegible] be found at Constantinople can restore the [illegible] Empire,' he was only giving expression to [illegible] which were beginning to dawn everywhere. It [illegible] pass, therefore, that when, after twenty years of [illegible] peace, and the command during that time of [illegible] sums of money which the capitalists of [illegible] poured into the lap of Turkey, her Government [illegible] worse and her corruption greater than before [illegible] people thought her case hopeless, and wisely [illegible] to let her get though her troubles with [illegible] sisted and alone.

But to return to 1856. Difficulties [illegible] respecting the execution of some of the [illegible] treaty of peace. A Turkish officer had [illegible] take possession of Serpent's Island, at the [illegible] Danube, and the Turkish flag was hoisted. [illegible] wards a party of seven Russian marines, [illegible] tenant, landed and occupied the island. [illegible] Government declined to remove them, on the [illegible] the question of its occupation was to be [illegible] Conference at Paris. The English admiral [illegible] tioned a vessel off the island, with orders to [illegible] force if necessary, all attempts to increase [illegible] force on the island. So matters remained [illegible] of the year.

Another point in dispute was as to the [illegible] of a place marked Bolgrad on the map. [illegible] said that the new frontier was to run 'south [illegible] When the commissioners met to mark it [illegible] covered that the real Bolgrad was much [illegible] south than the Bolgrad of the Conference [illegible] were unable, therefore, to agree, and [illegible] gether with the question of Serpent's Island [illegible] to a new Conference.

Lord Palmerston, in the following [illegible] recounts his first interview with the [illegible] bassador in London, and records [illegible] about these two disputed points:—

[illegible] Piccadilly, August 28, 1858. [illegible] this morning at half-past [illegible] by civil expressions of [illegible] acquaintance, to which I replied in [illegible] preliminary talk of this kind, I [illegible] our first interview on the renewal of [illegible] the two Governments, I should [illegible] of grievances. 'Well,' said he, [illegible] are they?' I said I was sorry to [illegible] since the conclusion of the treaty of [illegible] Government has been acting in a manner [illegible] engagements, and has in some instances [illegible] tried to evade them. That the treaty [illegible] the fortress and district of Kars are to [illegible] Turkey; in violation of which engagement the [illegible] demolished, and the Russian occupying [illegible] The treaty says that a portion of Bessarabia [illegible] to Turkey, and from the ratification of the [illegible] belonged of right to Turkey; but in [illegible] the Russians have destroyed the fortifications [illegible]. Here Count Chreptovitch interrupted me [illegible]. He said these things were done, whether [illegible], and there was no use in going back to past [illegible] we must look only to the future. I said I [illegible] from him; I thought there was great use in [illegible] past events, and that they had, as I would pre-[illegible] great bearing on the future. That I must be [illegible] him fully and plainly all I think on these [illegible] was for the purpose of doing so that I had asked [illegible] me; and that if he did not choose to listen to [illegible] go back to Petersburg. I then resumed. I [illegible] were not only at variance with the treaty, but [illegible] of a great Power like Russia. If Russia had [illegible] Congress of Paris to obtain stipulations that [illegible] no defensive works at Kars, and no fortifica-[illegible] and Reni, and that both those frontiers should [illegible] the future attacks of Russia—meditated attacks, [illegible] would lead us to think, though I did not ask him [illegible] such stipulations could have been obtained, [illegible] understood the value which Russia would have [illegible], and they would have been worth a struggle in [illegible] as no such stipulations were made, the only [illegible] Kars and Ismail and Reni would be to put

the Turks to some expense and trouble in re
these works, and the probable result would b
would be rebuilt upon a better plan. This, therefo
ebullition of ill-humour and revenge that might be
I said, however, that we were glad to find that one
grievance is about to cease, and that Kars and its
be immediately evacuated by the Russians. The
had to complain of was the attempt to take posses
pent's Island. When the east and west boundar
Russia and Turkey in Europe ran south of this
island naturally belonged to Russia; but now that
west boundary line will run a good way to the
island, the island must naturally belong to Turkey.
the island has no intrinsic value as territory; th
value is that it is, by means of its lighthouse, a guid
ships making the mouths of the Danube, and on that
must belong to the Powers to which the mouths of
belong. Count Chreptovitch said that the island is
tant for ships going to Odessa, because when they
frequently the case, to be blown to the southward
their course by adverse winds, the light on this
them where they are. I said that the light kept
nube would do equally well for Odessa; and that,
point, I would observe, in passing, that we have be
that the Russian detachment which landed to take
the island, finding a superior force of Turks there,
to induce the Turks to violate their duty, and either
and give up the island to the Russians, or to desert
Russian service. Count Chreptovitch seemed to ad
of the reasoning that the change of the boundary
quarters must throw this island into the Turkish

I then went on to Bessarabia. I said that th
Russia had formally accepted the Vienna propos
the new boundary between Russia and Mold
starting from a point north of the Pruth, and
along a chain of hills to Lake Salyick; that
pure deference to the wishes of the Emperor
from a desire to insist on nothing that had
value, the allies had agreed to a great modi
in favour of Russia; that the new line
plainly and clearly described by the treaty
from a point on the sea-coast beyond La
up to the Ackerman Road, and to follow

...the town of Bolgrad to the north of ... at the Congress a map had been produced, ... had been pointed out bearing the name of ... and which was designated as the town to ... the boundary line is to run, and between ... Lake Yalpouk there is space enough for the ... But, I said, when the commissioners came ... the Russians started a new Bolgrad on the ... new Bolgrad is much to the south of the Bolgrad ... and so close to Lake Yalpouk that there is ... boundary line between the town and the lake. I ... an unworthy deception which cannot be acquiesced ... the old Bolgrad, which was the town meant by the ... must be the Bolgrad to the south of which the ... to run. Count Chreptovitch said that in fact the ... is the real town, the old Bolgrad being only a ... deserted village; but nevertheless he admitted that ... Bolgrad, and not the new one, must be deemed the ... the treaty.

... that we had to complain of another proceeding of the ... commissioners. That the commission had agreed to ... general survey of the whole line in the first instance, ... go over it regularly, putting up landmarks as they ... That upon a great part of the line all are agreed; and ... commissioners proposed that upon those parts the land- ... should be fixed, leaving the other parts, as to which ... had arisen, to be landmarked afterwards, when the ... points should have been settled. That to this the ... have objected, and want to delay the whole till the whole ... upon. I said that in this way the season for opera- ... will be lost; winter will come on before the boundary is ...; and what will be the consequence? The Russians ... go out of the district to be ceded, because the boundary ... not settled and drawn; the Austrians will not go out of ... Principalities because the Russians are not out of ceded ...; and our fleet may probably not leave the Black ... the treaty is not executed. All this state of things ... contrary to the treaty; but the fault will be with ... and with her also the responsibility; and this we shall ... say when Parliament meets. Count Chreptovitch said ... delays were the fault of subordinate agents, and ... the Russian Government, who are anxious for a final set- ... I said that might be; but we cannot give orders to

these subordinate Russian agents, and th
ment can; and as that Government is the
orders to be obeyed, and we must therefo
ment answerable for the conduct of its ag
Count assured me, in the most positive te
ters shall be speedily and satisfactorily setti
they would, and that thus all difficulties v
That the information that Kars is immedi
to the Turks, had relieved us from an emb
felt as to whether Lord Granville should be
Moscow; and if those other points were wel
resume with Russia our former habits of
That we are plain and simple people, and
not to words; and that the sort of small att
which we understand they are lavishing
though with what success may be doubted—
thrown away upon us. That Prince Go
have expressed to Lord Granville some su
should have taken singly, in the Black Se
ence to a treaty to which England is only
tracting parties; but that Prince Gortsch
surprised if we continue to act in the same
any occasion for doing so should arise, inasm
that we have a right to do so, and we kno
power to do so.

I said that Baron Brunnow had often s
land and Russia hold to different princip
Russia is for despotic power; England fo
nevertheless the two countries have grea
mon, upon which abstract and theoretical di
have no direct bearing; and that, as long
land do not come into collision about the
the affairs of Persia, there is no reason w
act in concert on many important matter
that Russia would stick to her engagements
then there could be no differences on that
Persia, Russia had, during the war, done
had done in America, and what she had
that is to say, create for England as much
hostility as she could. That her instrume
become, or will become, her victims. That
President Pierce all chance of re-election
urged him to take towards England; and

shown great forbearance, the time is the Persian Government will see cause towards us, unless in the interval that entirely changed, and fully atoned for. I Ostreptovitch did not very much deny what of Russia in America and in Persia. I with great warmth of manner joined in the wish desire is to forget the recent past, and to former good relations. I said that, with regard it is unfortunate that so long a delay has between his nomination and his arrival, because it otherwise than as a mark of want of re- not perhaps on his part, but on the part of That in general, when a foreign Minister the Queen is at Osborne, such Minister is taken Secretary of State for Foreign Affairs, to have as his audience of Her Majesty at Osborne; but this practice will not be observed; and that, as so little *empressement* to pay his respects to the Majesty cannot be advised to show any *empresse-* him; and that he cannot have his audience till shall return to London.

arted with much mutual cordiality, and tender in- out mutual friends, English and Russian.

did not show herself so ready to support the council table as she had proved herself Lord Palmerston spoke frankly to the Ambassador. He pointed out that owing to assistance at the Congress, Russia had obtained ncessions to which she was not entitled: that, same, a Treaty had been concluded which was t, if loyally carried out; but that, on the con- was being evaded, and that the Russians pre- that they were secretly backed by France. He t, as to these two points of Bolgrad and the Isle it was absolutely impossible for England to pretensions of Russia. That England had to accept somewhat unsatisfactory con- peace, sooner than be the cause of a continu- curse of war, but that she was quite resolved to insist on the full and entire execution of those conditions, and that the only result of any failure of French co-operation would be a weakening of the honourable and advantageous alliance between France and England.

Count Walewski's answer was of a nature to draw from Lord Palmerston a very decided hint that England would take her own line, whether France went back or forward, and his firmness eventually carried the day.

During the session a resolution was introduced in the House of Commons alleging that 'the conduct of Her Majesty's Government in the differences with the United States on the question of enlistment has not entitled them to the approbation of the House.' We had been charged with violating the neutrality of the United States, by enlisting recruits for the British service. No doubt the laws of the States had in some respects been infringed, but not intentionally, nor by any authorised English official.[1] However, Mr. Crampton, our minister at Washington, received his passports from the President and left the country. Our Government did not retaliate for this act of diplomatic censure, but continued to receive Mr. Dallas in London. Both their original offence and their subsequent apologetic conduct formed the grounds of Parliamentary attack on the Government. Lord Palmerston, when the resolution was discussed, successfully pointed out the inconsistencies of its supporters. While with one accord they joined in aspirations for peace and goodwill between the two countries, they were doing all they could to create illwill.

These gentlemen, so anxious for peace, tell you that England has been insulted, treated with contempt, contumely, and indignity. What is the effect likely to be produced? Why, to excite a spirit of resentment towards our neighbours and kin-

[1] During the Crimean war we sent a remonstrance to Holland on her violation of neutrality in supplying arms to Russia, and then discovered that our own Ordnance Department had been ordering from the Dutch large quantities of gunpowder.

...States. Others, again, tell the Americans ... has been deluded, and persuaded to ... they ought not to have accepted, and that ... been intentionally violated by a foreign Govern- ... the way to create good feeling! Is that the ... the American people to cultivate the most ... with England!

... meet his critics.

... the end of the year Lord Palmerston visited ... and Liverpool, and received, amid much ... addresses from the corporations and other ...

... record of his life would be incomplete that did ... the death of his only brother, Sir William ... which occurred in London, in August of this ... Although Lord Palmerston was the older by not ... two years, he always treated his younger ... with the affectionate care which might rather ... from a father. Many of the most inter- ... his letters are those to his brother, who, being ... diplomatic service, lived much abroad, and ... Lord Palmerston therefore endeavoured, in spite ... work, to keep informed as to what was going ... A strong affection subsisted between them, ... their temperaments were very different; and ... William Temple's last illness in London, Lord ... passed a considerable time with him every ...

... future of Egypt must, for a long time to come, ... special interest for Englishmen. The following ... Lord Clarendon sufficiently explains itself, and ... as showing the head of the British Cabinet ... proposals coming from an unexpected quarter, ... to lead to the possession of Egypt by Eng- ... Lord Palmerston's opinions on this matter were ... repeated. He saw the paramount importance ... kept open for transit, but never encouraged ... of annexation. On one occasion, to Lord ... used a homely but apt illustration: 'We do not want Egypt,' he said, [illegible] more than any rational man with [illegible] of England and a residence in [illegible] wished to possess the inns on the [illegible] could want would have been, that [illegible] well kept, always accessible, and furn[illegible] he came, with mutton chops and post-[illegible]

Piccadilly [illegible]

My dear Clarendon,—As to the [illegible] Africa, the sooner Cowley sends in his [illegible] better. It is very possible that many parts of [illegible] be better governed by France, England, and [illegible] they are now; and we need not go beyond [illegible] Spain for examples. But the alliance of England [illegible] has derived its strength not merely from the mili[illegible] power of the two states, but from the force of the [illegible] ciple upon which that union has been founded. [illegible] for its foundation resistance to unjust aggression, [illegible] of the weak against the strong, and the mainte[illegible] existing balance of power. How, then, could we [illegible] become unprovoked aggressors, to imitate, in Afri[illegible] tition of Poland by the conquest of Morocco, for [illegible] Tunis and some other state for Sardinia, and of [illegible] England? and, more especially, how could England [illegible] who have guaranteed the integrity of the Turkish [illegible] round and wrest Egypt from the Sultan? A coali[illegible] a purpose would revolt the moral feelings of [illegible] would certainly be fatal to any English Governm[illegible] a party to it. Then, as to the balance of power [illegible] tained by giving us Egypt. In the first place, we [illegible] to have Egypt. What we wish about Egypt is [illegible] continue attached to the Turkish empire, which [illegible] against its belonging to any European Power. [illegible] trade with Egypt, and to travel through Egypt, [illegible] want the burthen of governing Egypt, and its [illegible] not, as a political, military, and naval question [illegible] in this country, as a set-off against the [illegible] by France. Let us try to improve all [illegible] general influence of our commerce, but let [illegible] a crusade of conquest which would call [illegible] tion of all the other civilised nations. [illegible]

¹ To Lord Cowley, Nove[illegible]

nest of Morocco was the secret aim of Louis Phi-
me of the plans deposited for use, as occasion may
rchives of the French Government.

nst the Emperor of the French, with the
aid a visit to the Queen at Osborne. The
on to be discussed was that of the Danubian
es. Russia, France, and Sardinia were in
e union of Roumania with Moldavia; Prussia
l; England, Austria, and Turkey were op-
By the Treaty of Paris their future con-
ad been left to be settled by the Treaty
r a Divan had been convoked in each of the
ces to ascertain the wishes of the people
There was little doubt as to what they
the elections in Moldavia resulted in the
nembers unfavourable to the union. The
accused of having obtained this result by un-
a demand was made for the annulling of the
der a threat of the withdrawal of the French
n ambassadors from Constantinople. This
and general confusion. Lord Palmerston's
was requested at Osborne in order to confer
matters, and a memorandum of the arrange-
d upon was drawn up by him. It was in
the Moldavian elections should be annulled;
wo Governments were to combine to secure
nty of the Sultan over the Provinces. The
ll, however, was, as we know, their union
uler, thereby affording another illustration of
of attempting in these days to sever by arti-
s countries which affinity, fellow-feeling,
phy combine to join. England gave herself
sion much trouble and incurred some risk,
le result of alienating from herself the sym-
the populations whose fate was involved.
l taken an opposite line, though, no doubt,
motives than pure affection for the Rou-
d Moldavians.

Lord Palmerston's character must have been quite a puzzle to the French Emperor, who found that he could neither intimidate nor cajole him, nor yet shake him off. No wonder that he sometimes showed a little temper.

'I am rather surprised,' says Lord Palmerston,[1] '[illegible] the Emperor should have spoken with so much bitterness [illegible] me, for nothing could be more personally friendly [illegible] manner at Osborne. But the fact, no doubt, is [illegible] much annoyed at finding that we did not give in to his [illegible] about driving the Mahomedans away from the southern [illegible] of the Mediterranean, and about giving an extension to [illegible] occupation in Africa. The fact is that, in our alliance [illegible] France, we are riding a runaway horse, and must always [illegible] our guard; but a runaway horse is best kept in by [illegible] hand and an easy snaffle. It is fortunate for us that [illegible] thus mounted, instead of being on foot, to be kicked at [illegible] same steed; and as our ally finds the alliance useful to [illegible] it will probably go on for a good time to come. The [illegible] and always has been, that France and Russia should [illegible] carry into effect some great scheme of mutual ambition [illegible] land and Germany would then have to stand out against [illegible] and Germany is too much broken up and disjointed [illegible] efficient ally.

We had this year a little war with Persia, [illegible] her occupation of Herat, contrary to the solemn [illegible] ments made with England in 1853. Alth[illegible] dispute did not attract much public atten[illegible] Palmerston was fully alive to the importan[illegible] issues involved. He foresaw that Khiva and [illegible] would shortly be occupied by Russia, and [illegible] and Candahar might, before very long, be [illegible] advanced outposts of British India. Whe[illegible] be better that Herat should remain a weak, [illegible] Government, or that it should be in the ha[illegible] able to defend it, like the ruler of Cabul, [illegible] geographical position, must attach himself [illegible] alliance, might be a moot point; but [illegible] clear that it must not be allowed to [illegible] About the general question he says to [illegible]

[1] To Lord Clarendon, September [illegible]

[illegible] February 17, 1857.

[illegible] as you say, that people in general are dis- [illegible] of our Persian war; that is to say, not [illegible] importance of the question at issue. Ellen- [illegible]: we are beginning to repel the first opening [illegible] India by Russia;[1] and whatever difficulties [illegible] make about Afghanistan, we may be sure that [illegible] prompter and secret backer. But that makes it [illegible] that we should carry our point on that [illegible] however, are our important points? The [illegible] by Persia of all claim over Herat and of all [illegible] or attempt to invade Herat. This is a *sine quâ* [illegible] of course, includes an acknowledgment of the inde- [illegible] of Herat, and includes it so completely that a dis- [illegible] acknowledgment of that independence seems hardly [illegible]. Any engagement on our part towards Persia about [illegible] relations with Affghanistan should be peremptorily [illegible]

[illegible] our mediation, as there is in most men's minds a [illegible] of ideas between mediation and arbitration, we might, [illegible] to it, substitute for mediation, a condition that if any [illegible] should arise between Persia and any of the Affghan [illegible] including Herat, Persia would, in the first place, ask our [illegible] to arrange the matter in dispute; and we might [illegible] to use our good offices to obtain a settlement just and [illegible] to both parties.

[illegible] treaty of peace between the Queen of England [illegible] His Majesty whose standard is the sun' was signed [illegible] on March 4. Persia renounced all claim or [illegible] over Herat and Affghanistan, and engaged (in [illegible] as were suggested in the above letter) to [illegible] any future differences she might have with the [illegible] states to the friendly offices of the British [illegible]ment.

[illegible] opportunity of this war was also taken to obtain [illegible] of slave trade in the Persian Gulf—an [illegible] consistent with the many former efforts of Lord [illegible] to put an end to traffic in human beings.

[1] [illegible] Ellenborough had just made a speech in the House of Lords [illegible]

[illegible] Khan, ambassador from Persia.

I append a letter which, on the occa[illegible] he wrote to the Sadr Azim[1] in reply [illegible] munication from that minister. It is [illegible] of the skill with which he could read [illegible] between the lines and of candid irony in [illegible] sentiments. Behind the diplomatic [illegible] Persian minister he discerned the true [illegible] motives of his correspondent, who had [illegible] bitter enemy of England. His courteous [illegible] very clearly that he knew it all, but that [illegible] soonest mended; only don't let it occur again [illegible]

London: Septem[illegible]

Excellency,—I have received with much plea[illegible] dated June 5 last, which you were so good as [illegible] me; and I have been much gratified by the friendl[illegible] which it contains. I rejoice, as your Excellency [illegible] treaty of peace, which has happily put an end [illegible] between England and Persia; and I hope that the [illegible] has thus been established may long continue for [illegible] advantage of both countries. I can truly assure you[illegible] lency that it is the wish of the English Government [illegible] English nation that Persia should be a happy, a pros[illegible] strong, and an independent state, and that the [illegible] friendship and the fullest confidence should prevail [illegible] the Governments of England and of Persia.

I am rejoiced to find, from your Excellency's lette[illegible] is your desire and intention to cultivate in futur[illegible] ship of England. But I should not be deserving of [illegible] opinion if I were to disguise from you the truth of [illegible] and there are parts of your Excellency's letter wh[illegible] me to speak frankly in reply.

Your Excellency says that, until now, out of [illegible] siderations, you have looked upon yourself as [illegible] out assistance in your endeavours to preserve the [illegible] the two Governments from injury. And you fur[illegible] you request me, and you entertain the firm hope [illegible] henceforward give my full attention to the [illegible] rules of friendship and unity between the two [illegible]

Now upon this I feel myself obliged to [illegible] which took place between our two countries [illegible]

[1] The 'Prime Minister' of [illegible]

[illegible] of the English Government of the [illegible] equity, but was occasioned solely and [illegible] Excellency's own unfriendly conduct, and by [illegible] which your Excellency displayed towards [illegible] and deed; and, therefore, so far from [illegible] been alone in endeavours to preserve [illegible] the two Governments, your Excellency [illegible] principal cause of the cessation of that

[illegible] that your Excellency, in seeking a quarrel [illegible] that you were promoting the interests [illegible] am bound to suppose that your Excellency [illegible] as performing on that occasion the part of [illegible] this belief on my part strengthens my con-[illegible] future maintenance of friendship between the [illegible] and countries, because the events of the war, [illegible] victories obtained by the British troops over [illegible] of Persian troops, must have shown and have [illegible] capacious mind and powerful understanding of [illegible] that the true interests of Persia are best pro-[illegible] friendship with England, and that the sure [illegible] of war with England must be defeat and [illegible] this conviction strongly impressed upon your [illegible] Excellency will, I am sure, like a good patriot, [illegible] what direction the welfare of your country lies, [illegible] direct your policy as minister of your Sovereign [illegible] that welfare. Therefore it is that, knowing the [illegible] qualities which so eminently distinguish [illegible], I feel satisfied that the alliance between our [illegible] will rest henceforward upon the basis of national [illegible] is a firmer foundation than the sentiments of [illegible] Ministers, however friendly and sincere those senti-[illegible]. With every wish for the health and happiness [illegible] Excellency, and with a fervent hope that the reign of [illegible] master and Sovereign the Shah of Persia may [illegible] prosperous,

I have the honour to remain,
Your Excellency's most obedient
and faithful Servant,
PALMERSTON.

[illegible] The SADR AZIM, &c.

CHAPTER XIII.

QUARREL WITH CHINA—RESOLUTION CARRIED BY MR. [illegible] AGAINST THE GOVERNMENT—DISSOLUTION—INDIAN [illegible] GOVERNMENT INDIA BILL—DEFEAT ON CONSPIRAC[illegible] RESIGNATION.

'HER MAJESTY commands us to inform you tha[illegible] violence, insults to the British flag, and infr[illegible] treaty rights committed by the local Chinese [illegible] ties at Canton, and a pertinacious refusal of [illegible] have rendered it necessary for Her Majesty's [illegible] China to have recourse to measures of force [illegible] satisfaction.' So ran the Speech from the [illegible] the opening of Parliament in February 1857. [illegible]

This was the affair of the lorcha 'Arrow,' [illegible] to attain some celebrity. It happened thus: [illegible] treaties with China, British vessels were to [illegible] to consular jurisdiction only. The 'Arrow,' [illegible] British register, was boarded by Chinese [illegible] junk and the crew carried off, on a charge [illegible] Sir John Bowring, Governor of Hong-Kong, [illegible] satisfaction from the Chinese Commissioner, [illegible] failing to obtain it, proceeded to use force [illegible] under Admiral Sir Michael Seymour. He [illegible] to his former demands one for the admission [illegible] ers to the port and city of Canton under [illegible] ments which had never been carried out. [illegible] by proclamations offering rewards for the [illegible] barbarians.

Such was the position of affairs [illegible] brought forward in the House of Commons [illegible] to the effect that 'the papers laid on [illegible] establish satisfactory grounds for the [illegible]

…ented to.' In the House of Lords a similar motion, brought forward by Lord Derby, had been rejected by a majority of thirty-six. The discussion in the Commons lasted four nights, and was marked by great ability. Mr. Gladstone, Sir James Graham, Lord John Russell, Mr. Disraeli, and Mr. Roebuck all joined Mr. Cobden in his attack upon the Government. As the debate proceeded it became evident that the fate of the Government was involved. Meetings were held, on the one hand by the Opposition, and on the other by the friends of the Government, at which resolutions to put forward all their respective strength were adopted. The ministerial phalanx had been lately weakened, many Liberals having grown apathetic, owing to the coldness shown towards the cause of Reform. The issue was up to the last doubtful. Lord Palmerston spoke vigorously, and concluded with some pointed strictures upon the combination of parties confederated against him, warning the House that it had in its keeping not only the interests and lives of many of their fellow-countrymen, but also the honour and reputation of the country. The resolution was, however, carried against the Government by a majority of sixteen.

'Let the noble Lord,' Mr. Disraeli had said in his speech, 'who complained that he was the victim of a conspiracy, not only complain to the country, but let him appeal to it.' Perhaps he little thought that he would be taken at his word. Anyhow, the next day but one, Lord Palmerston announced to the house that, as soon as the necessary business could be completed, Parliament would be dissolved. He was at once asked whether meanwhile the war, which had been condemned, was to be carried on, and whether the Governor, who had been censured, was to be retained. But Lord Palmerston was not a man to be awed by [illegible] into conclusions inconsistent with that policy which he was about to ask the nation to ratify. His answer to these challenges was that the policy of the Government, so long as it continued a Government would remain what it had been. That policy was [illegible] maintain the rights and defend the lives and prop[illegible] of British subjects; to improve our relations with [illegible] and in the selection and arrangement of the means [illegible] the accomplishment of those objects to perform [illegible] which they owed to the country.'

There never, perhaps, was a general election [illegible] turned more completely than this one of 1857 [illegible] personal prestige of a minister and the national [illegible] dence in one man. Lord Palmerston—after decli[illegible] overtures from the City of London and other [illegible] put forth his address to the country through the [illegible] of Tiverton, the Devonshire borough to which [illegible] wedded, both by ties of gratitude and of [illegible] In it he distinctly challenged the verdict of the [illegible] stituencies as one of confidence or no confidence [illegible] administration. But in a very short time there [illegible] doubt as to what the answer would be. Pe[illegible] was in the heyday of his popularity. The [illegible] remembered that when others had shrunk [illegible] responsibility of conducting the war with [illegible] had come forward and carried it to a successful [illegible] the face of great difficulties at home, in the [illegible] at the congress table. It appreciated his [illegible] versatility. It admired his good-humour [illegible] bearing in the face of opposition, and was [illegible] marvellous energy and boisterous fun in [illegible] advancing years. The news of a happy [illegible] the Persian war came in time to aid his [illegible] 'Palmerston!' became a rallying cry on every[illegible] The 'fortuitous concourse of atoms,' as he [illegible] termed his opponents when they denied [illegible] against him, was scattered to the winds. [illegible] leading Peelites lost their seats. Mr. [illegible] Milner Gibson were displaced at [illegible] [illegible] at Aylesbury, and Cobden himself [illegible] [illegible] field. The Opposition [illegible] [illegible] majority was [illegible] [illegible] Government.

Parliament met on the 30th of April; and ...diately after the commencement of business ...ston moved the Army Estimates, Sir John ...the Under-Secretary for War, not having had ...ake himself acquainted with the details of ... This short session was naturally not very ... of legislation. The silence of the Queen's ...n the subject of Parliamentary Reform had ...ngly commented upon in the discussion on the The murmurers had been quieted by Lord ...ton's assurance that before next year it would ...aty of the Government to take the subject into ...lest consideration, but that they felt no useful could be served by calling upon the House ...o brief a session to enter upon so large and ... a question. One of the principal measures ...was the Divorce Court Bill, which encountered ...ious opposition. Lord Palmerston met the ...f hurrying the Bill through Parliament by a ... rejoinder that, on the contrary, he was quite ... sit through September if it was desired to full discussion of all the details, and added, ...ghter and cheers, 'One prominent opponent of said to me on one occasion, "You never shall Bill." I replied, "Won't we?"' The ques-indeed occupied the attention of the Legislature ...any years, that it seemed likely to do so for ...ars longer. It was only the firmness and de-...ion of the Premier that carried it to a settle-

Palmerston varied his labours during the ...y a visit to Manchester, for the opening of the Exhibition, and by interviews at Osborne with ...eror of the French and the Grand Duke Con-... who both visited England this summer. He ...himself of his conversation with the latter to that the English Government could not con-the proposal which had been made to them ...Russian Government, namely, to limit British consuls to the southern districts of Persia, and [illegible] the Russian consuls in undisturbed possession [illegible] northern.

About the middle of June the news of the [illegible] mutiny burst upon the Government. Troops [illegible] once ordered to prepare for embarkation. The mail brought tidings of the death of General An[illegible] Commander-in-Chief. The news arrived on a [illegible] day. That same night Lord Palmerston had an [illegible] view with Sir Colin Campbell, who started [illegible] Sunday, to take the command in India.

Vigorous as were the efforts of the Governm[illegible] meet the crisis, they did not completely satisfy [illegible] natural anxiety of their Sovereign. The Quee[illegible] expressed her views to this effect in a letter [illegible] Palmerston, which drew from him the following [illegible] teristic answer:—

Piccadilly: 18th Ju[illegible]

Viscount Palmerston presents his humble du[illegible] Majesty, and has had the honour to receive your Maje[illegible] munication of yesterday, stating what your Majesty [illegible] said if your Majesty had been in the House of Com[illegible]

Viscount Palmerston may perhaps be permitted [illegible] liberty of saying that it is fortunate for those [illegible] opinions your Majesty differs that your Majesty [illegible] House of Commons, for they would have had to [illegible] formidable antagonist in argument; although, [illegible] hand, those whose opinions your Majesty approves [illegible] had the support of a powerful ally in debate.

But with regard to the arrangements in conne[illegible] state of affairs in India, Viscount Palmerston [illegible] Majesty that the Government are taking, and [illegible] continue to take, every measure which may appear [illegible] to the emergency; but measures are sometimes [illegible] to succeed which follow each other step by step.

This drew another and a more detaile[illegible] tion from the Queen, in which the milit[illegible] be adopted were urged at greater length [illegible] were not backward in seconding [illegible] Crown, and, 'step by step,' ha[illegible]

and avenging army was dispatched
. The first vessel had sailed from our shores
the 1st of July, and she was followed by
continuous succession, so that by the end of
eighty ships had left for India, with
30,000 troops on board. This rapidity and
but the fitting counterpart to the heroic
our fellow-countrymen in the East, who pre-
our empire in Hindostan. Lord Palmer-
the Lord Mayor's banquet on the 9th of
paid a tribute to the national spirit.

possible for any Englishman to allude to that which
achieved in India—not by soldiers only, but by
individuals, and by knots of men scattered over the
face of a great empire—without feeling prouder than
nation to which we have the happiness to belong.
was an instance in the history of the world of such
examples of bravery, of intrepidity, of resource, and
accomplishing such results as those which we
witnessed. The Government at home, on the other
justly pride themselves on not having been unequal
magnitude of the occasion. We took the earliest oppor-
despatching to India a great army—an army which
not arrived when those great victories were accom-
but which, when it shall arrive, will render that which
be done comparatively easy of accomplishment, and
cannot entertain the slightest doubt, re-establish the
d authority of England upon an unshakable basis
it the whole of our Indian empire. My noble friend
mure has alluded to the spirit which has been dis-
this country, and I am proud to say, that although
despatched from these shores the largest army that I
er at one time left them, we have now under arms
United Kingdom as many fighting men as we had before
of the mutiny reached us; and, therefore, if any
tion ever dreamed in its visions that the exertions
had been compelled to make in India had lessened
th at home, and that the time had arrived when a
bearing might be exhibited towards us from that
safe in the moment of our strength, the manner in
spirit of the country has burst forth, the manner in
r ranks have been filled, the manner in which our

whole force has been replenished, will teach [illegible] would not be a safe game to play to attempt to [illegible] of that which was erroneously imagined to be [illegible] our weakness. It has been the fashion among [illegible] the Continent to say that the English nation is [illegible] nation. In one sense, indeed—in their sense—[illegible] may be said to be true. An Englishman is not [illegible] people of some other countries are of uniforms, of [illegible] and of iron heels; but no nation can excel the [illegible] as officers or soldiers, in a knowledge of the dutie[s] [mili]tary profession, and in the zeal and ability with [illegible] duties are performed; and wherever desperate de[eds] accomplished—wherever superior numbers are [illegible] encountered and triumphantly overcome—wherev[er] are to be encountered—wherever that which a [illegible] confront is individually or collectively to be faced, [illegible] venture to say, there is no nation on the face of th[e] can surpass—I might, without too much national [illegible] believe that there is no nation which can equal— the British islands. But, my Lord Mayor an[d] while we all admire the bravery, the constancy, a[nd] pidity of our countrymen in India, we must not [illegible] justice also to our countrywomen. In the ordin[ary] life the functions of woman are to cheer the days [illegible] to soothe the hours of suffering, and to give additi[onal] to the sunshine of prosperity; but our countrywo[men] have had occasion to show qualities of a higher [illegible] and when they have had either to sustain the peril[s] to endure the privations of a difficult escape, to [illegible] sufferings in endeavouring to minister to the w[ants] the women of the United Kingdom have, wherev[er] been found in India, displayed qualities of the [illegible] such as never have been surpassed in the history [illegible] Henceforth the bravest soldier may think it no [illegible] to be told that his courage and his power of endur[ance] to those of an Englishwoman.

In Lord Palmerston's pocket-book I [illegible] about this speech: 'Gave much offence [illegible]

[illegible] with certain noisy bodies in France, [illegible] at the protection England afforded [illegible]; although Lord Palmerston, writing [illegible], says, 'My speech was pointed, not [illegible]ly, but at the whole Continent, [illegible] last six months, we have been talked of, [illegible] of, and printed of as a second-rate power. [illegible] Paris, since the fall of Delhi, no French- [illegible] ever mentions India.'[1]

[illegible] was, that not only our Indian empire, but [illegible] among nations was at stake during this crisis. [illegible] of this was Lord Palmerston that he steadily [illegible] offers of foreign assistance which [illegible] to the British Government, feeling that, [illegible] adopted abroad, it became necessary that [illegible] should triumph entirely 'off her own bat,' as [illegible] expressed it. Not only did Prussian officers [illegible] volunteer their services, but an offer was [illegible] two Belgian regiments to be taken bodily into [illegible]. The object in either case was, no doubt, the [illegible] to be gained by active operations in the [illegible] large scale, rather than any quixotic devotion [illegible] English cause. But, whatever the motives, Lord [illegible] steadily set his face against the proposals, [illegible] some in places of authority appeared inclined [illegible] the idea of a Belgian contingent. 'The more [illegible] of it,' he wrote to Lord Clarendon on Sep- [illegible] 29, 'the more I feel it is necessary for our [illegible] and reputation in the world that we should [illegible] this mutiny and restore order by our own [illegible], and I am perfectly certain that we can do it [illegible] we shall do it.'

[illegible]rliament was called together for the next session [illegible]cember 4, to pass a Bill of Indemnity for the [illegible] for having suspended the Bank Charter [illegible] the financial panic of the autumn. Lord [illegible] has a pithy note about the debate: 'Geo.

[1] To Lord Clarendon, November 16, 1857.

Lewis and J. Russell made good speeches. ... not having a clear idea, conveyed none.' ... Houses adjourned for Christmas, and met again ... usual time in February. On the first evening ... mier moved an address of congratulation to ... on the marriage of the Princess Royal and ... Prince of Prussia, stating that there had been ... since the marriage of her Majesty herself ... so much enlisted the feelings and so much ... interest of the whole British nation. With ... instinct as to what would be most pleasing to ... of England, he put into the foreground that ... not a marriage of mere political convenience, ... of mutual affection. The illustrious parties ... concerned, he added, 'have been more fortunate ... many royal personages. They, indeed, have ... to that class whom it is said—

> . . . . . "Gentle stars unite, and in one ...
> Their hearts, their fortunes, and their feelings ...

A few days later he introduced the Govern... which was to transfer the rule over India from ... Company to the Crown, it having been shown ... events of the past year that, to use his own ... the Queen, the inconvenience and difficulty of ... tering the government of a vast country ... side of the globe by means of two Cabinets ... responsible to the Crown and Parliament,' ... only responsible to the holders of India Stock ... for a few hours, three or four times a year ... longer tolerable. Many vested interests ... and, under a plea of delay, a strong opp... offered; but on a division the Ministry, ... general expectation, obtained the large ... 145.[1] Walking home with Lord Palm...

[1] The majority was even greater than had been ... how little credit is to be given to reports which ... drawing-rooms as to the probable result of ... (Lord Palmerston to the Queen, Feb. 18, 1858.)

Sir Richard Bethell, then Attorney-
to him that he ought, like the
triumph, to have somebody to re-
was, as a minister, mortal.
showed that no such reminder was
we must go back to recall the circum-
had prepared the ground for the cata-
was now imminent.

14 a most determined attempt had been
the Emperor Napoleon as he was
with the Empress to the Opera. Bombs
thrown under his carriage, shattering the
when they exploded and killing some twenty
Fortunately, the Imperial party escaped
trifling injuries. The gang who had perpe-
outrage, of whom the leader was one Orsini,
from London, where they had made their
ations for this atrocious attempt. Much indig-
was felt by the French that men should be able
such a diabolical deed under the protection
hospitality. It was felt to be unjust that
should be afforded by a Government—and still
a friendly Government—to the assassins of a
Sovereign. This very natural feeling found
in a despatch from the Minister of Foreign
at Paris to Count Persigny, the French ambas-
London. Count Walewski, after deprecating
tion to find fault with the right of asylum
England extended to political refugees, pointed
such as Pianori and Orsini were not mere
but were assassins :—

the English legislation, he proceeded, to contribute
designs and continue to shelter persons who place
beyond the pale of common right and under the ban
? Her Britannic Majesty's Government can assist
a repetition of such guilty enterprises by affording
of security which no state can refuse to a neigh-
and which we are authorised to expect from an
relying, moreover, on the high sense of the English

Cabinet, we refrain from indicating in any way the measures which it may see fit to take in order to comply with this wish. We rest entirely upon it for estimating the decisions which it shall deem best calculated to attain the object.

There was little in this document to arouse the susceptibilities of the nation; and the Cabinet, sensible of the justice of some of the observations contained in it, determined, without answering it officially, to introduce a measure the effect of which would be to make the crime of conspiracy to murder—which had hitherto been treated as a misdemeanour—a felony, punishable with penal servitude. Lord Palmerston's first idea was a measure to give power to the Secretary of State to send away any foreigner whom the Government might have good reason to suspect was plotting a scheme against the life of a foreign sovereign, the Government being bound to state the grounds upon which the person in question had been sent away, either to a secret committee of Parliament or to a committee composed of the three chiefs of the courts of law. This notion, however, was abandoned for the simpler form of Bill which would, it was believed, attain the object in view. The Bill, although strongly opposed, was read a first time by a majority of no less than 200. Meantime, however, events were occurring which rapidly altered the public tone. Addresses had been presented to the Emperor from members of the French army, which, while congratulating him on his escape, contained expressions and menaces but too well calculated to wound the pride and inflame the temper of the English people. Some of these 'French colonels'—as they were popularly designated—spoke of the English as 'protectors of assassins,' and uttered threats to the effect that 'the infamous haunt in which such infernal machinations were planned should be destroyed for ever.'

These ridiculous effusions would have passed unnoticed, unless with contempt, had not some of them, unfortunately, been inserted in the 'Moniteur,' the official organ of the French Government. In vain did the ambassador, by order of his Government, express regret at their insertion and explain that it happened through inadvertence, owing to the number of addresses which, according to the usual custom, required such official notification; in vain did Lord Palmerston urge the House that it would be unworthy of the nation to be turned from a course, otherwise proper, by the vapourings of irresponsible swashbucklers, and upon any paltry feelings of offended dignity or of irritation at the expressions of three or four colonels of French regiments, to act the childish part of refusing an important measure on grounds so insignificant and frippery.' The nation's back was up. The House repented of its former vote, and the leader of the Opposition, who had spoken for the Bill on its first reading, joined with the other malcontents in giving it its death-blow, by supporting Mr. Milner Gibson's amendment to the question that it should be read a second time. This amendment was: 'That this House cannot but regret that Her Majesty's Government, previously to inviting the House to amend the law of conspiracy at the present time, have not felt it to be their duty to reply to the important despatch received from the French Government, dated January 20.'

Verbal answers, fitting both in substance and in tone, had been given to the French ambassador in London and, through Lord Cowley, to the French Cabinet at Paris; but an official despatch, in reply, had been deliberately postponed, under the conviction that in the actual temper of men's minds, no advantage, but only exasperation, would be the result of any answer which the English Foreign Office could consistently give.

Report said that Lord Derby, sitting under the gallery of the House of Commons and watching the progress of the debate, saw the turn of the tide with the quick eye of an old parliamentary tactician, and sent hasty word to his lieutenants that they should take it at the flood which led to office. Anyhow, Mr. Disraeli plunged into the stream, and, declaring that while, on the first reading, the question was between England and France; on this the second reading, by some strange metamorphosis, it had become one between the House of Commons and the English minister, he announced that he sided with the House. Mr. Gladstone also threw in his lot with the Opposition in a powerful speech; Lord John Russell joined the Radicals; and when a division was called, Lord Palmerston's Government found itself in a minority of nineteen.

This defeat was a complete surprise. Ministers, when they went down to the House of Commons on the afternoon of this February 19, did not even anticipate a narrow division, much less a crisis. There were [illegible] causes, however, which had been gradually sapping Lord Palmerston's ascendency over the House of Commons. Some injudicious appointments had alienated not a few of his supporters, and his manner lately had certainly, for some reason or other, become more [illegible] and dictatorial than was altogether pleasing to the members. Many, however, of those who voted in the majority did not wish to overthrow his Government, and had he thought fit to appeal to the House of Commons for a vote of confidence, it would probably have accorded it, and have remained satisfied with the [illegible] already given by the public to the denunciations of the French army. But Lord Palmerston never showed any undue tenacity in the retention of office. He at once tendered his resignation to the Queen, and persisted, although Her Majesty at first declined to accept it.

Thus Lord Palmerston, after weathering [illegible] turbulent storm, was overthrown by a gust, and Lord Derby, being sent for, reigned in his stead. [illegible] Premier, with a candour which was very characteristic of him, soon acknowledged the hasty and [illegible] character of the vote which had proved [illegible] opponents, and to which he had so greatly [illegible] In the House of Lords, on March 1, Lord [illegible] who had been the Foreign Secretary of [illegible] [illegible]ment, fully vindicated their conduct [illegible] in reporting to the Queen the proceedings of the evening, said, 'Lord Clarendon made an admirable speech in explanation of the course which the late Government pursued, and which, had it been delivered in the House of Commons on the subject of the amendment, would probably have deprived Lord Derby of the honour of addressing your Majesty on the present occasion.'[1]

[1] Martin's *Life of the Prince Consort*, vol. iv. p. 190.

ies would be very seriously injured by such a step as the f his ambassador.

e find him availing himself of his comparative e to serve on a committee about the pollution of hames, to preside at the Royal Literary Fund r, to see Rarey, the horse-tamer, perform on a called Surplice at the Duke of Wellington's g-school, and to make notes afterwards about his a of breaking and the pedigree of the animal. variety of employment must have been to him new and refreshing.

November he went over to Compiègne on a visit Emperor Napoleon, and with both horse and ined in the sports of the French Court, though, e hunting days, a stag, and not a fox, was the r. He wrote to his brother-in-law: 'They are ry civil and courteous, and the visits of the ih to the Emperor serve as links to maintain and then English alliance.' I find a scrap of con-ion recorded which is amusing, as illustrating an ent of the French mind. While the dancing was on, Lord Palmerston and the Emperor walked d down an inner room, and the Imperial philo-r propounded his idea of an improvement upon xisting system of universal suffrage, namely, to the right of voting to married men. He said inmarried men do not feel the same sentiments their country as those who have a family stake and that such a voting qualification would shut oth priests and soldiers—classes which he would to see excluded. Lord Palmerston could only r that property of some sort ought, in his opinion, the real basis for the suffrage, and that while bachelors might own property, many a man oth wife and child might have none.[1]

[1] uring this conversation the Emperor also said that the Emperor ia had told him that he would spend his last rouble, and his last man, to prevent the establishment of a Greek empire

thing, that the most exacting elector could ... it amiss.

Rowcliffe said that as Lord Palmerston had talked a ... about Lord Derby's Reform Bill, he hoped his lord... favour the electors and non-electors with his views ... He would ask his lordship whether he would vote ... ballot, and whether he was in favour of manhood ... or 6*l.* franchise, or rating franchise. He was once a ... of the noble lord's committee, but finding his opinions ... of his lordship's, he refused to remain a member any ... The noble lord also said a great deal about the Con... Bill, but it was well known he was a pet of the Emperor ... French. (Laughter.) He believed that the noble lord ... downright Tory, and the best representative the Conserva... possibly have. He hoped his lordship would answer ... in a straightforward and honest manner.

Palmerston said he was delighted to find that his old ... however far advanced in years, retained that youthful ... which he possessed when first he knew him, and with ... he had retained also his prejudices and opinions. ... and a cry of 'No chaff.') His friend asked for a ...forward answer, and he would give him one. He totally ... with him in almost all his opinions. He (the noble ... the day would never come when he and his friend ... in political faith. His friend asked him what he ... many points. In the first place he would say he ... to the ballot. He was against manhood suffrage. ... 'How far will you go with the franchise?') He ... a straightforward answer to that. He would not ... (Laughter.) He held it was his duty, after the con... had reposed in him, to act according to his judg... measure relating to Reform. He hoped that the ... of Mr. Rowcliffe and himself would not alter ... friendship. He was sorry to disagree with his ... no man could agree with everybody. The man who ... with everybody was not worth having anybody to ... (Cheers and laughter.)

... were much influenced by the aspect ... affairs. On New Year's Day the French ... electrified Europe by addressing the ...bassador, at the usual reception of the

diplomatic corps, in a manner which betok
pleasant feeling between the two countrie
in so doing he was imitating his uncle, w
remark to the English minister at Paris
mediately preceded the rupture of the peac
was a matter for curious speculation; but
did not fail to excite general uneasiness. T
between Austria and Sardinia were kn
strained, owing to the impatience of the
the continuance of Austrian predomina
peninsula. Did these few words spo
Tuileries import that France would join
should hostilities break out? This prove
meaning, and, after a few months of suspe
fired the mine by a summons to Sardinia
On her refusal war was declared, and Fr
began to pour into North Italy, as alli
Emmanuel. This was the moment of
election in England. Lord Derby's Gover
rightly or wrongly, suspected of leanin
Austria, while public feeling was strongly
Italian independence. This sufficed to t
wherever parties were evenly balanced,
dissolution failed to give the Conservat
majority.

A renewed attempt was made to induc
merston to join the Government with th
of the House of Commons, but the Liber
meanwhile been engaged in preparing fo
by healing their dissensions and recon
leaders. Lord Palmerston and Lord John
come to an agreement that whichever of
charged with the formation of a Govern
receive the co-operation of the other.
meeting in Willis's Rooms, at which
Peelites were present, it was arranged
mediate vote of want of confidence in
be moved by Lord Hartington in the
mons. Accordingly, on June 10, in

[illegible] members, such a vote was carried by a ma- [illegible] in spite of Mr. Disraeli's amusing protest [illegible] scene of Almack's, where dowagers and [illegible] formerly held sway, having been turned into [illegible] the issuing of vouchers by political patrons. [illegible] Granville, to the astonishment of everybody, [illegible] with the construction of a Ministry, the [illegible] that 'to make so marked a distinction [illegible] in the choice of one or other as Prime [illegible] of two statesmen so full of years and honours [illegible] Palmerston and Lord John Russell, would [illegible] invidious and unwelcome task.' Lord Gran- [illegible] failure to make a Government under the cir- [illegible] is worth noting, as an illustration of the [illegible] of our form of government, and of the [illegible] the House of Commons is the ultimate de- [illegible] of the power that makes, as well as unmakes, [illegible]

[illegible] Palmerston consented to serve under Lord [illegible] for the reasons and under the limitations [illegible] in the following paper:—

94 Piccadilly: June 11, 1859.

Viscount Palmerston presents his humble duty to Your [illegible], and has the honour of assuring Your Majesty that he [illegible] it his duty to afford Lord Granville his assistance [illegible] in forming an administration in obedience to [illegible] Majesty's commands. Viscount Palmerston considered [illegible] to be promoting the public interest by taking an active [illegible] the late proceedings in the House of Commons tending [illegible] removal of Lord Derby's administration; but he feels [illegible] would have been inexcusable in him to have encouraged [illegible] those proceedings with a view to any personal [illegible] interests of his own. Those who unite to turn out [illegible] Government ought to be prepared to unite to form [illegible] Government than that which is to be overthrown; [illegible] in this spirit, and with a deep sense of what is due [illegible] men to Your Majesty and to the country, that Viscount [illegible] and Lord John Russell, before they called the meet- [illegible] Willis's Rooms, came to an agreement to co-operate with [illegible] in the formation of a new administration, whichever

of the two might be called upon by Your
Your Majesty's Government. That
to the case of any third person; but
conceives that the same sense of public
to enter into that engagement with Lord
also lead him to give assistance to Lord
execution of Your Majesty's commands. Vi
promise to Lord Granville has, however, been
thinks that it would be a great disappointment
the country if, on the overthrow of one admi
deliberate vote of want of confidence by a
of Commons, the overthrowing majority should
as not to be able to offer to Your Majesty a
tration than that which they have overthrown,
other hand, it would be injurious to the interest
and of the nation, that on such an occasion an
should be formed which, by the weakness of its
ments, should be destitute of the inherent strength
enable it to face and overcome the difficulties
must have to contend; and Viscount Palmerston
bound by his duty to Your Majesty, and by a
what he owes to himself, to say that to an
composed he would feel it impossible to belong.
therefore, which he has given to Lord Granville
conditional on Lord Granville's success in organi
ment so composed as to be calculated officially to
public service, and to command the confidence
and of the country.

This success did not attend Lord Granv
He found Lord John Russell reluctant to
leadership, with Lord Palmerston leading the
Commons; and as he met with insuperable
in the task which he had unwillingly und
resigned his commission. Lord Palmerston
then been sent for, constructed a Ministry
John Russell at the Foreign Office, and
at the Exchequer. He also offered the
to Mr. Cobden, who declined it. The
was looked upon as the strongest
so *far* as the individual talents of
concerned. Men of some political

subordinate offices. Thus Lord Pal- seventy-fifth year, again became Prime of the House of Commons. The his course was to be comparatively smooth. He was accepted by the country as the nation, and almost occupied a position the chances of party strife. Whatever had to contend with did not consist either or in parliamentary defeats at home. may have been, they were of a more hidden The events of this period are too recent to great detail in their history, or absence on the part of the historian.

in North Italy was sharp and short. The of Magenta and Solferino drove the Austrians famous Quadrilateral, and the last week in the French and Sardinians pausing in view formidable defences. The Emperor Napoleon learnt that Prussia was preparing to field and to march on Paris. He had lost and was anxious to make peace; and so it that, within a fortnight after accession to Lord Palmerston had to consider a proposal made British Cabinet that they should intervene be- the belligerents, and propose an armistice upon which were laid before them by the French am- These included the surrender of Lombardy Duchies to Sardinia, and the erection of Ve- an independent state under an Archduke, no provision for the Papal States. In the letter he gives his reasons for declining to England in such a false position :—

Piccadilly: July 6, 1859.

John Russell,—The more I think of Persigny's the less I like it, and the more I incline to the opinion ought to be very careful not to involve ourselves, and commit ourselves by hastily adopting it. Those who two belligerents on the point of fighting that they to an armistice, in order to negotiate a peace, ought to have settled in their own minds the [illegible] arrangement as might be proposed to the [illegible] chance of success; but we have no plan of our [illegible] asked to adopt as our own one sketched out by [illegible] gerent parties out of three. It would be [illegible] armistice to the Austrians, unless we gave them [illegible] terms to be the subject of negotiation; but if we [illegible] selves simply to the first condition, that Italy should [illegible] given up to the Italians, Austria would, of course, [illegible] refuse. If we were to go farther, and communicate [illegible] of the Persigny scheme, we should identify ourselves [illegible] and be committed to an approval of it; but that I [illegible] unwilling to do, though if such an arrangement [illegible] worked out as the result of the war, we should, of [illegible] quiesce in it, and say that matters might have turned [illegible] It is to be observed that we are not told that this [illegible] the assent of the Sardinians nor of the Italians general[illegible] would obviously fall far short of the wishes and expecta[illegible] Italy; and if we made it, we should be accused of havin[illegible] posed and stopped the allied armies in their career of [illegible] and of having either endeavoured or of having succeeded [illegible] on Italy a remnant of Austrian shackles, and of havi[illegible] trayed and disappointed the Italians at the very momen[illegible] their prospects were the brightest.

The scheme proposes to give Venetia and Modena [illegible] Austrian archduke, as an independent Sovereign, by [illegible] interposing some neutral state between Piedmont and A[illegible] But what would be the result? The same Austrian inf[illegible] and interference which have been the bane of Tuscany [illegible] soon afflict this new state. It would not be constitution[illegible] there would be worse neighbourhood between it and [illegible] tional Piedmont than there would be between Venetia [illegible] of Piedmont and Austria, because Venetia and Piedmont [illegible] be separated only by an imaginary line; whereas [illegible] would be a buffer between Venetia and Austria. [illegible] of Piedmont would excite the aspirations of the V[illegible] Discontent and disturbance would arise. Austria w[illegible] vene, she could not see an archduke in trouble [illegible] and help him. She would again be brought into [illegible] ference in Italian affairs; and if Modena were added [illegible] Austria would again take her place in Central [illegible] quarrels would arise because the old grievances [illegible] up anew, and fresh wars would inevitably [illegible]

[illegible] own, it is suggested by jealousy of [illegible] for the Pope; but we feel neither of [illegible] and are not bound to adopt them. The [illegible] throws wholly out of question the wishes of [illegible] and we are asked to propose to the [illegible] out of the nations of Italy, as if we [illegible] to dispose of them. I cannot be a party to [illegible]

[illegible] Emperor is tired of his war, and finds the [illegible] he expected, let him make what proposals he [illegible] whomsoever he pleases; but let them be made [illegible] formally and officially, and let him not ask us [illegible] suggestions, and make ourselves answerable for [illegible]

[illegible] French Emperor must have anticipated the [illegible] England to become his cat's-paw. Anyhow, [illegible] he acted for himself. On that day he sent [illegible] Fleury to the headquarters of the Emperor of [illegible] with a letter proposing an armistice. General [illegible] arrived at a late hour, and the night was spent [illegible] Emperor Francis Joseph in council with Count [illegible] Prince Metternich, and Count Mensdorff. [illegible] morning Napoleon received a reply accepting the [illegible] An interview took place on the 8th between [illegible] Emperors, and on the 11th, at Villafranca, a [illegible] treaty of peace was signed, containing as [illegible] creation of an Italian Confederation, under [illegible] presidency of the Pope, the cession of Lombardy [illegible] and the return of the Grand Dukes of [illegible] and Modena to their states. The Emperor [illegible] however, obtained from the Austrian Em- [illegible] verbal assurance that no force should be [illegible] to restore the Grand Dukes. The definitive [illegible] was to be settled in a Conference at Zurich. [illegible] withdrew from the Sardinian Ministry on the [illegible] of this peace, although the spirit, which [illegible] and left behind him, was not destined to [illegible] until, in defiance of the imperial compro- [illegible] Villafranca, it had worked out his project of a [illegible] Italian Kingdom. Lord Palmerston also lost

no time in expressing his disappointment at t
of the treaty:—

94 Piccadilly: juillet

Mon cher Persigny,—Si je comprends ce qui va
pour l'Italie, il est question d'une Confédération
l'Autriche prendrait place en vertu de la Vénétie
arrangement serait funeste, et mettrait l'Italie au dés

La plus grande partie des maux de l'Italie, et
volutionnaire qui s'y est montré, prennent leur
l'ingérence de l'Autriche dans les affaires des Etats
Pô. Jusqu'à présent cette ingérence n'a eu aucune
et un des buts que l'Empereur des Français se pro
teindre était d'affranchir l'Italie de cette ingérence
en des pays ne faisant pas partie des possessions de l'

Mais une fois que l'Autriche devient membre
fédération Italienne, toute l'Italie est livrée
liés à l'Autriche. Jamais l'Angleterre ne pourra
à un si mauvais arrangement. Au contraire, nous
croire de notre devoir de protester hautement
l'Europe contre un pareil asservissement des peuples
L'Autriche devrait au contraire être strictement
ingérence politique ou militaire en dehors de ses
si cela n'est pas fait, rien n'est fait, et tout sera
en fort peu de temps.

Confédération politique des Etats italiens,
une question qui mérite examen. Il y a du pour
Le Pape, Naples, Toscane, Modena seraient
l'Absolutisme. Le Piémont seul pour un
comment on parviendrait à s'entendre reste à

Union douanière de toute l'Italie avec un
libéral encourageant le commerce, quant à cela
du 'pour' parmi les hommes intelligents.
cette union, les relations de l'Autriche ne
celles d'un pays étranger faisant un pacte avec
n'est pas membre.

Soyez bien sûr que si l'Autriche n'est
exclue de toute ingérence, de toute espèce,
l'Italie, le sang français a été versé en
l'Empereur ne sera que de courte durée.

This scheme of an Italian Confe
proposed by Austria, but by Louis
been floating in his mind for

...Italian support of the Pope for the ... and Austrian troops. The English ... without delay, in a despatch to Paris, ... to it, which they felt sure the French ... would, on consideration, recognise.

... appeared likely that, in contravention ... engagement given at Villafranca, and ... to the text of the provisional treaty, ... attempt to employ her troops in re- ... archdukes. An official remonstrance was ..., in the month of August, by our Govern- ..., which declared that 'a provision for ... of French or Austrian forces to put ... clearly expressed will of the people of ... Italy would, in the opinion of Her Majesty's ..., not be justifiable. Great Britain would ... duty to protest against a supplement to the ... Villafranca of that nature, if such were even ...' The Emperor Napoleon also was urged ... firm on this point.

... doubt the French Emperor was in a dilemma, ... to England to extricate him from it. The ... over, but not the conflict. Neither Romagna ... Duchies would agree to a confederation of ... Austria would be the most powerful member, ... which the ecclesiastical domination of the ... was secured by the Presidency of the Pope. ...poleon had bound himself not to move forward ... only direction which would satisfy the national ... of the people whose cause he had espoused. ... turned to England with the hope that ... propose a Congress, which should take the ... off his shoulders. Mr. Theodore Martin, in his ... of the Prince Consort,' says that there was ... for anxiety lest the Prime Minister and the ... Secretary would, at this time, 'be carried into ... by their enthusiasm for the Italian ... If enthusiasm is the proper word to apply to ... in the matter, it was at any rate certainly not the ill-regulated and unreflecting s of youth, which often leads men to be it was the firm sympathy of experienced recognised in the Italian cause not only a but one destined by the very nature of the end, and involving meanwhile the perity of Europe. But there was no fear of England being led on where she would go, and the Cabinet declined even taking th proposals into consideration until the prelim peace had been reduced into the form of a Austria then expressed no objection to a C the British Government signified that they by any act of theirs be the means of preventi pean concert.

In the work already referred to the au implies that the Foreign Office at this junc unnecessarily eager to communicate its view parties concerned, and that it was no busines land to intermeddle in the bad peace which th Emperor had made, but that the proper cour to maintain was perfect silence. Lord John in a letter to Lord Palmerston, dated Aberge tember 11, 1859, stated in the following word met this criticism :—

I maintained that so far as regarded the Empero transfer of the province of Lombardy from one to th had never said a word. But the state of Italy w question. It had occupied our Government for yea during these years been a source of anxiety. To cause two Emperors had treated the question at Vill should suddenly become silent, and not try to prev newal of troubles, would be in my opinion to dese That the policy of the Cabinet was contained in two for each of which there was a cause. The cause of t an invitation on the part of France to join in a C which we had replied by objecting to certain peace, and supposed intentions of the Powers. second was the apprehension that Austria restore the Archdukes. Against such a

I was willing to keep within the line of these despatches. But conversations with foreign ministers abroad raised fresh questions, to which it was necessary to reply by fresh explanations.

Naturally all this caused Lord Palmerston to be represented as very hostile to Austria, just as was the case in the former revolutionary years. He denies it.

94 Piccadilly: August 22, 1859.

My dear Cowley,—I know that all the partisans of arbitrary government in Europe represent me as the bitter enemy of Austria, and I wish whenever you hear this to deny its truth. I am an enemy to bad government, to oppression and tyranny; and, unfortunately, the Austrian rule in Italy, as elsewhere, has been marked by those evils. I am an enemy, therefore, to the bad system of Austrian government, and heartily wish all Italians to be freed from the Austrian yoke. It would be better for Austria that this should be. It has been decided that Venetia shall still be a victim, but care ought to be taken that Austria be prevented, either as member of a Confederation, or in any other way, from interfering in the affairs of Italy beyond her own frontier. The Austrian Government is unfortunately hated in many Austrian provinces north of the Alps, and especially in Hungary and Galicia. I wish with all my heart she would change her system, and conciliate the goodwill of her subjects; for I hold a great and powerful Austrian empire north of the Alps to be of the utmost importance for the general interests of Europe.

Much is said at Paris of what are called the intrigues of Cavour—unjustly, I think. If it is meant that he has laboured for the enlargement of Piedmont and the freedom of Italy from foreign yoke and from Austrian rule, he will in history be called a patriot; but the means he has employed may be good or bad. I know not what they have been; but the end in view is, I am sure, the good of Italy. The people of the Duchies have as good a right to change their rulers as the people of England, France, Belgium, and Sweden; and the annexation of the Duchies to Piedmont would be an unmixed good for Italy, and for France, and for Europe. I hope Walewski will not sway the mind of the Emperor to make the enslaving of Italy the end of a drama, which opened with the declaration, 'Italy free from the Alps to the Adriatic,' and 'l'Italie rendue à elle-même.'

If the Italians are left to themselves all will go [illegible] when it is said that if the French garrison were [illegible] from Rome, all the priests would be killed, the [illegible] Bologna may be quoted, where the priests remain [illegible] and perfect order has been maintained.

When the French showed an evident [illegible] Austria during the negotiations at Zurich, L[illegible] merston pithily said that this famous [illegible] ‘l'Italie rendue à elle-même’ was being [illegible] ‘l'Italie vendue à l'Autriche.’

These negotiations proceeded very slowly, [illegible] not finished till the autumn. The Duchies [illegible] lutely refused to take back their sovereign[illegible] September Tuscany and Romagna had formally [illegible] their annexation to Sardinia. How, then, wi[illegible] employment of force, was the proposed Treaty [illegible] to be reconciled with the stipulations of Vill[illegible] Towards the end of October, therefore, France [illegible] more than ever urgent for a Congress. Mr. [illegible] his ‘Life of the Prince Consort,’[1] says that [illegible] Russell stated that Lord Palmerston and him[illegible] advise the Cabinet to accede to the French [illegible] proposal, and implies that, superior counsels [illegible] their intentions were fortunately overruled. [illegible] cult to reconcile this alleged statement of [illegible] Russell's with the following note from him [illegible] Palmerston and Lord Palmerston's endo[illegible] the same day:—

Pembroke Lodge: [illegible]

My dear Palmerston,—On reading the article[illegible] of Zurich and reflecting upon the figure we [illegible] Congress, I can see no reason sufficient to [illegible] one. We cannot object to the transfer of [illegible] clause about the Duchies and the article [illegible] especially objectionable. I cannot but think [illegible] a Congress we should give some sanction [illegible] trine of the divine right of kings. The [illegible] tion we have always scouted as a way [illegible] to the house of bondage.

[1] Vol. iv. p. [illegible]

I should therefore be inclined to say in answer to Walewski's despatch that our objections on the score of Venetia being part of the Italian Confederation are by no means removed—that the Pope's assurance that he will grant reforms when his authority is restored is of no value in our eyes, as we do not see how the authority of the Pope is to be re-established without the employment of foreign force—that to such employment of foreign force, either to re-establish the authority of the Pope or to restore the Archdukes in Tuscany and Modena, we have insuperable objections. The rights reserved to the Archdukes and to the Duchess of Parma by the Treaty of Zurich appear to us in the same light as the rights of the Count de Chambord and Prince Wasa—rights to respect and observance, but not to obedience and subjection on the part of France and Sweden. That if the independence of Italy mentioned in the Treaty of Zurich, is not to be illusory, the rights of the Italian people ought to be respected and observed. Yet if the Congress should decide to use force, what would be the position of Great Britain? She would only have to protest and withdraw. France would be in a similar position, but France has bound herself by engagements to which Great Britain is not a party. For these reasons, etc. Yours truly,

J. Russell.

Lord Palmerston's endorsement on this note is as follows: 'I entirely agree with John Russell, and had already come to the same conclusions.'—P. 21, 10–59.

It is true that a few days later these views were modified, but it is acknowledged how 'evenly balanced the arguments were on both sides.' The ground finally taken by the Foreign Secretary was that, as we already had differences with France about China, Morocco, the Suez Canal, &c., a blank refusal of her proposed Congress would be the prelude to a total divergence of views between the two countries. The decision, therefore, finally arrived at by the Cabinet was not to decline the Congress, if it were clearly understood beforehand that the declaration made against the employment of foreign force would be maintained and acted upon, and provided there was nothing in the invitation contrary to the already declared policy of England. This decision was made known to the French Gov[illegible] was to issue the invitations to the other [illegible]

There was a dispute this year bet[illegible] Morocco, which, as affecting English in[illegible] tracted Lord Palmerston's attention. Spain [illegible] a *rayon* of territory round her fortress of C[illegible] African coast. This was agreed to by the M[illegible] they could not come to a settlement a[illegible] should be the boundary lines of the territory [illegible] ceded.

Broadlands: October [illegible]

My dear John Russell,—It is plain that F[illegible] through Spain, at getting fortified points on each si[illegible] Gut of Gibraltar, which, in the event of war between S[illegible] France on the one hand, and England on the other, wo[illegible] cross fire, render that strait very difficult and dangerous [illegible] and thus virtually to shut us out of the Mediterranean [illegible] distance between part of the African coast and the S[illegible] coast is only eight miles. With a fortified port on ea[illegible] and guns that would carry three miles or more, a fleet [illegible] chantmen or of transports would have some difficulty in [illegible] out of fire, especially if on each side there were a flotilla of [illegible] boats, protected by the guns of the fortresses, firing [illegible] certain distance out from these fortresses, and presenting [illegible] small mark to any ships-of-war convoying the merchan[illegible] transports. As things now stand such vessels would [illegible] keeping well over to the African coast, but they would [illegible] be so if that coast belonged to France or Spain.

The French Minister of War or of Marine said [illegible] day that Algeria never would be safe till France p[illegible] port on the Atlantic coast of Africa. Against whom w[illegible] a port make Algeria safe? Evidently only against E[illegible] and how could such a port help France against [illegible] Only by tending to shut us out of the Mediterranean. [illegible]

I still think that the Spanish Government are d[illegible] to pick a quarrel with Morocco, and that their first [illegible] to take Tangier, and their *last* to evacuate it; and [illegible] way of preventing a serious difference between [illegible] would be to ask the Emperor of Morocco to [illegible] occupy Tangier in trust for him during hostilities [illegible] if war with Spain should break out.

was declared a few days after this. It was d to the Spaniards that if Tangier were occu- their troops, we could not permit the occupa- be prolonged after the close of the war. The Foreign Minister promised that Spain 'would e possession of any point on the Straits the of which would give her a superiority threaten- navigation.' On this assurance being given, undertaking being observed, Great Britain d neutral.

next letter refers to the fortifications which terwards constructed. It was a subject much ed at the time, and on which Lord Palmerston essively anxious.

re could be no question which so thoroughly he patriotism of a British statesman, because the was successful the less likely it was to be popu- he fact that we were placed in a state of ade- efence was precisely the fact that rendered any upon us unlikely; and if we were never attacked, ure to be said that our defences were uncalled t we must remember that though the boy who volf' did so often when the wolf did not appear, right in the main, for the wolf did come at last, flock was eaten because the cry had been dis- . We might as well have no locks on our doors bars to our windows, because thieves do not to break into our houses every night.

94 Piccadilly: December 15, 1859.

ear Gladstone,—Sidney Herbert has asked me to sum- abinet for to-morrow, that we may come to a decision tification question, and I am most anxious that the nent which he has proposed should be adopted.

main question is whether our naval arsenals and some portant points should be defended by fortifications or I can hardly imagine two opinions on that question. be clear that if, by a sudden attack by an army landed th, our dockyards were to be destroyed, our maritime ould for more than half a century be paralysed, and our colonies, our commerce, and the subsistence of a large [illegible] our population would be at the mercy of our enemy, who [illegible] be sure to show us no mercy. We should be reduced [illegible] rank of a third-rate power, if no worse happened to us.

That such a landing is, in the present state of [illegible] sible, must be manifest. No naval force of ours can [illegible] prevent it. Blockades of a hostile port are no longer [illegible] as of yore. The blockading squadron must be under [illegible] cause there would be no means of supplying it [illegible] enough to be always steaming, while the outrunning [illegible] come steaming on with great advantage, and might [illegible] moment when an on-shore wind had compelled the [illegible] to haul off. One night is enough for the passage to [illegible] and twenty thousand men might be landed at any point [illegible] our fleet knew that the enemy was out of harbour [illegible] could be no security against the simultaneous landing [illegible] thousand for Portsmouth, twenty thousand for Plym[illegible] twenty thousand for Ireland. Our troops would [illegible] scattered about the United Kingdom; and with [illegible] and Plymouth as they now are, those two dockyards [illegible] they contain would be entered and burnt before [illegible] sand men could be brought together to defend either [illegible]

Then, again, suppose the manœuvre of the first [illegible] repeated, and a large French fleet, with troops on [illegible] for the West Indies, what should we do? Would [illegible] satisfied to see our fleet remain at anchor at Torbay [illegible] leaving our colonies to their fate? And if we [illegible] French, they might be found to have doubled [illegible] returned to the Channel, and for ten days or a fort[illegible] the command of the narrow seas. Now the use of [illegible] is to establish for a certain number of days [illegible] thirty) an equation between a smaller inside and a [illegible] outside, and thus to give time for a relieving [illegible] This in our case would just make the difference [illegible] and destruction. But if these defensive works [illegible] is manifest that they ought to be made with [illegible] delay; to spread their completion over twenty [illegible] would be folly, unless we could come to an [illegible] chivalrous antagonist not to molest us till [illegible] we were quite ready to repel his attack. [illegible] works might, if money were forthcoming, [illegible] in three, or latest four years—long enough [illegible] state of imperfect defence.

money, estimated in round numbers at ten to be got? There are two ways: annual this purpose over and above all other ex- fourth of this sum, or the raising a loan for payable in three or four annual instalments, in twenty or thirty years. The first method be the best in principle, and the cheapest, but would be heavy, and the danger would be that after desire for financial relief might prevail over a of danger, and the annual grants would dwindle present insufficiency; and the works would thus unfinished. The second course has the of being financially as light, or nearly so, as the pre- because the annual repayment of principal and would be but little heavier than the present annual we should gain the same advantage of early com- works which would be secured by the greater financial of the first plan.

of this kind have been deemed, by the de- judgment and action of Parliament, wise and proper persons. Why should they not be so for a nation, to outlays of the same nature as those for which persons have been by law enabled to charge their . The objection to borrowing for expenditure is stronger than for a nation.

individual, if he went on borrowing for annual expenses, by having no income left to live upon or to assign lender. A nation would, perhaps, in the end come to standstill, but its power of increasing its income is than that of an individual; but still Parliament has and enabled private persons to borrow money for improvement of their estates, the money so borrowed in a limited number of years.

do not ourselves propose such a measure to Parlia- will infallibly be proposed by somebody else, and will not indeed against us, because I for one should vote proposer, whoever he might be, but with great dis- the Government for allowing a measure of this kind, one may say, the fate of the empire, to be taken out hands. People would say, and justly too, that we and ought to change places, and that he and his friends themselves fitter than we were to assume the re- of taking care 'ne quid detrimenti respublica capiat.'

In accordance with these views he moved a resolution in the following session providing nine millions for the purpose of fortifying our dockyards and arsenals. His proposals were founded on the report of a Royal Commission which had enquired, during the preceding autumn, into our means of defence. The resolution was adopted by the House by a large majority, and the results of his action are seen in our existing forts and lines round Portsmouth, Plymouth, Chatham, and Cork.

CHAPTER XV.

ITALIAN DUCHIES—SYRIA—EMPEROR NAPOLEON'S NEUTRALITY OF SAVOY—ATTITUDE OF FRANCE—THE OF 1860—CONFLICT BETWEEN LORDS AND COMMONS ON —DISCUSSION ABOUT THE 'PRESS.'

may have been the previous differences which between Lord Palmerston and Lord Russell in the of their long career, these two statesmen were, the years which covered the second Palmerston ation, thoroughly united, both in their general policy and also as to the best manner of giving effect.

year 1860, Italian affairs absorbed almost the interest of foreign events, and both ministers had one aim the speedy realisation of an independent ed Italy. In the following memorandum, drawn Lord Palmerston and circulated among his col- we find sketched out the policy which, in with the Foreign Secretary, he wished to We must, however, in order to appreciate it, the position of matters at the opening of the

Congress which, by the Treaty of Zurich, France Austria had engaged themselves to summon had postponed. The British Government had then forward and proposed that France and Austria agree not to interfere for the future by force in affairs of Italy, that the French Emperor concert with the Pope for the evacuation of that Sardinia should not send troops into Italy until its several states had voted as to destiny, she being at liberty to do so as soon as a vote for annexation to her was [illegible] proposals France had instantly [illegible] the Duchies had preserved internal order, [illegible] unmistakable signs of their intention [illegible] annexation to Sardinia if left to themselves [illegible] had demanded and was about to receive [illegible] Savoy from Sardinia as an equivalent for th[illegible] of territory which the latter was on the p[illegible] quiring. Lord Palmerston had foreseen [illegible] but, though deploring it, had considered that [illegible] of Northern Italy was cheaply purchased at [illegible] Lord Palmerston's memorandum was as follo[illegible]

Broadlands: Jan[illegible]

The affairs of Italy are coming to a crisis, and [illegible] pensably necessary that the English Government [illegible] without further delay to a decision as to the course [illegible] land is to pursue. But, in truth, that course has [illegible] marked out. The English Government might have [illegible] that, in regard to Italian affairs, England should [illegible] position as one of the great Powers of Europe. We [illegible] said that we live in an island, and care not what [illegible] on the Continent; that we think only of making [illegible] of defending our own shores; and that we leave [illegible] task of settling as they like the affairs of the [illegible] Europe. But such has not been the policy of th[illegible] greatest statesmen who have taken part in the g[illegible] this country. We might have deemed the prese[illegible] tional case; we might have said the Emperor [illegible] got into a scrape about Italian affairs; let him g[illegible] he can: it is not our business to help him. [illegible] considered that what is at issue is not the interest[illegible] peror Napoleon, but the interests of the people [illegible] through them, the welfare and peace of Europe[illegible] when a proposal was made that a Congress shou[illegible] sider how best the independence and welfare of [illegible] secured, and when England was invited to be [illegible] Congress, we accepted the invitation.

But it would have been unworthy of the [illegible] great Power like England to have accepted [illegible] without having decided upon the policy which [illegible] sue when in the Congress. We had a [illegible]

[illegible] policy known to the principal Powers in- [illegible]. That policy is in accordance with those [illegible] English statesmen in our times have professed [illegible] which are the foundation of public opinion [illegible] declared that in going into Congress we should [illegible] upon the principle that no force should be em- [illegible] of imposing upon the people of Italy any [illegible] or constitution, that is to say, that the [illegible] and especially of Central Italy, should be left [illegible] their own condition of political existence. We [illegible] into Congress, if Congress there is to be, not [illegible] into their box, discarding preconceived opinions [illegible] be determined by what we hear in Congress, but [illegible] with a well-matured and deliberately formed [illegible] with the intention of endeavouring to make that [illegible]. What is the best way of accomplishing this [illegible] Why, obviously to persuade those Powers to agree [illegible] are most able to sway the course of events in Italy [illegible] them to the result we wish for.

[illegible] those Powers? Obviously France and Sardinia. [illegible] Pope, and the King of Naples have views directly [illegible] ours; and the other states to be represented in Con- [illegible] far off to have the same influence as France and [illegible] Italian affairs.

[illegible] demonstrable, therefore, that we ought to endeavour to [illegible] an understanding with France and Sardinia, for the [illegible] common and united action with them in regard to [illegible] to be treated of in Congress. We need take little [illegible] about Sardinia, because we know that her views tally [illegible] own; we can have little doubt as to the inclination of [illegible] Napoleon, because he has declared over and over [illegible] manifestoes, in speeches, in letters and other communi- [illegible] his object is to free Italy from foreign domination, [illegible] Italy free from the Alps to the Adriatic, and to [illegible] l'Italie à elle-même.' There can be no reasonable doubt, [illegible] that both France and Sardinia would unite with Eng- [illegible] maintaining the principle that the Italians should be [illegible] against foreign compulsion, and should be left free to [illegible] according to their own will, what shall be their [illegible] political condition. But what is the best time for en- [illegible] to establish this understanding? Shall we take [illegible] or shall we wait till the Congress is assembled, and [illegible] proposal is made by Austria or by the Pope, or by some other Power, which would be at [illegible] Common sense seems to point out that if [illegible] is to be aimed at, we ought to endeavour to [illegible] delay, and not to allow France and Sardinia to [illegible] ignorant whether England would or would [illegible] ciently the principles which she has [illegible] put off endeavouring to establish an [illegible] and Sardinia till after the Congress had met [illegible] discussions, would be the most unbusiness[illegible] could well be imagined, and would, in all prob[illegible] to deserved disappointment. Austria does not [illegible] chapter of accidents, but has been actively [illegible] ing for support to her views.

But what is the understanding or agreement [illegible] ought to establish with France and Sardinia? [illegible] determination to prevent any forcible interference [illegible] Power in the affairs of Italy. This, it is said, would [illegible] against Austria. No doubt it would be, as far as [illegible] interference of Austria by force of arms in the affairs [illegible] and such a triple league would better deserve the [illegible] alliance than the league which bore that name.

But such an engagement might lead us into war [illegible] whom? War with Austria. Well, suppose it did, [illegible] war be one of great effort and expense? Clearly [illegible] Sardinia, and Central Italy would furnish troops [illegible] enough to repel any attempt which Austria could [illegible] erce Sardinia or Central Italy. Our share in such [illegible] be chiefly, if not wholly, naval; and our squadron [illegible] atic would probably be the utmost of our contrib[illegible] we were asked to lend a couple of regiments to [illegible] point on the Adriatic, which, however, we should [illegible] be asked to do, and if asked, we might not con[illegible] ought not to be frightened by words; we ought [illegible] things. But is such a war likely? On the con[illegible] the highest degree probable that such an engage[illegible] England, France, and Sardinia would be the [illegible] means of preventing a renewal of war in Italy [illegible] England keeps aloof, Austria may speculate upon [illegible] in a war between her on the one hand, and [illegible] on the other. It is so natural that we should [illegible] and Italy, that our holding back from doing [illegible] upon by Austria as a proof that there was [illegible] current which prevented us from doing [illegible]

[illegible] not unnaturally reckon that when the war [illegible] that undercurrent would drive us to side with [illegible]liance; and this speculation would be a great [illegible] to Austria to take a course leading to war. If, [illegible] we make it publicly known that we engaged [illegible]y on the side of France and Italy, it might be [illegible]dently as anything can be affirmed as to a future [illegible] there would be and could be no renewal of war in [illegible] triple alliance, while it would be honourable to [illegible] might say, the only course that would be honourable [illegible], would secure the continuance of peace in Italy, and [illegible] one danger to the general peace of Europe.

[illegible] said we cannot trust the Emperor Napoleon, and [illegible] had entered into this triple alliance, he would throw [illegible] make some arrangement of his own without con[illegible]. It is no doubt true that such was the course pur[illegible] Austria during the war which ended in 1815. Austria [illegible] subsidies, bound herself by treaty not to make peace [illegible] our concurrence, sustained signal defeat in battle, and [illegible] made peace without our concurrence. But on [illegible] has the Emperor Napoleon so acted? On none. [illegible] with us about certain conditions and the interpre[illegible] certain conditions of the treaty of peace with Russia, [illegible] points in dispute were settled substantially in confor[illegible] our views. There is no ground for imputing to him [illegible] in his conduct towards us as allies. But it is said that [illegible] steadiness of purpose, and the agreement of Villafranca [illegible] of this. That agreement was certainly much short of [illegible] of intention with which he began the war, but [illegible] difficulties of many kinds to contend with in further [illegible] the war; and though we, as lookers on, may think, [illegible] rightly, that if he had persevered those difficulties [illegible] have faded away, yet there can be no doubt that he [illegible] them at the time real; and he is not the only instance [illegible] sovereign or a general who has at the end of a war or a [illegible] accepted conditions of peace less full and complete [illegible] he expected or demanded when hostilities began.

[illegible] there is no ground for imputing to Napoleon unsteadi[illegible] purpose in regard to his views about Italy. I have, [illegible] last four or five years, had at different times oppor[illegible] of conversation with him upon many subjects, and, [illegible] others, upon the affairs of Italy, and I always found him [illegible]taining the same views and opinions which have filled his mind since January of last year, in regard to freeing Italy from Austrian domination, and curtailing the temporal sovereignty of the Pope. There seems, therefore, no reason to apprehend that if we came to an understanding with France and Sardinia, for the purpose of maintaining the principle that no force should be employed to coerce the free will of the Italians, the Emperor Napoleon should turn round and leave us in the lurch. There is every reason, on the contrary, to be confident that by such an agreement with France and Sardinia, we should without war complete a settlement of Italy highly honourable to the Powers who brought it about, and full of advantage, not to Italy alone, but to Europe in general.

I have argued thus far on the supposition that the Congress will meet, and I think it most probable that it will meet. Austria and the Pope look to the Congress (mistakenly, I trust and believe, and mistakenly if the proposed concert with France and Sardinia is established) as the means by which the Archdukes are to be restored and Romagna brought back to obedience. These two Powers will not lightly let the Congress slip through their fingers. The Emperor Napoleon also wishes the Congress to meet, in order to relieve him from responsibility as to the settlement of Italy. The probability, therefore, is that the difficulty arising out of the pamphlet will be got over, and that the Congress will meet. But if that difficulty should prove insurmountable, and the Congress should be given up, everything which I have said in this memorandum would equally apply, or rather I should say the necessity of coming to an agreement with France and Sardinia would be stronger still, for in that case matters would have to be settled by diplomatic negotiation or by force of arms, [illegible] an agreement between England, France, and Sardinia would [illegible] effect the objects which such an agreement might have in view.

It is said, however, that although the course now recommended might in itself be right and proper, it would not be supported by the country nor by Parliament.

My [illegible] is that it would be highly approved [illegible] the country, both on the general grounds of its own merits and [illegible]

[illegible]

… a rupture with France, and to secure … peace with our neighbour. I am equally of … would be approved by Parliament; but if, by … of parties, an adverse decision were come to, it … be the duty of the Government to appeal … to the country. My belief is that such an … be eminently successful; but if it were not, I … give up office for maintaining the principle on … which I recommend would be founded, than … by giving that principle up.

PALMERSTON.

… was no need, however, of any formal league … 'triple alliance.' The influence of the two … Powers sufficed to restrain any forcible inter… if such had been contemplated. In the … of March, Tuscany and Emilia declared by an … majority in favour of annexation to Sardinia, … Victor Emmanuel formally received them … Piedmontese monarchy. Italy was already … on her road to unity.

… massacre of the Maronites by the Druses with … of the local authorities in the neigh… of Beyrout and Damascus led this year to … of English ships and French troops to … under the provisions of a convention between the … and Turkey, after we had declined a pro… by France to invite the Viceroy of Egypt … Lord Palmerston consented, but unwillingly, … expedition, fearing lest there would be much … in getting the French out again. This was, … the case; for, although all danger of renewed … had passed away by the time they arrived on … it was not until the latter end of 1861 that … ; and during this interval continuous re… to urge their departure were deemed … by the British Government. Before they left, … the coercive influence of their presence had … the due punishment of the guilty, and had … the British and French Commissioners to establish a system of administration which about in the Lebanon a durable state of peace order.

Lord Palmerston had, no doubt, a personal p for Napoleon III., and fully acknowledged conduct had in many instances been that of an able ally, but he was not blinded to the tenden this active-minded Prince, whose youth had bee in schemes of personal ambition, had to the and nurturing of national projects which m more or less inconvenient to his neighbours; English Government under Lord Palmerston very desirous to be friendly, would not in an gency have been subservient to that of Fra short note to our ambassador at Paris may ser illustration:—[1]

John Russell has shown me his private letter concur in all he says. We must not take the Thouvenel or the Emperor as ordinances from the It is an old-established manœuvre to represent as inevitable that which one desires to accomplish beforehand to deaden resistance by making people hopeless.

The Emperor's mind seems as full of schemes is full of rabbits, and, like rabbits, his schemes for the moment to avoid notice or antagonism.

We had no ground for war, and no sufficient war about Nice and Savoy, nor could we by any have prevented their annexation; but other arise in regard to which England could not be

The illustration was very apt that French Emperor's mind to a rabbit warren constantly working underground, but at In 1863, for instance, conversing with lian minister at Paris, he told him that wanted to get Rome they ought never their capital, just as he himself, Brussels, never professed it openly,

[1] To Lord Cowley, Ap

[illegible], and that, in that way, he was more likely [illegible] if he raised opposition by talking of it! [illegible] Palmerston in the note quoted above pointed [illegible] in regard to which England could not re-[illegible]. One was the question of Genoa. When, [illegible], it was suspected that France was to be repaid [illegible] acquiescence in Garibaldi's conquest of Sicily [illegible] by the cession of Genoa or the Island of [illegible], he let it be understood that the fleet of [illegible] would not be a passive witness of the trans-[illegible]. If any such intention existed—of which there [illegible] evidence—his outspoken remonstrances acted [illegible] effectual check to it.

[illegible] was not so successful in his efforts on behalf of [illegible]land, whose position was greatly affected by [illegible] annexation of Savoy to France. The two districts [illegible] Chablais and Faucigny, bordering on the Lake of [illegible], had been declared by the treaties of 1815 to [illegible] in the neutrality of Switzerland. It was at [illegible] hoped that the Emperor would consent to hand [illegible] these two northern districts of Savoy to the Swiss [illegible]deration. When this expectation vanished, it [illegible] at any rate believed that France might be induced [illegible] cede a strip of territory, so as to leave the lake [illegible] to the Swiss, and to provide them with a strate-[illegible] line on the frontier of the Valais. Lord Palmerston [illegible] in this sense to the French Ambassador, and [illegible] with great tact to those considerations of [illegible] which, on paper at any rate, have so much [illegible] influence with Frenchmen.

94 Piccadilly: avril 17, 1860.

[illegible] cher Persigny,—Soyez bien convaincu que nous sou-[illegible] sincèrement de nous entendre avec la France sur cette [illegible] Savoyardo-Suisse, mais dans cette discussion la France [illegible] Angleterre ne partent pas du même point de départ; chez [illegible] ici, l'habitude est de considérer les questions politiques [illegible] ce que nous croyons leur résultat pratique, et chez vous, [illegible], c'est trop l'habitude de traiter toutes les questions [illegible], non pas sur le terrain du résultat pratique, mais sur le terrain de l'amour-propre national; et, si vous me p de vous le dire, c'est surtout, lorsque les arguments quent, qu'on se place à Paris le plus fortement sur le t l'amour-propre. Cependant ce n'est pas là la bonne d'envisager les questions de haute politique; mais amour-propre national ne doit-il pas conseiller à faire c juste et généreux et honorable? et n'est-ce pas que la j générosité et l'honneur conseilleraient à la France de aux réclamations légitimes de la Suisse? La France a à la Sardaigne une frontière stratégique pour la sécurité de la France. Est-ce juste que la France ôte à la S frontière stratégique que l'Europe, la France elle-même avait donnée à la Suisse pour la sûreté du territoire de fédération? Tous les arguments dont la France s'e pour justifier sa demande, soutiennent plus encore la d de la Suisse. Mais une grande Puissance et un grand S en traitant avec un voisin faible, devraient se montr seulement justes, mais généreux; il n'est pas une faibl d'agir ainsi, c'est une preuve de la conscience de sa for avec l'Empereur des Français ce n'est pas seulement u tion de générosité; la reconnaissance y entre pour C'est en Suisse que l'Empereur a fait ses premières é qu'il a commencé à développer ce caractère qui lui depuis, des succès si éclatants; c'est en Suisse plus tard des temps moins heureux que les dernières dix années, q pereur a eu à se louer des procédés de la Suisse à son é est impossible que l'Empereur ne sente pas de la bienv envers la Suisse. On croit en Europe que l'Empereur à espérer aux Suisses, qu'après que la Savoie lui au cédée par la Sardaigne, il donnerait à la Suisse les part tralisées; ne serait-ce pas inconséquent de leur refuse la frontière stratégique dont ils seraient contents? La du Lac de Genève et la ligne stratégique, qui couvre le paraissent essentiels pour la Suisse. Quant aux bords il est à remarquer que de toutes les raisons stratégiqu en avant par la France pour appuyer la demande de la de la Savoie, il n'y en a pas une qui s'applique aux b Lac de Genève, tandis que toutes ces raisons s'appliqu demande que fait la Suisse de ne pas avoir sur le Lac u aussi puissant que la France. Les stipulations dont o lesquelles la France s'engagerait à n'avoir aucun b sur le Lac, et de ne construire aucune forteresse ne pourraient guère être prises au sérieux: il y a

that it was necessary for France to obtain the Palatinate, and to acquire Saarbruck and Saarlouis, places which, indeed, became in 1870 the first point of his attack on Prussia. The general concurrence of many other [illegible] indications, some, no doubt, false, and each by [illegible] perhaps trivial, gave strength to the distrust [illegible] Lord Palmerston had already felt at the end of [illegible] previous year, when he wrote to Lord John Russell.

Broadlands: November [illegible]

My dear John Russell,—Till lately I had strong [illegible] in the fair intentions of Napoleon towards England, [illegible] I have begun to feel great distrust and to suspect [illegible] formerly declared intention of avenging Waterloo [illegible] dormant, and has not died away. He seems to have [illegible] that he ought to lay his foundation by beating, with [illegible] with our concurrence, or our neutrality, first Russia [illegible] Austria, and, by dealing with them generously, to [illegible] his friends in any subsequent quarrel with us. In [illegible] ever, he would, probably, find himself mistaken; [illegible] nations and governments resentments for former [illegible] gratitude for former benefits invariably give way to [illegible] tions of present and prospective interests; and Russia [illegible] and Austria certainly, would see no advantage in [illegible] lowering of England for the augmentation of the [illegible] of France. But this reasoning of mine may be [illegible] Russia, at least, might join France against us.

Next, he has been assiduously labouring to [illegible] naval means, evidently for offensive as well as [illegible] purposes; and latterly great pains have been [illegible] throughout France, and especially among the army [illegible] hatred of England, and a disparaging feeling of [illegible] and naval means. All this may be explained [illegible] be accounted for by other causes than a [illegible] hostility to England; but it would be unwise in [illegible] Government to shut its eyes to all these symptoms [illegible] make all due preparations for the gale which [illegible] meter thus indicates, though it may possibly [illegible] course we should take as 'argent comptant' [illegible] of 'alliance intime et durable,' as Walewski [illegible] China despatch; and the only expression [illegible] anything like suspicion should be in the [illegible]

...arrangements. In regard to them, however, ...overruled by financial economy.

...exertions which the French were ...place their navy upon the most complete ...footing did not tend to diminish the ...anxiety. It was under these circumstances ...Palmerston urged forward our defensive ...and the construction of fortifications, ...encouraged the development of the Volunteer ...movement. This was no mere 'invasion panic.' ...that the salutary and restraining action of a ...Power like England is not confined to the ...of physical force. If such a Power is ...to be strong within itself, and capable of ...when required, its diplomatic action will ...and attention, will often strongly influence the ...of events, and, by dealing timely with beginnings, ...prevent proceedings which, if unchecked, would ...great and disastrous international convulsions. ...Palmerston, however, also feared direct action ...England if we remained unprepared. He says ...letter to the Duke of Somerset:

...have watched the French Emperor narrowly, and have ...his character and conduct. You may rely upon it that ...bottom of his heart there rankles a deep and inextin-...le desire to humble and punish England, and to avenge, ...the many humiliations, political, naval, and military, ...since the beginning of this century, England has, by ...and her allies, inflicted upon France. He has sufficiently ...ed his military means; he is now stealthily but steadily ...ing his naval means; and, when all is ready, the over-...l be played, the curtain will draw up, and we shall have ...disagreeable melodrama.

...e following conversation with Count Flahault ...he letter to Count Persigny are very character-... Lord Palmerston had an enviable power of ...hard truths under a sense of duty, while he ...giving offence, owing to the frankness and ...of his manner:—

Memorandum of a Conversation with Count Flahault on Tuesday, March 27, 1860.

Count Flahault came to me at a quarter after four, [illegible] I was going down to the House of Commons. He said [illegible] going to Paris next morning, and he wished to know [illegible] should say from me to the Emperor. I said I could [illegible] minute, as I had to be in the House to answer a question, [illegible] that if he would go down with me in my brougham we [illegible] talk as we went along. To this he agreed. I then [illegible] what Lord John had said. He objected to that [illegible] saying that what had fallen from Lord John was [illegible] offensive to the Emperor. I asked what part. He said, [illegible] latter part, which related to concert with other Powers, [illegible] was political, and could not be objected to; but Lord John [illegible] expressed distrust of the Emperor. I said distrust [illegible] founded on either of two grounds: either upon the [illegible] of intentional deceit, or upon such a frequent change of [illegible] and of conduct as to show that no reliance could be [illegible] the continuance of the intentions or policy of the [illegible] Count Flahault must admit that, without imputing [illegible] there is ample ground for a feeling founded on the [illegible] sideration. Count Flahault said his great object was [illegible] war between the two countries. I said that I [illegible] Emperor and Thouvenel had schemes and views [illegible] to bring about that result, and might array [illegible] France. Count Flahault did not fear that, but [illegible] hensive that irritation on both sides might bring on war [illegible] England and France. I said that I was most anxious [illegible] such a war; but if it was forced upon England, [illegible] fearlessly accept it, whether in conjunction with a [illegible] alliance, or singly and by herself; that the nation [illegible] and rally as one man; although, speaking to a [illegible] ought perhaps not to say so, yet I could not [illegible] observing that the examples of history led me to [illegible] the result of a conflict between English and [illegible] thing like equal terms, would not be [illegible]

Count Flahault said that he had been [illegible]

battle of Blenheim: 'Vous venez, milord,' de battre les meilleures troupes de l'Europe.' replied Marlborough, 'celles qui les ont said Count Flahault, 'what I fear is an in- country, for which steam affords such facilities, would be disastrous to England.' I replied that ways, for defence as well as for attack; and invasion, though it would no doubt be a temporary under no apprehension as to its results. That a England and France would doubtless be disastrous countries, but it is by no means certain which of the suffer the most.

at the House of Commons, we took leave of each Count Flahault said he should not say anything to the calculated to increase the irritation which he expected would endeavour to calm. I said that of course Flahault would judge for himself what he should say, have observed what is the state of public feeling in this country. The conversation was carried on friendly manner, as between two private friends known each other for a long course of years.

Broadlands: octobre 18, 1860.

on cher Persigny,—Borthwick s'est rendu ici il y a jours, d'après votre désir, pour me donner communica- la conversation que vous avez eue avec lui.

substance de ce qu'il m'a raconté comme le résumé de ce lui avez dit est à peu près que l'Empereur souhaite, comme toujours, paix avec tous et alliance avec que le maintien de cette alliance dépend beaucoup Vous avez dit que dans les masses en France il y a vouloir envers l'Angleterre; que l'Empereur peut et contraindre ce sentiment, tant qu'il est aidé par amicale de la part du Gouvernement anglais, et qu'il faudrait de notre part, ce serait d'exprimer confiance, et de nous abstenir de toute tentative d'organiser européenne contre la France. Que si nous devions un autre et différent système, il y aurait danger de les deux pays, chose que vous considéreriez comme pour les deux. Mais vous avez ajouté que dans préparatifs et des moyens guerriers sur terre et sur pays, le résultat d'une telle guerre ne serait peut-être pas favorable pour nous; qu'avec vos bâtiments [illegible] vous pourriez détruire nos chantiers, et que le résult[illegible] telle lutte serait peut-être de mettre la France à la tê[illegible] coalition européenne dirigée contre l'Angleterre, isolé[illegible] politique autant que par la géographie, et finalement vo[illegible] suggéré l'idée que, lorsque je vais à Leeds vers la fin d[illegible] prochain, je pourrais utilement pour les deux pays pr[illegible] l'occasion pour exprimer dans un discours notre confia[illegible] intentions pacifiques et désintéressées de l'Empereur.

Eh bien! je suis toujours bien aise d'apprendre, [illegible] discours de l'Empereur, soit parce qu'on nous rapport[illegible] conversations, que la politique extérieure de la Fr[illegible] pacifique et désintéressée; et quant à la question de [illegible] guerre entre nos deux pays, vous pouvez être sûr qu[illegible] personne en Angleterre qui voudrait la guerre, et qui n[illegible] pas la paix.

Mais pour ce qui regarde la guerre, l'histoire du [illegible] rassure quant aux chances de l'avenir. Il n'y a cert[illegible] pas de nation qui puisse se vanter d'être plus brav[illegible] nation française, mais je crois que nos hommes ont [illegible] dix minutes de ténacité de plus que les vôtres; et [illegible] courage est égal des deux côtés, c'est la ténacité qui [illegible] sort du combat. Pour ce qui regarde l'application de [illegible] et des arts mécaniques à la guerre, je crois qu'il n'y a [illegible] différence entre les deux pays, soit pour les opération[illegible] soit pour celles sur mer; mais nous avons plus [illegible] charbon que vous, et notre industrie en ces matière[illegible] développée que la vôtre.

La grande différence entre les deux pays consi[illegible] que tous nos préparatifs, soit militaires, soit naval[illegible] tiellement défensifs, tandis que les vôtres ont [illegible] parence d'être destinés pour des opérations offensiv[illegible]

Si par conséquent les autres gouvernement[illegible] commencent, non pas à se coaliser pour attaqu[illegible] chose à laquelle la démence seule pourrait [illegible] s'entr'aider dans le cas où la France devenait [illegible] les actes récents de la France et son attitude [illegible] en sont les causes. Mais ceci ne donne à la [illegible] sujet de plainte. Il n'y a pas un homme [illegible] songerait à organiser une coalition pour [illegible] tranquille et paisible; mais il n'y a pas [illegible] son possible pour organiser une coalition [illegible] France ambitieuse et envahissante.

[illegible] tout ceci, que l'Empereur a entre ses mains [illegible] paix ou de guerre pour l'Europe. J'espère [illegible] la paix, et si cela est, nous l'aiderons de tout [illegible] à la maintenir.

[illegible] très-bien que, parmi les masses en France, il y [illegible] vouloir envers l'Angleterre. Il n'est pas surprenant [illegible] haineuses des nos guerres aient survécu plus [illegible] en France que chez nous. Dans notre pays toute la [illegible] est si activement occupée de la vie politique du [illegible] qu'elle oublie bien vite le passé, et ne porte ses regards [illegible] petite distance dans l'avenir.

[illegible]s vous en France, les masses ne prennent que peu de [illegible] la vie politique du présent, et par conséquent elles re-[illegible]t beaucoup plus longtemps les souvenirs du passé, et [illegible]rnent leurs regards plus activement vers l'avenir. Mais [illegible]us dire franchement la vérité, il nous revient de plusieurs [illegible] que les agents du Gouvernement français ne se [illegible] pas fâchés de voir ce mauvais vouloir se propager, [illegible] et se perpétuer.

[illegible] à Leeds, j'y vais pour rencontrer des ouvriers, et pour [illegible]rler ménage et éducation, et non pas pour faire un dis-[illegible]olitique.

Mille amitiés,
PALMERSTON.

[illegible] the same time he acquaints the English Am-[illegible]dor at Paris with the correspondence that had [illegible] place.

Broadlands: November 2, 1860.

[illegible] dear Cowley,—As you say that Persigny has only sent [illegible]s from my letter, I think it right to send you a full copy [illegible]hich I wish you to show to Thouvenel, because the first [illegible] the letter accounts for my having written at all, and for [illegible]hich I did write.

[illegible]ould not consider Persigny's message, coming as he did [illegible]t from Paris, in any other light than as a sort of semi-[illegible] communication, and it was necessary for me to answer [illegible]ly but firmly. I believe that I was not wrong in con-[illegible]g the communication as coming from superior authority [illegible]s, though possibly Persigny, in his zeal, may have added [illegible]ing of his own. He wrote me an answer, in which he [illegible] well admitted that Borthwick had faithfully rendered [illegible]bstance of what had been said to him. I purposely omitted to allude to one thing which Persigny had ... was that if I did not adopt a friendly course towar... should be turned out at the beginning of next ... coalition of Tories and Radicals upon the cry of ... what they would represent a policy calculated to ... war with France. Other things which I have ... me that Persigny spoke by order and according to ... therefore, the Emperor and his ministers ought no... or offended at the answer which it was impossible f... give. If Persigny had been able to come down h... logue would have been by word of mouth instead ... and it would, therefore, have been less formal. But ... the Emperor that my great wish and that of all ... is to maintain the closest relations of friendship ... with France, and that it will certainly not be our f... should take a different course. But they must kn... fidence depends upon facts, and not upon words ... which have happened, and language which has b... some time past could not fail to inspire distrust as t... but that distrust has not been accompanied by ... feeling of hostility to France, and is purely and ... ing of a defensive character.

The Emperor and those about him fancy we a... coalition to attack France. We should be insan... What would be the object of such an attack, and w... hopes would anyone have of success!

France is an essential element in the balance ... Europe, and, I may say, in the world. All the... that France should be content with what she is... not take up the schemes and policy of the first Na... many things of late lead us to think she has an ... do. Of course if that system were again to b... it would be resisted now as it was before, but ... success. The seizure of Savoy and Nice and ... promise towards Switzerland about the cession ... of the neutralised district are matters which ... easily.

At Leeds he did not make a politic...

[illegible] his own sphere, and that while the mechanic [illegible] of place as Prime Minister, the Premier [illegible] as a weaver, Lord Palmerston quickly re-[illegible] general laughter, 'Oh, my business is not [illegible], but to unravel!'

[illegible] was one confederacy of a totally different [illegible] any that came across the path of his official [illegible] which baffled his 'unravelling' powers this [illegible] When the much-coveted 'blue riband' of the [illegible] just within his grasp, his horse Mainstone—[illegible] the betting—unaccountably broke down, with [illegible] suspicion of foul play. The entries in his list [illegible] views on the morning of Monday, May 21, are [illegible] by their variety:—

[illegible] Day and Professor Spooner about Mainstone: settled [illegible] run on Wednesday.—Shaftesbury about Church ap-[illegible]ments.—Powell, to ask about Mainstone.—Sir Robert ditto.—Bernstorff to read me a despatch.—Sidney Herbert his evidence to be given to-morrow before committee on organisation.—Deputation from Manchester against in-[illegible] of the House of Lords to throw out the repeal of the duty on paper.

[illegible]he Derby Day being the next but one, we may be [illegible] that on this morning the trainer and the veterinary received with even more interest than the Prus-[illegible] ambassador and the deputation. In spite of [illegible] report from the stable, Lord Palmerston rode [illegible] to Epsom on Wednesday to see Thormanby [illegible]and his own horse only come in somewhere about [illegible]. It was a great disappointment to him. He [illegible] never been so near taking the great prize of the [illegible] and he was convinced that if his horse had been [illegible] dealt with, it would at any rate have made a good [illegible] to the front. Lord Palmerston's connection with [illegible]urf extended over a long period, commencing in [illegible], with a filly called Mignonette, at Winchester, [illegible] only ending with his death. He seldom betted, [illegible] raced from innate love of sport and horses. He usually bred his animals [illegible] after his farms. A visit to [illegible] Broadlands made his favourite [illegible] The interest he took in Turf [illegible] ance which he gave to those [illegible] were signally recognised when the [illegible] passed an unanimous resolution that [illegible] be offered to him for his invaluable [illegible] the laws of the Turf, and that he [illegible] to become an honorary member of [illegible] been elected unanimously by a [illegible] Changing his trainer after this [illegible] feeling very much disgusted at the [illegible] revealed, as he considered, by the [illegible] horse, he had no animal of any merit [illegible] Baldwin,[1] which he disposed of shortly [illegible] in the manner shown by the following [illegible]

94 Piccadilly: July [illegible]

My dear Lord Naas,—I have been obliged [illegible] horse Baldwin out of training, in order to prevent [illegible] regularly lame.

I mean to devote the rest of his days to the [illegible] good horses, and, if you like to accept him as a stall[illegible] Palmerstown breeding stud, I will gladly make him [illegible] to that establishment, on the single condition [illegible] time you found that he did not suit, he should [illegible] me.

If you take him, you should send some [illegible] Broadlands to give him over to Ireland, and [illegible] better.

The session of 1860 offered many [illegible] which the tact and good humour of the [illegible] House of Commons were required. [illegible] these was the dispute about the [illegible] threatened to disturb the mutual [illegible]

[1] Baldwin was named by Lord [illegible] Baldwin Walker. The Admiralty had [illegible] fetch Sir Baldwin back after he had [illegible] could not catch him.

... The Upper House had thrown out, by ...y, the Bill for the repeal of the excise ..., and, by so doing, they undoubtedly ...power which, by the spirit of the Constitution, ...ight be its letter, rested solely with the .... Lord Palmerston was not inclined to ... misunderstanding to grow into a quarrel. ... for a committee to enquire into precedents, ... its report, proposed three resolutions which ... that the right of granting aids and supplies is ...Commons alone, and that although the Lords ...cised on some occasions the power of rejecting ...relating to taxation by negativing the whole, the ... viewed such acts with peculiar jealousy, and ...ed in their own hands the power so to frame Bills ...pply as to maintain their rights inviolate. He ... these resolutions on the acceptance of the House ...great dexterity and, as it proved, with entire suc- ... His position was difficult. There was indeed no ...or a resolution at all; but while he wished to ... a bridge for the retreat of the Lords, he had two ...gues in his Cabinet who were committed far too ...y by their expressions of wrath at what they ...d an outrageous invasion of the liberties of the ...e to permit of their passing the matter over in ...e. So he had, as a wise and moderate counsellor, ...dicate in his speech the rights of the Commons ... sparing the susceptibilities of the Lords. The ...tions were adopted, the question rested for the ...nder of this session, and the Bill passed the Upper ...e in the next.

...nother matter of smaller moment served to illus- ...his happy art of putting things. Mr. Horsman ...ised a discussion which involved allusions to the ...ction between the Government and the press, and ...uated that the social influences of Cambridge ... helped to sway the political leanings of one of ...hief organs of public opinion. Lord Palmerston ...ed him as follows :—

My right honourable friend has stated that he d
what the influence was which drew one of the edit
gers of the 'Times' to me; and if by that statemen
to imply a wish on my part to exercise any influen
line of conduct which is pursued in the case of th
can only say in answer to that charge, in the wo
Malaprop, that I should be but too glad to plead g
soft impeachment, and to know that the insinuati
involves was really founded on fact. If there ar
which, as the right honourable gentleman says, have
led Mr. Delane to me, they are none other than th
of society. My right honourable friend has obser
glowing address which he has just delivered, that t
tors to the press are the favourites and the ornam
social circles into which they enter. In that opin
seems to me, perfectly correct. The gentlemen
refers are, generally speaking, persons of great attai
information. It is, then, but natural that their so
be agreeable. My acquaintance with Mr. Delane i
that character. I have had the pleasure of m
frequently in society, and he has occasionally d
honour to join in society under my roof; that so
may add, composed of persons of all shades of pol
various pursuits. I need hardly say I feel proud w
so honour me without undertaking any other engag
that which Mr. Delane always makes good—of ma
selves agreeable during the time of their stay.

A tribute paid by the Lord Chancellor
Palmerston's conduct of public affairs du
session is so forcible and compendious th
insert it. Lord Westbury writes to him in
of August:

I cannot close this note without expressing to yo
most unfeigned sincerity, my admiration of yo
leadership during this most difficult session. Great
great judgment, great temper and forbearance, h
and tact, matchless courtesy, and great oratorical
with each important occasion, have in a most
marked your conduct of the Government and
of the House of Commons. Those who know
Cabinet must feel that none but you could ha

But what I esteem most is that happy quality you possess by which, whilst you receive the admiration, you at the same time win the affection of all around you.

We must remember that during all these years the Liberal party had only a small nominal majority of twenty in the House of Commons, and that the Cabinet, containing statesmen of marked individual importance, contained also strong elements of divergence, whether on matters of finance, of reform, or of foreign affairs. Lord Westbury was right in thinking that none but a minister possessing peculiar talent for reconciling, cementing, and commanding diverse idiosyncrasies could have overcome such obvious difficulties.

CHAPTER XVI.

STATE OF PARTIES—LORD WARDENSHIP OF THE
CIVIL WAR IN AMERICA—COTTON SUPPLY—
—VISIT TO HARROW—FATHER DALY—
SORT—'TRENT' AFFAIR—NATIONAL
PATRONAGE.

POLITICAL parties were in a singular
period which we have now reached.
tives, alarmed at the 'advanced' ten
Chancellor of the Exchequer, promised
all attempts to turn out the Liberal Pre
would resist 'democratic' budgets, and
from any violent action against Austri
say that Lord Palmerston was too loy
any such secret understanding. The
other hand, hopeless of any effective p
part, and impatient of the laggard ste
Cabinet, offered to help the Tories
existing Government, and to give the
which would succeed a two years'
They anticipated that by that time the
be ready for such a Government and
Bill as they would themselves desire.
that the Conservatives were not an
accept such an alliance. The upshot
Palmerston, although with a small
continued to hold an unassailable
House and the country.

The very ancient and dignified
den of the Cinque Ports becom
of Lord Dalhousie in the

y, had disappeared. Lord Palmerston's installa- ok place at Dover with pomp and circumstance. the antiquarian care of the town-clerk all the ditions had been unearthed and rusty ceremonies ished, and the new Lord Warden was conducted Bredenstone with due solemnity to take the of office at a grand Court of Shepway. Lord rston entered into the thing with proper spirit, ade an appropriate speech at the inaugural ban- in which reminiscences of the past mingled with tations to the practice of modern patriotism.

it another penalty attached to the acceptance of ord Wardenship. It was a 'place of profit' gh of small profit) 'under the Crown.' So during aster recess he had to vacate his seat in Parlia- and was compelled to enjoy what the newspapers day called his 'favourite relaxation, when he had ng else particular to do'—namely, the being re- d for Tiverton. Of course the redoubtable Row- was on the watch, and from an open window near ustings upbraided the Premier for his lukewarm- about reform. 'You come to Tiverton to gull the e, but you don't gull me. I have given the Whigs g trial, but now I throw them over. Go back to ing Street, and bring in an honest Reform Bill, let us have no more double shuffle.' At the sound of the crowd, turned his tormentor inside out, and then went down, shook hands with him, and gave him a receipt for the gout. This Tiverton butcher was a vulgar specimen, eager for notoriety; yet the spectacle of a Prime Minister, at the height of his power and popularity, giving himself as much pains to answer these taunts as if they had come from the Leader of the Opposition had its moral. In some countries [illegible] would have been ejected, or at least hustled; [illegible] England his rights as an elector were recognised [illegible] by the mob and the minister.

The great event of this year was, undoubtedly, [illegible] outbreak of the civil war in America. The [illegible] Government, though it recognised the South[illegible] belligerents, proclaimed its neutrality and [illegible] it in spite of many temptations and frequent [illegible]tions to take a different course. Not only were [illegible] to that effect pressed upon them in both H[illegible] Parliament, but similar proposals were made [illegible] by the French Government; but they early [illegible] that, if the war was to cease in any other way [illegible] the complete success of the North, it was [illegible] that it should so cease owing to a conviction [illegible] sides that they could never live again [illegible] community, than that the termination of [illegible] should be brought about by the mediation [illegible]ference of any European Power. The senti[illegible] inspired the Cabinet may be gathered from [illegible] the following short note, which I insert as [illegible] the generally received impression of Lord [illegible] hostility to the American Republic. It [illegible] that he entertained a feeling of contemp[illegible] dislike, for many of the men who from [illegible] occupied public positions in connection [illegible] States Government. He thought [illegible] honesty and offensive in tone—in short, [illegible] in the sense which is independent of [illegible] solely upon character; but for [illegible] apart from its politicians, he [illegible] regard which his truly English nature would necessarily feel for a free and kindred nation. To his correspondent who had been urging proposals for our mediation he writes:—

94 Piccadilly: May 5, 1861.

My dear Ellice,[1]—The day on which we could succeed in putting an end to this unnatural war between the two sections of our North American cousins would be one of the happiest of our lives, and all that is wanting to induce us to take steps for that purpose is a belief that any such steps would lead towards the accomplishment of that purpose, and would not do more harm than good. The danger is that, in the excited state of men's minds in America, the offer of anyone to interpose to arrest their action, and disappoint them of their expected triumph, might be resented by both sides; and that jealousy of European, especially of English, interference in their internal affairs might make them still more prone to reject our offer as impertinent.

There would, moreover, be great difficulty in suggesting any basis of arrangement to which both parties could agree, and which it would not be repugnant to English feelings and principles to propose. *We* could not well mix ourselves up with the acknowledgment of slavery and the principle that a slave escaping to a free soil State should be followed, claimed, and recovered, like a horse or an ox. We might possibly propose that the North and South should separate amicably; that they should make some boundary line, to be agreed upon, the line of separation between them; and that each confederation should be free to make for its own internal affairs and concerns such laws as it might think fit—the two confederations entering, however, into certain mutual arrangements as to trade and commerce with each other.

[illegible] you think the time is come for any arrangement of such [illegible]? or is it not in the nature of things and in human [illegible] that the wiry edge must be taken off this craving appetite [illegible] conflict in arms before any real and widespread desire [illegible] peace by mutual concession can be looked for?

[illegible] those who looked ahead the civil war threatened [illegible] blow to English interests in the shape of the [illegible] our cotton supply. Lord Palmerston writes to

[1] Right Hon. Edward Ellice, M.P.

[illegible] for the preservation of the rights of [illegible] Porte, Lord Palmerston had, of course, [illegible] to keep a watchful eye on the proceedings [illegible] in Syria. He now writes to the British [illegible] at Constantinople, and bases on the success [illegible]eavours in that quarter an exhortation to the [illegible] to abandon the architects and builders of [illegible]d for nobler agents and objects more worthy [illegible]ightened ruler. The years which have since [illegible] have sufficiently shown how vain were the hopes [illegible] such change; but it cannot be too clearly re[illegible]ed that the keynote of Lord Palmerston's [illegible] policy at the time of the Crimean War and for [illegible] after was a sincere belief in the possibility, [illegible] the probability, of the complete regeneration of [illegible], if the opportunity were offered to her. He [illegible]fore the experiment could be finally pronounced [illegible].

94 Piccadilly: June 26, 1861.

[illegible] dear Bulwer,—I am heartily glad we have got the [illegible] out of Syria, and a hard job it was to do so. The [illegible]ment made for the future government of the Lebanon [illegible] say, work sufficiently well to prevent the French [illegible]ing any pretext for returning thither. But the death [illegible] Sultan and the accession of the present one are the [illegible] important events of the day, as bearing upon Eastern [illegible] Abdul Mejid was a good-hearted and weak-headed [illegible] was running two horses to the goal of perdition—his [illegible] and that of his empire. Luckily for the empire, his [illegible] won the race. If the accounts we have heard of the [illegible]an are true, we may hope that he will restore Turkey [illegible]per position among the Powers of Europe. If he will [illegible] the system of Liberal toleration and progressive in[illegible]provement established by his predecessor on paper, and [illegible]cases and places carried into execution, and if he will [illegible] his empire the well-regulated economy with which he [illegible] have managed his own private affairs, he may be able [illegible] his country from the downfall with which it has lately [illegible] be threatened.

[illegible] will, of course, encourage him to follow such a course, [illegible] present Grand Vizier will be a useful instrument for such a policy. But the Sultan must begin by closing his Harem, dismissing his architects and builders, and turning out his robber ministers. The natural resources of the empire, intellectual, physical, and material, are great; and, if brought out and turned to account, would render Turkey a powerful and important state.

Lord Palmerston always entertained a great affection for Harrow, the place of his early education. Many a time did he ride down in the course of his life to revisit the old scenes, and this year he was present at an interesting ceremony, for he undertook to lay the foundation stone of the School Library, erected in honour of Dr. Vaughan, who had recently retired from the head-mastership. In spite of the pouring rain he went down on horseback, and was received by the assembled boys with great enthusiasm. He reminded them, in his speech, that the strength of a nation consists not so much in the number of the people as in the character of the men; and then, turning the subject to account, went on:—

We ought to pay due respect to those who form the minds of the rising generation; who instruct them that self-denial is better than indulgence; who tell them that labour is to be preferred to pleasure; and that whereas mere amusement may be compared to the southern breezes, which, though they may be enjoyed, yet pass away and leave no trace behind, honourable exertion, on the contrary, may be compared to the fertilizing shower which, though it may, as you all know at the present moment, not be agreeable to those who are exposed to it (laughter), yet nevertheless leaves, by enriching and fertilizing the soil on which it falls, solid marks behind it in the rich and abundant harvest which it helps to create. ... Harrow man, be permitted to say that Harrow has ... in public estimation and public service by furnishing ... tinguished the most in all the careers which ... chosen for their future life. We have ... tinguished in arms. We are proud of one ... Byron—who here imbibed the first elements ... attainment which afterwards led to his high ... boast—I speak now as a Harrow boy— ...

[illegible] four Harrow boys[1] have attained the post which I now [illegible] the honour to hold, and I trust that there are many other [illegible] Harrow boys who are destined to become distinguished [illegible] like those to whom I allude.

After this he rode back in the rain to pass the rest of the day and night on the Treasury Bench; being at the time close upon seventy-seven years of age.

The manner in which from his place on that bench he, this session, countermined the workings of an unscrupulous intriguer deserves notice as illustrative of his readiness of resource and knowledge of human nature. The Government had announced the withdrawal of a grant given by the Derby administration towards the maintenance of a mail-packet service between the port of Galway and the United States. Great indignation was excited by this withdrawal in those parts of Ireland which had expected to profit by the scheme; and a certain Father Daly, armed with credentials from influential quarters, came over to England, with the avowed design, by means of the Irish vote, to put the Government in a minority should it refuse to give way. He had an interview with Lord Palmerston, and threatened him with this party defection on the forthcoming Budget. Lord Palmerston merely replied, that he should go straight down to the House of Commons and relate exactly what had just passed between them. He did so in a manner both frank and amusing, and with such effect, that the Irish Liberals, even had they secretly nursed any thoughts of playing traitor to their party for the sake of local emoluments, became ashamed to appear as dancing to the wire-pulling of an Irish priest, and the Budget was saved.

Some of Lord Palmerston's views about contemporary Italian and American affairs are given in the following letter:—

[1] Perceval, Goderich, Peel, Aberdeen.

Broadlands[illegible]

My dear Russell,—First, as to Rome, I [illegible] in not instructing Cowley to make, at present [illegible] gestion to the Emperor as to a final arrangement [illegible] tion about the Pope. We could not suggest any [illegible] which was not founded on the basis that Rome [illegible] territory should be evacuated by the French; [illegible] should have no temporal dominion over any part [illegible] of Italy, and that the city of Rome should be the [illegible] Italian kingdom. But the first of these conditions [illegible] once stop the discussion of the other two. [illegible] ing the affected regret of the Emperor at [illegible] led to occupy Rome, it is, I think, pretty clear [illegible] to the occupation of that central part of Italy, as [illegible] him great military and political advantages which he [illegible] determined not at present to give up. He is [illegible] with his army of twenty-five thousand men, [illegible] being increased to any amount, either to take [illegible] of any successful disturbance in the Neapolitan [illegible] or to turn the flank of the Austrians in Venetia, [illegible] pass over to Dalmatia, whenever it may suit him [illegible] with Austria—and he may very possibly do so next [illegible] But at all events his occupation of Rome, and the [illegible] which he thus affords to Antonelli, the Pope, and King [illegible] in their intrigues, retards the consolidation of the [illegible] and holds out to him a still glimmering ray of hope [illegible] succeed in his own scheme of an Italian confederation [illegible] an united kingdom. The course of events will settle [illegible] question. Peter's pence will at last begin to fail; [illegible] Pope will only put forth a few more allocutions, [illegible] Catholics will become reconciled to the cessation of his [illegible] power. I think you are right in believing that [illegible] will turn Austria out of Venetia before he turns [illegible] Rome; and there can be little doubt that he remains [illegible] for the purpose of being more easily able to turn Austria [illegible] Venetia.

The arrangement you suggest by which Turkey [illegible] Herzegovina to Italy, and Italy would give it to [illegible] change for Venetia, would be a very good one, [illegible] hard to accomplish. Turkey would not easily [illegible] sell Herzegovina, and Austria would not [illegible] to take that province in exchange for Venetia [illegible] foolishly attaches great military importance [illegible]

... give up Venetia till compelled to do so for ... in war. It might be worth considering ... concerned might be sounded about some such ..., because the first cession would be made by

... America, our best and true policy seems to be ... have begun, and to keep quite clear of the con... North and South. It is true, as you say, that ... cases in Europe in which allied Powers have ... parties, like the man in the 'Critic,' 'In the ... I bid you to drop your swords;' but those cases ... peculiar. The love of quarrelling and fighting is ... man, and to prevent its indulgence is to impose ... on natural liberty. A state may so shackle its own ..., but it is an infringement on national independence to ... other nations. The only excuse would be the danger ... interfering parties if the conflict went on; but in the ... case this cannot be pleaded by the Powers of Europe. ... agree with you that the want of cotton would not ... such a proceeding, unless, indeed, the distress created by ... was far more serious than it is likely to be. The ... is that some cotton will find its way to us from ..., and that we shall get a greater supply than usual from ... quarters.

... only thing to do seems to be to lie on our oars and to ... pretext to the Washingtonians to quarrel with us, while, ... other hand, we maintain our rights and those of our ... countrymen.

...wards the end of the year 1861 two events, very ... in their nature, but alike sudden and startling, ... excited the public mind. I refer to the illness ... death of the Prince Consort and the seizure of the ...federate envoys on board the British mail-steamer ...,' which brought us to the verge of a war with United States. During the simultaneous interval ...uspense, Lord Palmerston was laid up with an ...ck of gout, the worst in his whole life. No doubt ...ymptoms were aggravated by the anxieties of the ...; and I remember that both his hands and both ... were completely crippled, and that he was unable ... fortnight even to open a letter for himself. Yet he never abandoned his post. Daily [illegible] with the physicians in attendance at W[illegible] perhaps with unnecessary precaution, [illegible] of additional advice, daily communicati[illegible] views with those charged with the duties of [illegible] or of preparation for war, showed that [illegible] not daunted by the pain and prostration [illegible] He felt the death of the Prince Consort [illegible] and looked upon it as an irreparable loss [illegible] dispute with America, he regarded the despatch [illegible] Guards and other troops to Canada before [illegible] of a reply to our demand for a surrender of the [illegible] as the best means of averting war, and so it [illegible] Although by certain organs of the peace party [illegible] denounced as an irritating measure, it was [illegible] thing, but the one way of showing, without [illegible] the United States Cabinet, that England was in [illegible] It was only by extraordinary exertions that the [illegible] ships were enabled to reach the St. Lawrence before [illegible] river navigation was closed by ice.

During these years there was constant friction [illegible] work between the two wings of the Liberal party [illegible] the national expenditure; both parties [illegible] agreeing as to the ends to be attained, but di[illegible] to the necessary means. In 1862 Mr. St[illegible] spokesman of the one section, moved a resolution [illegible] House that the national expenditure was cap[illegible] duction without compromising the safety [illegible] mate influence of the country. Lord Palm[illegible] this by a counter-resolution, by which [illegible] acknowledging the obligations of economy, [illegible] bind themselves to any declaration beyond [illegible] such further reductions might be made [illegible] state of things might warrant. The [illegible] letters refer to this question of outlay [illegible] and navy, and to his disinclination to [illegible] and chances when the position of E[illegible] cerned :—

94 Piccadilly: January 8, 1862.

My dear Mr. Cobden,—I have many apologies to make to you [illegible] having sooner acknowledged the memorandum which you [illegible] me some time ago suggesting an understanding and agree[illegible] between the Governments of England and France about [illegible]umber of ships of war which each of the two countries [illegible] maintain. It would be very delightful if your Utopia [illegible] be realised, and if the nations of the earth would think [illegible] but peace and commerce, and would give up quarrel[illegible] fighting altogether. But unfortunately man is a fight[illegible] quarrelling animal; and that this is human nature is [illegible] by the fact that republics, where the masses govern, [illegible] more quarrelsome, and more addicted to fighting, than [illegible], which are governed by comparatively few persons. [illegible] long as other nations are animated by these human pas[illegible] a country like England, wealthy and exposed to attack, [illegible] by necessity be provided with the means of defence, and [illegible] expensive these means may be, they are infinitely [illegible] than the war which they tend to keep off.

94 Piccadilly: April 29, 1862.

My dear Gladstone,—I read with much interest, as I came [illegible] by the railway, your able and eloquent speeches at [illegible]; but I wish to submit to you some observations [illegible] financial part of the second speech. You seem in that [illegible] make it a reproach to the nation at large that it has [illegible] you say it has, on the Parliament and the Govern[illegible] high amount of expenditure which we have at present [illegible] for. Now I do not quite agree with you as to the [illegible] admitting it to be as you state, it seems to me to be [illegible] a proof of the superior sagacity of the nation than a [illegible] reproach.

[illegible] main sources of increased expenditure have been army, [illegible] education. As to education, the increase has arisen [illegible] working of a self-acting system. We may not have [illegible] value of our money, but we have derived great [illegible] from the outlay.

[illegible] to the augmentation of our military and naval [illegible], I cannot give to the nation, contradistinguished [illegible] and Government, the exclusive merit of hav[illegible] them. It appears to me that the merit, as I call [illegible] be shared by the nation, Parliament, and Go[illegible] Governments have taken the lead by proposing to Parliaments such estimates as, [illegible] responsibility, they thought needful for [illegible] successive Parliaments have sanctioned [illegible] nation has ratified those acts by their approval. [illegible] fore, a mistake to say that this scale of [illegible] forced upon Parliament or upon the Gov[illegible] still greater mistake to accuse the nation, as Cob[illegible] having rushed headlong into extravagance [illegible] of panic. Panic there has been none on the [illegible] There was for a long time an apathetic blind[illegible] the governed and the governors as to the [illegible] the country compared with the offensive [illegible] acquiring by other Powers. The country at last [illegible] its lethargy, not indeed to rush into extravagance [illegible] for exertions, but to make up gradually for [illegible] and so far, no doubt, to throw upon a shorter [illegible] expenses which earlier foresight might have spread [illegible] length of time. The Government, the Parlia[illegible] nation acted in harmonious concert; and if any[illegible] wanting that the nation has been inspired by a [illegible] sagacious appreciation of its position with [illegible] Powers, that proof has been afforded by the [illegible] well-sustained sacrifices of time and money [illegible] made by the 160,000 Volunteers, and by those [illegible] tributed to supply them with requisite funds.

But have the Government, or rather have both [illegible] Conservative Governments, have the Parliament[illegible] been wrong, and have Bright and Cobden been [illegible] ture to think that the Government, the Parlia[illegible] nation have taken the juster view of what the [illegible] required.

We have on the other side of the Channel a [illegible] what they may, hate us as a nation from the [illegible] hearts, and would make any sacrifice to inflict [illegible] tion upon England.

It is natural that this should be. They are [illegible] and their passion is glory in war. They cannot [illegible] Aboukir, Trafalgar, the Peninsula, Waterloo, [illegible]

Increased commercial intercourse may [illegible] mutual interest between us and them; [illegible] is a link that snaps under the pressure [illegible] Witness the bitter enmity to England [illegible] now with difficulty suppressed, by [illegible]

[illegible] have had a most extensive commercial [illegible], at the head of this neighbouring [illegible] nothing so well as a retaliatory blow [illegible] an able, active, wary, counsel-keeping [illegible] sovereign; and we see this sovereign organis[illegible] including his reserve, is more than six times [illegible] than the whole of our regular forces in our [illegible] the same time labouring hard to create a [illegible] superior to ours. Give him a cause of [illegible] foreign Power may at any time invent or [illegible], give him the command of the Channel, which [illegible] accidental naval superiority might afford him, and [illegible] if you can—for it would pass my reckoning power [illegible] disastrous consequences to the British nation [illegible] of an army of from one to two hundred thou[illegible] would bring with it. Surely even a large yearly [illegible] for army and navy is an economical insurance [illegible] a catastrophe.

[illegible] argument that, ample financial means being [illegible] for national defence, we should devote our [illegible] attention during peace to the husbanding of [illegible], he used to reply, that if a war should [illegible] come, as it might have come, with France [illegible] Tahiti, or with America about the 'Trent,' the [illegible] ships, troops, guns, and dockyard defences [illegible] ill made up for by the fact that some hundreds [illegible] and manufacturers had made large for[illegible] for that this 'would only be offering to the [illegible] a well-fatted calf instead of a well-armed bull's [illegible] When it was urged that our measures of prepa[illegible] made the French angry, he answered that it was [illegible] because these preparations rendered us secure [illegible] the effects of French anger. 'The anger of a [illegible] no stronger than ourselves may be borne, with [illegible] no doubt, but without alarm. The anger of a [illegible] greatly and decidedly stronger must cause ap[illegible], and is likely to lead to humiliation or [illegible].'

[illegible] was also very watchful at this time for the se[illegible] of our Canadian frontier, in presence of the strife

in the United States, and insisted on
regular force in Canada, in order, by
the United States Government in
and confidence to our own people in the
to take the best chance for the continu

Towards the end of the session Mr.
vigorous attack upon Lord Palmerston and
of affairs. The Prime Minister was accused
false to the professions of Reform which
alleged, been freely made, if not by himself
by many of his followers, when Radical
wanted to oust the Tories. He was charged
his retention of power to the support of his
adversaries, who had more confidence in him
their own leader. Mr. Cobden asserted that,
fortifications, ironclads, wars in China, and
ments sent in haste in every direction,
Canada, during the 'Trent' affair, or elsewhere
Palmerston had cost the country one hundred
which, he maintained, was too heavy a price
such a bargain. Lord Palmerston replied with
confidence and imperturbable good humour.
the charge of lukewarmness about Reform as
which the country, and not he, was responsible
acknowledging the other points, he sarcastically
Mr. Cobden most warmly for having drawn
to the successful efforts which the Government
made for the preservation of the honour,
and the interests of the empire. The very
Mr. Cobden urged as calling for censure he
those which deserved the chief approbation
House, which, nothing loath, testified their
this view. Both sides of the British House
mons are always ready to support a Minister
travagance, even if it deserve that name
belief honestly intended for the maintenance
national interests, and not merely for
the interests of a class or a party. . . .

¹ To Duke of Newcastle: September

[illegible] which Lord Palmerston ad[illegible] his two premierships was so large, [illegible] on which he declared himself to act, [illegible], he consistently did act, is worth [illegible] words. I can certainly of my own [illegible], that the one way in which a clergy[illegible] certain that he would not get pre[illegible] commence his letter of application by a [illegible] his political opinions, thus making them [illegible] claim. Lord Palmerston writes to Lord [illegible] Lord-Lieutenant of Ireland:—[1]

[illegible] never considered ecclesiastical appointments as [illegible] be given away for grace and favour, and for per[illegible] political objects. The choice to be made of persons to [illegible] in the Church must have a great influence on many [illegible] matters; and I have always endeavoured, in making [illegible], to choose the best man I could find, without [illegible] to the wishes of those who may have recommended [illegible] choice.

[illegible] this chapter with a short but suggestive [illegible] Slavery and the Board of Admiralty:—

August 13, 1862.

[illegible] Russell,—No First Lord and no Board of Admi[illegible] ever felt any interest in the suppression of the slave [illegible] taken of their own free will any steps towards its [illegible], and whatever they have done in compliance [illegible] wishes of others they have done grudgingly and [illegible]. If there was a particularly old slow-going tub in [illegible] she was sure to be sent to the coast of Africa to try [illegible] fast-sailing American clippers; and if there was [illegible] notoriously addicted to drinking, he was sent to a [illegible] rum is a deadly poison.

[illegible] go on better now; but still there is at the Admiralty [illegible] aversion to the measures necessary for putting [illegible] slave trade. These prejudices are so strong with the [illegible] of the Board, that the First Lord can hardly be [illegible] to be swayed by them.

[1] Walmer Castle: August 17, 1862.

For nothing will Lord Palmerston be more honourably remembered than for his long and successful efforts for the suppression of the slave trade and the discouragement of slavery. From the moment that he was called to the Foreign Office in 1830, he entered warmly into the subject, and with his whole heart laboured for their extinction. He sought to engage all maritime states in one great network of treaties for the combined annihilation of this nefarious traffic in human beings, and to a large extent he succeeded. Some of the Spanish and other diplomatists used to be quite surprised at what they thought his craze, and were fain to humour him on, what they considered, so insignificant a matter. When action succeeded to negotiation—as, for instance, in the decisive blow dealt in 1840 at the Portuguese slave-dealers by the destruction of their barracoons on the West Coast of Africa—he never allowed any consideration for the susceptibilities or anger of foreign Governments to induce him to halt in his course. On the contrary, when the country, sick with deferred hopes and aghast at the expense of the necessary squadrons, seemed at one moment disposed to flinch, his earnest language, conveying lofty aspirations, maintained its spirit and strengthened it for renewed efforts.

CHAPTER XVII.

[illegible]POLAND—VISIT TO SCOTLAND—PROPOSED CONGRESS—[illegible] AND SLESWIG-HOLSTEIN—LONDON CONFERENCE—[illegible] DEBATE—VISIT TO NORTHAMPTONSHIRE—CRIMINAL [illegible]—CUBAN SLAVERY—IRISH CATHOLICS—CONVOCATION—[illegible] AND DEATH.

[illegible]mier, Lord Palmerston kept a watchful eye over [illegible] proceedings of all the departments of his Govern[illegible] and was an unwearied attendant on the sittings [illegible] House of Commons, ready at any moment to [illegible] a difficulty or avert a storm. But he was very [illegible] of speech; and when there was nothing particu[illegible] to say he did not attempt to say it. The session [illegible] was entirely deficient of any subject of debate, [illegible] or foreign, which could call for any lengthened [illegible]position on his part, with the exception of the question of Poland; and while this was being discussed [illegible] was kept away by an attack of his old enemy the [illegible].

The immediate cause of the Polish outbreak was a [illegible] by the Russian Government of all the young [illegible] in the cities whom they had reason to believe were [illegible]affected, and their enrolment in the ranks of the [illegible] under the name of a conscription, or 'partial re[illegible]ting.' In fact, to use the words of our ambassador [illegible] Petersburg, it was 'a simple plan, by a clean sweep [illegible] the revolutionary youth of Poland, to kidnap the op[illegible]sition and to carry it off to Siberia or the Caucasus.' [illegible] wonder that this produced resistance. Those who [illegible] took to the woods and organized themselves in [illegible] bands.

Lord Palmerston writes to 'condole' with the [illegible] sian ambassador :—

[illegible]

Mon cher Brunnow,—Je regrette beaucoup les [illegible] tions qui ont éclaté en Pologne et en plusieurs des [illegible] la Russie, parce que ces mouvements produiront de [illegible] heurs dans le pays, et parce que beaucoup d'hommes [illegible] vraient se rendre utiles à leur patrie payeront de [illegible] par l'exil, la révolte dont ils ont été coupables.

Mais, quant au Gouvernement russe, je considère [illegible] rections comme une juste punition du Ciel, pour [illegible] dont ce Gouvernement a été coupable, pour [illegible] printemps des révoltes et des insurrections dans [illegible] chie, en Servie et en Bosnie, contre le Sultan.

. . . . . . Non lex est justior ulla,
Quam necis artifices arte perire sua.

Il est vrai que ces insurrections, ou éclatées, ou [illegible] ne menacent de mort ni l'Empire russe ni l'Empire [illegible] la Russie saura mettre ordre dans les provinces [illegible] saura apprendre à Couza, au Prince de Servie et [illegible] qu'il est mieux de rester fidèle à son Souverain que [illegible] conseils subversifs d'un voisin ambitieux.

Mais, pour le moment, la Russie souffre dans son [illegible] mal qu'elle a l'intention d'infliger à un voisin [illegible] concevez bien que je parle maintenant des cent mille [illegible] fusils que le Gouvernement russe a envoyés en [illegible] Bosnie par des chemins détournés, et avec toutes les [illegible] pour cacher, autant que possible, ce que l'on [illegible] allusion aussi à cette nuée d'agents provocateurs [illegible] la Russie, abondent et travaillent dans les [illegible] péennes de la Turquie. Si le Prince Gort[illegible] autant à moi comme vous l'êtes, je me [illegible] lieu de vous écrire, mais j'aimerais beaucoup qu'il [illegible] sion que sa politique a faite sur nous.

[illegible]

General disgust had been excited [illegible] by the Prussian Government having [illegible] vention with Russia whereby the [illegible] authorised to cross the frontier, and [illegible] [illegible] into the territory of [illegible] [illegible] from a letter to the King [illegible]

[illegible] much Lord Palmerston disapproved of [illegible] assistance being given by Prussia to one of [illegible] contending parties, he was not going in conse[illegible] allow England to become the cat's-paw of an [illegible] neighbour:—[1]

> [illegible] Majesty will have learnt that we declined to fall into [illegible] which the Emperor of the French laid for us by his [illegible] for a violent identical note to be presented to the [illegible] of Prussia.
>
> [illegible] was evidently intended that the demands of such a note [illegible] refused, or evaded, a pretence would thereby have been [illegible] to France for an occupation of the Prussian Rhenish [illegible], and the French Government have shown much ill-[illegible] at the failure of that scheme. But the danger to [illegible] and to other States is not over. If the Polish Revolu[illegible] goes on, and Prussia is led to take an active part in any [illegible] against the Poles, the Emperor of the French is sure, [illegible] or later, and upon some pretext or other, to enter the [illegible] provinces as a means of coercing Prussia to be neutral. [illegible] Majesty would render an essential service to Prussia and [illegible] Europe if you could exert your influence with the King of [illegible] to abstain from any action of any kind whatever beyond [illegible] frontiers of his own territory.

During the ensuing months the British and Russian [illegible] Governments were engaged in a long correspondence. [illegible] Russell proposed a suspension of arms, and a con[illegible] of the eight Powers to settle the affairs of [illegible], on the basis of national representation, liberty [illegible] conscience, establishment of a legal system of re[illegible], and Polish administration of the country. The [illegible] communications which were exchanged were couched [illegible] friendly, though very frank terms, but they yielded [illegible] visible fruit, Russia declining to accede to the Eng[illegible] proposals. At one moment England, France, and [illegible] contemplated combining together in order to [illegible] a semi-detached state in Poland, but as Austria [illegible] drew back the project fell to the ground. The [illegible], however, which the reports of Russian misdeeds [illegible] Poland, whether exaggerated or not, had excited in

[1] To the King of the Belgians: March 13, 1863.

the public mind, compelled the organ of the Bri Government to put on record such observationsha considered himself entitled to make, England ha been a party to the Treaty of Vienna whereby Po was secured to Russia.

In the spring of this year Lord Palmerston wa Scotland to deliver an address on being install Lord Rector of the University of Glasgow. He visited Edinburgh, where he received the freedo the city and an honorary degree at the University, was received everywhere with marked enthusiasm. went down the Clyde in a small steamer to Gree both banks of the river were lined with thousand workmen, who had left their work to catch a gli of the Premier on the paddlebox, and to cheer hi he passed. The captain of the guard-ship, anxio do honour to the occasion, was hindered by the that a Prime Minister was not recognised in the naval salutes; but he found an escape from his ma in the discovery that Lord Palmerston was First Lord of the Treasury, but also Lord Warden Cinque Ports, for which great officer a salute of guns was prescribed—an apt instance of the anomalies of the Constitution under which we

Before the end of the Glasgow visit an incid curred which illustrates the fun and simpli characterised Lord Palmerston to the end of A number of gentlemen had confederated together under the title of the 'Gaiter' Cl power to add to their number. This club ha habitation, but only a name. Its objects, mild pedestrianism, were left undefined, but all that could be comprised under the my far-reaching head of 'gaiterdom.' This bo to entertain at a breakfast one of their return from China, namely, that disting Admiral Sir James Hope, and they deter by the opportunity to invite Lord Pal a 'Gaiter.' He entered with bec

At Edinburgh Lord Palmerston [illegible] of Arthur's Seat, and wrote to his [illegible] he really felt very little more difficulty [illegible] when he used to mount it daily sixty years [illegible] past was also recalled to him by a visit [illegible] to an old woman named Peggie Forbes, [illegible] servant at Dugald Stewart's when he [illegible] there in 1801. She produced an old box of [illegible] she had preserved all these years because it [illegible] the property of 'young Maister Henry.'

The French Emperor now sent letters to the [illegible] sovereigns of Europe, proposing the assembling [illegible] Congress, and suggesting Paris as the place of [illegible] ing. 'It is on the Treaty of Vienna,' he said, '[illegible] reposes the political edifice of Europe, and yet [illegible] crumbling away on all sides.' The British Gov[illegible] declined the invitation. Some of Lord Palm[illegible] remarks upon it are contained in the following le[illegible]

94 Piccadilly : November 1[illegible]

Sire,—The subject to which Your Majesty's letter [illegible] one of very great importance and deserving of mature [illegible] ration. Our answer to the Emperor's proposal has [illegible] substance, that we do not admit that the Treaties of V[illegible] have ceased to be in force, inasmuch as, on the contrary [illegible] are still the basis of the existing arrangements of [illegible] that, with regard to the proposed Congress, before we [illegible] to any decision about it, we should like to know wh[illegible] it is to discuss, and what power it is to possess to giv[illegible] its decisions.

My own impression is that the Congress will [illegible] and that the Emperor has no expectation that it sho[illegible]

The truth is that the assembling of a Congress [illegible] measure applicable to the present state of Europe.

In 1815 a Congress was a necessity. France [illegible] all Europe, had overthrown almost all the former [illegible] arrangements, and had established a new order of [illegible] came the returning tide of the Allied Armies [illegible] everything which France had created, and est[illegible] moment, military occupation of the greater part [illegible]

[1] To the King of the Belgi[illegible]

[illegible] necessary to determine to whom, and in what [illegible] on what conditions, the vast regions reconquered [illegible] should be thenceforward possessed. The Powers [illegible] had made this reconquest were the natural and [illegible] only arbiters; and they had, by their armies, the [illegible] carrying their decisions into effect.

[illegible] of the kind exists in the present state of Europe. [illegible] no doubts as to who is the owner of any piece of [illegible], and there are not even any boundary questions in [illegible].

The functions of a Congress, if now to be assembled, might [illegible], and would bear either on the past or on the future, [illegible] both. Drouyn says that the Congress might take up the [illegible] of 1815, go through them article by article, strike out [illegible] has been repealed or set aside, and re-enact the [illegible] as the Treaty of 1863–64, the name of which would [illegible] disagreeable to France than that of the Treaty of 1815, [illegible] brings to mind Waterloo and St. Helena. This may be [illegible] feeling for France; but it is no good reason why all the rest of Europe should meet round a table to please the French nation; and those who hold their estates under a good [illegible], now nearly half a century old, might not be particularly [illegible] of having it brought under discussion with all the alte[illegible] which good-natured neighbours might wish to suggest [illegible] their boundaries.

No doubt there have been some not unimportant changes made in the territorial arrangements of Europe established by the Treaty of 1815; but some of these were made regularly by treaty at the time, and the others, not so made, some of the Parties to the Congress might not like to sanction by treaty acknowledgment.

Chief among the first class is the separation of Belgium from Holland; but that was solemnly sanctioned by negotiations the length of which I cannot easily forget, and by a treaty between the five Powers and Holland and the German Diet. That transaction requires no confirmation. Chief among the second class was the absorption of Cracow by Austria without any treaty sanction; and to that transaction the British Government, which protested against it at the time, would not be greatly desirous of giving retrospective sanction by treaty now. Then come the cession of Lombardy to Italy, and of Savoy and Nice to France. These were legally made by the rightful owners of the ceded territory, and no confirmation can be required. There was indeed, in [illegible] omission to attach to the territory [illegible] condition of neutrality as to Chablais and [illegible] which the King of Sardinia held Savoy; [illegible] whether France would consent to [illegible] and its real value, either for Switzerland or [illegible] all, be trifling. Then comes the absorption [illegible] of Italy of Tuscany, Parma, Modena, [illegible] Sicily. These were all violations of the Treaty [illegible] done without treaty sanction; but they were [illegible] people of those countries. Those transactions [illegible] virtually sanctioned by all the Powers who have a[illegible] the King of Italy; and if Victor Emmanuel is wi[illegible] be content with leaving those matters as they a[illegible] especially because if a new European treaty wer[illegible] the kingdom of Italy as it now is, that treaty would[illegible] renunciation by the King of Italy to any claim to [illegible] Rome. On the other hand, Austria and the Pope [illegible] be prepared to give their formal sanction to the[illegible] made by the Italian kingdom.

As to the past, therefore, the functions of [illegible] would either be unnecessary or barred by ins[illegible] difficulties.

But then as to the future? Would the Cong[illegible] range over the wide and almost endless extent of [illegible] possible changes, or would it have to confine itself [illegible] now practically pending? There are but two su[illegible] the one relating to Poland, the other to the differ[illegible] the German Confederation and Denmark about [illegible] Lauenburg and about Sleswig. As to Poland, wou[illegible] more likely to yield in a Congress than she has s[illegible] to be in a negotiation? I much doubt it. A[illegible] question between Germany and Denmark, a small[illegible] than a European Congress might surely be suffic[illegible] that question.

But if the Congress were to enter upon th[illegible] proposed and possible changes of territory, wha[illegible] animosities would ensue! Russia would ask to [illegible] lost by the Treaty of Paris; Italy would ask [illegible] Rome; France would plead geography for the [illegible] Rhine; Austria would show how advantage[illegible] Turkey to transfer to Austria Bosnia [illegible] Greece would have a word to say about [illegible]

... how England could think of retaining ... would say that Sleswig is geographically ... and that, as Jutland is an integral part of ... ought Sleswig to be so too; Sweden would claim ... some of the greater German states would strongly ... expediency of mediatising a score of the smaller ...

... members of the Congress should be unanimous in ... any of these proposals, of course there would be no ... for carrying a unanimous decision into effect; but if a ... were one way, and a minority, however small, the ... that minority including the party by which a con... was to be made, is it intended that force should be used, ... Congress to remain powerless to execute its own ...

... the face of all these difficulties, my humble opinion is ... Congress will meet; and I shall be glad to think that ... Emperor will have mended his position at home by making ... proposal, while its failure will have saved Europe from ... danger and much embarrassment.

... Lady Palmerston desires me to tender to your Majesty her ... thanks for your condescending message; and we both ... greatly delighted at the prospect which your Majesty's ... holds out to us of the possibility of having, in the course ... the winter, the honour of receiving your Majesty at Broad-...

And a fortnight later he writes to Lord Russell:—[1]

The state of Europe in 1815 was wholly different from ... it is now. At that time the success of French arms had ... swept away most of the territorial boundaries and separate ... sovereignties which existed before 1792. The tide of conquest ... which at first ran from west to east, then returned back from east ... to west, and swept away almost all that France had established. ... Europe was a political waste, and required the action of a ... body of inclosure commissioners to allot the lands, and to give ... binding titles. This was done at Vienna in 1814 and 1815. ... But nothing of the kind exists in 1863, and nobody wants an ... improved title to any possession except those who ought not to ... have it; as, for instance, Russia to the kingdom of Poland, ... Austria to Cracow, France to Savoy without neutrality, and ... the Pope to what he holds and as much as he could get back.

[1] December 2, 1863.

It is quite certain that the deliberations of a Cong consist of demands and pretensions put forward by resolutely resisted by others, and that, there being authority in such an assembly to enforce the decisions of the majority, the Congress would separa many of the members on worse terms with each o when they met.

I think it seems pretty clear that, among othe which the Emperor had for the Congress, there was that there should be given to the Pope a European for his unmolested possession of the territory now he by the French troops, which then might have been w France and all the Catholic Powers would willingly l in such an arrangement, and Russia might have don complaisance to France. Italy would have been en but might have been overruled. We should have b in a disagreeable dilemma, having either to refuse a openly a position hostile to the Pope and distaste Catholic fellow-subjects, or to give our formal an guarantee to the permanence of the temporal power o against which we have not hesitated to declare our o

This, however, was probably only one of the traps l poleon for the silly birds he was trying to lure into h

Several of the other great Powers also decli Congress, the project fell through.

An account of the intricate proceedings c with the Sleswig-Holstein question cannot con either the scope or the space of this book; but which Lord Palmerston's Government took in th must be briefly narrated.

The real dispute between Denmark and dated from the year 1848, when an insurr party in the former declared their grieva appealed to Germany for aid in establishing of Holstein and Sleswig with a constitution ence separate from the rest of the monarch many assisted the insurrection, and at the Berlin in 1850, although nothing was was understood that the Danish Monarchy reconstructed with a view to satisfying

Holsteiners. Negotiations followed, which, as Sleswig was concerned, were of an international character, and not merely between Denmark and the Germanic Diet. It was on the interpretation and fulfilment of the engagements contracted by Denmark that the result of these negotiations that the dispute with Germany turned, which, while at its height, assumed a new and more complicated aspect by the sudden death of the King of Denmark. In conformity with the Treaty of London, 1852, Prince Christian ascended the Danish throne, including that of the Duchies, as King Christian IX.; but the Duke of Augustenburg, though his father had renounced for himself and his family, insisted on being recognised as Duke of Sleswig-Holstein. Some of the smaller German states, in spite of the treaty to which many of them had acceded, were disposed to go with him on the ground that the treaty of 1852 was not binding unless the other engagements alleged to have been entered into by the Crown of Denmark at an antecedent time and upon another subject were also fulfilled. To state such a proposition was to refute it; and the British Government had common sense and common justice on their side when they urged that every consideration of honour and good faith demanded the acknowledgment of King Christian as King Duke of all the territories which were under the sway of his predecessor, and that there would then be a responsible sovereign from whom might be claimed the fulfilment of any and every engagement taken by the late King and not made good. The German Diet, however, decreed a federal execution in Holstein—that is to say, an administration of the Government by commissioners—and, though this was nominally done only in the interests of the Holsteiners, it was undisguised intervention in behalf of the Duke of Augustenburg, who made his appearance at Kiel, and was greeted as the rightful Duke. The close of the year saw the Danish and German troops confronting one another on opposite banks of the Eider.

Austria and Prussia were at [illegible] abide by the Treaty of London; [illegible] Diet acting upon their mutual [illegible] of each lest it should jeopardise [illegible] combined to drive them along the [illegible] The first to suffer was the Diet [illegible] was taken out of their control, and a [illegible] and Prussian force advanced [illegible] Sleswig. On February 2 the [illegible] Dannewerke, on which so much [illegible] placed, and fell back upon Düppel. [illegible] might have been expected, there had [illegible] England a strong feeling of indignation [illegible] offered to little Denmark by the two [illegible] powers. It was suggested that France and [illegible] should offer their mediation on the basis of [illegible] of the Danish monarchy and the [illegible] and that, if such mediation were refused by [illegible] Prussia, England should despatch a [illegible] hagen, and France a corps d'armée to the [illegible] frontier of Prussia. The following letter [illegible] Lord Palmerston said about this proposal:—

94 Piccadilly: February [illegible]

My dear Russell,—I share fully your [illegible] conduct of Austria and Prussia is discreditably [illegible] both of them will suffer for it before these [illegible] I rather doubt, however, the expediency of taking [illegible] moment the steps proposed. The French [illegible] probably decline it, unless tempted by the [illegible] should place an armed force on the [illegible] event of a refusal by Austria and [illegible] ought to reckon upon as nearly certain.

The objections which might be urged [illegible] suggested as the consequences of the [illegible] Prussia may be stated to be: First, that we [illegible] weeks to come send a squadron to the [illegible] step would not have much effect upon [illegible] were understood to be a first step [illegible] and I doubt whether the Cabinet [illegible] prepared for active interference. [illegible]

[illegible] with all Germany on continental ground [illegible] undertaking. If Sweden and Denmark were [illegible] with us, our 20,000 men might do a good [illegible] and Prussia could bring 200,000 or 300,000 [illegible] and would be joined by the smaller German [illegible]

[illegible] though it is very useful to remind the Austrians [illegible] privately of the danger they are running at [illegible] in Italy, Hungary and Galicia; Prussia in her [illegible] provinces—yet it might not be advisable nor for our [illegible] to suggest to France an attack upon the Prussian [illegible] territory. It would serve Prussia right if such an [illegible] made; and if Prussia remains in the wrong we [illegible] take part with her against France. But the conquest [illegible] territory by France would be an evil for us, and would [illegible] affect the position of Holland and Belgium. On the [illegible] I should say that it would be best for us to wait awhile [illegible] taking any strong step in these matters.

[illegible] English Government was, in fact, not only [illegible], but fettered by the refusal of Russia and [illegible] to join heartily with her. Russia acted, it may [illegible] supposed, from the same motives which have hitherto [illegible] kept her from breaking with Prussia; France [illegible], no doubt, from pique at our refusal the previous [illegible] to agree to her Congress. It might, of course, [illegible] been very different could England have consented [illegible] French conquest on the Rhine as the price to be paid [illegible] French assistance.

Lord Palmerston, however, was anxious to do all [illegible] could for Denmark within the bounds of what was [illegible] statesmanlike and possible. He wrote to the First [illegible] of the Admiralty:—[1]

I own I quite agree with Russell, that our squadron ought [illegible] to Copenhagen as soon as the season will permit, and that [illegible] ought to have orders to prevent any invasion of, or attack [illegible] Zealand and Copenhagen. It is not unlikely that Austria [illegible] Prussia, reckoning upon our passive attitude, contemplate [illegible] occupation of Copenhagen, and think to imitate what the [illegible] Napoleon did at Vienna and Berlin, and mean to dictate

[1] To the Duke of Somerset: February 20, 1864.

at the Danish capital their own terms of peace,
laughed at if we stood by and allowed

The Prussians took Düppel in April,
a solitary gleam of sunshine for the
monotonous gloom of their reverses, and
naval success against the Austrians off
two following letters tell Lord Palmerston's
action in case of the Austrian Government
to reinforce their fleet in the Baltic:—

94 Piccadilly: May 1, 1

My dear Russell,—I felt so little satisfied with the d
of the Cabinet on Saturday, that I determined to make a
off my own hat, and accordingly I wrote this morni
Apponyi, asking him to come here and give me half an
conversation. He came accordingly. I said I wished t
some friendly and unreserved conversation with him,
between an English minister and the Austrian ambassad
as between Palmerston and Apponyi; that what I
to say related to serious matters; but I begged that
might say should be looked upon as a threat, but only
explanation between friends on matters which
disagreements, and with regard to which, unless timely
tion were given as to possible consequences of
a reproach might afterwards be made that timely
might have averted disagreeable results. I said that
from the beginning taken a deep interest in favour of
—not from family ties, which have little influence
policy, and sometimes act unfavourably—but, first,
have thought from the beginning that Denmark
harshly and unjustly treated; and, secondly, we
integrity and independence of the State which
entrance to the Baltic objects of interest to England.
abstained from taking the field in defence of Denmark
reasons—from the season of the year; from the
our army, and the great risk of failure in a
Germany by land. That with regard to operations

[illegible] the Baltic to help in any way the German operations [illegible] Denmark, I should look upon it as an affront and insult [illegible] England. That I could not, and would not stand such a [illegible]; and that, unless in such case a superior British squadron [illegible] to follow, with such orders for acting as the case might [illegible], I would not continue to hold my present position; and [illegible] case would probably lead to collision—that is, war; and [illegible] opinion Germany, and especially Austria, would be the [illegible] in such a war. I should deeply regret such a result, [illegible] it is the wish of England to be well with Austria; but [illegible] confident that I should be borne out by public opinion. I [illegible] begged that he would not consider this communication as [illegible], but simply as a friendly reminder of consequences [illegible] might follow a possible course of action.

[illegible] Apponyi, having listened with great attention to what I [illegible] replied that the considerations which I had pointed out [illegible] not new to his mind; that they had been forcibly dwelt [illegible], among other persons, by the King of the Belgians. [illegible] he was quite aware that, if the Austrian ships entered [illegible] Baltic, an English squadron would follow them; that in all [illegible] one of two things would happen—either that the [illegible] squadron would be destroyed, or that it would be [illegible] by orders from the English admiral to leave the [illegible]. Thus they would run the risk of a catastrophe or a [illegible], and they did not wish for either. That, therefore, [illegible] may have been said by Rechberg in his note, we [illegible] sure that the Austrian squadron will not enter the [illegible]. This is satisfactory, as far as Apponyi may be con[illegible] the organ of the Austrian Government; but I think [illegible] to have something more positive in writing than we [illegible]

[illegible] state to the Cabinet to-morrow the substance of my [illegible] with Apponyi.

[illegible] same time he wrote to the First Lord of the [illegible]:—

May 4, 1864.

[illegible] Somerset,—It seems to me that we ought to insist [illegible] ships of war shall at any time, or under any [illegible] during the war, enter the Baltic. We have never [illegible] neutral in this war: we have declined, for [illegible], to take a part in it; but we have done our [illegible] by diplomatic interference.

The reasons which opposed military interference on our part do not apply to naval aid; and, so far as forbidding the Austrians to enter the Baltic at any time during the war, we are rendering valuable aid to the Danes, without any great effort to ourselves.

I should be much disposed to allow the Danes to have their ironclad. I am satisfied that a manifestation of good-will on our part towards the Danes must contribute much to make the Germans more reasonable in negotiation. They have been encouraged hitherto by a belief that nothing would induce us to interfere; and this belief has been much strengthened, unfortunately, by letters and language received in England.

In the meantime the British Government were making active exertions, by a conference of the Great Powers, to put a stop to the further prosecution of the war; and after much trouble they persuaded the belligerents to come into such a conference to be held in London. It met on April 25, and, after proclaiming an armistice, proceeded to business. But no agreement could be arrived at as to the future frontier between Denmark and the Duchies. The victorious Germans were exacting; the desperate Danes were obstinate; and after sitting for two months the conference broke up without any result of their labours. On June 24 an informal application was made by our Government to the French Emperor, again seeking for his active alliance to defend Denmark. Louis Napoleon unhesitatingly declined giving any such assistance. He was not inclined to incur the cost and risk of a war with Austria and Germany, without the prospect of compensation on the banks of the Rhine. He showed at the same time the strongest desire that England should undertake the task, promising any amount of 'moral' support. It is clear that he had hopes that, should such a war spread, and naval operations begin in the Adriatic, it would turn to his advantage in his cherished object of procuring the freedom of Venetia. He urged upon the British Government that, England having no frontiers to be concerned about, it was for her to stand forward as the champion of the Danes. But with no [illegible] save Sweden the Cabinet did not think this country bound to enter the lists, when the independent existence of the Danish monarchy was not at stake, but only its rights and dominion over the provinces in dispute. The peremptory refusal of France caused the abandonment of the plans which England had conceived, and no renewed proposal for active assistance was made to Russia. Had Great Britain, in alliance with France and Russia, succeeded in arresting the proceedings of the German Powers, there can be but little doubt that she would have made radical reforms by Denmark in her administration of the subject provinces a *sine quâ non*. If, however, she had single-handed defended Denmark by arms she would have been looked upon as the upholder of Danish policy towards the Duchies in its entirety—a policy which was at total variance with the principles by which she had been hitherto guided; for though the accounts of Danish oppression might have been exaggerated, there was no doubt that the Duchies had good cause for complaint. Hostilities were quickly renewed, and Denmark was compelled to sign a peace at Vienna, by which she finally surrendered to Germany the Duchies of Sleswig, Holstein, and Lauenburg.

Parliament now intervened to call Ministers to account for their conduct of these affairs. During the whole of the session there had been frequent interpellations and fragmentary debates upon this Dano-German question; but in the beginning of July a simultaneous attack was made in both Houses upon the policy of the Government. In the House of Lords the resolution moved by Lord Malmesbury was carried by a majority of nine, and in the House of Commons Mr. Disraeli proposed a similar resolution. He asked the House to join with him in expressing the opinion that the course pursued by Her Majesty's Government had 'lowered the just influence of this country in the councils of Europe, and thereby diminished the securities for peace.' This was a distinct vote of censure, and was accepted

the crowd assembled in Pala
last night. As the success
party debate, involving the fa
on this occasion was his last
though he spoke at the end
weary sitting, his old vigour
not deserted him. He had,
There had been a conspicuo
there could be no doubt. A
cumstances had proved adve
failure could not publicly be
with the exception of a dexte
of the resolution as 'a gratuit
by a great party who hoped to
the House long on the points
dropping the Danish matter
into a history of the financial
ment. What has this to do
impatient Tories. But it ha
question, for it decided the vo
caring little about Sleswig-H
about English finance. Anyh
for the Government got a maj
renewed their lease of power.

Germany was still undecided, though with little hope that right could prevail over might. The Danish Government, both under the late and under the present King, undoubtedly committed many mistakes, both of commission and omission, and they showed throughout these affairs, from beginning to end, that inaptitude to deal with great concerns which might, perhaps, have been expected from a nation shut up in a remote corner of Europe, and not mixed up or practised with the general politics of the world. It was, however, an unworthy abuse of power by Austria and Prussia to take advantage of their superior enlightenment and strength to crush an antagonist utterly incapable of successful resistance; and the events of this Danish war do not form a page in German history which any honourable or generous German hereafter will look back upon without a blush. I wish that France and Russia had consented to join with us in giving a different direction to those affairs; and I am convinced that words from three such Powers would have been sufficient without a recourse to blows. One consequence is clear and certain, namely, that if our good friend and neighbour at Paris were to take it into his head to deprive Prussia of her Rhenish provinces, not a finger in England would be stirred, nor a voice raised, nor a man nor a shilling voted to resist such retribution upon the Prussian monarch; and when France and Italy shall be prepared to deliver Venetia from the Austrian yoke, the joy with which the success of such an undertaking will be hailed throughout England will be doubled by the recollection of Holstein, Lauenburg, Sleswig, and Jutland.

He went to the North after the session, visiting Bradford, where he had a very cordial reception, and afterwards proceeding to Hereford, to uncover the statue erected in memory of Sir George Lewis. The enthusiasm with which he was received drew the following from Lord Russell:—[1]

Let me congratulate you on the reception you have met everywhere since the prorogation. It is clear your popularity is a plant of hardy growth and deep roots, as the real embarrassments of the Danish question have not shaken it. I still believe that with a less timid cabinet we might have been able to deter Austria from the Danish war, and shown that it was in our power 'pacis imponere morem.' But the risk was some-

[1] Sept. 8, 1864.

thing, and the course pursued justifiable, though not so justifiable, though not so splendid as one could have wished.

In reply to this note of congratulation from the Foreign Secretary, Lord Palmerston writes as follows :—[1]

Many thanks for what you say about my August
tions; they were not sought for by me, but they were
not simply as regards myself, but as relates to the Government; and I may safely affirm that our general conduct has been approved by the country, and especially the management of our foreign affairs, notwithstanding the run made against us on that point in Parliament. You say that with less timidity around us we might probably have kept Austria quiet in the Danish affair. Perhaps we might; but then we had no equal pull upon Prussia, and she would have rallied all the smaller German Powers round her, and we should equally have failed in saving Denmark.

As to Cabinets, if we had colleagues like those who sat in Pitt's Cabinet, such as Westmoreland and others, or such men as those who were with Peel, like Goulburne and Hardinge, you and I might have our own way on most things; but when, as is now the case, able men fill every department, such men will have opinions, and hold to them; but unfortunately they are often too busy with their own department to follow up foreign questions so as to be fully masters of them, and their conclusions are generally on the timid side of what might be the best.

Before going to Bradford he went with Lady Palmerston to visit her estates in Northamptonshire, and to assist her at Towcester to cut the first sod of a railway from Northampton to Stratford-on-Avon. Of course he was well received; and the county member,[2] in his speech at the banquet, very happily hit off the popular sentiment about the Premier, illustrating as follows the way in which his personal influence buoyed up the Ministry, and the exceptional position which he held with all parties in the state :—

The noble lord and his Ministry seem to be always engaged in the game of chuck-farthing, and it is invariably with 'Heads

[1] To Lord Russell: September 11, 1864.
[2] Mr., now Sir Rainald, Knightley.

I win, tails you lose.' (Cheers and laughter.) Whenever it comes up 'head,' the noble Viscount very properly has all the credit; when it comes up 'tail,' the rest of the ministers get the blame. I do not mean to say that the noble Viscount is guilty of unfair play, but the people, it is evident, are determined to give him all the halfpence, and the rest of the Ministry all the kicks. (Great laughter.)

His own speech on this occasion is an instance of how genially he could touch the veriest commonplace. It was after dinner, and his topic was the advantages of railways. Instead of giving a laboured dissertation on steam and civilisation, he brought home to the country squires, in the following words, what they would gain by a new railroad:—

In former times a gentleman asked his friend in London to come down to him in the country, and the friend came with things to last him a fortnight or three weeks, and he took, perhaps, a week on the journey. Now, if a friend meets another in St. James's Street and says, 'I shall have some good shooting next week; will you come down to me and spend a few days?' the friend says, 'Oh, by all means; I shall be charmed. What is the nearest station to your house?' 'Well,' the friend says, 'I am not very well off at present with regard to railway communication; the nearest station is sixteen miles from my house; but it is a good road: you will get a nice fly, and you will come very well.' Upon which the invited guest says, 'Did you say it was Tuesday you asked me for?' 'Yes,' says the countryman; 'and I think you told me that you were free on that day.' Upon which the other replies, 'I have a very bad memory. Upon my word, I am very sorry, but I have a particular engagement on that day. Some other time I shall be happy to come down to you.' Then he offers himself as a visitor to some other friend, who has a station within one or two miles of his house. (Laughter.)

This autumn Lord Palmerston became eighty years old. Traits of physical vigour at such an advanced period of life are always interesting and generally instructive, as teaching us how best to preserve and enjoy those bodily faculties which we receive at our birth. Lord Palmerston was endowed with an excellent constitution, and was very temperate both in eatin drinking; but he maintained his freshness, both of and body, to a great degree by the exercise of hi He never gave anything up on the score of age. rate, he never owned to that as a reason. He used out partridge-shooting long after his eyesight w dim to take a correct aim, and persevered in his outdoor pursuits. Twice during this year, starti nine o'clock and not getting back till two, he rod from Broadlands to the training stables at Littlet see his horses take a gallop on Winchester racec He rode down in June to Harrow speeches, and himself to trot the distance from Piccadilly to the master's door, nearly twelve miles, within the hou accomplished it. On his eightieth birthday, in Oc he started at half-past eight from Broadlands, his horses by train to Fareham, was met by En officers, and rode along the Portsdown and Hils of forts, getting off his horse and inspecting them, crossing over to Anglesey forts and Gospo not reaching home till six in the evening—an of such combined energy both of mind and cannot in the nature of things be very comm fourscore.

The opening of the session of 1865 found Palmerston still maintaining his ground in dence of the nation. Party spirit was not it was certainly dormant, and there was a quiescence in the opinion that the veteran be trusted with the honour and interests of and that he should be left undisturbed during remainder of his career. The Parliament, Everybody thus was looking to the future the present, and the session—the last which ter was destined to see—was, therefore, Among the minor topics which Lord Pal in discussing was that of the condition of repeated on this occasion his favourite 'tenant's right is landlord's wrong;

only meant the extreme demands of the Irish agrarian party, who claimed for the tenants the right of dealing with the landlord's property, not only without but against his sanction, coupled with the condition that at some future period they might compel the landlord to pay for alterations to the making of which he had protested when being made. Lord Palmerston, however, spoke with great warmth of feeling and affection for the Irish people, lamenting the want of capital in Ireland, the influx of which was prevented, as he maintained, by the sense that there was not the same security for property as elsewhere, and by the alarm and distrust which had been engendered by political and religious feuds.

Lunacy, when pleaded as an excuse for crime, has been frequently handled as a subject for discussion. Lord Palmerston had at any rate distinct notions as to how he should meet it, as is seen in the following extract of a letter to the Home Secretary. The occasion that elicited this letter was the reprieve of Victor Townley, who had murdered Miss Goodwin because she had broken off her engagement with him. Neither the presiding judge nor the Commissioners of Lunacy reported to the Home Office in terms sufficient to justify an exercise of the prerogative of the Crown, but three justices and two medical men obtaining access to the condemned man, sent in a certificate to the effect that he was insane. This certificate had been prepared in conformity with an Act of Parliament, which, when thus put in force, Sir George Grey conceived he had no alternative but to comply with. The convict was accordingly respited. Lord Palmerston, after saying that the statute could never have been intended to act in this way, and that it ought to be altered, went on:—[1]

For my part I never have had but one opinion upon the manner of dealing with murderers said to be insane. It seems to me that if a man is sufficiently in possession of his reasoning

[1] To Sir George Grey.

faculties to be able to take care of himself, and not attempt to kill himself, he is, and ought to be, made for taking away the life of another person.

The object of punishment is not vengeance on the but deterring example to others. Madmen are cunning, and are perfectly able to calculate and can be swayed like other people by the fear themselves resulting from violence committed upon doctrine set up in the Townley case seems to me most to the general interests of society. Here is a man much deliberation, commits a barbarous murder, h about and mixed in society without being reputed he is rescued from the hands of justice, and from t of the law, because four gentlemen choose to say imperfect notions of the distinction between right and because he chose to maintain that he had a right victim to death. Why what murderer would not demnation, and in order to save his own life, make declaration? And what an encouragement it is to let it be known that by such means a man may penalty of the law. Again, the doctrine of these b mongers is that the more atrocious the deed, the m be the impunity to the doer; because, the greater of the crime, the more certain it must be that the out of his mind, for no man in his right senses would of such a crime.

What is called in such cases mercy to the guilty cruelty to the nation at large, by taking away restraints which the laws impose on the bad and vici of mankind. The true test, as it appears to me, the culprit, after condemnation, chooses to say admit the difference between right and wrong, but the time of committing the crime, he knew that punishment would follow.

The sympathy which the Government for Italian unity—the realisation of which hateful to the Papacy—had deprived tent of the Liberal Irish vote. Lord P of this in the following letter:—[1]

[1] To Mr. Chichester Fortescue

September 10, 1864.

[illegible] very glad to have the support of the [illegible]land; but as their political action is regu[illegible] they receive from time to time from Rome, [illegible] Government is pleased to deem us its enemy, [illegible] opinion that Italian unity would be a good [illegible] we could do with propriety in Ireland would [illegible] influence upon the Irish Catholics. If they [illegible] degree capable of political gratitude they would [illegible] the Whig Government; but two Monsignores [illegible] a 'Grandis Epistola' from the Vatican, array [illegible] men in the House of Commons who call them[illegible] but who are ready to vote as Tories in obedience [illegible] injunctions. This, it is true, was foretold by the [illegible] the Catholic Emancipation, and we who supported [illegible] derided the prediction. By though I am sorry to [illegible] this respect a false prophet, I do not the less rejoice [illegible] of sound policy and strict justice.

[illegible] two days later he says to the same:—

[illegible] invariably endeavoured to deal with equal impar[illegible] between Protestant and Catholic, but there is no shutting [illegible] the fact that in Ireland, as elsewhere, the Catholic [illegible]—and through them a portion of the laity—while [illegible] a desire for religious equality, aim at nothing less [illegible] domination, and strive to transfer the source and [illegible] centre of that domination to a foreign authority.

[illegible] connected with this subject was that of [illegible] Colleges—a matter which has already caused [illegible] debate, and may cause much more. His view of [illegible] matter is thus conveyed to the Lord-Lieutenant of [illegible]:—

July 28, 1865.

My dear Wodehouse,—The new arrangement to be made [illegible] the Catholic College will require much circumspection. [illegible] required is that young men brought up in that estab[illegible] should have the means of being examined for a Degree. [illegible] the Irish Catholics want to accomplish under cover of [illegible] reasonable purpose, is to substitute their Sectarian College [illegible] for the Queen's Colleges, which are founded on the [illegible] of mixed education. This is an aim which we must [illegible] them to accomplish. Their scheme of affiliation, plausibly recommended, tends to that end. My opinion, on the contrary, is that the aggregate University body of these Colleges should examine for Degrees all comers, wherever educated. It is said that this would not give any security for moral character, but that might be required from the [illegible] of each candidate; and it may safely be inferred that a man, who by study and application has qualified himself for a Degree, must be possessed of sufficient self-control to [illegible] to be a well-conducted young man. What the Catholic [illegible]hood want is that this Catholic College should be the [illegible] of education for the young Irish Catholics, and that it [illegible] be, like Maynooth, a place where young men should be [illegible] up to be bigoted in religion, to feel for Protestants [illegible] hatred, and to feel political hatred for England. It is [illegible] to put a number of lay Catholics into the council of the [illegible]gate University. This would be quite right, but would be [illegible] check upon the priests and bishops. How could such [illegible] O'Hagan and Monsell be expected to stand up against [illegible] and others upon any important religious matter? They [illegible] make a good fight about Euclid and algebra, or [illegible] astronomy, but upon all questions involving the real [illegible] the Catholic priesthood they would give way. The [illegible] I come to is, that we ought to give the students of the [illegible] College the means of obtaining Degrees, if they are [illegible] instructed to pass examination; but that we ought not [illegible] to the Catholic College a University condition of [illegible]. Therefore, if it should be necessary to give that College a [illegible] of incorporation, such charter should be limited to the [illegible] capacities of suing and being sued, and should not [illegible] power of holding lands, either by purchase, grant, or [illegible] and of course should not give power to confer Degrees.

Clerical rule he regarded as very objectionable [illegible] whatever communion it might be found; and [illegible] to the Home Secretary about Convocation:—

[illegible]

I see that Convocation have been very active [illegible] posing to draw up a Reform Bill for themselves [illegible] is that, unless kept very tight and within the [illegible] Convocation would become a nuisance, and [illegible] disposed to consent to any alterations which [illegible] them a more real and practical experience [illegible] hint be given them to check their [illegible]

[illegible], who was not addicted to unnecessary [illegible] them about their business one time when [illegible] to be meddlesome.

[illegible] letters about foreign affairs will, I think, [illegible]ing :—

September 8, 1865.

[illegible]wley,—The Duke of Somerset writes me word [illegible] were surprised, during the recent meeting at [illegible] to find how real the cordiality was with which [illegible]ived. If this should happen to be mentioned or [illegible] to you by any of the French ministers, it might [illegible] that you should explain to them that we English-[illegible] two distinct entities in France, the nation and the [illegible]. Towards the French nation we all feel that [illegible]ndship which was expressed by words and deeds [illegible] late meetings; all old sentiments of rivalship and [illegible] as between Englishmen and Frenchmen are, on our [illegible]nguished. But with regard to the French Govern-[illegible] see, from time to time, measures taken and schemes [illegible]d which, whether framed or not in hostility to Eng-[illegible], in our opinion, calculated to be injurious to our [illegible] interests. Such schemes, therefore, we do our best to [illegible] to defeat; not, as some French agents endeavour to [illegible], from hatred to France and to everything French, but [illegible] that watchful care of the interests of our country [illegible] it is the duty of every Government to exert. The result [illegible] on the one hand, the French nation ought not to see in [illegible]ional opposition to the schemes of their Government [illegible] inconsistent with the friendly feelings manifested in [illegible] meetings of the two navies; and, on the other hand, the [illegible] Government should not infer, from the friendliness of [illegible]ption of their fleet, that we shall be more likely to give [illegible] any matter in which the interests of England are [illegible]ed.

September 13, 1865.

[illegible] dear Russell,—It was dishonest and unjust to deprive [illegible] of Sleswig and Holstein. It is another question how [illegible] two Duchies, when separated from Denmark, can be dis-[illegible] best for the interests of Europe. I should say that, [illegible] view, it is better that they should go to increase the [illegible] of Prussia than that they should form another little state [illegible] to the cluster of small bodies politic which encumher Germany, and render it of less force [illegible] the general balance of power in the world [illegible] as she now is ever to be honest or indep[illegible] and, with a view to the future, it is desir[illegible] the aggregate, should be strong, in order [illegible] ambitious and aggressive powers, France and [illegible] upon her west and east. As to France, we [illegible] and aggressive she is, and how ready to break [illegible] for the Rhine, for anything she would be likely [illegible] too great an exertion. As to Russia, she will [illegible] become a power almost as great as the old [illegible] She can become mistress of all Asia, except [illegible] whenever she chooses to take it; and when [illegible] rangements shall have made her revenue propor[illegible] territory, and railways shall have abridged distances [illegible] mand of men will become enormous, her pecuni[illegible] gigantic, and her power of transporting armies [illegible] distances most formidable. Germany ought to be [illegible] order to resist Russian aggression, and a strong [illegible] essential to German strength. Therefore, though [illegible] condemn the whole of the proceedings of Austria [illegible] about the Duchies, I own that I should rather see [illegible] porated with Prussia than converted into an additi[illegible] in the system of Europe.

As the foregoing pages do not profess [illegible] 'history of the times,' but only those events [illegible] dents in which Lord Palmerston individually [illegible] marked share, a very rapid retrospect of a more [illegible] character over the period dealt with in this vo[illegible] not be out of place.

The years of his last administration of [illegible] Office have this peculiar feature about them [illegible] form the last period of active intervention [illegible] in the affairs of other countries. We appear [illegible] moved from that epoch by a vast interval [illegible] difficult for us now to imagine the despatch [illegible] legion to assist a sovereign against a [illegible] subjects, to realise a Quadruple Alliance [illegible] land should join to secure the succession [illegible] throne, or even to believe in the adv[illegible] fleet to protect a weak neighbour fro[illegible]

...such a foreign policy requires a man like ...on to carry it out successfully, and such ...e. His was not a flash policy, sacrificing ... to appearance, constructed merely to suit ...poses, and casting aside while still incomplete ... and undertakings, as soon as they had ...ir turn. On the contrary, he worked quietly ...everingly, keeping always in view 'British ...ts,' but not ostentatiously thrusting them into ...ground on every occasion, and thus defeating ...ject. So much was this the case, that during his ... career he incurred temporary unpopularity for ...which, if they had been puffed and heralded, or, to ...w a word from the Stock Exchange, properly ...d,' in the more modern fashion, would have ...d immediate and general applause.

Another element of his success lay in such circum-...ces of comparative freedom to act without check ...erference as can hardly be the lot of any minister, ...ever able, now-a-days, when foreign matters are ...e as familiar to the peasant, if he can only read, as ...etime to the prince. The doctrine of 'non-inter-...tion' and the penny press have rapidly and simul-...ously grown into favour with the British public; and the activity which characterised the Foreign Office under the Palmerstonian *régime* is a thing of the past. Yet the fruits which Lord Palmerston was able to show as the results of his energy and determination were well worth some risk and trouble in the cultivation. Peace between nations was preserved right through an era of revolutions; constitutional government was planted in a great part of Europe; and, meanwhile, England was known, respected, and dreaded wherever the name of Palmerston had penetrated; and that was—everywhere.

Of course the enemies of such a policy became countless. Disturbers of the peace must dislike the ...table; neither despots nor their friends relish con-...tions; bullies, whether high or low, hate those who keep them in order; and the selfish or [illegible] home grow weary of being constantly called [illegible] exertions on behalf of objects which, however [illegible] not affect their immediate interests. These [illegible] antipathies, foiled in 1850, made a renewed attack following year, and, as they hoped and believed, [illegible] ceeded in crushing Lord Palmerston. Had he [illegible] mere partisan, relying for his position solely [illegible] connection with a great party, the blow might [illegible] have proved as fatal as it was intended to be; [illegible] strength lay, as he well knew, in the country [illegible] which saw in him a statesman, not indeed [illegible] blemish, but who maintained the honour of [illegible] extricated her from innumerable difficulties [illegible] drawing the sword, and extended abroad those [illegible] ciples of civil and political liberty which are [illegible] Englishmen.

During the greater part of Lord Palmerston's [illegible] term of office questions relating to Turkey [illegible] Crimean war filled up the foreground of [illegible] have seen that, from the first, he foresaw [illegible] was so bent on an aggressive movement, [illegible] diplomatic remonstrances would not [illegible] her, and that nothing would stop her in [illegible] conviction that she would have to face [illegible] French alliance. The success with which [illegible] to the head of affairs, he finished the [illegible] the terms of peace greatly consolidated [illegible]

The short interval which separated his [illegible] [illegible] sufficed to enable him [illegible]

[illegible] Government not only quickly established [illegible] with France, but, by its influence, greatly [illegible] people to become a nation; and, in [illegible] were undoubtedly acting in harmony [illegible] general feeling of the English people.

[illegible] Louis Napoleon had taken the French [illegible] for Italy, he was in no way desirous of [illegible] unity such as it exists to-day. He wished [illegible] and Southern Italy, with a Papal sove- [illegible] between them; and this was the secret of his [illegible] retention of French troops at Rome. He [illegible] large force there, in order to hold for the Pope [illegible] to him, and in the hope also of being [illegible] set up some nominee of his own as King of [illegible] if Ferdinand became impossible. Italy would [illegible] have been divided into three portions, each too [illegible] to resist his influence. But the march of events [illegible] too strong for him; and although the frank and [illegible] representations which Lord Palmerston used to [illegible] against the continued occupation of Rome failed [illegible], his Government was of signal service to the [illegible] cause, both when there was a question of re- [illegible] the Grand Dukes after the Peace of Villafranca, [illegible] on when Garibaldi was helping to crown the [illegible]. So sensible were the Italians of this that, after [illegible] of Naples, addresses of thanks poured [illegible] Lord Palmerston from all parts of Italy.

[illegible] of the earliest and most beneficial results of the [illegible] to power of a Liberal Ministry was the con- [illegible] of a commercial treaty with France, which was [illegible] at home in spite of strong resistance from the [illegible] Opposition. The treaty was signed in [illegible] 1860; and to Mr. Cobden, its distinguished [illegible], Lord Palmerston offered, as an acknowledg- [illegible], in the name of the Queen, the choice of a [illegible] or a seat at the Privy Council; but Mr. [illegible] declined to receive any titular distinction.

[illegible] general financial achievements of Lord Palmer- [illegible] Government, with Mr. Gladstone as Chancellor

of the Exchequer, cannot be forgotten,
they did extensive relief to trade, industry,
by the remission of taxation, simplification of
and reduction of debt. Notwithstanding the
famine and the war in America, the nation, du
period, made great progress in wealth and
In the early part of 1860, the Imperial
China having shown its determination still to
treaty engagements, a second Chinese war was
taken in conjunction with the French. Lord
sent out from England to co-operate with Bar
and, finally, the success of the allied forces
us at last to obtain regular diplomatic interco
the Court of Pekin.

Overtures were soon after made to this
France, the object of which was to persuade
them in obtaining some compensation, if possib
losses sustained by the holders of Mexican bond
restore peace to Mexico, long distracted by
lution. The Palmerston Ministry, though
to aid in operations at Vera Cruz, where the
of the customs were seized, wisely declined
any further intervention, even though our
intimated that they would be satisfied if
consisted merely of black troops. The Fr
took the hopeless task of establishing
country and placing an Austrian Emperor
but the Spaniards and men of Spanish
disorder, and hated both French and Au
the remainder were weak and helpless,
Mexican leaders each was for himself
the others. The only class, therefore,
could find to back them was the Pri
were thus obliged either to join in
liberty and restoring intolerance and
quarrel with their own supporters.
failure which ensued. The discomfi
and the sad fate of the Archduke
accepted the imperial crown

[illegible] the British Government were in their [illegible] in Napoleon's scheme, which, hatched [illegible] but a bad imitation of his uncle's earlier [illegible] on the Spaniards of old Spain a king of [illegible] of their choice.

[illegible] through the bad government of King Otho, [illegible] scene of revolution, and was for some time [illegible] of anarchy. At last our Government and [illegible] France determined on a friendly intervention, [illegible] in 1862 to find a new king for the Greeks, who [illegible] an English prince. Any member of the English, [illegible] or Russian royal families was, however, excluded [illegible] agreement to that effect; and finally, after [illegible] fruitless search for a fit man, Prince George of [illegible]mark accepted the crown, and the Ionian Islands [illegible] handed over by England to the reconstituted [illegible]dom. This cession evoked a considerable amount [illegible] opposition at the time; but as these Islands formed [illegible] part of the dominions of the British Crown, and as [illegible] protectorate which we exercised had long been to [illegible] a source of annoyance, this gift to the Greeks was [illegible] politic measure. It was hoped that not only would [illegible] kingdom thus be strengthened, but that such a [illegible] of our goodwill would tend to rivet their attach[illegible] to England. But this was not all: Lord Pal[illegible]'s Government at the same time strenuously [illegible] Turkey to give Thessaly and Epirus over to the [illegible], but, as the map of Europe still indicates, with[illegible] success.

We have seen how the Polish rising began, and also the attack on Denmark by Germany. In both these cases Lord Palmerston could easily have stirred up a cry for war. English feeling was much excited on either question; but it was felt that neither the English interests involved, nor our available means of offence, were sufficient to justify an appeal to the national sentiment. In July 1865, Parliament having nearly reached its full term of existence, had been dissolved. There was a contest at Tiverton, and Lord Palmerston went down

most touching and characteristic feature of his bearing at this time was his solicitude to avoid adding to Lady Palmerston's anxiety, and the cheerfulness which he assumed in her presence. Indeed, consideration for others was, as in life so in death, one of his finest qualities. I remember that, only a few days before his end, when, so far as the aspect of his face could betoken illness, he appeared as ill as a man could be when about and at work, Lady Palmerston, at breakfast, alluded to the cattle plague, which was then making great havoc in England. He at once remarked that all the symptoms of the disorder were described by Virgil, and repeated to me some eight lines out of the Georgics descriptive of the disease. He then told us a story of a scrape he got into at Harrow, for throwing stones; and the excess of laughter, which he was unable to restrain, with which he recalled the incident, was the only token that could have betrayed to Lady Palmerston how weak he was.

A chill caught while out driving brought on inflammation of the kidneys, and on October 18, 1865, within two days of completing his eighty-first year, he closed his earthly career. The half-opened cabinet-box on his table, and the unfinished letter on his desk, testified that he was at his post to the last.

I here quote a letter written very shortly before his death, as it shows him, instead of being engrossed in his own state of health, solicitous and active about the health of a subordinate. On Sir Arthur Helps, as Clerk of the Council, had come a great influx of business, owing to the outbreak of rinderpest, and Lord Palmerston had already volunteered to help him by undertaking some of the work:—

Brocket: October 3, 1865.

My dear Gladstone,—I have this morning received the enclosed from an eminent physician of Southampton. The report he makes of the health of Helps and of the state of the Council Office Establishment seems to me to require immediate and effective action. I have, therefore, written to Helps positively to forbid his going to Balmoral; and, as it seems that his second in command, Harrison, is also knocked down by [illegible] and as the limited establishment of the Council Office [illegible] too small and weak for the daily work pressing in [illegible] reason of these cattle, sheep, and pig diseases, [illegible] threatening of extension to horses, I have written to W[illegible] to request him to send some Home Office clerk to [illegible] officiate at the Council.

I have also told Helps that, as head of the Gover[illegible] authorise him to take, without any delay, such steps [illegible] necessary to procure additional assistance for his [illegible] this great influx of daily business continues to press [illegible] have told him that I will write to you to ask you to [illegible] necessary directions for an official sanction to the [illegible] but I have said that he ought not to delay taking [illegible] steps for obtaining relief by additional assistance.

That, in spite of the depressing influence [illegible] illness, he was also fully alive to any new [illegible] which might arise, is shown by the next letter [illegible] same date, to the Home Secretary, about the [illegible] movement in Ireland:—

Brocket: Octo[illegible]

I am clearly for sending to Ireland a regiment [illegible] to take the place of the one which it seems was [illegible] away from Ireland, and whether Rose[1] is for [illegible] ment or against it. If the question was reversed [illegible] considering whether a regiment could be spared [illegible] we could not properly decide to diminish the Irish [illegible] the full assent of the general commanding; but [illegible] being whether we could add to the existing force [illegible] highly satisfactory to find that Sir Hugh Rose [illegible] sider any addition necessary, we ought nevertheless [illegible] Sir Hugh Rose has been accustomed to walk [illegible] and everybody opposed to him; but in this [illegible] not the only thing to be provided for. If [illegible] break it will begin by partial risings in [illegible] small numbers, but yet numbers sufficient [illegible] no protecting force, to murder, burn, and [illegible] villages and landlord residences. A [illegible] of rapid movement, would do what [illegible] cases, and cavalry would be well [illegible]

Fenians, moreover, may have arms for infantry, and may, by possibility, have guns, though that is unlikely, but cavalry they cannot have; and a Fenian put suddenly on horseback, even if they could so fit out some of their men, would not be a cavalry soldier. Then, upon the general principle, we should be inspiring confidence in the loyal, and be giving a useful warning to the Fenians by showing that we could, if needed, add to the regular force now in Ireland.

The same week he is writing to the Secretary of State for War to inquire into the provision of arms and ammunition in Canada, and to suggest heavier armaments for the works around Quebec. Three years previously he had urged successfully that these fortifications should be restored and enlarged, so as to provide some place of strength for our small body of regular troops to fall back upon, should a sudden invasion take place from the United States. This did not then appear an unlikely event. It was very widely anticipated, at the time, that the civil war would end in the separation of South from North, and that the North would want compensation and some triumph over somebody to wipe away the stain of failure. The invasion of Canada, if it could be followed by the conquest of the province, would have satisfied both requirements, and, had we been unprepared, the temptation might have been overpowering. Matters, however, took a different turn, and the defeat of the Southerners not improbably saved the Canadians from attack. But during the summer of 1865 alarm had been renewed by the threatening aspect of the Federal Government, as manifested by a notice to the British Government of the abrogation of the Treaty of 1817, and by the establishment of a system of passports between Canada and the United States. The Federals were flushed with success; they had many men under arms, and many grudges against the Canadians. Lord Palmerston was fully alive to all this, and was anxious, by assisting the colony in her fortifications, and by maintaining an efficient flotilla on the lakes, to back that spirit of self-reliance which alone, in the moment

body was accordingly moved up to his town resi-
e in Piccadilly, and the funeral took place on the
of October. The whole distance to the Abbey was
by a dense crowd of interested and sympathetic
ators, and the sacred building itself was filled
all that was most distinguished and most repre-
tive. The Houses of Parliament, although their
on was over, were amply represented, and through
ense crowd that surrounded the entrance into the
y Church all his late colleagues of the Cabinet
hed as pallbearers. In the north transept, near
grave of Pitt, were laid the mortal remains of
erston.

CHAPTER XVIII.

CHARACTER—CHARACTERISTICS OF STYLE OF WRITING [illegible] SPEAKING.

LORD PALMERSTON'S character has been so fre[illegible] discussed—its many-sidedness offering to such [illegible] dispositions some point or other of attraction— [illegible] may seem superfluous in me to attempt a repet[illegible] a similar kind. Yet, in closing this history, I [illegible] resist the desire to put, however imperfectly, o[illegible] the impressions made upon me by seven years [illegible] intercourse, both private and official. Biograph[illegible] proverbially partial; and it is, on the whole, [illegible] credit that they should be so. Retrospect shou[illegible] fasten on the good than the evil. But, on the [illegible] hand, indiscriminate and extravagant praise i[illegible] real as it is unsatisfactory; and whoever unde[illegible] inform his fellow-countrymen is bound to [illegible] judgment as well as his affection into play.

Lord Palmerston, then, was a great man [illegible] the sense that he was so complete a man. [illegible] racter deserves our attention more from [illegible] combination of good qualities than from [illegible] presence of any one great quality or attri[illegible] about him neither the glories nor the [illegible] genius; but he possessed, in rare har[illegible] teristics which are generally in anta[illegible] great pluck, combined with remarkab[illegible] good-temper, associated with firmness [illegible] to obstinacy. He was a strict dis[illegible] ready above most men to make allow[illegible] ness and shortcomings of others. He loved hard work in all its details, and yet took a keen delight in many kinds of sport and amusement. He believed in England as the best and greatest country in the world, while he had not confined his observation to her affairs, but knew and cared more about foreign nations than any other public man. He had little or no vanity in his composition, and, as is seen in several of his letters to his brother, he claimed but a modest value for his own abilities; yet no man had a better opinion of his own judgment, or was more full of self-confidence. It was amusing to notice the good-natured pity with which he quite unconsciously regarded those who differed from him in questions whereon he had made up his mind. He never doubted for an instant in such a case that he was right, and that they were wrong.

This gave him great tenacity of purpose, and helped him through many difficulties, and even mistakes, which would have swamped a weaker man. He seems almost to be describing himself when, writing to Sir Stratford Canning in December 1850 about the Turkish Ministers, he says: 'I believe weakness and irresolution are, on the whole, the worst faults that statesmen can have. A man of energy may make a wrong decision, but, like a strong horse that carries you rashly into a quagmire, he brings you by his sturdiness out on the other side.' During the critical moment before the breaking out of the Franco-Austrian war in 1859, M. Drouyn de Lhuys, talking to Lord Clarendon, used the same simile:—

'I sigh,' he said, 'for one hour of Palmerston. No one knows better than I do his faults. I have often suffered by them, and so has England, and so has Europe. But his merits, his sagacity, his courage, his trustworthiness, are invaluable when you want

"A daring pilot in extremity;"

with whom one feels as if one was mounted on a first-rate hunter, who pulls, indeed, and rears and kicks, but never swerves, never starts, and carries you over everything as long as you give him his head.'

He liked office and the possession of pow
statesman showed more indifference to its
so cordially detested the flatteries which it
quently attracts. Perhaps his strongest dis
affectation of any sort. He could not abide
and never even dreamt of it for himself.

He was, for instance, always above the
feeble tone of those who think it necessa
coyness with respect to office, and who
nothing else but the sacrifice they made
the last occasion of accepting it. His la
always frankly to the effect that office is
and proper object of a public man's ambiti
sphere in which he can most freely use
for the interest and advantage of his coun
Palmerston never pretended to dislike it.

Who, again, at a social party, ever saw
into a corner with a colleague or a diplom
by mysterious looks and enigmatical gestu
an admiring curiosity among the bystande
an ambassador of the old school must have
at his own discomfiture, but he was indeed a
who could 'buttonhole' Lord Palmerston at
party, unless he really had something very
say. She also was a clever woman who coul
draw him on to politics, with a view to
other guests with the high range of the con
the head of the table. The easy interchang
talk on social subjects being the appropri
the payment of what is due to society, L

[illegible] were held in suspense, and he himself mis[illegible]. His manner, arising from an instinctive [illegible] pomposity or affectation, created a belief in [illegible]; his good-humour and forbearance, a belief [illegible] indifference; his reticence, a belief in his paucity [illegible]. A passage from 'Greville's Memoirs,' under [illegible] of August 7, 1836, shows however that, what[illegible] was the judgment of the public, his talents were [illegible] recognised by competent judges:—

[illegible] is surprising to hear how Palmerston is spoken of by [illegible] who knew him officially. Lady Granville a woman [illegible] in judging, thinks his capacity first-rate; that it approaches [illegible] greatness from his enlarged views, disdain of trivialities, [illegible], decision, confidence, and above all, his contempt of [illegible] and abuse. She told me that Madame de Flahault [illegible] a letter written by Talleyrand soon after his first arrival in [illegible], in which he talked with great contempt of the Ministers [illegible], Lord Grey included, and said there was but one [illegible] among them, and that was Palmerston. His ordinary [illegible] exhibits no such superiority; but when he takes [illegible] pen in his hand, his intellect seems to have full play, and [illegible] when engaged exclusively in business.

Perhaps the most valuable quality for a commander, [illegible] in the field or the Cabinet, is 'knowledge of [illegible].' To be able to choose fit instruments is often [illegible] battle half won; to be able to test reports that are [illegible] in is often a defeat half saved. For both these [illegible] knowledge of character is indispensable—[illegible] gleaned not from laborious investigations, [illegible] which there is seldom time, but from that instinc[illegible] judgment which is a gift in itself, and which only [illegible] for its exercise a few moments' conversation [illegible] the person whose character is to be learned. This [illegible] Lord Palmerston had in a large degree. The con[illegible] of its possession led him, no doubt, on some [illegible] occasions, to be over-hasty in condemnation; but [illegible] of a new-comer is for a Minister a safer fault [illegible] blind confidence.

At the time when the Greeks were being urgently

pressed to satisfy certain Engli[illegible] the banker, came to Lord Nor[illegible] Coletti had, without any warning, [illegible] 500,000 francs in favour of the [illegible] the Greeks availing themselves of [illegible] on his part; that it would cost him [illegible] provide the money at once, and that he [illegible] a request to the British Government to [illegible] months, so as to spare him this loss. The [illegible] bassador, in a letter home, recapitulated [illegible] statements of the financier, and was evide[illegible] his appeal. Not so Lord Palmerston:—

C. G.: A[illegible]

My dear Normanby,—I have received your [illegible] account of your interview with Eynard. I [illegible] what Lowther used to call *débuted* in London [illegible] as an amateur actor; and he seems, according to [illegible] not by any means to have trained off in his perform[illegible] ance in that line. He did his part throughout the [illegible] admirably, and the only pity was that there were no[illegible] to crown him with applause. But as the report of [illegible] acted scene never can produce the same effect as the [illegible] hearing would, just as the best speech is tame with[illegible] habitumque hominis,' so I am concerned to say [illegible] Eynard's generosity, nor his impending loss of 80,0[illegible] nor his desertion by Guizot, nor his European rep[illegible] his Philhellenic enthusiasm, can light one spark of [illegible] my cold and gloomy mind, and I feel as stone-hear[illegible] himself, even after reading your letter to an end. [illegible] Eynard as well as you do, and therefore, perhaps, [illegible] better. Rely upon it that in all these matters he [illegible] instrument of humbug in the hands of other perso[illegible] are too old birds to be caught by such chaff. [illegible] tell Eynard, in such civil terms as you think be[illegible] nothing to do with him in this matter, and [illegible] communication with him on the subject. Our [illegible] the Government of Greece, and not with [illegible] Government. We mean to settle our affairs [illegible] the Greek Government, and he will, of [illegible] with Greece with the Greek Governme[illegible] settle our affairs with Greece with him, [illegible] with us. Depend upon it, the money his pocket, but from the till of Louis and Co., and they sent him to you to bamboozle us. But, even if this were not so, and natured, soft enthusiast he represents himself result would be that Greece would have to pay francs which he *says* he is going to lose, if that All this is nothing to us, and we have nothing to do with the matter. It is a question entirely be-Greek Government and Eynard.

the most steadfast and loyal of chiefs to served under him. 'There is the devoted who stands or falls by one, like the noble Lord.' satirically, the leader of the Opposition, re-to Lord Palmerston, in the debate of June 16, But the party sneer contained an acknowledged whose universal acceptance did Lord Palmerston honour and good service during his long career. served with zeal because the absent knew that would shirk no difficulties in their defence, and that would listen to no depreciatory tales against them, accompanied by substantial proofs.

Lord Howden, British Minister at Madrid, begs him to attend to private and slanderous reports about The reply is as follows :—

Broadlands: September 7, 1850.

My dear Howden,—I have received your letter of the 25th month, and beg you not to trouble yourself about the to which it relates. If I had not full confidence in you, would not have recommended you to the Queen for the post occupy; and when I have confidence in a man, I do not that confidence to be shaken by the tales of intriguers and biters, even if such should reach my ears, which in your they have not and probably will not. I say will not, the commercial principle that supply follows demand to other matters besides trade; and when certain sup-are known to be discouraged and rejected, they are apt to withheld. In fact, the usual effect of underhand attempts to a man is, with me, to make me more disposed to take his I have some little experience in my own proper person of the way in which falsehood is enlisted into the [illegible] sonal pique or unfounded resentment.—Yours sin[illegible]

P[illegible]

This is a letter which deserves to be rem[illegible] account of the truth which it contains. [illegible] found no market for their goods in Lord [illegible] study, and so did not attempt to smuggle t[illegible]

Nor was he more willing to yield to the [illegible] of those in high places who sought to pers[illegible] sacrifice his agents abroad to their prejudice[illegible] 'Pray make him clearly comprehend,' he [illegible] English Minister abroad, 'that I will never [illegible] British diplomatic officer, high or low, [illegible] and caprices of any foreign prince or potent[illegible]

When the Greek Court used its person[illegible] with our Court at home to bring pressu[illegible] Foreign Office for the removal of Lord [illegible] Athens, he writes to Lord John Russell:—

Broadlands: Au[illegible]

Otho's dislike to Lyons is not personal, but p[illegible] not that Lyons is disagreeable in himself, but the [illegible] advice which he has been always instructed to [illegible] political principles and party which he has been [illegible] support, are odious to Otho, and he hates Lyons [illegible] principle that a dog snaps at a stick. You woul[illegible] feeling by changing the stick. It is the establis[illegible] proceeding in such matters to run down the m[illegible] method than combating his policy, or, rather, the [illegible] he is the organ. I think it is very unwise to [illegible] intrigue; to do so is a proof either of great [illegible] weakness of character; and when people once [illegible] bringing a certain amount of combined intrigue [illegible] a given individual, or upon a given object, they [illegible] point, either by imposing upon belief or by [illegible] their system of political tactics is reduced to [illegible] with which a general can tell you the [illegible] which it will take him to capture a fortr[illegible]

[1] To Sir J. Milbanke, January 31, 18[illegible] ment asked for the removal of the English [illegible]

When a public servant is molested abroad he speaks out plainly, and sends a direct message to the responsible authority:—

Broadlands: October 29, 1849.

My dear Moncorvo,[1]—I am sorry to say that the last Lisbon mail brings me another correspondence which has taken place between Mr. Howard and Count Tojal upon the subject of another act of petty vexation on the part of Dr. Moacho, the Guarda Mor of the Health Department at Belem, towards Mr. Phillipps, our Vice-Consul. I confess I am astonished that the Portuguese Government should permit one of their inferior officers to continue to carry on this system of malicious annoyance; but pray make Count Tojal clearly understand (which you will best do by sending him this note) that it is quite impossible for me to permit a deserving servant of the British Crown to be the victim of the low rancour and vulgar malignity of any Guarda, whether he be 'Mor' or not; and I do intreat the Portuguese Government not to allow this ill-conditioned Doctor to bring on a quarrel between England and Portugal.—Yours sincerely,

PALMERSTON.

F. O.: March 10, 1851.

Dear Gordon,[2]—I have received your letter about the attacks made upon Sir E. Lyons, and I request you will tell Baron Sterngeld in plain terms that I will not stand a continuance or renewal in Sweden of those base intrigues which were got up against Sir E. Lyons at Athens. We have chosen for the Queen's representative at Stockholm an able and distinguished diplomatist, and a brave and honourable naval officer. We expect and require that he shall be received at Stockholm with all the courtesy which is due to his personal merits, and to the respect which is owing to the Government and country which he represents; and if the Swedish Government attaches any value to the maintenance of its friendly relations with England, it will take proper care that we shall have no just cause of complaint on that score. Pray read this letter to Baron Sterngeld.

The staunch support, which he was thus wont to give to all his fellow-workers, did not spring from a mere generous impulse, but was based upon wide expo-

[1] Portuguese Minister in London.
[2] British Minister at Stockholm.

rience of the world and upon a practical knowledge of its ways and difficulties. He well knew that none but the men who are actually engaged in the conduct of an affair can justly understand all the bearings of the circumstances, and the full value of all the separate incidents of which it consists; and that the tendency of the minds of one's best friends always is to think that one has done too much rather than too little, when difficulties arise which are connected with what has been done; and, on the contrary, to think that too little has been attempted, when difficulties arise in consequence of what has been omitted. But men must be taken as Nature made them, and it is well to make the best of things as they are. His own words constantly repeated this, and he added on one occasion that it was 'the duty of those who are charged with the conduct of a branch of the service *to support those who are acting with them, and to back them up well through the difficulties to which they may be exposed; and you may rely upon it that I shall always do that, which I hold to be the* sine quâ non *condition upon which the co-operation of men of honour can be expected.*'[1]

Not that he omitted to convey privately to his agents very plain expressions of his opinion if in any respect he considered that they had failed in judgment or energy; but such rebukes created no ill-feeling when the motive was not to shift blame but to discharge a duty. In the case of minor errors he managed to intimate his opinion without giving offence. 'But we must suspend our judgment and decision,' he writes to Lord Normanby, 'till we know exactly what has happened; and if a friend of mine had done so in his communications on these matters with the French Government, he would not have found himself so [illegible] placed thereby in subsequent discussions.'[2]

Nothing more annoyed him than that an [illegible] show indifference to the ill-treatment of [illegible]

[1] To Lord Normanby, March 5, 1848.
[2] Idem, May 10, 1850.

ject; and he pushed this laudable feeling at times further perhaps than the general principles of international law would strictly allow. An Englishman who goes to reside in a foreign country must be held undoubtedly subject to the laws of that country, and can strictly only claim that such laws in his case should be fairly carried out. But Lord Palmerston did not always abide by that rule. 'As to the laws of Venezuela,' he observes in one instance, 'the people of Venezuela must of course submit to them; but the British Government will not permit gross injustice to be done or gross oppression to be exercised on British subjects under the pretence of Venezuelan law.'

When a timid, hesitating Ministry is fearful of using the power confided to it, there is always a reason found for not doing so. Either the Government we have to complain of is powerful—and it would be imprudent to exact reparation from a State which might resent our demands and defy our power; or the Government we have to complain of is weak—and then it is beneath our dignity to force a nation so inferior to our own to do us justice. Lord Palmerston had none of these scruples. Right, in his eyes, was right; and if he insisted upon it when a formidable enemy might be provoked, he treated with becoming scorn the argument that we should deal more gently with an inferior delinquent.

'What!' he used to say; 'we are to tax our people for the purpose of giving them a strong Government, and then we are not to maintain the rights of our people because their Government is strong? The weaker a Government is, the more inexcusable becomes its insolence or injustice.' This mode of reasoning is in truth incontrovertible. Whenever it is asserted that we are to put up with a wrong or an affront because it comes to us from a contemptible antagonist, it is generally easy to recognise an attempt to cover an act of cowardice by an assumption of magnanimity.

Neither does it appear to signify much when once reparation has been demanded whether the act which called for that reparation concerns a great inte small one. The only question is, whether re was justly demanded or not. Our honour is pl obtain satisfaction when we once demand it wit and equity on our side. Our honour is tarnish we demand it without such advocates in our be

I have already alluded to his thoughtfulne others. With this was combined that atte details which alone makes such thoughtfulness practical utility. To the Commander-in-Chief gests that the Guards should be relieved of so weight of their headgear:—

There is another subject which seems deserving Royal Highness's attention. When your Royal Hi any other sportsman, goes out shooting, whether in summer, carrying no other load than a double-barr weighing about eight pounds, and intending to walk only a few hours, the lightest possible wideawake is the head, and a loose jacket and trousers leave the lim as possible; but when a soldier of the Guards is order long and fatiguing march, or has to make all the bodil required on the field of battle, as if his tight clothin musket, knapsack, ammunition, and other things, probably about sixty pounds, were not sufficient rest muscular exertion, he has to carry on his head a gre cap, weighing, it is said, about two pounds four ou a far lighter headgear, even if made of bearskin, w every purpose, and relieve his head and brain from th pressure of the present head-dress. I would ventur for your Royal Highness's consideration that a partly bearskin, if that must be, but smaller and the Artillery busby, would be a great relief to Guards; and that after such an improved head into use everybody would wonder that the heavy cap had ever been worn.[1]

In another letter to Mr. S. Herbert of State for War, after asking whether preparing a little book of instructions lunteers, he adds, 'Have you been

[1] To Duke of Cambridge, No

Barrack Department to provide the sleeping rooms of the soldiers with decent civilized arrangements of utensils for night wants?'

When the rage for competitive examination for clerkships in our public offices first broke out he watched with anxiety its detailed development; and, wishing himself to revise the Papers of Questions on which the examinations were conducted, he writes thus to the Home Secretary:—

They (Civil Service Commissioners) continue to put the most absurd questions, which tend to throw ridicule upon the whole system, and answers to which are no more a test of the capacity of a young man to be a clerk than would be his happening to know the exact dimensions of one of the great craters in the moon.

This absurd pedantry is injurious to the interests of the public service. Would it suit you to appoint them to meet us in the Cabinet room in Downing Street on Wednesday at three? If so, I wish you would appoint them, and request them to bring with them their Papers of Questions for all the public departments for which examinations take place.'[1]

When, for the purpose of preparing papers for Parliament, or from any other cause of pressure, the hours of work in some department of the Foreign Office were unusually prolonged, he used to send for a list of the clerks who had been so detained, and would convey to them individually his thanks and his appreciation of their work. I find notes put away, docketed "Names of Foreign Office Clerks who sat up" for such and such a purpose. It is not every chief who, in the middle of all his engrossing employments, would trouble himself about the share which each individual under him had taken in the general work.

During a fit of the gout he hears that a colleague is also laid up. Straightway, thinking of his friend's health, and not absorbed only in his own, he sends him the following letter:—

[1] To Sir George Lewis: Dec. 6, 1856.

Piccadilly: May 2[illegible]

My dear Clarendon,—Sympathy between colleag[illegible] good thing, but it may be carried too far, and I am [illegible] hear that you have pushed it to the point of joining [illegible] touch of gout.

Peel said that no man should give advice till he is [illegible] and you have not called me in; but I am called i[illegible] interest which we all take in your health. What, the[illegible] be your objection to the following suggestion?

You want more air and exercise. Much you can[illegible] a little you might have, and every mickle makes a mu[illegible] a little every day tells in the course of the year. Wh[illegible] you not provide yourself with a steady hack, with ge[illegible] who would give you no trouble when on him, and no[illegible] you from thinking over the draft you are next going [illegible] Why should not the aforesaid quadruped be at your d[illegible] morning just as you finish your breakfast, and why s[illegible] not ride him to the end of Hyde Park and back again, [illegible] to the Office, making a slight deviation by the way? [illegible] take you only half an hour, but you would soon find the [illegible] of that half-hour, if daily taken.—Yours sincerely,

PALM[illegible]

He himself practised what he preached. Hi[illegible] relates that often in his early days the horses w[illegible] waiting at the door of the Foreign Office up [illegible] eleven o'clock at night, so that, at any rate, [illegible] merston might ride home, and so observe [illegible] daily exercise on horseback. He was fond [illegible] that 'Every other abstinence will not make [illegible] stinence from exercise.'

Although, perhaps, almost too hard in [illegible] during the combat, he was, after it was [illegible] free from petty malice or lasting rancour. [illegible] always a desire to forgive and forget wi[illegible] of what was just. This won him at length [illegible] ment even of his political foes. 'He was [illegible] generous enemy,' said Cobden on his d[illegible]

He had a wonderful faculty of d[illegible] mind any matter, however anxious, [illegible] it was disposed of, and his disposi[illegible]

feel perfect confidence in his subordinates so long as they had done nothing to forfeit it. These two qualities were mighty aids to him in his work, as they not only assisted his power of concentration, which was already naturally strong, but freed him from that perpetual head-worry which has worn out so many busy men. It is almost needless to add that, in spite of his long official habits, he never succumbed to that infirmity of small minds which is well described and well understood by the term 'red-tapeism.'

Fearless truthfulness was one of his distinctive characteristics, which, while it made him some enemies, in the long run won him more friends. In his intercourse with foreign Ministers, however, it sometimes served a purpose which he at the time little anticipated. I have heard him say that he occasionally found that they had been deceived by the open manner in which he told them the truth. When he had laid before them the exact state of the case, and announced his own intentions, they went away convinced that so skilful and experienced a diplomatist could not possibly be so frank as he appeared, and imagining some deep design in his words, acted on their own ideas of what he really meant, and so misled their ownselves.

A distinguished author of an essay on the working of the English Constitution lays down that a statesman who aspires to be a leader must also be an unflinching partisan. This appears to be so far true that it would, perhaps, be impossible to name any other man than Lord Palmerston whose life has been an illustration of the contrary; but he never seemed to take much interest in purely party politics, and party spirit influenced few of his acts. It used to be said of an eloquent Conservative leader that he led the Opposition with the spirit and keenness of a jockey riding a race; every nerve was strained, and every legitimate means resorted to, to 'dish' his opponents. Lord Palmerston, on the contrary, once owned, in a letter to his brother, that he was not fit to be a leader of Opposition, because, as he said, 'I have not faction enough in my composition.'

But if in public life he was genial, straightforward, and considerate, in his private life these qualities were equally marked. As an English country gentleman—that type of landed proprietor which foreigners recognise as peculiar to this country, and by which so many of our best qualities are fostered—he took a keen interest and a personal share in all rural pursuits and business. Sports or meetings, farmers' dinners or agricultural shows, village schools, where he sometimes himself examined the children, or labourers' teas, when he always had a cheery word ready, and friendly advice mingled with fun—as on one occasion, when handing to a man a prize of twenty-five shillings, given for the tidiest couple, he added: 'Scripture says that a virtuous woman is a crown to her husband; but in your case, you see, she is five crowns'—into each and all he threw himself with unaffected zest and enjoyment; for intercourse with his fellow-creatures, of whatever degree, was a positive pleasure to him, and in this Lady Palmerston resembled him. Her memory, cherished by his private friends, should not be less preserved in connection with his public career. Her assemblies—neutral ground where distinguished persons of all parties, whether foreign or domestic, met for social intercourse, forgetting for the moment their political differences—were a powerful aid to him as head of a Government. Shortly after her death, Mr. Disraeli, in a speech at Glasgow, while alluding to the happy circumstance of public life in England that we do not as a rule permit our political opinions to interfere with our social relations, recalled in the following words one of his reminiscences:—

If you are on the Continent and wish to pay your respects to a minister and go to his reception, you are invited by the minister. The consequence is that you find no one there except those that follow him. It is not so in England. I remember so[illegible]ars ago meeting, under the charming roof of one of the most accomplished women of the time, the most celebrated diplomatist of certainly half a century, and he said to me, 'What a wonderful system of society you have in England! I have not been on speaking terms with Lord Palmerston for three weeks, and yet here I am; but you see I am paying a visit to Lady Palmerston.'

The manner in which she performed what Lord Palmerston, in reply to a complimentary letter from the American Minister, once termed her 'portion of our joint duties,' sufficiently proved that to the refinement and kindliness of a 'grande dame' she joined the genial and sympathetic nature of her husband. Both host and hostess succeeded in pleasing because they were pleased themselves; for age had not blunted their delight in the society of their fellow-men, or their pleasure in seeing others happy. By a natural law these hospitable efforts strengthened their influence in the political world, for the very reason that such was not the sole object they had in view when they threw open their doors not grudgingly or of necessity, but because they liked it.

Let two instances suffice to illustrate Lord Palmerston's considerate kindness to those round him in the country:—One day Lady Palmerston brought him home word that during her drive she had heard of one of his tenants having met with a serious accident. Although it was late, and the hour for his daily work in his library, he instantly ordered his horse, left his despatches, and within half-an-hour was by the side of what proved to be a dying man. Again, when, in 1859, he presented the parish clergyman, Mr. Moore of Romsey, to the living of Sutterton, knowing that Mrs. Moore had indifferent health, and was anxious about the quality of the water in her future home, he directed specimens of it to be sent to him out of Lincolnshire, and himself forwarding them for analysis to the Royal College of Chemistry, obtained a satisfactory report, which he handed to Mr. Moore.

Lord Palmerston was not a Democrat. He did not

think a democracy the best government for a people, and he wished to maintain an aristocracy as a part of ours. But all his feelings and sympathies were of a broad popular kind. Instances appear through his correspondence, when Secretary of War, of his interest in the private soldier's comfort and moral improvement. As a landlord he showed a constant attention to the comfort, education, and improvement of the peasantry. But nowhere could be found a more complete exemplification of his feelings as to the happiness and enjoyment of the great masses of the population than in the letters to Sir Benjamin Hall, at that time First Commissioner of Works, with respect to the management of the parks.

94, Piccadilly: Oct. 31, [illegible]

My dear Hall,—I cannot agree with you as to the [illegible] on which the grass in the park should be treated. You [illegible] to think it a thing to be looked at by people who are to be confined to the gravel walks. I regard it as a thing to be [illegible] upon freely and without restraint by the people, old and [illegible] for whose enjoyment the parks are maintained; and [illegible] hurdles would turn the parks into so many Smithfields [illegible] entirely prevent that enjoyment. As to people making [illegible] across the grass, what does that signify? If the parks [illegible] to be deemed hayfields, it might be necessary to prevent [illegible] from stopping the growth of the hay by walking [illegible] grass; but as the parks must be deemed places [illegible] enjoyment, the purpose for which the parks are [illegible] marred and defeated when the use of them is [illegible] number of straight gravel walks.

When I see the grass worn by foot traffic, I [illegible] as a proof that the park has answered its purpose [illegible] done its duty by the health, amusement, and enjoy[illegible] people.

In the college courts of Cambridge a man is [illegible] crown who walks over the grass plots, but that is [illegible] dent to be followed.

94, Piccadilly [illegible]

My dear Hall,—I have been much [illegible]

a right to expect that essential alterations should not be made in the spaces allotted for the enjoyment and recreation of the public without my previous sanction and concurrence, and I entirely disapprove of the restrictions which you are imposing upon the free enjoyment of the Green Park and Hyde Park by the public.

Your iron hurdles are an intolerable nuisance, and I trust that you mean shortly to remove them. To cut up the Green Park into enclosed shrubberies and plantations would be materially to interfere with the enjoyment and free recreation of the public; and I must positively forbid the prosecution of any such scheme. As head of the Government, I should be held by the public to have authorised these arrangements, and I do not choose to be responsible for things which I disapprove.

There is earnestness and determination here. There might have been a different way of looking at the subject. It might have been contended that pleasure may be derived from the eye—that the working man might be gratified by seeing pretty patches of flowers, and walking down nicely-gravelled walks; and the popular philosopher might have theorized on this subject with much grace and plausibility. But what the simple glance of Lord Palmerston saw was the labouring man, relieved from his toil, strolling with his wife as he listed along the broad common, sitting down under the trees, playing with his children, enjoying the free air and the open space in careless independence; and when he says that he likes to see the grass worn because it is a proof that the people have been enjoying themselves, we feel how completely his heart beat, even on the most ordinary questions, with the great public heart of the country—how much in reality he was one of the many, and concentrated in his own mind the feelings of the many.

It was this identity which he felt with the English people that made him so proud of their strength and so jealous of their honour.

It is singular how this feeling in a Minister—this feeling which distinguishes the great Minister from the ordinary one—raises his country, and elevates all those in its service by a sort of magical influence [illegible] both at home and abroad. Chatham was in the [illegible] Wolfe, and his son in that of Nelson. Mr. Can[illegible] high bearing and splendid words gave to a few [illegible] sent to Lisbon a force which may be said [illegible] paralysed the power of the great military [illegible] Europe. Lord Palmerston had not the genius of [illegible] men, but he had the spirit and the sentiment, [illegible] took care that no one who served under him [illegible] without them.

Lord Palmerston's correspondence, [illegible] serves to account at the same time for his [illegible] and his authority: the mixture of [illegible] satire—of good humour with censure—of [illegible] with command. The kindly tone of [illegible] and ample expression of thanks, combine in a [illegible] manner to exhibit the Minister who [illegible] our imagination as the ideal of a statesman, [illegible] hero, satisfied our mind with the reality of [illegible] practical, good-tempered man who loved his [illegible] and his countrymen, did his business with [illegible] pleasure, liked a joke, would not be trifled [illegible] never showed a disposition either to cringe or [illegible]

In short, there was a genuine desire to [illegible] agreeable impression as to themselves on [illegible] took away that character of selfishness [illegible] attaches to what a man when receiving [illegible] an obligation usually says, and that makes [illegible] the person who got the letter addressed to [illegible] have felt lighter and happier on the [illegible] ceived it.

It is said that M. de Talleyrand had [illegible] answering literary men who sent him [illegible] usually wrote that he received them [illegible] which he felt sure would be increased [illegible]

But Lord Palmerston had no set [illegible] himself in his correspondent's [illegible] self the trouble to realise the [illegible] the person he was addressing. [illegible]

[illegible] appointment, the other expressing regret at not [illegible] so—are models of their kind. The gentleman who got the appointment, and who might have thought [illegible] through a private friendship for his father, is [illegible] told that he owes it to his own merits; and the gentleman who is not appointed would have shown this refusal with as much pride to his mother or his wife as if it had been the offer of a lucrative place.

94, Piccadilly: Dec. 14, 1859.

My dear Sir,—Many thanks for your note of the 12th. I can assure you that it gave me great pleasure to find myself able to do that which was agreeable to the son of a much esteemed and highly valued friend; but at the same time it is due to you to say that I should not have been guided by my personal feelings in this respect, if I had not thought that you were the fittest person I could choose for the office to which you have been appointed.

Piccadilly: June 24, 1859.

My dear Sir,—I return you the enclosed, and beg at the same time to express my regret that it has not been possible for me to avail myself of your very valuable assistance in regard to the arrangement which I have had to make, as I am well satisfied that any public duties which you might have consented to undertake would have been performed by you with that ability which you are known to possess.—Yours faithfully,

PALMERSTON.

He had a good-natured, gay way of giving reproofs when he did not mean them to be severe, of which everyone who had much correspondence with him will recollect some example. 'Put a little more starch into your neckcloth, my dear ———,' he said to a favourite diplomatist who he thought did not hold up his head high enough at the court where the Minister represented us.

It must often happen to a diplomatist who has any intellect to differ from some of the views which the Minister of Foreign Affairs may have conceived, because the Minister cannot know all the local circumstances to which his views have to be applied so well as the man

on the spot. Such independence never dre
Lord Palmerston's displeasure. At times he
or modified his previous instructions; at first
sisted in them; but he never rebuked an agent, w
anything to justify his sentiments, for expressin

But he hated anything like a subterfuge, an
once through a device which some clever dipl
practice of putting their own opinions into s
else's mouth.

On one occasion a *chargé d'affaires* who wa
carry out instructions he disapproved of rel
conversation with the Minister on whom he wa
urge them, and gave the Minister's arguments
with all the skill and force he could supply.

Lord Palmerston, after answering these ar
with his usual ability, closed his despatch by the
observations:—

> It may be, and no doubt is, the duty of a diplo
> reporting a conversation with a member of the Gover
> which he is accredited to report the arguments, howev
> may be, that may be said to him, but it would be m
> credit of his own sagacity if he took care in making
> not to let it be supposed that he did not see the ab
> the things that had been said to him.

To one gentleman who was perpetually pre
him some claims of his father to a peerage, whic
had been frequently put aside by him, after re
his correspondent courteously of this fact and
reasons for it, he writes, as if relieving himsel
disagreeable thought: 'I confess I cannot s
advantage or satisfaction can accrue to you
from drawing from me at repeated intervals
tion of this statement.'

Lord Palmerston's style of writing illust
character, and may be studied with advantage.
be borne in mind that the letters which have be
in these volumes were for the most part written
amid the press of business, and always without

or correction. Great simplicity, fun, and clearness convey the true impression of a straightforward correspondent whose object in writing is not a display either of wit or of erudition, but the communication of what he has to impart in as short and as easy, but in as effective a manner as possible. As a pompous and reserved statesman too often gets, among the vulgar, the credit of wisdom, so a dark and heavy writer is supposed to be profound. If he is clear and light-hearted, he is often regarded as shallow. No greater mistake. Lord Palmerston's letters survive as a protest against any such false judgment.

He wants a reform both in the manner and substance of a young diplomatist's reports; so he says to Lord Normanby:—[1]

> Your new man sends a long bavardage in an illegible hand. Pray tell him that his reports are of no use if they cannot be read, and that unless he encloses a couple of spare half-hours with each report he had better keep them to himself. The F. O. is not a spelling school. He should write a larger hand, throw over his reflections, and state his facts concisely like a table of contents.

He is tormented by the difficulty of reading the faded colour of the Vienna despatches, so through Lord Ponsonby he takes the mission to task:—

> Your attachés put me out of all patience by the paleness of the ink in which they write out your despatches. Pray give them my compliments, and say I have put them all at the bottom of their respective lists, and if they do not mend their ways I shall be obliged to send you in their stead another set who will pay more attention to writing that which can be read.[2]

His own language being simple and accurate, he was apt to speak out when he came across sentences of a different quality.

> Lord Palmerston desires me [writes his secretary][3] to hint

[1] March 7, 1849.
[2] To Lord Ponsonby, February 8, 1849.
[3] Sir G. Shee to Mr. Morier, April 22, 1834.

to you privately that he has great objection to the of any Gallicism into a despatch which may ha before Parliament. He observes, for instance, that word *adhesion*, which he says is not an English sense in which you use it; and he considers the applicable to the phrase, *It may be permitted to do* also employed.[1]

To the Home Secretary he conveys a con view about the supposed claims of civic func marks of royal favour :—

Novemb

My dear Grey,—It seems to me that there are tions to giving Baronetcies to Mayors and Lord the first place, it would be opening a door withou to say how many would have to enter by it; for begin, it would be difficult to draw a line of distinc cases to be accepted and cases to be refused. I would be handing over to municipal corporations disposing of dignities granted by the Crown; an that all the magistrates of Edinburgh express a wi may be allowed to make a Baronet.

Municipal corporations exercise their own pr conferring upon one of their members the dignit and the Crown exercises its prerogative in conferrin whom it deems worthy of it the dignity of Barone

But each party should keep within its own corporations should not try to make Baronets, an the Crown should try to make Mayors.

He declines to forward an oft-repeated re tion from the Lord-Lieutenant of Ireland, which is quite a model of brevity, because t

[1] So, also, once in a speech in the House of Commons, voice against a common error of expression:—'We ha term ally and allies rung in our ears by those who ei ignorant of the slipslop expression they were using, or what I must admit to have been its general acceptatio they were using a totally unmeaning term. Why, wh An ally is a Power allied by treaty engagements in active operation, political or otherwise. But to call a merely because it is in a state of friendship with

[illegible] civil—a point in the letter being that the 'sarcastic critic' whom he was 'remembering' happened to be Lord Carlisle himself to whom he was writing :—

Broadlands : April 24, 1862.

My dear Carlisle,—I have received your letter of the 19th. I remember a sarcastic critic exclaiming, 'Here comes Dudley Stuart with his eternal Poles.' I shall parody the exclamation by saying, Here comes Carlisle with his eternal X—— ; but I think the Poles better entitled to their freedom than X—— is to the Commandership, and so let us adjourn the debate.

He was often very happy in the phrases with which he described a man's failings. Of a diplomatist who would obstinately stick to his own idea in spite of instructions from home, and for whom he was meditating a rebuke, he says, 'S—— is like a bad retriever, that will not let go his game till he gets a rap on the nose.' Of another, whose charity was not so large as his egotism :—

I wish B——'s letters were not so full of backbiting : however, he makes up for his disparagement of others by his praises of himself.

There is a whole type of diplomatists described in the following sketch of a foreign ambassador :—

Colloredo is agreeable in private society, but diplomatically he is a very unsatisfactory man to deal with. He seems always in a fright lest he should say anything that would commit him ; he is ever on the defensive, and there is no discussing any matter on equal terms with him. He ends a long conversation by saying, 'Mais souvenez-vous que je ne vous ai rien dit,' and while he is talking seems to fancy that there is a shorthand writer behind the screen taking down what he says.[1]

'What energy,' he once said, speaking of the Turks, 'can be expected of a people with no heels to their shoes ?' And when a message was sent to him from a foreign sovereign, asking that a baronetcy might be conferred on an Englishman for whom that sovereign professed an attachment, the only remark he made was

[1] To Lord Ponsonby, October 19, 1849.

that while titles and honours were said to be the cheap rewards bestowed by princes, they certainly were cheapest of all when borrowed from a neighbour.

Sir John Bligh, our Minister at Hanover, writes to complain that the King will persist in giving balls on Sunday, and asks for Lord Palmerston's approval if he leaves the palace when the band strikes up. The Foreign Secretary, in reply, sanctions the conduct of the English Minister, but so words his communication as to check any disposition that might exist to make too grave a matter of the affair:—

It is certainly somewhat singular that the King of Hanover, who lays so much stress upon religion, should choose Sunday of all days in the week for his ball-night, and in this respect he seems to be the reverse of Lord Fitzhardinge, who said to somebody, that, to be sure, he had not much religion, but that what little he had was of the best quality. The King of Hanover professes to have a great deal; but its quality seems rather indifferent, and I should think that his friends in England would not be much edified by hearing of his Sunday-evening polkas. However, I think you are quite right in making your bow at these parties, and in then going away.[1]

His illustrations, often homely, generally went to the root of the matter, as, for instance, when discussing the policy of insisting on reciprocity from France before throwing our markets open to her, he thus condemned the notion:—

I look on the tariffs of the two countries as if they were two turnpikes, one on each side of a river dividing two counties, both of which require payment from all passing across. Who would not laugh at county A. if it were to insist on continuing to pay the turnpike on its own side, unless it were also relieved from paying the turnpike on the B. side of the river? But high customs duties are like turnpike tolls, a charge making passage more expensive for everything that comes in.

As a public speaker, Lord Palmerston's success was very great, and surely results are good tests of merit in the art of persuasion. He always contrived to serve up

[1] Foreign Office, October 26, 1847.

food for every palate the best suited to his audience for the moment, whether learned, municipal, political, or artisan. He certainly never aspired to the lofty rank of a great orator, nor to the magic wand of a great master of phrases; but in the power of conveying abundant knowledge in an apt, logical, and convincing form, he yielded the palm to none. I find traces of careful preparation for the speeches of his earlier years; but during the latter half of his life he made little or none. The great changes in the constitution of the House of Commons which successive Reform Bills have made must never be forgotten by those who would compare the Parliamentary speakers of the present with those of a former generation. The House of Commons of the nineteenth century, for a variety of reasons, all perhaps excellent, gives no encouragement to oratory. A man may succeed in spite of it if he possesses knowledge of details sufficient to redeem his defect; but if he cherishes the models studied by Pitt and Fox he bears about him rather a burden than a source of power.

Shortly after Lord Palmerston's death there appeared a short criticism on his public speaking which is so good, as far as it goes, that I here insert it. It is taken from the columns of a newspaper[1] which, as a Radical organ, had been very hostile to him. The tribute to his powers is all the more impartial:—

Lord Palmerston was successful chiefly because he always made it his business to understand the temper of his audience, and accommodate himself to it. He was not an orator in any critical sense of the word. He never made the slightest attempt to rival such men as Pitt and Fox, as Gladstone and Bright, in eloquence. But few men were ever more successful in effecting, by means of public speaking, the objects at which they aimed. Lord Palmerston never indulged in any attempts at fine language. He studied nothing of elocution except the art of speaking out distinctly. His action was generally monotonous. Although fluent, he had a fashion—perhaps an affectation—of

[1] The late *Morning Star*.

interjecting occasionally a sort of g
words, which must necessarily have be
true oratorical effect, but which somehow
peculiar effectiveness of his unprepared,
Certainly the occasional hesitation, real or
much to increase the humour of some of
which Lord Palmerston so commonly d
seemed to be so entirely unpremeditated;
kept for a moment in such amusing suspense,
was apparently turning over the best way to
when at last it came it was enjoyed with the
jokes were always suited to the present capacity
he happened to address.[1] If the House seemed
for mere nonsense, then Lord Palmerston
nonsense. He had the happy art of making
seem effective. He never rose above his audience;
vexed their intellect by difficult propositions or
ments. Unless where he purposely chose to be
intelligible, he always went straight to the
in homely, vigorous Saxon English. He never
he never by any chance wearied his audience. H
as if instinctively, what style of argument
any given moment tell upon the House. He
upon every debate an unsurpassed tact, and a
rivalled. He could reply with telling effect, and
to a lengthened attack from an enemy, without
note or memorandum of any kind. When
employed broad, rough English satire. He was
was never ineffective; he was never uninter
rough and ready speeches helped to carry many
Burke would have turned friends into foes
tience, and when brilliant eloquence of any
been as dangerous to play with as lightning.[2]

[1] Having, on one occasion, to make an open-
stituents while suffering from a bad cold, he le
be guessed by his hearers, and said, amid much
you will allow me to address you with my hat
be your true representative, for I see that you a

[2] As a chance illustration of his after-dinne
an extract from one of the last he made,
Fishmongers' Company in 1864. He follow
descanted learnedly on the blessings of the
Palmerston spoke more appropriately of
believe that one of the functions of this

But whatever his merits as a speaker, it was to the general confidence felt in his judgment, motives, and character that Lord Palmerston owed the great position which he latterly occupied in the country. Public confidence is, for a statesman in a free community, one of the first requisites for success; and if this be wanting no amount of brilliancy in speaking will long supply such a capital defect. There have, no doubt, been temporary exceptions; but leaders of party in England, and above all, leaders of the Liberal party, must command the moral trust as well as the intellectual homage of thinking men. It was felt that Lord Palmerston, with all his vigour of action and desire for personal distinction, which alone can give the necessary stimulus to exertion, was yet never moved by love of display, whether personal or national; that, having a full sense of responsibility, he despised no details; and therefore, while limiting the objects to be aimed at by a careful consideration of the means at his disposal, he would launch the country on no enterprise until he saw clearly how it should be carried through without being abandoned half-way. His calm judgment made him independent of the forces which so often act on our public men, namely, the taunts and reproaches of foreign statesmen and writers, whose interests are certainly not British interests, and who generally give us their warmest approval when we are playing their game and not our own, or at any rate are satisfying their feelings of not unnatural jealousy. In short, Lord Palmerston's

ticularly connected with the position of the country to which it belongs, because in an island country it is natural that one of the first functions of an efficient civic corporation should be to regulate the immigration of the vast multitude of the inhabitants of the ocean that come in contact with the population (laughter). That duty has been from time to time most worthily performed by this corporation; and I am told that to this day the inhabitants of this great metropolis are weekly and daily indebted to its guardian care; for that there are multitudes of immigrants that come here from the depths of the ocean unfitted to mix with the population of this island, and being unable to obtain the necessary passport are refused an entrance through the vigilance of this ancient corporation (laughter).'

character, free from bombast, tho[illegible] self-assertion, was typical of the [illegible] inspired the confidence which it deserved [illegible] his papers the following passage, copie[illegible] from some essay which he had been [illegible] Witt, Grand Pensionary of Holland. [illegible] an appropriate ending to this story of [illegible]

The statesman who, in treading the slipper[illegible] is sustained and guided only by the hope of fame [illegible] of a lofty reputation, will not only find himself [illegible] sant temptations to turn aside from the line of [illegible] but the disappointment he is sure to meet with [illegible] drive him to misanthropy, perhaps even irritate [illegible] by vindictive treachery a virtue founded upon [illegible] enduring principle. But the statesman who looks [illegible] performance of his duty for consolation and support [illegible] the toils and sufferings which that duty may [illegible] encounter, who aims not at popularity, because [illegible] that continued popularity rarely accompanies [illegible] unyielding integrity; who, as he is urged to [illegible] measures by the hope of fame, so he is deterred fro[illegible] are just by the fear of censure, such a man may [illegible] course through the shoals and breakers of the [illegible] and whether he meet with the hatred or [illegible] countrymen is to him a consideration of minor [illegible] reward is otherwise sure. He has laboured with [illegible] great objects; he has conferred signal benefits upon [illegible] men; nobler occupation man cannot aspire to; [illegible] it would be very difficult to obtain.

This extract bears date 1843. Did Lord [illegible] make these maxims his own? His public [illegible] ture to think, proves that he did.

INDEX.

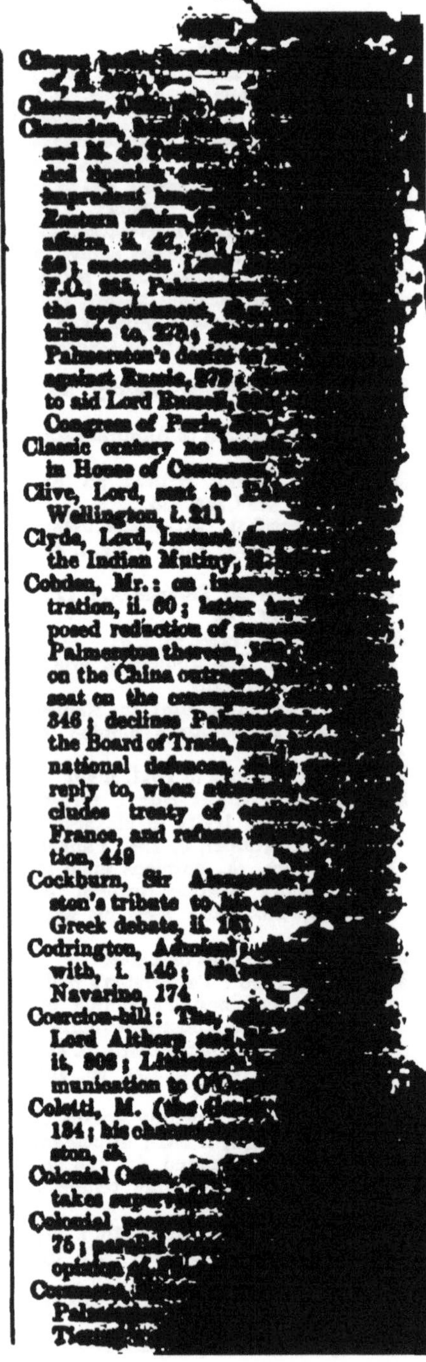

LIB MAG

PAL.

PAL

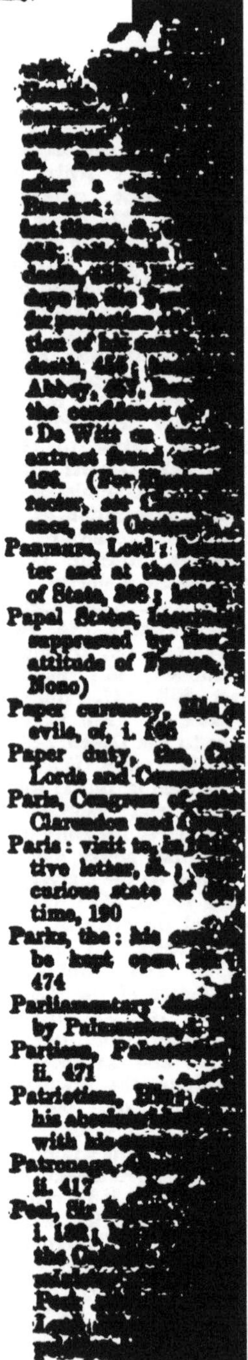

THE END.

SOME STANDARD WORKS

PUBLISHED BY

RICHARD BENTLEY & SON.

PROFESSOR MOMMSEN'S HISTORY of ROME, from the Earliest Time to the Period of its Decline. Translated (with the Author's sanction, and Additions) by the Rev. W. P. DICKSON. With an Introduction by Dr. SCHMITZ. 4 vols. crown 8vo. £2. 6s. 6d. Or separately, Vols. I. and II., 21s.; Vol. III., 10s. 6d.; Vol. IV., with Index, 15s.

Also, a LIBRARY EDITION, in 4 vols. demy 8vo. £3. 15s. These Volumes not sold separately. The Indices to the Two Editions separately, each 3s. 6d.

PROFESSOR CURTIUS'S HISTORY of GREECE. Translated by A. W. WARD, M.A. Vols. I. and II., each 15s.; Vols. III., IV., and V., with Index, each 18s.

SIR EDWARD CREASY'S RISE and PROGRESS of the ENGLISH CONSTITUTION. Post 8vo. 7s. 6d.

SIR EDWARD CREASY'S FIFTEEN DECISIVE BATTLES of the WORLD, from Marathon to Waterloo. Crown 8vo. with Plans, 6s. Also, a LIBRARY EDITION, 8vo. with Plans, 10s. 6d.

FIFTH EDITION OF

SIR EDWARD CREASY'S HISTORY of the OTTOMAN EMPIRE. Crown 8vo. 6s.

The HISTORY of ANTIQUITY. Translated from the German of Professor MAX DUNCKER, by EVELYN ABBOTT, LL.D., M.A. of Balliol College, Oxford. The First Volume contains: Book I., Egypt; Book II., the Semitic Nations. Vol. II. demy 8vo. 21s. The Second Volume contains an Account of the Rise of Assyria, of the Phœnician Colonies, the Hebrew Monarchy, and the later Pharaohs.

The LIVES of the ARCHBISHOPS of CANTERBURY, from St. Augustine to Juxon. By the late Very Rev. WALTER FARQUHAR HOOK, D.D. Dean of Chichester. 11 vols. demy 8vo. £8. 5s. Or sold separately as follows: Vol. I., 15s.; Vol. II., 15s.; Vols. III. and IV., 30s.; Vol. V., 15s.; Vols. VI., and VII., 30s.; Vol. VIII., 15s.; Vol. IX., 15s.; Vol. X., 14s.; Vol. XI., 15s. The Second Series commenced with Vol. VI.

THE THIRD EDITION OF

DEAN HOOK: his Life and Letters. By his Son-in-Law, the Rev. W. R. W. STEPHENS, Author of 'Memorials of the See of Chichester,' and 'Life of St. John Chrysostom.' 2 vols. 8vo. with two Portraits, 30s.

The NAVAL HISTORY of GREAT BRITAIN, from the Declaration of War by France in 1793 to the Accession of George IV. By WILLIAM JAMES. With a Continuation of the History down to the Battle of Navarino, by Captain CHAMIER. 6 vols. crown 8vo. with Portrait, 36s.

THIERS' HISTORY of the GREAT FRENCH REVOLU-TION, 1789–1801. Translated by FREDERICK SHOBERL. 5 vols. small crown 8vo. with 41 fine Engravings and Portraits of the most eminent Personages engaged in the Revolution, engraved by W. Greatbach, price 30s.

The HISTORY of the INDIAN NAVY: being an Account of the Creation, Constitution, War Services, and Surveys of the Indian Navy between the years 1613 and 1863 (when it was abolished). From Original Sources and hitherto Unpublished Documents. By Lieut. CHARLES RATHBONE LOW, (late) Indian Navy, F.R.G.S. 2 vols. demy 8vo. price 36s.

The HEAVENS: an Illustrated Handbook of Popular Astro-nomy. By AMÉDÉE GUILLEMIN. Edited by J. NORMAN LOCKYER, F.R.A.S., F.R.S. New and revised Edition, embodying the latest Discoveries in Astronomical Science, demy 8vo. with over 200 Illustrations, price 12s.

RICHARD BENTLEY & SON, New Burlington Street,

Publishers in Ordinary to Her Majesty the Queen.

OR,

MIRTH AND MARVELS.

I.

THE ILLUSTRATED EDITION.

With Sixty Illustrations by Cruikshank, Leech, and Tenniel; cover designed by John Leighton, F.S.A. Crown 4to, cloth, bev[elled] boards, gilt edges, 21s.; or bound in the Ely pattern, white [illegible] suitable for presentation, 22s. 6d.

'A series of humorous legends, illustrated by three such men as Cruikshank, L[eech] and Tenniel—what can be more tempting?'—Times.

'Abundant in humour, observation, fancy; in extensive knowledge of books and [illegible] in palpable hits of character, exquisite grave irony, and the most whimsical indulge[nce] [illegible]. We cannot open a page that is not sparkling with its wit and hu[mour] that is not ringing with the strokes of pleasantry and satire.'—Examiner.

II.

THE ANNOTATED EDITION.

A Library Edition, with a History of each Legend, and other N[otes] and some original Legends now first published. In 2 vols. demy [8vo] with an original Frontispiece by George Cruikshank; and all [the] Illustrations by Cruikshank and Leech, including two new ones by [the] latter artist. Edited by the Rev. Richard Dalton Barham. 24[s.]

III.

THE BURLINGTON EDITION.

In 3 vols. fcp. 8vo., with no Illustrations. 10s. 6d.

IV.

THE CARMINE EDITION.

In crown 8vo. With 17 Illustrations by Cruikshank and Leech. [illegible] gilt edges and bevelled boards. 10s. 6d.

V.

THE EDINBURGH EDITION.

In crown 8vo. with 32 full-page Illustrations by Cruikshank, Le[ech] Tenniel, and Du Maurier, especially re-engraved for this editi[on by] George Pearson. An entirely new Edition in large type. [illegible] [illegible]ly. Price 6s.

VI.

THE TAPPINGTON EDITION.

Crown 8vo. 3s. 6d.

VII.

THE 'VICTORIA' (POCKET) EDITION

In fcp. 8vo. 1s.

AT EVERY BOOKSELLER'S.

[RICHAR]D BENTLEY & SONS, New Burlington Street

Publishers in Ordinary to Her Majesty the Queen.